D1083327

WITHDRAWN

# THE HERMENEUTICS READER

# THE HERMENEUTICS READER

## Texts of the German Tradition from the Enlightenment to the Present

*Edited, with an
introduction and notes, by*

Kurt Mueller-Vollmer

Continuum • New York

1985

The Continuum Publishing Company
370 Lexington Avenue, New York, NY 10017

Printed in the United States of America

*Library of Congress Cataloging in Publication Data*

Main entry under title:

The Hermeneutics reader.

Bibliography: p. 347
Includes index.
1. Hermeneutics—Addresses, essays, lectures.
2. Philosophy, German—Addresses, essays, lectures.
I. Mueller-Vollmer, Kurt.
BD241.H374   1985     121'.68'0943     85-461
ISBN: 0-8264-0208-9

# Contents

v

# Preface

CONCERN FOR HERMENEUTIC PROBLEMS has become quite common in recent decades, and the term hermeneutics and its derivatives have been used more and more frequently by representatives of the social and human sciences. What seemed at first a strictly continental affair has come to occupy an important place in the general discussion about the very nature of these disciplines, their methodologies, and their underlying philosophical assumptions. Today the term hermeneutics denotes a concern that is shared by members of such diverse fields of knowledge as philosophy, sociology, history, theology, psychology, jurisprudence, literary criticism, and the humanities at large. Yet, many of the issues raised today have had a long-standing history on the Continent. This has been true ever since Schleiermacher in the early nineteenth century and Dilthey in the latter half of that century and the early years of our own century succeeded in transforming hermeneutics from the study and collection of specialized rules of interpretation for the use of theologians or jurists to that of a genuine philosophical discipline and general theory of the social and human sciences.

The aim of this volume is to make available to students of the humanities and social sciences a number of texts which will enable them to become acquainted with some of the important ideas and issues raised by the writers of the nineteenth- and twentieth-century hermeneutic tradition in the German language. A first-hand knowledge of these issues seems indeed necessary and desirable. For in recent debates certain names, terms, and concepts derived from this tradition have been used, often without a sufficient grasp of their meaning and the context they imply. Even the term hermeneutics itself is frequently found to have contradictory or at least ambiguous connotations. For some it designates a movement in twentieth-century philosophy (Heidegger, Gadamer) or theology (Bultmann and the "New Hermeneutic"). Others, literary students for the most part, see in it a special

ix

method of interpreting literary texts, while still others use the term to refer to those disciplines in the human and social sciences (as opposed to the natural sciences) which make use of the methods of understanding and interpretation (Von Wright). In some quarters, the word "hermeneutics" has assumed the character of a voguish term as if we were dealing with a new movement or intellectual trend like "structuralism" or "poststructuralism" which would provide us not merely with a fresh vocabulary but with an alternative methodology as well. Gadamer and the students of philosophical hermeneutics have always insisted, of course, that hermeneutics has nothing to do with the creation or validation of specific methodologies of any kind. They may be overstating their case, for there exists and has existed an active reciprocal relationship between hermeneutics on the one hand and the rise and development of specific methodologies on the other, as we shall point out later. But their insistence should at least discourage those who are all too eager and ready to seize and popularize what seems to them a new and useful paradigm.

The problem is that hermeneutics is both a historical concept and the name for an ongoing concern in the human and social sciences; and for the historical aspect of hermeneutics a simple definition will not do. As Nietzsche succinctly put it: "all concepts in which an entire process is semiotically concentrated elude definitions; only that which has no history is definable."* It was this editor's task, therefore, to present to his readers texts which would allow a sufficient grasp of the hermeneutic enterprise in its various aspects.

A few additional words about the principles which guided this selection. It has not been my intention to document a full history of hermeneutic theory during the past two centuries. This would have been a task far beyond the limits set by this single volume. Instead, I have attempted to include texts characteristic of those positions which have been or still are significant for the hermeneutic debate. Hence, my main attention was focused on a notion of general hermeneutics rather than on that of a particular discipline with its narrower interests and perspectives. The texts represented here were written by members of different disciplines and fields of inquiry—philosophers, historians, philologists, theologians, social scientists—and constitute significant contributions to their individual disciplines. But at the same time, they transcend the boundaries of these disciplines and raise issues of much larger import and thus form part of what might rightfully be called the mainstream of hermeneutic tradition. I hope that this mainstream and its concerns will become evident to the reader. To simplify matters it makes sense to identify two distinct phases in the development of the modern German hermeneutic tradition: the philological and the philosophical phase or school of thought. The first is represented by such names as Schleiermacher, Ast, Droysen, Humboldt, and Boeckh; the second includes Dilthey, Husserl, Heidegger, and

*On the Genealogy of Morals* (Vintage Books, 1967), p. 80.

Gadamer and their respective followers. This is a useful distinction. It does not mean, however, that the philological hermeneutics of the nineteenth century was unphilosophical or antiphilosophical. On the contrary. Some of the most radical arguments of twentieth-century philosophical hermeneutics derive from the insights first articulated by the nineteenth-century writers, even though they were primarily interested in the problems of philology and the cultural sciences. Similarly, the writings of the hermeneutic philosophers invariably display a deep concern for the problems facing these disciplines. In addition, writers like Heidegger or Gadamer have exercised a considerable influence upon the way in which students of literature read and understand poetic texts and speak about their understanding. Of course, hermeneutics did not begin with the nineteenth-century philologists and historians, and we must consider some important writers from the eighteenth century and earlier in any serious study of the history of hermeneutics. But since this reader is to serve as an introduction to modern hermeneutics, only one eighteenth-century author, Chladenius, was chosen to illustrate the state of hermeneutic thought at that time. The hermeneutics of Schleiermacher and the Romantics that would follow afterwards represents a complete and radical break from the older tradition. With Schleiermacher, modern hermeneutics begins.

For the occasion of this book a number of the contributions have been translated for the first time, or were retranslated. When necessary, existing translations were corrected and changed to assure accuracy of terminology and of the ideas expressed. I owe thanks to Professor Jerry Dibble and to my former students Carrie Asman-Schneider, Barbara Hyams, and Linda DeMichiel for having undertaken the translation of some exceedingly difficult texts, a task whose successful fulfillment represents a hermeneutic accomplishment in its own right. I am also indebted to Robert Leventhal for his suggestions in rendering some of Dilthey's terms and phrases. The bibliography at the end was not meant to be exhaustive. It is intended for the reader who wants to follow up on the various problems raised by the different texts and who would like to have a fair and accurate overview of the current debate. Emphasis has been placed on English language titles. I should like to thank my publishers for the support which they lent to this project in the face of many difficulties. Last but not least, I wish to thank my wife, Patricia Ann Bialecki, whose continued assistance and numerous helpful suggestions I deeply appreciate.

KURT MUELLER-VOLLMER
*Stanford, California*

# Introduction

# Language, Mind, and Artifact: An Outline of Hermeneutic Theory Since the Enlightenment

I

> They mean by that the messenger of the gods who, according to the opinion of these heathens, must proclaim to the humans the will of the gods.
>
> Johann Heinrich Zedler, *Grosses Vollständiges Universallexicon aller Wissenschaften und Künste*, vol. 12 Halle-Leipzig, 1735

THE ETYMOLOGY OF THE TERM hermeneutics carries an obvious relation to Hermes,[1] the messenger god of the Greeks, and suggests a multiplicity of meanings. In order to deliver the messages of the gods, Hermes had to be conversant in their idiom as well as in that of the mortals for whom the message was destined. He had to understand and interpret for himself what the gods wanted to convey before he could proceed to translate, articulate, and explicate their intention to mortals. To describe the different facets of Hermes' task, modern mortals have at their disposal a whole set of terms such as linguistic competence, communication, discourse, understanding, interpretation. Looking at Hermes' task may give us a clear warning as to the complexities underlying the term hermeneutics and the hermeneutic enterprise itself. In antiquity the term hermeneutics occurred only sporadically. Aristotle used it as a title for one of his works, *Peri Hermeneias*,[2] in which he dealt with the logic of statements: the grammatical structure by which subject and predicate are united in human speech to reveal the character of things. In order to avoid confusion, the history of the term and the history of that which

1

it has come to designate today should best be kept separate. Interpretation was performed in various ways since late antiquity, as for example, in the school of Alexandria. It later became an integral part of the theological culture of the Middle Ages, but it was not until the Renaissance, Reformation, and thereafter that hermeneutics as a special discipline came into being. Against the Catholic insistence on church authority and tradition in matters of understanding and interpreting the Holy Scriptures, which was reaffirmed at the Council of Trent in 1546, the Protestant reformers advanced the principles of perspicuity—*perspicuitas*—and of the self-sufficiency of the holy text. Thus the need existed for the reformers to develop the means of demonstrating the basic intelligibility and noncontradictory nature of the Scriptures. The most important Protestant theorist and apologist of biblical interpretation was Matthias Flacius Illyricus with his work *Clavis Scripturae Sacrae* (1567).[3] Drawing on the Aristotelian rhetorical tradition and the entire tradition of patristic Bible exegesis from Origen to his own days, Flacius laid a firm basis for the development of Protestant hermeneutics. Over the next hundred years his *Clavis* went through ten editions. Flacius advanced two principal arguments which proved important for subsequent developments. First, he argued that if the Scriptures had not yet been understood properly, this did not necessarily imply that the church ought to impose an external interpretation to make them intelligible; it merely reflected the insufficient knowledge and faulty preparation of the interpreters. A thorough linguistic and hermeneutic training could remedy the situation. Second, Flacius claimed, in accordance with the opinion of the other reformers, Luther and Melanchthon, that the Scriptures contained an internal coherence and continuity. He thus asked the interpreter to explicate each individual passage in the light of the whole continuity of the Scriptures. If Flacius believed that he had freed biblical interpretation from the norms and restrictions of church authority and tradition, he did not realize that he himself was instrumental for the introduction of a new system of norms with its own body of hermeneutic rules, which would insure a necessary degree of consent in matters of scriptural exegesis. Without such consent the unity of the Protestant church would have faltered.

Besides the sacred hermeneutics of the Protestant reformers, three other tendencies were instrumental for the rise of modern hermeneutics: developments in classical philology, jurisprudence, and philosophy.[4]

A resurgence of interest in the study of the classical texts from Greek and Roman antiquity occurred during the Renaissance. Humanist scholars and their successors at universities and academies produced an arsenal of philological-critical methods (*Ars Critica*) whose object was to establish the authenticity of a given text and to reconstruct as much as possible its original or correct version. Philological criticism and its concerns became an important source for the subsequent development of systematic theories of interpretation. The humanist hermeneutic tradition stayed alive well into the eighteenth century, as is testified by the frequent reediting of relevant works by writers like Vives, Scioppius, and Johannes Clericus.[5] For some time, the theory of translation was subsumed under the category of interpretation as, for example, in works by the English humanist Laurentius Humphrey in the sixteenth century and by the French Bishop Huet in the seventeenth century.[6]

The revival of interest in Roman law, which began during the so-called twelfth-century Renaissance in Italy with the concomitant efforts of scholars to elucidate the Code of Justinian (A.D. 533), led to the development of a special hermeneutics of jurisprudence. This special hermeneutics would soon spread across the Alps to the rest of Europe. In 1463 Constantius Rogerius, in his *Treatise concerning the Interpretation of Laws*,[7] summarized the main tenets of these interpretive efforts which had their center in Bologna. Rogerius wanted to explicate and harmonize the various parts of Justinian's code. He introduced a fourfold distinction of forms of legal exegesis which he termed "the corrective," "the extensive," "the restrictive," and "the declarative" interpretations. This distinction remained in force until the beginning of the nineteenth century when traditional legal hermeneutics was replaced by the historical school of Savigny and his followers.[8] The rise and development of legal hermeneutics was intimately connected with the rise of philology, and we can witness a frequent transferal of ideas and concepts from one field to the other. Thus, in his *Iurisconsultus* of 1559, the humanist Franciscus Hotomanus viewed grammatical interpretation as the basis of legal explication.[9] In fact, grammatical interpretation remained an essential category for most writers in legal hermeneutics. In his *Treatise on the Science of Interpretation* (1689), the German jurist Johannes von Felde attempted to establish interpretive principles which would be valid for all classes of text, both literary and legal. He also offered a definition of hermeneutics which Chladenius would incorporate into his hermeneutics. To interpret, for von Felde, meant but to explicate to someone that which proves difficult for him to understand.[10] The jurist Thibaut — the last writer in the humanist and Enlightenment tradition— in 1806 defined the relationship between grammatical and other kinds of legal interpretation in the following manner. Grammatical interpretation should be directed solely at the literal sense of a given law. It finds its limits only where the meaning of a law cannot be understood from ordinary linguistic usage. At this point, the "purpose" (*Absicht*) of the law and the intention of the lawgiver have to be considered ("logical interpretation").[11]

Finally, with the desire of Enlightenment philosophers to proceed everywhere from certain principles and to systematize all human knowledge, hermeneutics became a province of philosophy. Following the example of Aristotle, who had analyzed the problems of logic in his treatise *On Interpretation* (*Peri hermeneias*), Enlightenment philosophers viewed hermeneutics and its problems as belonging to the domain of logic. This was an important event in the history of hermeneutic thought. For even though many writers of special (technical) hermeneutic texts—

theologians, jurists, and philologists— would frequently allude to generally applicable principles and concepts in their works, it was not until the philosophers of the Enlightenment made hermeneutic problems their own concern that the discipline of general hermeneutics came into being. Their contention was that like logic itself hermeneutics rested on certain generally applicable rules and principles which were valid for all those fields of knowledge which relied on interpretation. Although the claim for universality of twentieth-century philosophical hermeneutics radically differs from the Enlightenment position, thinkers like Heidegger and Gadamer in some fundamental respect still follow the example of their eighteenth-century predecessors. Thus, for Gadamer general hermeneutics is part of philosophy because it transcends the confines of individual disciplines and deals instead with their foundations.

Christian Wolff, probably the most prolific and influential of the eighteenth-century enlightened philosophers, included in his widely read work on logic several chapters in which he dealt with hermeneutic problems, among them, "On reading historical and dogmatic books" and "On interpreting the Holy Scriptures."[12] Since a good deal of our knowledge comes to us through books, Wolff contended, we must rely on our critical judgment concerning their truth character. He divided all writings into "historical" or "dogmatic" kinds. Works belonging to the latter category must be judged on the strength of their arguments, their truth content, and the knowledge of the subject matter displayed. Historical writings on the other hand should be judged according to the "completeness" of the historical account which they offer and according to their "truthfulness" and "sincerity," since we no longer have access to historical truth once the events referred to are past.[13] The completeness of the account can be ascertained only by referring to the author's intention. The notion of authorial intention (*Absicht*) as used by Wolff, Chladenius, and other Enlightenment theorists does not, however, carry a psychological meaning as it does today. Nor can it be taken in the sense in which Schleiermacher and the other Romantics would soon understand a literary work, as the expression of its author's individuality. For Wolff and his contemporaries, the author's intention is not an expression of his personality but relates to the specific genre of writing he intended to produce. There were, according to Wolff, in addition to the system of rules and principles governing all fields of knowledge, particular discursive forms in which this knowledge should be presented. The opinion, the intention of the author, carries foremost an objective and generic denotation. Consequently, Wolff discusses different classes and kinds of historical writings in terms of the different intentions which govern them. He distinguishes among the intentions of natural history, church history, secular (political) history, and the "history of learning." To judge a book by its authorial intention thus meant to ascertain the degree to which its author had succeeded in adhering to the generic requirements of the particular discourse he had chosen. The meaning of a given text or passage for Wolff was not an issue. Words and sentences—if used correctly—would always convey the meaning which the author intended. If a text appeared obscure or ambiguous, this was because the writer did not succeed in the correct use of language, the correct explanation of terms, or in the proper construction of his arguments. Wolff's theory is strongly normative not only with respect to how books should be read but also how they should be written. His arguments contain *in nuce* many of the ideas which were elaborated much more fully a few decades later in the first formal work on general hermeneutics written in the vernacular.

## II

Many centuries ago, scholars considered the production of interpretations to be one of the most prestigious endeavors, and because there were no principles which would have enabled these to be done reasonably, one can not be surprised that many interpretations ended unhappily and that the disciplines which were built on interpretations were completely devastated. This is proven in the case of Philosophy by the unfortunate interpretations made of Aristotle, by the glossaries for jurisprudence and by the interpretations of the Fathers and the Scholastic teachers. Finally, there was no alternative but to toss out all these interpretations and to start all over again

Johann Martin Chladenius

Chladenius (1710–1759), who had made a name and a living for himself as a university teacher and scholar in such diverse fields as philosophy, history, theology, and rhetoric, published his *Introduction to the Correct Interpretation of Reasonable Discourses and Books* in 1742.[14] He wanted to provide a consistent theory of interpretation together with a body of practical rules for the students of those disciplines which derived their knowledge by interpretation. Chladenius did not consider philosophy one of these disciplines. For the philosopher was not concerned with the interpretation of the meaning of statements but rather with the critical examination of what they claimed was true. On the other hand, the study of poetry, rhetoric, history, and the Ancients, together with all those disciplines which comprised the "sciences of beauty" (the humanities), had to rely on the art of interpretation (*Auslegekunst*). Hermeneutics for Chladenius is but another name for this art. Since "to be understood" was in the nature of an utterance, Chladenius defined hermeneutics as the art of attaining the perfect or complete understanding of utterances (*vollständiges Verstehen*)—whether they be speeches (*Reden*) or writings (*Schriften*).[15]

Chladenius's use of the term art reveals the extent to which his hermeneutic enterprise was still rooted in the Aristotelian rhetorical tradition. For the term does not carry any aesthetic or artistic connotation, but refers to the teaching and mastery of a specific area of knowledge as, for example, in the liberal arts, the disciplines of rhetoric, grammar, and dialectic. Drawing his inspiration from Wolff and other predecessors in the field of logic, Chladenius set out to develop in a rational and systematic fashion the principles, rules, and techniques governing the art of interpretation as he knew it. But he was concerned only with "reasonable speeches and writings." By this he meant those utterances which observe the rules of reason in language and thought, and among those he singled out historical writings. To the readers of his *Introduction* he promised the publication of a hermeneutics of poetic discourse in the future—a promise which he did not keep.

Chladenius's *Introduction* is significant not only because of its systematic exposition of Enlightenment hermeneutic theory.[16] It also raises, often inadvertently, a great many problems and issues which were to become dominant themes for writers in the nineteenth and twentieth centuries. But those who have seen in him the founder of a modern-day hermeneutics of the human sciences are largely mistaken. To the careful reader of his work it should be obvious how far removed his ideas are from those of the Romantic and post-Romantic schools of hermeneutic thought. His position can be made sufficiently clear by considering three aspects of his theory which are closely interrelated: his concept of hermeneutics, his implied notion of the nature of verbal meanings, and his theory of the "point of view" (*Sehe-Punckt*) with respect to historical writings.

If the purpose of the art of interpretation is to help us attain "perfect understanding," it must be the task of the hermeneutic philosopher to describe the aims of this understanding, the obstacles which have to be overcome, and the methods which must be used to achieve the desired goal. These are precisely the issues which Chladenius's *Introduction* addresses. Chladenius believed that there were primarily two criteria by which one could determine whether perfect understanding had been attained. This is the case whenever we have grasped the intention of the author and whenever we are able to think in our minds all that the words of the author are able to arouse in us according to the "rules of reason" and of the mind itself. What is meant here by authorial intention, namely, the generic choice of discourse by the author rather than his psychological state of mind, was explained in our discussion of Wolff's hermeneutics. In the same vein, the second criterion does not carry a psychological connotation or imply the idea of a relativization of meaning of a given utterance. The rules of reason were considered unchangeable by Chladenius and guaranteed the stability of meaning and the possibility of its objective transfer through verbal expressions. If an utterance was only constructed reasonably and in accordance with the appropriate rules of discourse, and if the writer had succeeded in making his ideas clear, his words on the page would give rise to a correct and perfect understanding: author and reader alike shared in the same rational principles.

We can see why the notions of understanding and of meaning did not pose a particular philosophical problem to the author of the *Introduction*, as it would later to the Romantics and the moderns. These notions were simply taken for granted by him. Given the skill and expertise of the interpreter, all hermeneutic problems appeared solvable to him simply because all reasonable utterances had to be intelligible. For Chladenius, as for the enlightened mind in general, the grounds for a correct interpretation and for understanding resided in reason itself. It was shared by writer and reader and was found embodied in the text.

Chladenius is best known for his notion of point-of-view or perspective (*Sehe-Punckt*) which he introduced into historical methodology. If one historian's account differs considerably from what another historian tells us about the same events, this does not necessarily mean, Chladenius argued, that there is a contradiction between the two accounts; or that only one version of the story could be true and that the other had to be rejected. For it is a characteristic of human nature, Chladenius believed, that an individual would perceive the events and happenings surrounding him from his own particular perspective or point-of-view. This relativity of perspective was, however, no cause for anxiety for Chladenius, because each observer would still perceive the same event. Taking into account the viewpoint of a given observer, I can still judge the truthfulness of his statements. When I place myself into his perspective, I can compare what I perceive through his account with what I know from other sources. This notion of perspective, Chladenius tells his readers, was derived from Leibniz's *Optics*. But it reminds us even more strongly of the same philosopher's *Monadology* in which each monad always perceives the same universe, but from its own perspective and according to its own abilities. Similarly, for Chladenius, each historical account (*perception*) would differ from another, since it reflected the observer's personal perspective, but it would still refer to the same event.

His introduction of the notion of perspective opened new dimensions which could have led to important changes in the assumptions of eighteenth-century hermeneutic theory—possibilities which Chladenius himself did not perceive. In our age of post-Nietzschean criticism the concept of interpretation itself has become thoroughly perspectivist, and there are, in the eyes of many—as Nietzsche once put it—no facts but only interpretations, where each interpretation represents one of the many possible "meanings" of a given text. It must be pointed out that any suggestion of a relativity of meanings and of interpretations was far removed from Chladenius's mind. Even though some of his modern interpreters have not resisted the temptation of reading a twentieth-century meaning into his notion of perspectivism, Chladenius did not proclaim the relativity of meaning or of interpretation, but merely the relativity of the account.[17] Despite its perspectivism, a given text remained for him transparent and unambiguous with regard to its referent and its meaning. It was the task of the interpreter to make the reader realize and restore wherever necessary this textual transparency; that is, whenever he

encountered difficulties in understanding. To put it briefly, the interpreter functioned as the mediator between the writer of a story and his perspective, and that
of the reader who may find the story unbelievable or untrue at first. Hermeneutic
difficulties for Chladenius always resided in individual parts of a given work, in
certain words, expressions, passages. A work in its entirety or in its total meaning
did not come into question. It was only for the Romantics later that such concerns
would become important. Hermeneutics, for Chladenius and his contemporaries,
had to provide for the students of the "beautiful sciences" a rational account of
the techniques and strategies to be applied to those parts of a given work which
appeared obscure or simply difficult to understand; they would yield their meaning once the right kind of knowledge and information had been brought to bear
upon them. In essence, then, interpretation is but verbal explication for Chladenius, and its end is clearly pedagogical and pragmatic: "Interpretation [*Auslegung*] therefore is nothing other than teaching someone the concepts which are
necessary to learn to understand or to fully understand a speech or written work."

<br>

## III

> Two definitions of understanding. Everything is understood when nothing
> nonsensical remains. Nothing is understood that is not construed.
> Friedrich Schleiermacher, Notes, 1809

<br>

Schleiermacher's contribution represents a true watershed in the development of
hermeneutics. He brought together and synthesized the major trends from the
older schools and, at the same time, laid the foundations for a new departure.
Both the philological and historical hermeneutics of the nineteenth century and
the hermeneutic philosophy of the twentieth century are indebted to him. Yet it
seems that a full and appreciative exploration of his monumental achievements
has hardly begun even today. For many decades Dilthey's pronouncements regarding Schleiermacher's hermeneutics had canonical value and were generally
accepted. In his essay "The Origin of Hermeneutics" (1900)[18] Dilthey depicted
Schleiermacher mainly as advocating a theory of psychological empathy—empathy with an author's creative personality as expressed in his works. In addition,
Dilthey maintained that Schleiermacher had defended divination as the highest
principle of understanding. Dilthey's essay was responsible for spreading a one-
sided and distorted notion of Schleiermacher's theories. Enraptured as he was by
the concerns of his own "philosophy of life," he failed to pay attention to essential
parts of Schleiermacher's hermeneutics, especially Schleiermacher's grounding
of the hermeneutic enterprise in a conception of language and human linguisticality.[19] Dilthey also failed to elaborate on Schleiermacher's substantial contributions

to the theory and practice of textual interpretation. Even though the philologists of the nineteenth century—notably Boeckh—absorbed many of Schleiermacher's concerns, they also lost an awareness of Schleiermacher's discovery of the linguistic dimensions of human understanding and its importance.

Schleiermacher did not create his hermeneutics in a vacuum. His endeavors must be seen as part of the early Romantic movement which, from 1795 to 1810, revolutionized the intellectual life of central Europe. A new aesthetics and poetics created by philosophers such as Fichte and Schelling, by critics such as Friedrich and August Wilhelm Schlegel, and by the poets Novalis, Tieck, and Wackenroder opened new dimensions and produced new tasks for hermeneutic thought. From now on hermeneutics concerned itself with the idea of the author as creator and of the work of art as an expression of his creative self. In harmony with the poets and philosophers of the period, the hermeneutic thinkers advanced the conception of the organic unity of a work, subscribed to a notion of style as the inner form of a work, and adhered to a concept of the symbolic nature of art which gave rise to the possibility of infinite interpretations.[20] The ancient task of interpreting and explicating texts suddenly appeared in a new and pristine light. Even more important than the ideas of the new aesthetics was the transcendental turn hermeneutic thinking underwent in the hands of the Romantic theorists—particularly F. Schlegel, Schleiermacher, and Wilhelm von Humboldt. Already Kant's Copernican revolution of thought had brought about a new and different usage for the term understanding. From the viewpoint of the *Critique of Pure Reason,* understanding (*Verstand*) appeared as an underlying capacity for thought and experience, and acts of understanding (*Verstehen*) which were present in all thinking and experience were an expression of man's rationality.[21] Fichte radicalized the Kantian position and in his *Doctrine of Science* (1795) attempted boldly to deduce the entire system of human knowledge from the operations of the mind itself. Following Fichte's example, F. Schlegel and, subsequently, Schleiermacher,[22] attempted to ground hermeneutics in a concept of understanding. Since then, "understanding" has become the cornerstone of hermeneutic theory.[23] For Schleiermacher, hermeneutics was no longer occupied with the decoding of a given meaning or with the clearing away of obstacles in the way of proper understanding, but was above all concerned with illuminating the conditions for the possibility of understanding and its modes of interpretation. Against the assumption of the older hermeneutics that a reader would understand everything unless or until he encountered contradictions or a nonsensical passage, Schleiermacher advanced a radically different position. From the point of view of hermeneutics we cannot claim to understand anything that we "cannot perceive and construct as necessary. In accordance with this maxim, understanding is an unending task."[24]

The student of Schleiermacher's hermeneutics is faced with singular difficulties which result from the particular form in which his ideas have been transmitted to us. When he taught his famous course on hermeneutics at the University of Berlin, Schleiermacher always relied on a set of notes which contained an outline of the course and its main ideas in an extremely condensed form. He would then develop his lectures from these notes before his audience. After his death these lectures, as culled from students' notebooks and Schleiermacher's own notes, were published as part of his collected works.[25] Schleiermacher's own manuscripts have only recently been published in their entirety in a reliable edition, enabling the reader to study Schleiermacher's own texts for the first time.[26] These texts do not make easy reading. They are often fragmentary and abound in cryptic statements in which the most important insights are revealed, thereby keeping the reader on his toes and forcing him to make the necessary connections himself. But it cannot be denied that these texts contain one of the richest and most profound contributions to hermeneutic theory. Their peculiarly aphoristic style reflects the lightning like quality of suggestiveness and openness found also in the literary fragments of the brothers Schlegel and Novalis. The fragment, as we know, constituted an important genre for the Romantic writer.

New and decisive in Schleiermacher is not merely the transcendental turn toward the process of understanding, but the linguistic interpretation he gives to it.[27] Understanding, for Schleiermacher, was an activity analogous to that of speaking. Both derive from man's linguisticality or capacity for speech (*Sprachfähigkeit*), that is, his knowledge of language (*Sprache*), and his mastery of speech (*Rede*). Schleiermacher thought that every human being was equipped with a basic linguistic disposition, which had to be realized by acquiring a given language at a particular moment of its history, and by internalizing its grammatical rules. Knowing a grammar for Schleiermacher was therefore the same as knowing a language. Men express their linguistic competence in speech acts (*Sprechacte*) which produce utterances (*Rede*); similarly, their linguistic competence enables them to understand the utterances of others. Thus speech acts and acts of understanding closely correspond to each other: "Their correlation consists in that every act of understanding is the reverse of an act of speaking, and one must grasp the thought that underlies a given utterance."[28]

At this point Schleiermacher introduces a distinction of momentous importance for his hermeneutics. He believed that understanding an utterance, whether spoken or written, necessarily involved a double aspect, namely, the coalescence of two entirely different planes. The first concerned the understanding of an expression solely in terms of its relationship to the language of which it is a part. Each utterance must be seen as forming a part of the given interpersonal linguistic system (*Sprache*). But at the same time, the expression must also be understood as a part of the speaker's life-process, his internal or mental history. Understanding, for Schleiermacher,

takes place only in the coinherence of these two moments:

1. An act of speaking cannot even be understood as a moment in a person's development unless it is also understood in relation to the language. . . .
2. Nor can an act of speaking be understood as a modification of the language unless it is also understood as a moment in the development of the person.[29]

To these two sides of understanding correspond two distinct modes of interpretation (*Auslegung*), which Schleiermacher called grammatical and psychological or technical. If each would occur without the other (in reality they never occur independently of each other), the grammatical interpretation would exclude the author, and the psychological one would ultimately disregard language. Under the label psychological or technical interpretation, Schleiermacher gathered all those aspects of verbal understanding which are not strictly grammatical in nature but make up the individual character of an utterance, that is, how this utterance relates to its author's individuality, its particular genre, and the historical circumstances it embodies. Boeckh, Schleiermacher's student, would later differentiate more accurately among generic, individual, and historical interpretation.[30]

Both aspects of the act of speaking and of understanding point to the primordial speech act of a speaker in whom the meaning of a text is grounded. To understand Schleiermacher's concept of the author (speaker) and to avoid attaching the label of Romantic subjectivism to it, this concept must be seen within the context of linguisticality as he conceived it. The primordial author is not a fixed substance — as little as the "I" in Fichte's *Science of Knowledge*[31] — but rather something fluid and dynamic, something mediated, an act rather than a substance. It is the act from which the work originates. This authorial act constitutes itself in the creation of the work. It is the act which synthesizes the two planes mentioned earlier: the system of language and the inner system of thought. Man, the linguistic being, can be seen as the place where language articulates itself in each speech act and where each spoken utterance can only be understood in relation to the totality of language. But man is also a constantly evolving mind and his speaking can only be understood as a moment in his mental life (*Tatsache im Denkenden*). Schleiermacher thus combines— to use contemporary terminology— a structural and a phenomenological viewpoint. To interpret what he means by a moment in one's mental life in strictly psychological terms is therefore not admissible. Through verbal articulation the mental fact becomes exemplary. This is so because for Schleiermacher mental facts articulated as speech are not independent of language. Or, in Schleiermacher's own words: "Speech as mental fact cannot be understood if it is not understood as linguistic signification [*Sprachbezeichnung*], because the innate nature of language modifies our mind."[32]

What this means ultimately is that the traditional label of the psychologism of Schleiermacher's position can no longer be maintained. Even the purely intentional mental side of speech—speech as a mental phenomenon—is not free from language. It is always conditioned and modified by its linguistic form. At the same time, Schleiermacher does not condemn man to the prison house of language as some of our modern theorists do. For language itself, according to Schleiermacher and also to Wilhelm von Humboldt, while it forces its formal patterns upon thought, in return must suffer the influence, the labor of thought upon it.

Schleiermacher viewed hermeneutics as the "art of understanding" where "understanding" is elevated to the art of a scholarly discipline. He thought hermeneutics should not, however, concern itself with the specific body of rules found in the hermeneutic treatises of the theologians or jurists. Nor should it include the presentation of what one has understood to others. The latter was relegated to the sister discipline of rhetoric. Schleiermacher argued that presentation amounted to producing another text which itself would become an object of hermeneutic concern—but which was not part of hermeneutics. However, it seems doubtful whether hermeneutics, by excluding from its agenda the element of presentation, can still fulfill the task which Schleiermacher envisions. For the art of the philologist consists largely in generally accepted procedures, assumptions, verbal strategies, an institutionalized body of knowledge and the tacit agreement on standards for hermeneutic competence. The presentation of one's understanding is an integral part of the art in question. Schleiermacher does not offer us a clear distinction between understanding and interpretation (*Auslegung*). He often implies that the art of understanding is also the art of interpretation. He does not see that interpretation as explication (*Auslegung*) is necessarily verbal and thus discursive. Thus, while founding modern hermeneutics on the concept of understanding, Schleiermacher also imparted to this concept a basic ambiguity which is still with us today.


IV


> However, language is never a mere tool of communication, but an imprint of the mind and the world-view of its speakers. Sociability is the necessary means for its development, but by no means the only purpose behind its labors, because this purpose is found after all in the individual as its end-point.
>
> Wilhelm von Humboldt


The historian Droysen has called Wilhelm von Humboldt "the Bacon of the historical sciences" and understood his own theory of history and human culture as an application and further elaboration of Humboldt's ideas.[33] Humboldt's importance for the development of the hermeneutics of the human sciences has been considerable indeed and is still increasing. Besides Droysen, the names Dilthey and Cassirer immediately come to mind. Early in his career Dilthey declared that he intended to emulate Humboldt's approach to the study of men and human speech in his own studies of religion. And he thought his attempt to ground his notion of understanding in human nature was in harmony with Humboldtian principles.[34] Cassirer's project of a philosophy of symbolic forms assigned a special status to language which provided the key to man's entire range of symbolic creations. Cassirer defines language strictly in Humboldtian terms, and the first volume of his *Philosophy of Symbolic Forms* can be read as an interpretation of Humboldt's philosophy of language for the purpose of providing an epistemological basis for Cassirer's own theory of the human sciences and their modes of operation.[35] The reception of many of Humboldt's ideas by various schools of linguistics in the last decades not only has created a new interest in Humboldt's linguistic writings but also, due to the increasing attention linguistics has been given by many social scientists in recent years, has led to a renewed relevancy of Humboldt's linguistics and philosophy of language for social and historical sciences. Yet there has been no recent study on Humboldt's contribution to modern hermeneutics.[36] This is doubly surprising because, in addition to the aforementioned names, the representatives of philosophical hermeneutics— notably Heidegger and Gadamer— often refer to Humboldt and lay claim to certain of his ideas.

Two different aspects of Humboldt's work must be considered in order to assess his contribution to modern hermeneutics: the hermeneutic dimensions of his views on language which form an integral part of his linguistics and philosophy of language; and, subsequently, his own application of some of his hermeneutic insights to historical writings— in particular, his introduction of the concept of understanding into the study of history. With Schleiermacher Humboldt shared certain fundamental beliefs regarding the nature of language, its relation to human nature, and the structure of the human mind. Their beliefs form part of what we might rightfully call the Romantic linguistic paradigm since it is shared to various degrees by other writers as well: A. W. and F. Schlegel, the poet Novalis, and philosophers like Bernhardi or Schelling.[37] In our own century the Swiss linguist Ferdinand de Saussure has been generally credited for having introduced a decisive distinction into linguistics between language as a system (*langue*) and language as speech or utterance (*parole*). Yet a very similar— if not the same— distinction was generally accepted by both Schleiermacher and Humboldt. However, in addition to viewing human linguisticality (*Sprachvermögen*) both as language (*Sprache*) and speech (*Rede*), Humboldt also used the distinction between language as *energeia* (process) and as *ergon* (objectified product) to characterize linguistic phenomena. This latter distinction cuts across both *langue* and *parole*— since both can be seen from the angle of either process or product.

Understanding for Humboldt was grounded in language and linguisticality and was seen by him (as by Schleiermacher) as the correlative of speaking. But for him speaking and understanding were necessarily connected with a third term: that of active linguistic competence (*Sprachkraft*) which occurred in both speaker and listener. "One can understand a word which one hears only because one could have spoken it oneself," Humboldt wrote.[38] This is an important idea, because it puts an end to the older notion which saw in language some neutral means of transporting "meanings" from the mind of one person into that of another. We found this transportative view of language to be operative in Chladenius's theory of interpretation. It was shattered with the advent of transcendental idealism and its application to the philosophy of language. There can be nothing in one's mind, Humboldt asserted, echoing Fichte's theory of knowledge,[39] except one's own spontaneous mental activity. Meaning cannot be transferred from one speaker's mind to that of another. In fact, meaning in this objective and naive sense did not exist at all for Humboldt. Meaning must be seen rather as the coproduction of speaker and listener where both share in the same active power of linguistic competence. Humans can understand each other, Humboldt argued, because they produce (*erzeugen*) and understand speech (*Rede*) according to the same underlying principles: those of the mind and those embodied in the grammar of the language which they share.

Even though certain universal principles were to be found in all languages (an idea which many latter-day "Humboldtian" linguists seem to have forgotten), each language, Humboldt believed, constituted through its grammatical form a unique manner and way of perceiving the world. The linguist's occupation, therefore, had a decidedly hermeneutic aspect to it: studying another language meant to liberate oneself to some degree from the fetters of one's own and to gain through the other language another perspective on the world. This process of understanding would repeat itself in one's own language as well: from the understanding of the verbal utterances of others to the written word, culminating in works of literature and philosophy. Each utterance, each work in a given language is the product of an individual mind and retains an aura of individuality. For this reason every act of understanding, Humboldt thought, was in some way also necessarily a non-understanding.

Humboldt believed that this shortcoming of all human language could be compensated for to some degree on another level. For language in its fullest sense— language as process (*energeia*)— only occurred in the societal context.[40] Societies are internally linked through language, which constituted not only a cultural force but a cultural product as well. Human beings can only understand themselves, according to Humboldt, if they test the intelligibility of their words against other humans. Objectivity of understanding, in other words, can be obtained to a certain degree if the utterance I have produced through my own mental activity resounds from the mouth of another person. What Humboldt is trying to say is that there are certain elementary forms of linguistic understanding and communication which occur in all human societies. These might in turn serve as a basis for achieving objectivity in the human sciences and the humanities. Humboldt's position thus anticipates the solution to a problem which Dilthey later tried to solve from an essentially different and extralinguistic point of view: that of determining the nature of understanding and of objectivity in the cultural sciences (*Geisteswissenschaften*).

Humboldt's essay "On the Task of the Historian" has been a favorite classic among German historians from Gervinus and Droysen to Dilthey, Troeltsch, and Meinecke; many commentaries have been written about it—including a recent one by the American historian Paul Sweet.[41] What interested historians principally was Humboldt's notion of the role which ideas play in history, and the relation between the craft of the historian and that of the poet. Beginning with Meinecke's research into the rise of the modern historical consciousness, Humboldt's position has often been viewed within the context of nineteenth-century historicism.[42] Whether or not this is an accurate assessment, the essay with its complex and multifaceted argumentation certainly offers a wealth of insights from the many different perspectives which one might take. Most important, it presents to the reader not only a philosophy of history and a theory of historical research but also offers a theory of historical understanding of great subtlety. This theory already indicates the direction which hermeneutics would later take in the writings of Droysen, Dilthey, and even Heidegger and Gadamer. Against two of the schools of historical thought which would become dominant in the nineteenth century, the teleological one (which includes Hegelian, Marxist, and positivist historians) and the objectivist academic school, represented by Ranke and his followers, Humboldt developed his own hermeneutic approach to history. Humboldt maintained that a teleological view of history does not attain to the "living truth" of real history. Because the teleologically oriented historian looks in vain for "final causes" in the concrete phenomena of history, he feels obliged to search for an ultimate purpose of history in "lifeless institutions," and in the "notion of an ideal whole" or in the attainment of a "state of perfection of civil society or some ideas of this sort." Such teleological constructions were totally erroneous for Humboldt, because he thought that historical truth could only be found in the concrete individual phenomena themselves.[43] Yet the deceptively simple definition (à la Ranke) of the historian's task, with which Humboldt begins the essay, leads to more and more complex questions: for what actually happens in history is only partially accessible to the glance of the historian. The historian merely perceives some scattered and isolated events and never the coherence or nexus between them. The historian himself must supply the inner coherence and unite the individual events without which these events would be meaningless. Thus there existed for Humboldt an inner affinity between the artist and the historian and their respective crafts: both have to rely on their creative imagination to produce a guiding vision which would unite all individual elements into a cohesive whole.

This creative notion of the task of the historian implies still another idea which would acquire great importance in hermeneutic thought. If the historian must interpret individual phenomena in the light of an overriding cohesive whole which itself is not directly observable, he must supply the idea of this whole himself. In other words, the historian is involved in what later generations will call the hermeneutic circle. This means that in any process of understanding the parts must be understood in relation to the whole, just as the whole can only be understood in relation to its parts. In actuality this apparent paradox is always overcome by the historian, because he begins his work with an intuition of the invisible coherence which unites the individual event.

If Droysen perceived Humboldt as the latter-day Bacon of the historical studies, it is not surprising that he owed to Humboldt one of his most famous and influential distinctions which he passed on to the emerging hermeneutics of the human sciences. I am referring to Droysen's designation of the term "understanding" (*Verstehen*) to define the nature and method of the historical sciences as opposed to those of the natural sciences.[44] Through Droysen understanding became a technical term which stood for a view widely held since the latter part of the nineteenth century of the dichotomy between the natural sciences and the human sciences. According to this view, the former engage in causal explanation (*Erklärung*) and the latter were identified with "the method of understanding" (*Verstehen*). At the end of the nineteenth and the beginning of the twentieth centuries Dilthey would provide the theoretical underpinnings for this view and transform Humboldt and Droysen's historical method into that of the human sciences at large (*Geisteswissenschaften*).

Humboldt maintained in his essay that the historian should above all study the "form" of that which happens in history. This alone would enable him to understand what in fact can be profitably investigated. For the historian understanding and investigation go hand in hand (we shall find these two terms again in Droysen) and help him to recognize what he would not have learned from his mere use of reason (*Verstandesoperationen*). What is required is that the historian's "investigative capability" (*forschende Kraft*) become assimilated with the object under investigation. Only when this takes place is he able to bridge the gap between himself and the historical phenomena, between subject and object. But how does the historian attain to the form of an event? Humboldt's answer—by drawing it from the events themselves—seems contradictory at first. But this contradiction disappears upon closer examination. According to Humboldt, every act of comprehension (*Begreifen*) "presupposes, as a condition of its possibility, the existence of an analogue" in the person who is comprehending and in the phenomena actually comprehended by him. This analogue constitutes what Humboldt calls a "precursive primary correspondence between subject and object."[45] In the case of linguistic understanding, as we have seen, this primary correspondence is to be found in the commonality of the language shared by speaker and addressee, in their common linguistic competence. When it comes to historical understanding, the gap between historian and event, between subject and object is bridged in a similar manner. It is not by reaching outside or abstracting from his subjectivity that the historian comprehends something, or by passively letting the object affect him. Subject and object, historian and historical phenomenon, for Humboldt stand in a pregiven correspondence to each other. This correspondence, which he also calls the "preexisting basis of understanding" (*vorgängige Grundlage des Begreifens*), results from the fact that what is effective (*wirksam*) in world history is also active within man himself. Thus an inner bond exists between the spirit of a nation or a community, as expressed in its history and the historian investigating this history. With reflections like these Humboldt clearly anticipates Heidegger's and Gadamer's respective notions of an ontological or historical preunderstanding as the basis of all formal understanding and interpreting in the human sciences. In fact, we can discern in his ideas a close anticipation of Gadamer's view of understanding as a fusion of two horizons: that of the interpreter ("Subject") and the phenomenon ("Object") which share a common effective historical coherence (*wirkungsgeschichtlicher Zusammenhang*).

## V

Understanding is the most perfect knowledge that is attainable for us humans.

Johann Gustav Droysen

Even though many of Humboldt's ideas can be interpreted in the light of later developments—as we have just done ourselves—it would be a serious mistake to view his contributions merely as an anticipation of certain twentieth-century schools of thought. Humboldt's hermeneutics rests on its own feet and must be understood in its own terms before its relation to other schools of thought can be properly explored. The same is also true of the historical and hermeneutic theories of Johann Gustav Droysen. Droysen's intellectual fortunes have been on the rise in recent years. Hayden White believes that in Germany today Droysen is "ranked with Marx and Dilthey" and equals their importance as an historical thinker.[46] The work upon which Droysen's reputation rests is his *Historik, or Lectures on the Encyclopedia and Methodology of History*.[47]

Droysen developed the *Historik* over many years from 1852 until 1882 to 1883 when he taught this course at the University of Berlin for the last time before his death. In the Anglo-Saxon world Droysen is mainly known as the leading historian of the Prussian school of historiography, whose adherents interpreted German history from the point of view of Prussia's mission to bring about the unification of Germany.[48] But besides his work on German history, Droysen also distinguished himself in the field of ancient history, where he is best known for his work on Alexander the Great and the late Greek civilization. (It was he who coined the term Hellenism.) His outspoken political engagement as an historian made for a conception of the historian's task which was radically different from that of Leopold von Ranke and his school. Droysen did not believe that the historian should or would ever be able to write objective history and to recreate the past as it actually happened: given the nature of human life the past will always remain inaccessible to us. On the other hand, the historian finds himself surrounded or affected by events and forces which originated in the past. These constitute the proper object of his investigations. In short, it is the past within the present which makes us ask historical questions and pursue our work as historians. We must interpret remnants of the past— documents, books, monuments, records of legal or economic systems— in order to attain an understanding of what they reveal about the past. The task of the historian is first of all a hermeneutic one for Droysen. Consequently, hermeneutics for him is an integral part of a comprehensive historical theory. This theory is concerned with the subjective and objective conditions of historical understanding and research, with the nature of the historical object, and with the methodology which the historian ought to pursue.[49] As a student Droysen had attended Hegel's Lectures on the Philosophy of World History, and he undoubtedly learned from Hegel's notion of historical reality. There is a certain similarity between Hegel's notion of an "objective spirit" (*objektiver Geist*) which he introduced to describe social, political, and cultural systems, and Droysen's term for these entities, "ethical powers" (*Sittliche Mächte*). But Droysen rejected Hegel's teleological scheme of world history as the self-realization of spirit and, instead, opened himself to the quite different ideas of Humboldt and of Schleiermacher, particularly their notion of understanding.

Droysen defined the historical method as "understanding by means of investigation" (*forschendes Verstehen*). For him there were three distinct methods for obtaining knowledge, each characterized by its own mode of cognition resulting from the nature of the objects of knowledge and of the human mind:

> the speculative (philosophically or theologically), the physical, and the historical. Their essence is to find out [*erkennen*], to explain [*erklären*], to understand [*verstehen*].[50]

These methods represented three different and independent paths to knowledge, Droysen believed. None was privileged, but each presented reality from a different perspective. Drawing his inspiration mainly from Humboldt's posthumous work, *Introduction to the Kawi Language* (1836),[51] Droysen added a new and important dimension to the concept of understanding. He thought that one should go beyond the purely semantic or "rational" meaning of an utterance and consider its expressive functions as well; that is, its psychological, emotional, and spiritual (*geistige*) content. An utterance, in order to be fully understood, must also be comprehended as an expression of something "internal" which discloses to the historian—besides its obvious meaning—the attitude, intention, or state of mind of its originator. According to Droysen the historian is able to understand all of these things because he is dealing with nothing alien to him but with an expression of man's inwardness and inner nature. In his own manner Droysen restated and laid a new foundation for the notion of historical understanding first expressed by Vico in his *New Science* of 1724. Vico maintained that we can have a true understanding only of the world of history (and not of nature), because in history we can comprehend what man has made himself; only here do truth and fact (*verum et factum*) coincide.[52] In his *Historik* Droysen writes:

> Understanding is the most perfect knowledge [*das vollkommenste Erkennen*] that is attainable for us humans.[53]

And in another place:

> The possibility of this understanding arises from the kinship of our nature with that of the utterances lying before us as historical material. A further condition of this possibility is the fact that man's nature, at once sensuous and spiritual, speaks forth every one of its inner processes in some form apprehensible to the senses, mirrors these inner processes, indeed, in every utterance.[54]

Behind these and similar formulations we can trace Humboldt's description of the expressive side of language. The extent to which the Romantic linguistic paradigm is still alive for Droysen can be gathered from his equation of the historical and linguistic modes of understanding. "Our historical understanding is quite the same as when we understand someone who is speaking to us," he writes.[55] In this same vein Droysen also mentions the connection between the whole and its parts which is operative in any process of understanding. Formulations like the following would frequently be reiterated in the future by other writers: "The part is understood within the whole from which it originated, and the whole is understood from the part in which it finds expression."[56]

If Droysen called the historical method "understanding by means of investigation," this means that for him understanding per se did not constitute this method except insofar as it was combined with the craft of the practicing historian. This craft rested on two procedures: criticism and interpretation. The first, which was derived from the philological tradition of the *Ars Critica,* was intended to secure the truth status and authenticity of the historian's sources and purported facts. The second was concerned with the evaluation and explication of what the sources had yielded as historical facts according to specific modes and classes of interpretation. Droysen distinguished four types of historical interpretation: pragmatic, conditional, psychological, and ethical interpretations.[57] Consequently, Droysen thought that interpretation must always tend toward explicitness; that is, it must find expression in the historian's account of his findings. For this reason he included in his *Historik* a section called "Topics" (after the Aristotelian rhetorical tradition) with specific guidelines and rules of presentation for the historian to follow.[58] We can say, therefore, that in order to function properly as a methodological concept, understanding has to find its appropriate expression. This was an important discovery. In this respect, Dilthey's version of the same concept represents a step backwards from Droysen's. The discursive aspects of "understanding" and of "interpretation," which begin to emerge in Droysen's hermeneutics, disappear again and are replaced by another view of the matter.

## VI

Of the varied signs and symbols in which the human spirit expresses itself, the most adequate to express knowledge is speech. To study the spoken or written word is, as the name philology testifies, the earliest philological activity whose universality and meaning are clear: without communication knowledge and life itself would fare ill. Philology is actually one of the prime conditions of life, an original element in the depth of human nature as well as in the chain of culture. It rests upon a basic pursuit of cultured people; to philosophize is possible for uncivilized nations, but to practise philology is not.

August Boeckh

Before taking up the beginnings of philosophical hermeneutics in Wilhelm Dilthey's work, it is necessary to focus on the contributions which the classical scholar August Boeckh has made to hermeneutics. To him we owe the most comprehensive and carefully elaborated theory of interpretation in the nineteenth century from the perspective of a philologist.[59] Boeckh was an heir to the philological traditions of eighteenth- and early nineteenth century classical scholarship of central Europe. He combined a grasp of the achievements of the older humanist scholarship with the new encyclopedic and methodological concerns of the age of Romanticism. With the philologists F. A. Wolf and F. Ast he shared a vital interest in the hermeneutic problems raised by their work in classical antiquity which embraced its linguistic, literary, and cultural aspects.[60] But he rejected many of their assumptions and, instead, closely followed the ideas and principles set forth by his teacher Schleiermacher, whose hermeneutics became the theoretical basis for his own system, contained in his monumental *Encyclopedia and Methodology of the Philological Sciences*.[61]

Boeckh developed his hermeneutic theory within the context of his *Encyclopedia* because he considered it the necessary basis for philology. Philology, in turn, constituted for him the matrix of all human sciences. To understand Boeckh's hermeneutic system and his complex theory of interpretation we must first explain his notion of philology. Boeckh defines the task of the philologist as "achieving knowledge of what is known" (*Erkennen des Erkannten*), a formulation which has given rise to much criticism and contradictory interpretations. Since I think that he explained quite well what he meant by that definition, I should like to quote his own words:

> The genuine task of philology seems, then, to be the knowledge [*das Erkennen*] of what has been produced by the human spirit, i.e., the knowledge of what is known [*des Erkannten*].[62]

This means that philological knowledge is concerned with the knowledge invested in the cultural creations of mankind as they have come down to us. Boeckh is not advocating simply a rethinking or a reconstruction of an original meaning. In order to make the knowledge invested in cultural artifacts the object of philological knowledge, the philologist must go beyond the obvious meaning which the original author intended and uncover the formal and material conditions behind them. These conditions are often hidden to the author, Boeckh thought, or lie unconsciously in his mind. Because all philological knowledge is based on understanding as its mode of cognition, it follows that the philologist must aim at understanding a work or cultural phenomenon not only differently but also "better" than its author or producer.

Boeckh believed that the most adequate expression of knowledge available to man was language. Philology, which deals primarily with the spoken and written word, was therefore the basis of all human sciences for him. This history of science and of learning is essentially "philological." History itself as a discipline is not possible without philology. But philology is also "historical": a strict separation between the two disciplines is, according to Boeckh, not possible. For example, the grammar of any given language which the philologist studies is also a historical phenomenon. It contains the linguistic system of a nation as it has historically evolved (*historisch gewordene Sprachsystem*), and the philologist may study it either diachronically or in a definite synchronic state of its history.

Philology for Boeckh was both a universal human science and the science of the culture of antiquity. Since in both instances the understanding of verbal and linguistic phenomena constituted the core of the philological activity, hermeneutics had to occupy a prominent position within his system. Following Schleiermacher, Boeckh argued for a general hermeneutics which could provide a comprehensive theory of understanding rather than a hermeneutics consisting of practical rules and precepts. Boeckh's hermeneutics is concerned with studying the art of understanding and interpretation as practiced by the philologist. This study was necessary because the philologists themselves were not aware of the

hermeneutic principles inherent in their philological work. These principles had
to be made explicit—and this was the task of hermeneutic theory:

> Correct understanding, like logical thinking, is an art, and therefore rests
> in part on a half-conscious competence. Hermeneutics is the methodical
> development of the principles of understanding [*Gesetze des Verstehens*].[63]

As a classical philologist Boeckh was aware that the operations of understanding associated with his craft required a number of specific competencies if the
historical gap which separated the researcher from the object under investigation
was to be successfully bridged. For these competencies he used the term interpretation. Interpretation, in other words, constituted the necessary condition for an
adequate or correct understanding of a given cultural artifact. Boeckh distinguished—as we mentioned in our discussion of Schleiermacher—four classes of
interpretation which constituted a totality of closely interrelated and interacting
operations. In analyzing our understanding we can find, he thought, these four
distinct interpretive operations at work: the grammatical, the historical, the
generic, and the individual. Each can be isolated and made a topic of study. But
in actuality all of them interact: there can be no understanding of a text without
the presence of all four modes of interpretation. Without grammatical understanding the text would remain mute, but grammatical understanding without
reference to the historical element in the language of the text would not be
possible. The historical understanding, in turn, would be blocked without also
comprehending the generic characteristics of the text, and so forth. In short, each
of the four modes of interpretation modifies and presupposes all the others, and
represents a specific competence which the philologist must acquire as part of
his craft.

In his *Encyclopedia* Boeckh introduced another important distinction, namely,
the distinction between interpretation and criticism which E. D. Hirsch in his
book *Validity in Interpretation*[64] has recently resurrected. Boeckh argues that all
acts of understanding can be viewed in two ways. First, understanding may be
directed exclusively toward the object itself without regard to its relationship to
anything else; and second, it may be directed only toward the relationship in
which the object stands to something else. In the first instance, understanding
is absolute and functions solely as interpretation; that is, one concentrates on
comprehending the object and its meaning on its own terms, that is, intrinsically.
In the second instance, one's understanding is purely relational: one concentrates
on the relationship which the object entertains with other phenomena, such as
its historical circumstances, the linguistic usage of its time, the literary tradition
in which it stands, and the value systems and beliefs which are contemporary
to the interpreter. In his actual work the philologist must continually rely on both
interpretation and criticism. His understanding would be uncontrolled and

unmethodical if he were not always aware of the interrelationship between the two.

Boeckh's hermeneutic theory contains a wealth of important insights. Many of these are of great relevance today when we are faced with the problem of establishing a literary hermeneutics.[65] The New Critics in this country and their continental counterparts fostered a narrow view of interpretation as the purely literary and aesthetic exegesis of a literary work selected from the canon of high literature. Following the demise of New Criticism and the rise of structuralist and post-structuralist methodologies, the notion of interpretation itself has been rejected by many. Boeckh's hermeneutics, on the other hand, demonstrates the full range of interpretative operations found in literary studies, operations which these studies share with the other human sciences and which should be made the object of renewed study if a truly literary hermeneutics is to become a reality.

## VII

Understanding and interpretation constitutes the method used throughout the human sciences. It unites all of their functions and contains all of their truths. At each instance understanding discloses a world.

Wilhelm Dilthey

Dilthey's hermeneutics represents the watershed between the nineteenth-century theories, which were an outgrowth of Romanticism, and those of the twentieth century which comprise philosophical hermeneutics and the methodological concerns of the social and historical sciences. But in some respect Dilthey still has his feet in both centuries, a fact which helps explain the often disconcerting complexities of his thought. His program for an "analysis of human life" (*Lebensanalyse*) and his concept of historicity presented Heidegger with an important impetus to develop his own existential hermeneutics in *Being and Time*. Yet at the same time, Dilthey remained a student of Schleiermacher and maintained a profound interest in his ideas throughout his life. After having studied Schleiermacher's thought in its various aspects for many years, he published in 1871 his monumental *Life of Schleiermacher*. This work was an attempt to portray the cultural and intellectual makeup of the entire age of early German Romanticism as it related to the inner and outer biography of the protagonist. This task, however, proved overwhelming in its scope even for the protean abilities and boundless energy which were the characteristics of Dilthey's intellect, and only the first volume of the *Life of Schleiermacher* was published during his lifetime. Meanwhile, there was hardly an area in the human and social sciences in which Dilthey did not maintain an active interest.[66] He published widely in such diverse fields as cultural anthropology, education, legal history, literary history and criticism

(German and comparative), psychology, intellectual history, the history of science, the history of historiography, musicology, and, last but not least, philosophy and the history and methodology of the human sciences. In many of these areas, particularly in psychology, intellectual and literary history, sociology and philosophy, his contributions permanently influenced the development of the discipline. An interest in hermeneutic problems pervades Dilthey's entire work, from his first youthful notes and essays to his extensive *opus posthumum* concerning a *Critique of Historical Reason*. His hermeneutic interest asserted itself in his attempt to provide a philosophical foundation for the human sciences and to secure for their methodology the highest possible degree of certainty. In 1883 he published his *Introduction to the Human Sciences*. The subtitle of this work spelled out the task which Dilthey had set for himself: an "Attempt at a Foundation for the Study of Society and of History."[67] Dilthey maintained that the human sciences formed a "totality" of their own with a body of knowledge, which was independent from that of the natural sciences. The human sciences should not borrow their methods from these, as the advocates of positivism had claimed. Droysen had already vigorously protested the positivistic treatment of history by the English historian Henry Thomas Buckle and had opposed his own method of investigative understanding to the method of explaining historical events through fictitious "laws of history" which were patterned after the mechanical laws of the natural sciences.[68] Dilthey went beyond Droysen and made the concept of understanding the cornerstone of his theory by attempting to secure its epistemological basis. At the same time he enlarged its applicability to include the entire spectrum of the social and human sciences (*Geisteswissenschaften*). The first volume of the *Introduction to the Human Sciences* set forth the problems in detail and traced the evolution of the historical consciousness in the human sciences. But a second volume with the promised solution to the problems raised in the first one never appeared. It had become increasingly difficult for Dilthey to elaborate the desired epistemology of understanding which would make this concept into a methodological basis for the human sciences and confer validity to the knowledge produced by the humanist and human scientist in their work.

In keeping with the beliefs of his age, Dilthey thought at first that psychology could provide a firm basis for his enterprise. But since the kind of psychology which Dilthey needed did not exist, he began to create his own. Against the psychology of his day with its mechanistic models of explanation he proposed a new analytical and descriptive psychology which aimed at investigating the structures of human mental activities and their inherent order.[69] Dilthey was determined to supplement Kant's *Critique of Pure Reason* with a *Critique of Historical Reason*. If the former had dealt with reason in the world of nature (scientific reason), the latter was to be concerned with reason as it manifested itself in the human world. However, Dilthey's efforts to transform psychology into an instrument for epistemological analysis remained fruitless or inconclusive at best.[70] It was only late in his life that he was able to make some significant headway. This occurred under the impact of Edmund Husserl's *Logical Investigations* (1899–1901), whose importance for his own enterprise was immediately apparent to Dilthey.[71] Returning to his earlier studies on Schleiermacher and adopting Hegel's theory of the "objective spirit," Dilthey now proceeded to develop his hermeneutics of the human sciences from the phenomenological vantage point made available to him by Husserl. He produced numerous studies, drafts and treatises for his *Critique of Historical Reason*. In 1910—one year before he died—his pioneering treatise *On the Construction of the Historical World in the Human Sciences* appeared.[72]

At first glance, Dilthey seems to follow closely in the footsteps of his nineteenth-century predecessors by emphasizing, as they had, the concept of understanding. But compared to Schleiermacher, for example, a radical shift, with far-reaching implications, occurred in his position. Dilthey abandoned Schleiermacher's contention that understanding was primarily rooted in language and man's linguistic nature, an idea still present in Boeckh's view of "grammatical interpretation," and he embraced instead a very different conception.[73] In Dilthey's view, understanding as a methodological concept has its roots and its origin in the process of human life itself: it is primarily a "category of life" (*Lebenskategorie*).

What is meant by "category of life"? Dilthey maintains that in their daily lives human beings find themselves in situations in which they have to "understand" what is happening around them so that they may act or react accordingly. Thus, their actual behavior reflects their lived understanding and comprehension of their social or cultural environment. Dilthey claimed that all "higher" or complex manifestations of understanding, including those found in the human sciences, derived from those "lower" or primitive forms of comprehension. We can detect in Dilthey's position a definite affinity with the views of the later Wittgenstein, according to whom the meaning of words and statements rests ultimately on a specific practice or "form of life" (*Lebensform*).[74] This affinity between Wittgenstein's analytic philosophy of language and certain tenets in the hermeneutic tradition will become more apparent as we move on to other writers. The philosopher K.-O. Apel, for example, made it the starting point toward a new linguistically and socially oriented hermeneutics, as is evident from his essay which is included in this *Reader*.

In order to grasp the full dimensions of Dilthey's concept of understanding, we must examine it within the context into which he placed it. According to Dilthey, what we understand as humanists or human scientists is always a manifestation of human life, a "life-expression" (*Lebensäusserung*). But understanding itself is a manifestation of life; acts of understanding are lived by us, they constitute "lived experience" (*Erlebnis*). The concept of "lived experience" functions as the middle ground in Dilthey's system.[75] A "life-expression" points back at a "lived experience" as its source, and we understand its expressed meaning (*Ausdruck*) in the form of a "lived experience" again. It seems appropriate at this point to comment briefly on Dilthey's use of terms if we want to avoid some of the common misunderstandings and confusions arising from his use of terminology. In view of the importance of the points at issue, I hope the reader will forgive me for the short philological observations which follow.

Dilthey uses both terms "life-expression" (*Lebensäusserung*) and "expression" (*Ausdruck*). Even though both are usually rendered into English as "expression," there is a significant difference in German between *Äusserung* and *Ausdruck*. The first, *Äusserung,* is related to *aussen,* "outside," "external"; its cognate verb is *äussern, sich äussern,* which has the basic meaning of "to externalize." According to Dilthey, what humans "externalize" in their actions is their particular state of mind, their emotive and mental attitude. But *äussern* also means "to utter"; an *Äusserung* therefore can be an utterance. In English usage the terms to utter and utterance designate verbal expressions, whereas the German *Äusserung,* as Dilthey uses it, can refer to every possible mode of expression, from gesture, voice, movement, rhythmic patterns, visual forms and arrangements to verbal expressions, actions, and attitudes. An *Äusserung,* then, should be viewed in relation to the individual who produced it, as an expression of his life.

To shed some additional light on Dilthey's position, let me in conclusion to these philological remarks relate his notion of life-expression to ideas which are central to the German intellectual tradition in the nineteenth century, and which can be found in both Hegel's idealism and Marx's dialectical anthropology and sociology. In a famous couplet the poet Goethe once commented upon the relation between "essence" and "appearance," claiming that we could not conceive of one as existing without the other:

> Appearance—what would it be without essence?
> Essence—could it ever be—if it did not appear?

> Der Schein, was ist er, dem das Wesen fehlt?
> Das Wesen, wär es, wenn es nicht erschiene?

In agreement with this opinion, in his *Phenomenology of the Spirit,* Hegel asserted that the power of the mind could only be as great as its power of expression (*Äusserung*). Consequently, the *Phenomenology of the Spirit* itself can be interpreted as a systematic exploration and exposition of the powers of the human spirit through its expressive manifestations. It was Marx who later credited Hegel with having discovered through his notion of expression (*Äusserung*) the idea of labor as constitutive force in human life. For Marx, this very notion of labor as human self-expression (*Äusserung*) becomes a central category for his entire theory of history and of society. As he put it in *The German Ideology:* "As individuals express their lives—so they are. What they are, therefore, coincides with their production, both with what they produce and how they produce."[76] Against this background we can easily discern that it was Dilthey who uncovered the hermeneutic dimension of this notion of expressive manifestation or *Äusserung*. If we were to rephrase the Marxian dictum from Dilthey's hermeneutic perspective, it would therefore read: "As individuals express their lives— so they can be understood by others."

Dilthey distinguishes expression (*Ausdruck*) from life-expressions as a class of hermeneutic objects that carry a meaning independent from the individuals who produced them and whose life-expressions they once were. These may be meaning complexes such as legal or economic systems which result from human interactions, or works of art which Dilthey believed to be the highest form of expression. In the human sciences, "understanding" becomes formal and methodical (*wissenschaftlich*) once it is directed at a specific class of hermeneutic objects. In the actual work of the humanist, understanding becomes explication. It is noteworthy that Dilthey considered the highest forms of explication those dealing with life-expressions of a written nature:

> Because our mental life finds its fullest and most complete expression only through language, explication finds completion and fullness only in the interpretation of the written testimonies of human life.[77]

Paul Ricoeur has recently restated Dilthey's idea of hermeneutic primacy of the written word and developed a model of textual interpretation as a foundation for a general hermeneutics of the human and social sciences.[78] But Ricoeur's notion of interpretation is not identical with Dilthey's "explication." For Dilthey, the student of Droysen, the human sciences had as their object the interpretation of all phenomena, nonverbal as well as verbal, and the latter required their own specific methods of investigation.

Commencing with Dilthey, the term "understanding" has assumed the meaning of a "category of life" or an existential principle without ceasing to be considered a methodological concept in the human sciences. The difficulty is that a gap has arisen between the two which neither Dilthey nor the adherents of philosophical hermeneutics have been able to bridge satisfactorily. Moreover, the practitioners of contemporary hermeneutic philosophy who have followed Heidegger have not been very successful in delineating the difference between the existential and the methodological aspect of understanding. Consequently, the distinction between understanding and interpretation which, we found, was frequently ambiguous in the texts of classical hermeneutics has become all but obliterated. One recent German writer, Bubner, has reduced hermeneutics itself to a "doctrine of understanding."[79] Dilthey, in contrast, had still maintained, as we have learned, that hermeneutics is both the art and science of understanding and interpretation.

Thus, for Dilthey, it was the task of the hermeneutician to make understanding and interpretation, as it has evolved in the disciplines of the sciences of man, the object of cognitive analysis. For this reason, Dilthey's ideas have maintained their vitality and presence in the methodological disputes among social scientists, historians, and literary students today.

VIII

> The essence of meaning is seen by us, not in the meaning-confering experience, but in its "content," the single, self-identical intentional unity set over against the dispersed multiplicity of actual and possible experiences of speakers and thinkers.
>
> Edmund Husserl

> Any understanding of the semantic units in the literary work (words, sentences, and complexes or structures of sentences) consists in performing the appropriate signitive acts and leads thereby to the intentional projection of the objects of these acts, or the intentional objects of the semantic units. Hence it appears, at first glance, that the understanding in ordinary reading suffices to constitute for the reader the objectivities of the work. But a closer look shows that this is not the case.
>
> Roman Ingarden

Dilthey in his later years came to appreciate through Husserl's teachings the avoidance of psychologistic reasoning and the importance of the idea of evidence and strict methodological procedure in cognitive analyses. He was not to remain the only thinker who benefited from the new phenomenological way of thinking. However, it would be a serious error to judge Husserl's importance for hermeneutic theory solely historically, that is, in terms of the impact he has had on Heidegger's thought, notably in *Being and Time*. Husserl's importance for hermeneutics and its further development is of a manifold and far-reaching nature. The *Logical Investigations*,[80] his first major work, sets forth nothing short of a new foundation for hermeneutic theory. It has exercised a strong influence on different writers from Ingarden in Poland and E. D. Hirsch in America to M. Leibfried in Germany.[81] Other works of Husserl which have had a momentous effect upon the development of twentieth-century hermeneutics include his *Phenomenology of Internal Time Consciousness* (1929), and his late works, *The Crisis of the European Sciences* (1936) and *Experience and Judgment* (1938).[82] In the latter two books Husserl introduced the notion of a "life-world" and laid the ground for a phenomenology of human social behavior. Subsequently, his student Alfred Schutz elaborated Husserl's ideas in sociological terms and fashioned from them his influential interpretive sociology.[83] In recent years, numerous volumes of Husserl's posthumous works have appeared under the sponsorship of UNESCO. These contain an untapped wealth of insights and ideas waiting to be studied in a hermeneutic context.[84]

Hermeneutic philosophy following Heidegger has prided itself on having established the prescientific ontological basis for the human sciences. But it has not succeeded, as we pointed out, in bridging the gap between this "foundation" and the critical epistemological function which notions like understanding and interpretation must fulfill in the actual work of the human scientist and humanist. Husserl and the adherents of his "strict" phenomenology have made their decisive contribution precisely at this junction. The *Logical Investigations* mark a new beginning for hermeneutic theory, because they are much more than an exploration of logic or the logical syntax of language. They are also concerned with the ontological conditions of meaningful discourse and the structure of those acts of consciousness which make it possible for our words "to point beyond themselves to things in the world."[85] By virtue of these acts alone there arises a world for us together with other humans with whom we can communicate. In the first of the *Investigations* Husserl offers a probing description of meaning-constituting acts as they occur in us and presents an outline of a theory of meaning and understanding. This theory is developed from the structures of the subjective phenomenological experience. But it is directed, at the same time, toward establishing the grounds for an intersubjective validity of "meaning," the mere possibility of which seems anathema today to many of our poststructuralist critics who themselves, nevertheless, take for granted the intersubjective meaningfulness of their own utterances.

The significance of Husserl's approach is that it is aimed at disclosing the common ground for the possibility of meaning and understanding in both the nonverbal and verbal realms, the worlds of actions and of language. Husserl is concerned with the description of intentional acts, in other words, acts whose meaning presents itself only in their actual performance (*Vollzug*). A phenomenological study and description of these performances necessarily involves the interpretation and explication of their implicit meaning—a meaning which is also accessible to other subjects. Hence we can discover in Husserl's phenomenological procedure itself an essentially hermeneutic quality of a paradigmatic nature.[86]

I do not wish to discuss Husserl's arguments in any detail or even to restate the results of his *First Investigation*. For our particular context it appears feasible, however, to underscore the importance of some of the distinctions which Husserl sets forth in this text. To begin with, there is the distinction between an act, its psychological content, and what the act intended, its meaning. If the intended meaning is fulfilled, it thereby becomes the meaning of the act and subsequently leads to the apprehension and perception of something in the real world, or to the expression of an utterance, or an understanding of an utterance's expressed meaning. Husserl would later introduce the terms *noesis* and *noemata* to distinguish between act and intended meaning. The point is, of course, that *noesis* and *noemata,* although genetically related, both have their own structures, which should not be confused. In a given expression one must distinguish, according to Husserl, between its expressed meaning and the object meant by it. The expression through its meaning always refers to its object as its referent. By its very nature, an expression possesses always an objective correlate, or, in other words, it projects the object meant in the meaning-fulfilling act. This correlate does not have to be a real object "out there" in the world in order for the expression to be meaningful. One is mistaken, Husserl argued, to identify the meaning of the expression with the object meant by it. Expressions like "round square" or "golden mountain" are not meaningless. Husserl's reasoning here parallels arguments set forth today by the generative linguists who maintain that seemingly nonsensical expressions are nevertheless meaningful and can be understood if their structure is grammatically acceptable.[87]

It is evident for Husserl that one and the same meaning can be meant or intended in different acts and by different subjects. This notion has some consequence for interpretation theory. Some members of certain contemporary schools of literary criticism seem to be committing the error, in Husserl's language, of identifying the act of meaning-fulfillment with the meaning of the act itself. The American critic Stanley Fish, for example, in a well-known essay, "Literature in the Reader: Affective Stylistics,"[88] eagerly identifies the meaning of a literary text with the total reading experience, that is, the total effect of that experience. According to Husserl, such assumption must be considered an error which can be explained by the fact that we ordinarily do not pay attention in our mind to the difference between the act of fulfillment and the meaning itself which is realized in this act. This is so, Husserl argues, because "in the act of fulfillment the act of intention coincides with the fulfilling act," so that "it readily seems as if the experience first got its meaning here, as if it drew meaning from the act of fulfillment. The tendency therefore arises to treat the fulfilling intuitions . . . as meanings."[89] The clarification of these relationships is precisely what Husserl's phenomenological analyses are all about. Studying the "total effect" of a reading experience may be of interest for developing a psychology or sociology of the reader, but it does not offer a way to discern and interpret methodically the meaning of the text which is concretized in this experience. Husserl's personal student, the late Polish philosopher and aesthetician Roman Ingarden, elaborated these distinctions in two important works, *The Literary Work of Art* (1929) and *On the Cognition of the Literary Work* (1968).[90]

The contributions of Ingarden to contemporary aesthetics can be evaluated variously from the point of view of the philosopher or that of the student of aesthetics and literary theory. In the first instance, Ingarden's position may be explained as a corrective for Husserl's division of reality into "real" and "ideal" entities. An investigation of the mode of being of the aesthetic object, which does not belong to either of the two divisions, offered an obvious approach to the problem of the Husserlian dichotomy. This view coincides with Ingarden's original intention.[91] In the second instance, we can cite the reception of his work by contemporary literary scholarship in various countries—by the Czech structuralists Mukarovsky and Vodicka, the German receptionist critics Iser and Warning, and by René Wellek in America. However, Ingarden's work must also be studied in the light of its significance for hermeneutic theory. Both of his major works, if seen together, represent a coherent and innovative approach to a number of the problems which classical hermeneutics tried to solve. Part of its importance results from the fact that Ingarden, by relying on the conceptual tools of phenomenology, did not employ the traditional hermeneutic concepts and terminology, but instead introduced a complex set of distinctions and a method of investigation which opened entirely new vistas. In his *Literary Work of Art* he developed an elaborate theory of the linguistic and nonlinguistic structures of literary works. In the sequel volume, *On the Cognition of the Literary Work,* he investigated the complex and highly structured acts through which literary meanings are understood and the literary work is concretized (i.e., actualized) in the reading experience. The important point for our context is that the meaning-apprehending acts and their inherent structures are studied by Ingarden in relation to the architecture of the literary work. He provides pioneering insights and descriptions of those processes and operations which lie at the bottom of the distinctions that classical hermeneuticians, such as Schleiermacher and Boeckh, made in the nineteenth century. The significance of Ingarden's work for developing a literary hermeneutics has hardly been realized.

In *The Literary Work of Art* Ingarden treated the structures of a work of literature in a seemingly objective fashion and abstracted from the fact that a work of art constitutes an object only for a given subject. In the sequel volume he undoes this abstraction and studies the work in relation to the different attitudes which we assume as readers. The analysis of the process of "understanding" and "concretization" reveals certain structural elements and typical qualities. Their description by Ingarden can be seen as an explicit exposition of those interpretive acts which mediate our understanding of literary texts. Literary understanding is possible only through interpretation as "silent" mental activity. The rules and classifications of classical hermeneutics intimated this state of affairs, though in an unreflected manner. Thus, the division by Boeckh of "interpretation" into grammatical, historical, generic, and individual categories implied the existence of certain correlative acts through which the constitutive elements of interpretation can now be studied and described. A phenomenologically-oriented hermeneutics would have to replace the mere enumeration of "kinds of interpretation" with the description of the constitutive acts from which they arise; such a description must be directed at these operational acts, as well as at the literary objects themselves which are constituted through them. These operational acts of the mind and the resulting modes of interpretation cannot be viewed as separate aggregates. They are parts of a unified process. Schleiermacher was aware of this fact when he stated that the division into grammatical and psychological interpretation was merely a useful heuristic device, for "understanding is nothing but the identity of these two moments."[92]

## IX

With the term "understanding" we have in mind a fundamental *existentiale*, which is neither a definite *species of cognition*, distinguished, let us say, from explaining and conceiving, nor any cognition at all in the sense of grasping something thematically. Understanding constitutes rather the Being of the "there" in such a way that, on the basis of such understanding, a *Dasein* can, in existing, develop the different possibilities of sight, of looking around, and of just looking. In all explanation one uncovers understandingly that which one cannot understand; and all explanation is thus rooted in Dasein's primary understanding.

                                                    Martin Heidegger

Heidegger did not stop . . . with the transcendental schema that still motivated the concept of self-understanding in *Being and Time*. Even in *Being and Time* the real question is not in what way being can be understood but in what way understanding *is* being, for the understanding of being represents the existential distinction of *Dasein*.

                                                    Hans-Georg Gadamer

The philosophical hermeneutics of recent decades has derived much of its inspiration and conceptual framework from Martin Heidegger's ontology of human existence or *Dasein* (being-there) as he expounded it in *Being and Time* (1927).[93] This truly ground-breaking book, certainly Heidegger's most sustained effort, has made its mark over the years on the entire spectrum of the social and the human sciences from philosophy, psychology, jurisprudence, and theology to sociology and literary criticism. From the point of view of hermeneutics, it presents a new departure in more ways than one. First of all, Heidegger has given a new meaning to the term hermeneutics by associating it closely with his specific philosophical endeavor. By defining his own task as a philosopher as a hermeneutic one, he has transformed the character of philosophy itself from its previous occupation with metaphysical, ethical, epistemological, and aesthetical questions. But in doing so, he relied on the ideas found in the classical hermeneutic tradition and utilized for his own purposes the vocabulary which was developed by the classical writers in that tradition— Schleiermacher, Humboldt, and Boeckh— within the context of textual and philological hermeneutics. It may seem strange at first to encounter familiar terms like understanding, interpretation, and explication within the rather different context of Heidegger's fundamental ontology of human existence. These terms actually assume a key position in Heidegger's philosophy of *Being and Time*. On the other hand, it is not surprising that Heidegger's investigation into the foundation of the familiar hermeneutic concepts has changed the very character of traditional hermeneutics itself and disclosed new vistas for it, moving it away from traditional methodological concerns.

The principal task of the book was to offer an analysis of human existence so that eventually the horizon could be established for "an interpretation of the meaning of Being as such." In other words, the existential analysis necessarily had to precede and clear the way for the attack on the true problem at hand, the problem of Being (*Frage nach dem Sein*), that is, "the interpretation of Being." As we know, the "second part" of *Being and Time*, which was to contain this "interpretation," never appeared. Yet the ideas set forth in "part one" represent a hermeneutic philosophy in its own right par excellence. If, in comparison with other beings, human existence possesses an ontological priority with respect to the question of Being because of an intrinsic human concern with Being, the investigation and analysis of human existence in relation to Being necessarily involves, Heidegger maintains, interpretation. For, in fact, *Dasein*'s own specific state of Being remains concealed from it most of the time. Yet *Dasein* is also, as Heidegger puts it, "ontologically closest to itself," despite its ontological distance from itself. Heidegger contends that human existence embodies in its ontic constitution, as part of its Being, a preontological understanding of self and of the world in which it finds itself. The aim of *Being and Time* is to expose precisely this preunderstanding which *Dasein* possesses with respect to its Being.

Heidegger rejects Descartes's notion of the Ego—the thinking subject as a foundational category. For our hermeneutic context this means that he also rejects the Romantic notion of the sovereignty of the author as the subjective creator of his work, as well as that of the reader who, through the work, "understands" the author. Heidegger grounds his concept of understanding no longer in the subject; he considers it no longer an attribute of the Cartesian *res cogitans*, the thinking I, but grounds it instead in man's "Being-in-the-World." To explicate the meaning of this proposition we shall have to glance at the kind of phenomenological method Heidegger pursues in his analyses.

It is fair to say—if we are familiar with Husserl's work—that Heidegger restructures the latter's phenomenological method to fit his own purpose. In one section of the book, which is deservedly famous for the brilliance of its exposition, Heidegger discusses his notion of phenomenon and of phenomenology.[94] He charges phenomenology with the job "to uncover what is not immediately apparent." This means, for the enterprise of *Being and Time*, the methodical uncovering of the concealed structures of human existence in the world. In other words, the phenomenological task set forth in *Being and Time* is fundamentally a hermeneutic one: "the methodological intent of phenomenological description is to interpret," and "the Logos of the phenomenology of human existence has the character of *hermeneuein*," (Greek, "to interpret"). For all practical purposes, phenomenology and hermeneutics become identical in *Being and Time*:

> The phenomenology of Being-there is hermeneutic in the original sense of the word, because it signifies the business of interpretation.[95]

But this is not all. We noted that for Heidegger phenomenological hermeneutics is concerned with the disclosure of the basic existential structures of human existence (*Dasein*) as a necessary precondition for pursuing the question of Being. We can say, therefore, that hermeneutics has taken the place which, in traditional philosophy at least since Kant, was occupied by the transcendental critique in its various forms. Hermeneutics now has become the cornerstone of philosophy, the prolegomena to a true ontology as interpretation of Being. Meanwhile, hermeneutic questioning had to bring to an ontological understanding that understanding which *Dasein* possessed already as part of its Being. Thus, what the hermeneutic philosopher must explicate and understand is not external and alien to him. According to Heidegger, there is a certain primary existential understanding that is constitutive for man's being-in-the-world. It forms the basis for the concept of understanding as a methodological category as we know from the human sciences. With this position Heidegger goes several steps beyond that of Dilthey, from whom he undoubtedly learned. Dilthey, as we saw, interpreted the hermeneutic operations performed by the historian, social scientist, and humanist scholar as derivative from certain elementary acts of understanding found in everyday life. Heidegger, in contrast, views all acts of understanding from the elementary to the most complex kind, as springing from a primordial mode of understanding which is part of *Dasein*'s Being. *Dasein* is that kind of being to whom Being discloses itself. This disclosure lies at the heart of *Dasein*'s primordial understanding.

As a constitutive element of man's being-in the world, understanding bears an inner relationship to his temporality. According to Heidegger, man's being is essentially temporal: his lived horizon includes past, present, and future, but he projects himself primarily toward the future. Understanding is that mode through which the possibilities and potentialities of his life are disclosed to a person. In a primordial sense, understanding for Heidegger is both existential and hermeneutic; man interprets Being in terms of his projects in relation to the world. "Understanding," as it points toward a projected future possibility, calls for the realization of this possibility, for its fulfillment. For this kind of fulfillment Heidegger introduces the term "explication." Thus, *Dasein* always projects itself in an act of understanding toward self-realization, which is the unfolding or explication of this understanding. Consequently, interpretation originates in understanding and is always derived from it. This is an important stance. Heidegger and, following him, Gadamer insist that all forms of interpretation in real life and in the human sciences are grounded in understanding and are nothing but the explication of what has already been understood.

We must consider still another element of "understanding" in *Being and Time*. This element, Heidegger maintains, is responsible for the phenomenon of the hermeneutic circle which we discussed earlier; namely, the fact that we understand something only in relation to the whole of which it is a part, and vice versa. This paradox is only apparent, for the so-called hermeneutic circle reveals to us the nature of all understanding and interpretation. According to Heidegger, interpretation occurs only within a given horizon of preunderstanding. There can be no understanding and interpretation on the part of *Dasein* without such preunderstanding. These ideas would later be reapplied to the human sciences and the humanities and their history by Gadamer in his attempt to investigate their operations in order to determine their underlying structures of preunderstanding.

Heidegger, too, deals with the nature of interpretive statements, the kind we expect to find in the works of historians, social scientists, or literary critics. Interpretive statements or "assertions," as he calls them, are a derivative mode of interpretation for him.[96] Given that the nature of interpretation itself is an outgrowth of understanding, it follows that verbal explications and assertions are but the fulfillment of "understanding." They are the forms which understanding takes in the human sciences.

Words like "statement" or "assertion" indicate that the analysis has moved into a new plane: that of language and speech. Assertions which are made for the purpose of communication depend on speech. Speech and language for Heidegger are equally as important as understanding itself. We are told, in fact, that speech possesses a foundational quality of its own. Speech is the ordering and structuring power which dwells in our understanding, and for that reason becomes the basis for interpretation and assertion. Echoing Humboldt's ideas on language and linguisticality (*Sprachkraft*), Heidegger argues that understanding itself is of a linguistic nature. The essential structures of understanding and interpreting in the final analysis turn out to be intimately connected with language and speech.

However, Heidegger in *Being and Time* does not elaborate further on the linguisticality of understanding. This has something to do with the main argument of the book. Having established the relationship between understanding and speech, Heidegger moves on to demonstrate how inauthentic existence masks itself in alienated speech (*das Gerede*).[97] Only many years later, after his "ontological turn" (*Kehre*), did Heidegger return to the positive aspects of linguisticality in his essays on poetry and language. But then he no longer ventured to speak on this topic with the kind of rigor and determination that characterizes his diction in *Being and Time*. It was up to Gadamer to develop more fully the notion of the linguisticality of understanding which Heidegger had suggested.

The impact of Heidegger's existential hermeneutics went far beyond the confines of academic philosophy and can be detected in such diverse works as the Swiss critic Emil Staiger's influential *Fundamental Principles of Poetics* (1946)[98] or the psychiatrist Ludwig Binswanger's trend-setting *Basic Forms and Analysis of Human Existence* (1942).[99] In French and Anglo-Saxon literary criticism today Heidegger's ideas have gained a new momentum of actuality which still seems to be growing. But while this development is still in flux, it seems appropriate at this point to discuss Heidegger's relationship to theology as it evolved from *Being and Time* and, in particular, his relationship to the theology of Rudolf Bultmann and the so-called school of the New Hermeneutics. This New Hermeneutics is, above all, a theological movement which drew substantive inspiration from Heidegger's existential analysis, while it also attempted to revitalize some of the older Protestant hermeneutic traditions.[100] But we are interested not in the strictly theological concern of the movement, but rather its implications for the enterprise of general hermeneutics. In this one respect, the New Hermeneutics resembles Schleiermacher and his *Hermeneutik* despite the "new" hermeneuticians' general opposition to the latter's theology. Bultmann's point of departure is the ontology of *Being and Time*, the existential interpretation of man's being-in-the-world. Heidegger's concept of understanding in particular and his hermeneutic approach to the problems of philosophy were important for Bultmann in two different ways: for the philosophical substance and direction and for the methodology which Heidegger offered. Regarding the first, Bultmann believed that the message of the Holy Scriptures lies in its existential appeal. This appeal, he argued, is clothed in a mythological form of discourse, an expression of the world view and thinking of the times in which the Scriptures were written. The business of the contemporary theologian, Bultmann maintained, is to penetrate via interpretation this mythological shell, in other words, to pass through what is merely said to what is actually meant—the existential core of the text. Theological interpretation, as Bultmann once put it, "distinguishes what is said from what is meant and measures the former by the latter."[101] Bultmann's "what is meant," that is, the true kernel of the Scriptures, is essentially "what is meant" also by Heidegger's existential hermeneutics. Philosophy and theology for Bultmann ultimately have the same object: man and his existence. But these disciplines pursue their tasks in different ways. Philosophy, Bultmann believes, inquires "ontologically into the formal structures of human existence," whereas theology speaks about the "concrete man insofar as he is faithful."[102]

As interesting as the relationship may be from the standpoint of theology, between the philosophy of Martin Heidegger and the theology of Rudolf Bultmann and followers of the New Hermeneutics like Fuchs and Ebeling, the second, the methodological aspect of Bultmann's thinking, reaches clearly beyond the theological aspects of the debate. Bultmann was a student of Heidegger (with whom he was closely associated during their stay at the University of Marburg in the

1920s); but he was also an independent thinker in matters of hermeneutics and was thoroughly familiar with the history of the hermeneutic tradition in its major theological and secular representatives. Many of his ideas parallel or anticipate those of Gadamer or point beyond the position which the latter expounded in *Truth and Method.* We can find in Bultmann's writings concrete directions toward a general hermeneutics which is both philosophical and methodological in its intent. An essay published in 1950, "The Problem of Hermeneutics," contains an outline of his position. Developing his views out of and against those of Dilthey and Heidegger, Bultmann states that in any interpretation one must consider first the vital existential relationship (*Lebensbezug*) which both the author and the interpreter share with respect to the matter at hand expressed in the text. In all cases the interpreter's specific interest in what the text says determines the course of the interpretation. Thus, for Bultmann, the interest of the interpreter— in addition to his preunderstanding which he brings to his task— decides upon the nature and the direction of the interpretation.

> From the interest of the subject arises the nature of the formulation of the enquiry, the direction of the investigation, and so the hermeneutic principle applying at any given time. . . . The object of interpretation can be established by the *psychological interest.* . . . The object can be given by the *aesthetic interest . . .* lastly, the object of interpretation can be established by *interest in history as the sphere of life in which human existence moves.*[103]

There are, therefore, no historical facts or phenomena *per se* out of which knowledge could be fashioned. In formulations which echo those of Droysen in his *Historik,* Bultmann states emphatically that facts of the past turn into historic phenomena only "when they become significant for a subject which itself stands in history and is involved in it.[104] Bultmann's position represents an interesting link between the existential hermeneutics derived from Heidegger and the sociological views expounded later by Habermas and his followers.

## X

> In fact the horizon of the present is being continually formed in that we have continually to test all our prejudices. An important part of this testing is the encounter with the past and the understanding of the tradition from which we come. Hence the horizon of the present cannot be formed without the past. There is no more an isolated horizon of the present than there are historical horizons. Understanding, rather, is always the fusion of these horizons which we image to exist by themselves.
> Hans-Georg Gadamer, *Truth and Method*

When Hans-Georg Gadamer's *Truth and Method— Outline for a Philosophical Hermeneutics* appeared in 1960,[105] it evoked an immediate and lively response not only from philosophers but also from historians, social scientists, and humanists from various disciplines. Its appearance set a new pace and gave new directions for the study of the hermeneutic tradition and of the hermeneutic enterprise itself. Whereas Heidegger in *Being and Time* had fashioned hermeneutics into a philosophical tool for uncovering the ontological structure of human existence (*Dasein*), Gadamer now turned the new philosophical hermeneutics around and carried it back to its traditional grounds in the human sciences and to the problems which they faced. The ideas and arguments he espoused in *Truth and Method* and elsewhere constituted a powerful ingredient in the ideological and methodological debates which took place in West Germany in the 1960s and early 1970s. His exchange with Habermas— the major statements of which have been included in this anthology— proved to be of far greater interest in the long run than the widely publicized "positivism dispute" between the late T. W. Adorno on the one side and Karl Popper and Hans Albert on the other.[106]

To appreciate Gadamer's position it may be helpful first to characterize his relationship to the hermeneutic tradition. This relationship comprises elements of both continuity and rupture. Like his predecessors, Gadamer ascribes primary importance to the concept of understanding. But in contradistinction to Schleiermacher, Droysen, or Boeckh, who conceived of understanding as a means of overcoming the historical distance between the interpreter and the historical phenomenon, Gadamer maintains the historical nature of understanding itself. Any interpretations of the past, whether they were performed by an historian, philosopher, linguist, or literary scholar, are as much a creature of the interpreter's own time and place as the phenomenon under investigation was of its own period in history. The interpreter, Gadamer claims, is always guided in his understanding of the past by his own particular set of prejudices (*Vor-urteil*). These are an outgrowth and function of his historical existence. The philosophers of the Enlightenment and the objectivist school of historiography of the nineteenth century erred if they thought that prejudices were something purely negative which had to be and could be overcome by the historian in his search for objective truths. On the contrary, Gadamer maintains, prejudice is a necessary condition of all historical (and other) understanding. Acts of understanding or interpretation— both are essentially the same for Gadamer— always involve two different aspects: namely, the overcoming of the strangeness of the phenomenon to be understood, and its transformation into an object of familiarity in which the horizon of the historical phenomenon and that of the interpreter become united.

Moreover, understanding is only possible, according to Gadamer, because the object to be understood and the person involved in the act of understanding are not two alien entities that are isolated from each other by a gulf of historical time. Rather, they initially stand in a state of relatedness to each other. The historical object and the hermeneutic operation of the interpreter are both part of an overriding historical and cultural tradition or continuum which Gadamer calls "effective history" (*Wirkungsgeschichte*). This effective historical continuum is the ultimate cause of the prejudices (positive and negative ones) which guide our understanding. Because prejudices function as a necessary condition of historical understanding, Gadamer argues, they should be made the object of hermeneutic reflection. To engage in such hermeneutic reflection and to determine our own hermeneutic situation is what Gadamer refers to in an almost untranslatable term as the development of one's "effective-historical consciousness" (*wirkungsgeschichtliches Bewusstsein*), that is, of one's consciousness of the effective historical continuum of which he is a part.

It was this notion of an effective historical continuum which served as a point of departure in the 1960s for the debates between the adherents of philosophical hermeneutics on the one side and the representatives of orthodox and neo-Marxist philosophy on the other.[107] But it was also a point of convergence between hermeneutics and the critical theory of the Frankfurt School. This becomes evident in Habermas's critique of the objectivist creed of contemporary social sciences, when he raises the question of whether "the social sciences—like the humanities—are not bound by a certain implicit pre-understanding when they attempt methically to delineate their subject matter."[108]

But before we can discuss any of the issues raised by the Gadamer-Habermas debate, it is necessary to treat, however briefly, another essential element in Gadamer's notion of understanding: his view of the linguistic nature or linguisticality (*Sprachlichkeit*) of understanding. One recent American writer has gone so far as to claim that Gadamer's "most original contribution" to hermeneutics was his "linguistic turn" which supposedly distinguishes his views from those of the nineteenth-century writers.[109] Gadamer himself never made such claims. On the contrary, he often stressed the significance of Schleiermacher's and Humboldt's contributions to hermeneutics which lay precisely in their discovery of the linguisticality of understanding.[110] However, to the reader of Gadamer's *Truth and Method* and many of his other studies, it is quite obvious that his concept of the linguistic nature of understanding is not identical with that of Schleiermacher or Humboldt, but deviates from theirs in some essential ways. Gadamer does not clearly distinguish—as did Schleiermacher and Humboldt—between language (*Sprache*), speech (*Rede*), and linguisticality (*Sprachvermögen*), which denote different aspects of linguistic phenomena. Gadamer generally uses language (*die Sprache*) to cover a variety of meanings and thereby allows contradictions and ambiguities to enter. According to Gadamer, the possibility for all understanding rests ultimately in language itself (*die Sprache*). The peculiar function (*eigentliche Leistung*) of language is to bring about the fusion of the horizons of the interpreter and of the historical object, which characterizes the act of understanding. But how is language able to fulfill this hermeneutic function? Gadamer does not provide us with a phenomenological or linguistic analysis of this all-important performance of language. In this respect both Schleiermacher and Humboldt have gone further than Gadamer. Instead, Gadamer conceives of language and linguisticality in an *en-bloc* fashion as a total historical-linguistic event which envelops both the interpreter and his object. It would appear that for Gadamer language and linguisticality, which seem to fuse into each other, in some ways resemble Heidegger's *Being (das Sein)* which hides itself in the very closeness of things that are (*das Seiende*). But instead of a "history of Being" (*Seinsgeschichte*), Gadamer posits rather a "history of language," or, more specifically, a linguistic historicity which enwraps our entire culture. Understanding and interpretation for Gadamer constitute the mode of being of all our cultural traditions. These traditions are necessarily embedded in language (*die Sprache*). It follows, therefore, that understanding and interpretation are, above all, events in an historical process. Only secondarily do they constitute a specific method of the human sciences.

Gadamer's discussion of the principal hermeneutic terms has largely determined their usage in contemporary discussions. This usage extends not only to the social philosophers and sociologists who have aligned themselves with the theories of the Frankfurt School. In literary studies the receptionist approach developed by Jauss and others has incorporated ideas taken from Gadamer's hermeneutics. Although Gadamer does not make any specific methodological claims, his argumentation has led to certain methodological consequences in the human and social sciences nevertheless. For example, Gadamer denies an actual distinction between understanding and interpretation or explication (*Auslegung*). He claims that "Romantic hermeneutics" has taught us that "in the final analysis, understanding and interpretation are one and the same."[111] In another passage in *Truth and Method* Gadamer retracts part of this statement and maintains that, during certain "acts of immediate comprehension, explication is only partially contained in these acts."[112] Explication thus merely brings understanding to the fore. It follows that "explication is not a means to aid understanding, but has itself entered into the meaning [*Gehalt*] of that which is being understood." In other words, "explication has become part of that which is understood."[113] Interpretation, however, for Gadamer is always explication expressed through language and hence linguistic explication must be considered "the very essence of explication." It seems obvious, as our discussion of the hermeneutic theories of Schleiermacher, Humboldt, and Boeckh has sufficiently demonstrated, that understanding is never identical with interpretation. It is certainly not identical with interpretive discourse (explication). The interrelatedness of certain hermeneutic phenomena and operations does not support the view of their identity, but instead calls for an investigation into the nature of their interrelatedness.

It is not difficult to see how certain key assumptions made by the receptionist school of literary history point at Gadamer's hermeneutics as their source of origin. For in Gadamer's view, explication, as the linguistic side of an act of understanding, constitutes the actual fulfillment of this act. This fulfillment, he claims, is "nothing but the concretion of meaning itself." If explicating a given text and speaking about its meaning really leads to the "concretion of meaning itself," as Gadamer insists, the meaning of the text must be viewed as embedded in its explications. The historical chain of such explications is what Gadamer calls "the tradition" (*die Überlieferung*). Literary works live through their explications (their reception) and form part of an historical continuity which, sustained by a speech community, is itself of a linguistic nature. Gadamer's position—if developed to its extreme—would allow the meaning of a work or a text ultimately to appear only as embedded in its different explications, its specific receptions. Thus, there would no longer be textual meanings to be understood, only explications to be explicated. In all fairness, it must be stated that Gadamer himself maintains the view of the normative character of the text vis-à-vis the interpreter and his changing interpretations. Nevertheless, his claim that understanding and interpretation are the same leaves his position in a state of ambiguity for the student of hermeneutics.

## XII

The legitimate claim which hermeneutics brings forth against the absolutism of a universal methodology of the experiential sciences with all its practical consequences does not dispense us from the business of methodology altogether. This claim, I am afraid, will either become effective in these sciences—or not at all.

Jürgen Habermas

The difference between Gadamer's and Habermas's positions in regard to fundamental hermeneutic notions, as one recent commentator has remarked correctly, becomes almost negligible once we have penetrated to the roots of the arguments presented in their public exchange.[114] It seems as though in the course of the debate Habermas defined his own views more and more in harmony with those of the Heidelberg philosopher. What is significant in this exchange is not merely the respective merit and persuasiveness of the arguments presented by the two participants but, over and above all, the renewed sense of actuality which hermeneutics received under their hands. Moreover, both men proved thoroughly familiar with the hermeneutic tradition. We must remember that in *Truth and Method* Gadamer had set forth his own views largely through a critique of the main authors of this tradition from the Enlightenment to Dilthey. In a similar vein, Habermas used ideas derived from the hermeneutic theorists for his critique of the various schools of contemporary social sciences and their methodologies. In his study *On the Logic of the Social Sciences* (1967)[115] he confronted the positivist and analytical theories in these sciences with the views of some of the principal hermeneutic writers. He does not agree with all of their assumptions and is quite critical of the hermeneutical philosophers' attitude toward methodological problems and issues. To understand the point of departure of the Gadamer-Habermas debate, therefore, it is necessary to look at Habermas's reception of the hermeneutic tradition and of Gadamer's views in particular.

The hermeneutic component in Habermas's critical theory can be plainly identified in his critique of Max Weber's conception of sociology, which he finds both deficient and ambiguous. In his *Economy and Society: An Outline of Interpretive Sociology* Weber defined sociology as "a science concerning itself with the interpretive understanding of social action and thereby with a causal explanation of its course and consequences."[116] In this definition the two methods, understanding and causal explanation, stand in an uneasy relationship to each other and, according to Habermas, give rise to uncertainty and confusion. He argues that Weber did not distinguish properly between the understanding of motivations that reenact the subjective meaning underlying a given social act and the hermeneutic understanding of meaning (*hermeneutisches Sinnverstehen*). The latter term stands for the appropriation of a meaning which has been objectified into events, institutions, or works of culture. Furthermore, Habermas argues that modern positivist and empiricist sociologists, by turning all history into a static present, run into a serious methodological problem. They reduce the meaning of social and cultural phenomena that have come down to us from the past to the status of mere empirical facts which can be subjected to causal explanation. Thus, the traditional dualism between the methods of the natural and the human sciences which contemporary scientists and humanists seem to have quietly accepted in their daily work erupts again, this time in the very center of the social sciences. For this reason, Habermas directs attention to the works of Dilthey, Schutz, and others whose methodological ideas quite ostensibly went beyond Max Weber's conception of a scientific sociology.

In a section of his study *On the Logic of the Social Sciences,* entitled "The hermeneutic approach," Habermas discusses Gadamer's *Truth and Method.* He singles out Gadamer's notion of "effective history" which according to him had all the earmarks of a methodological principle applicable to textual interpretation in the human sciences. Gadamer had never claimed such functional status for his notion. Nevertheless, Habermas reproaches him for wanting to reduce hermeneutics to a mere investigation of the transcendental conditions of understanding. He thereby neglected, Habermas claimed, both the methodological demands of the human and social sciences and the concrete social and material conditions which have determined the development of these sciences. Habermas believes that Gadamer is still a prisoner of the ideas of the Neokantianism of the Marburg school, an imprisonment which he allegedly shares with his teacher Heidegger. In Heidegger's existential ontology Habermas perceives but another version of traditional Kantian philosophizing in a priori principles. He charges that Gadamer was unwilling to change "from analyzing the transcendental constitution of historicity to considering universal history where these conditions first constitute themselves."[117]

Upon closer examination Habermas's position, too, remains equivocal. If the hermeneutic categories, as he believes, are constituted by and form an integral part of "universal history" viewed in a Hegelian-Marxian manner, it is difficult to see how the actual methodological problems of the different human and social sciences can be met successfully on that basis. There does not seem to be a necessary connection between Habermas's historical and political philosophy and the epistemological requirements that accompany the creation of a specific hermeneutics. This raises an important question: Can hermeneutics ever be more than an abstract call for "critical" reflection on one's social and historical conditions, if we do not submit its constitutive categories to epistemological analysis and description?

It is notable that Habermas has appropriated Gadamer's belief in hermeneutics as an historical and critical metatheory, while, at the same time, he hopes that this metatheory will provide guidance for the development of specific hermeneutic categories. These categories are needed, Habermas believes, in order to rid the social sciences of their domination by empiricist reductionist methodologies. Among these hermeneutic categories Habermas counts the concepts of language and linguisticality and those of communication and interaction. He elaborated the latter two partially by relying on the views of Dilthey, Schutz, and, finally, the later Wittgenstein.

G. H. von Wright, in his book *Explanation and Understanding* (1971),[118] has drawn our attention to two specific features which the hermeneutic movement on the Continent shares with analytic philosophy as it evolved from the later works of Wittgenstein in England. These are the central role accorded to the idea of language and language-oriented notions (such as meaning, understanding, and intentionality), and the ongoing concern for methodological problems in the social and the human sciences. The affinity between the two schools of thought did not remain unnoticed. Habermas, in his attempt to enlarge the scope of his critical theory, was quite aware of the contributions of the analytic philosophers to social thought. But he was not the first to point out the hermeneutic component in analytic philosophy. In his argumentation he follows the suggestions advanced by the philosopher K.-O. Apel who has made the relationship between analytic philosophy and the hermeneutic tradition one of his important concerns.

Apel was most qualified to explore the common hermeneutic concerns of the continental and Anglo-Saxon schools of thought since he combines the competency of a philosopher with that of a historian of science and of ideas, in addition to being a social theorist in his own right. As a philosopher he is indebted to Heidegger's fundamental ontology and to phenomenology. But he has also appropriated the historical consciousness and methodological concerns of Dilthey and his school, which his teacher E. Rothacker, the author of some important studies on the logic of the human sciences,[119] had embodied for him. In one of his early studies Apel traced the development of the concept of understanding as it manifested itself in philosophy, scientific thought, and in the human sciences from the late Middle Ages and Renaissance through the eighteenth and nineteenth centuries.[120] A few years later he published another important work, *The Idea of Language in the Humanist Tradition from Dante to Vico* (1963, 1975).[121] There Apel deals with a central hermeneutic aspect in the humanist tradition, shedding new light and, at the same time, adding a necessary dimension to the hermeneutic discussions in the human sciences. He was thoroughly familiar with the linguistic dimensions of the fundamental notions of hermeneutics when he undertook his examination of the philosophy of the later Wittgenstein and other analytic philosophers. His important contributions on the subject include "Wittgenstein and the Problem of Hermeneutic Understanding" (1966) and "Analytic Philosophy of Language and the *Geisteswissenschaften*."[122]

Apel's role in the contemporary discussion is that of a synthesizing and highly perceptive thinker who refuses to let himself be caught in sterile positions or ideological stances. While he accepts the idea of a common ground for the sciences of nature and those of man and society, he refuses to subordinate the latter to the infertile idea of an all-encompassing "unified science" as the neopositivist theorists wanted to have it. In this very important respect, Apel continues in the central tradition of the classical hermeneuticians by maintaining—as did Droysen and Dilthey before him—the autonomy and nonreductive nature of the human sciences. But at the same time he does not wish to reject the scientific attitude which characterizes the natural sciences and which can be found also in certain segments of the social sciences. For Apel, the hermeneutic and the scientific attitudes do not exclude but rather complement each other. For example, the fact that a natural science requires the existence of a linguistic community of communication as an a priori for its own existence cannot be grasped scientifically but must be understood hermeneutically. Apel is critical of Gadamer's metahermeneutic stance and defends the idea of the objectifying role of interpretation in the human sciences. The history of these sciences teaches us, according to Apel, that interpretation is not merely an activity which mediates between present and past, a fusion of horizons, as Gadamer had argued, but also a process by which knowledge is produced. The knowledge brought about by the human sciences and by the natural sciences are mutually complementary at every stage in our cultural history in Apel's view. He believes that both have their roots in the intersubjective sphere of a given speech community as their common *a priori*.

It follows that for Apel the task of hermeneutics must always be twofold. It must be concerned with the a priori conditions of all understanding together with the special hermeneutic problems of the individual disciplines. This means that hermeneutics must be transcendental and general as well as special and particular. In other words, Apel does not dissolve hermeneutics into metahermeneutical reflection, nor does he allow its absorption into a branch of critical sociology or into the methodology of the social sciences. It seems to me that this basic view of hermeneutics is well taken, even if one does not agree with certain of Apel's ideas or objects to his often ingenious interweaving of threads from different traditions and different disciplines.

Looking backward once more at the various positions we have examined from the eighteenth to our own century, one thing has emerged persuasively; namely, that general (or philosophical) and specific hermeneutic endeavors are dependent upon each other. Schleiermacher's *Hermeneutik* was as much specific as it was intended to be general and universal. Droysen and Boeckh produced their theories for their own disciplines of history and classical philology respectively. Their specific focus arose from and was an expression of a general philosophy of man, culture, and history. The predominant position of philosophical hermeneutics in recent decades may have deepened our interest in hermeneutic problems or, in some instances, opened our eyes to them. But there can be no doubt that it has also been detrimental for the advance of a genuine hermeneutics in individual disciplines, as, for example, in literary studies. To be sure, there have also been promising new beginnings, mainly in the social sciences. But on the whole these have remained relatively unnoticed outside their own disciplines. What is necessary today is the serious pursuit of hermeneutic questions from within or, at least, from the viewpoint of the different disciplines of the social and human sciences. This pursuit must be theoretical, pragmatic, and historical in outlook, for it must deal both with general philosophical questions and with the particular methodological issues facing these discipines today. One might envision, furthermore, a critical history of hermeneutics, the study of its basic principles and strategies as they have evolved as parts of different systems of discourse.

Terms like understanding, explication, and interpretation must be comprehended as sharing different historical and discoursive contexts. Apparent contradictions and the frequent overlapping in the use of terms which we have observed can be explained by tracing the changes and transformations these terms underwent within different hermeneutic systems. In the course of our historical discussion we have discovered, for example, that the term understanding may signify at least three different, though semantically related meanings.[123] In accordance with our findings we must distinguish the understanding which one might gain from reading a given text or listening to someone's speech from the interpretive operation, also called understanding, which led to this understanding. These two meanings in turn must be differentiated from understanding used as an equivalent for hermeneutic competence, that is, the abilities and skills required for a proper understanding of a given linguistic or other human cultural expression. A writer may address himself to quite different hermeneutic phenomena while using one and the same word. To speak of hermeneutics as the "method of understanding" is therefore quite misleading.

Modern hermeneutics from the Enlightenment to the present has continued to display the tendency to combine theoretical and philosophical with practical and critical concerns (the texts which follow will amply illustrate this point). In fact, throughout that period the hermeneutic enterprise seems to have received guidance and orientation from two different directions. First, from a desire to account for and secure the procedures of a particular discipline (i.e., history, biblical scholarship, classical philology, theology, jurisprudence, aesthetics, or linguistics). In this context hermeneutics can be seen in relation to the history of a particular discipline or a group of disciplines. Second, from a more general philosophical concern that transcended the boundaries of a particular discipline and its limited methodological interests. The borderline between these two orientations is, however, often fluid and anything but distinct, as can be witnessed in the writings of Schleiermacher, Droysen, Humboldt, or Boeckh. This state of affairs can be explained in part by the fact that hermeneutic concerns almost inevitably lead us back to the consideration of epistemological problems, and these tend effectively to undermine any purely pragmatic way of dealing with the methodology of a given humanistic discipline. Instead of a method or the method of understanding, hermeneutics should better be conceived of as a logic of the humanities and human sciences, which would complement the notion of a logic and theory of the natural sciences.

In order to function as a logic of the human sciences, hermeneutics must add yet another dimension to its traditional areas of concern. K.-O. Apel is right when he sees the rise of the human sciences from the eighteenth to the twentieth century in connection with the break-up of the institutionalized transmission of our cultural traditions which was effectively valid up to the French Revolution and the rise of industrial capitalist society:

> The process of the communication of tradition, without which man would indeed never be able to exist, must in fact assume a different form in our posthistorical age than in the time prior to the rise of the historical-hermeneutical cultural sciences. The immediacy of the dogmatic-normative (institutionally established and socially binding) "application" of the understanding of tradition—as it functioned up into the time of the Enlightenment in Europe and up to the present in most non-European cultures—cannot be restored. The process of the communication of tradition must become a complicated, scientifically mediated process.[124]

In an age where the mediating process of the transmission of cultural knowledge has become the central task of the human and historical sciences, hermeneutics must go one step further and attempt to mediate for the present the different hermeneutic standpoints that it finds embodied in the history of these sciences. Methodological and critical concerns by themselves no longer suffice. The history of hermeneutic thought itself is in need of hermeneutic attention, because the history of the human and cultural sciences has become problematical during the past half century. It is a history which has been eclipsed by a steady stream of always changing "new" approaches, trends, and current movements that "reinterpret," that is, usurp and absorb, the past, from their single-minded points of view. On the other hand, the achievements contained in the various hermeneutic positions of the past (which accompany the history of the human and cultural sciences) constitute a body of knowledge and insight which we can ill afford to overlook. It is a body of knowledge that can give us a fuller grasp and understanding of the present state of our human sciences, their historical, epistemic and epistemological make-up, and the multi-dimensional nature of the problems with which they have to deal.

## Notes

1. A concise discussion of the etymology and history of the term hermeneutics and its cognates can be found in G. Ebeling's article "Hermeneutik" in the encyclopedia *Religion in Geschichte und Gegenwart,* 3rd ed., vol. 3, pp. 243–62.

2. Aristotle's *"Categories" and "De Interpretatione,"* trans. with notes by J. L. Ackrill (Oxford: Oxford University Press, 1963).

3. For the early history of hermeneutics the reader is referred to G. Ebeling's article (n. 1) and the bibliography supplied by him. Of particular interest are the valuable observations by L. Geldsetzer in his various introductions to the reprints of important historical texts which he has reissued. Among these: G. Fr. Meier, *Versuch einer allgemeinen Auslegungskunst,* Neudruck der Ausgabe Halle 1757 (1965); Flacius Illyricus, *De vera ratione cognoscendi sacras literas,* Neudruck aus dem *Clavis Scripturae Sacrae,* 1567; J. M. Chladenius, *Einleitung zur richtigen Auslegung vernünftiger Reden und Schriften,* Neudruck der Ausgabe Leipzig 1742 (1969).

4. See L. Goldsetzer in the Preface to Meier's *Versuch* (n. 3), p. VIIIff.; H.-G. Gadamer in *Seminar: Philosophische Hermeneutik* (1976) (Sect. C, Bibl.), pp. 7–30; K. Weimar, *Historische Einleitung zur Literaturwissenschaftlichen Hermeneutik* (1975) (Sect. B, Bibl.).

5. Johannes Ludovicus Vives, *De ratione studendi ac legendi interpretandique auctores,* 1539; Scioppius (Kaspar Schoppe), *De Arte Critica,* 1597; Johannes Clericus, *Ars Critica,* 1697.

6. Laurentius Humphrey, *De ratione interpretandi,* 1559; Petrus Daniel Huet, *De interpretatione libri ii,* 1661.

7. This treatise was published only in 1559: Constantius Rogerius, *Singularis Tractatus de Iuris Interpretatione.*

8. A brief history of legal hermeneutics is provided by L. Geldsetzer in his introduction to the reprint of A. F. J. Thibaut's *Theorie der Logischen Auslegung des Römischen Rechts*

of 1806 (1966), pp. V–XLIII.

9. Franciscus Hotomanus, *Iurisconcultus sive de optimo genere iuris interpretandi,* 1559.

10. Johannes von Felde, *Tractatus de scientia interpretandi cum in genere omnis alias orationis, tum in specie leges romanas,* 1689, p. 3.

11. Anton F. J. Thibaut (n. 8), p. 16.

12. Christian Wolff, *Vernünftige Gedanken* (1713), in *Gesammelte Werke,* I. Abteilung, vol. I, chaps. 10, 11, 12 (Sect. B, Bibl.).

13. This and the following arguments were developed by Wolff in chap. 10, entitled "How to pass Judgements about writings," op. cit., pp. 219–26.

14. Johannes Martin Chladenius, *Einleitung . . .* (1742) (see Acknowledgements). For works about Chladenius's hermeneutics, see Sect. A, Bibl.

15. See in particular ## 148, 149, 176, 192.

16. It was Chladenius's intention to emancipate hermeneutics from the study of logic to that of an autonomous discipline, see # 177.

17. J. Wach in vol. III of his monumental study of the history of hermeneutics in the nineteenth century places major emphasis on Chladenius's theory of perspective and interprets his views in the context and the light of nineteenth-century historicist thinking; J. Wach, *Das Verstehen* (Sect. B, Bibl.).

18. Wilhelm Dilthey, "Die Entstehung der Hermeneutik," *Gesammelte Schriften,* vol. V; published in English as "The Development of Hermeneutics," in H. P. Rickmann, *Wilhelm Dilthey. Selected Writings* (Sect. A, Bibl.).

19. Dilthey was still aware of the linguistic dimensions of Schleiermacher's notion of understanding in his early studies of Schleiermacher's thought. But he disregarded this important element in Schleiermacher's theory of understanding when he worked out his own approach to hermeneutics. See Wilhelm Dilthey, *Gesammelte Schriften,* vol. XIV, p. 707 (Sect. A, Bibl.).

20. Regarding the aesthetic and literary ideas of the early German Romantics, see René Wellek's *History of Modern Criticism, 1750–1950,* vol. II, *The Romantic Age* (1955), chaps. 1–3, 12 (Sect. B, Bibl.).

21. In his *Logic* Kant wrote: "To understand something [*intellegere*] means to know or to conceive of something through the understanding [*Verstand*] by means of our concepts." *Kants Werke,* Akademie-Textausgabe (Berlin, 1968), p. 65. My translation.

22. On this issue, see the works by J. Forstman, H. Patsch, and P. Szondi in Sect. A, Bibl.

23. J. Wach treated the entire history of hermeneutics in the nineteenth century under the heading of "understanding," i.e., *Das Verstehen* (Sect. B, Bibl.).

24. *Hermeneutics, The Handwritten Manuscripts,* ed. H. Kimmerle, trans. by J. Duke and J. Forstmann, p. 41 (Sect. A, Bibl.).

25. *Hermeneutik und Kritik,* ed. F. Lücke (Berlin, 1838). This edition has been included in M. Frank's recent publication *Schleiermacher: Hermeneutik und Kritik* (1977) (Sect. A, Bibl.).

26. Ed. H. Kimmerle; Eng. trans. by J. Duke and J. Forstman (Sect. A, Bibl.).

27. See M. Frank's study *Das individuelle Allgemeine* and his introduction to the volume *Schleiermacher: Hermeneutik und Kritik* (1977) (Sect. A, Bibl.).

28. See Schleiermacher selection below, p. 74.

29. Ibid., p. 75.

30. See Boeckh selection below, p. 135f.

31. J. G. Fichte, *Science of Knowledge, Wissenschaftslehre, with First and Second Introductions,* trans. and ed. P. Heath and J. Lachs (1970) (Sect. B, Bibl.).

32. Schleiermacher selection in this reader, p. 75.

33. In his *Historik* (see n. 47 below), p. 324.

34. *Der junge Dilthey.* Ed. Clara Misch, 2nd ed. Göttingen: Vandenhoeck & Ruprecht, 1960, p. 76.

35. See Sect. A, Bibl.: "Humboldt."

36. The only extensive discussion of Humboldt's hermeneutics is by J. Wach in *Das Verstehen* (1926) (Sect. A, Bibl.).

37. On the Romantic language paradigm see my contribution in *Der Transzendentale Gedanke* (1981) (Sect. B, Bibl.).

38. Wilhelm von Humboldt, *Gesammelte Schriften,* vol. 5, p. 382 (Sect. A, Bibl.).

39. See n. 37 above.

40. The societal aspect of language was elaborated by Humboldt as early as 1801 to 1806 in his studies on the Basque language; *Gesammelte Schriften,* vol. 7, pp. 593–608.

41. Paul Sweet, *Wilhelm von Humboldt: A Biography* (1980) (Sect. A, Bibl.).

42. Friedrich Meinecke, *Historicism* (1972) (Sect. B, Bibl.). A discussion of the various interpretations of Humboldt's essay can be found in P. Sweet's biography (n. 41), vol. II, p. 428ff.

43. Humboldt criticized the teleological view of history in two essays, "Observations on the effective causes in World History" (1818) and "Observations on World History" (1814). See *Gesammelte Schriften,* vol. 3, pp. 360–66 and pp. 356–59 (Sect. A, Bibl.).

44. See selection below, pp. 121,123. G. H. von Wright, the title of whose book *Explanation and Understanding* (1971) (Sect. B, Bibl.) is evidently indebted to Droysen, offers a brief discussion of Droysen's distinction and its importance for later developments in hermeneutic theory. Von Wright, however, uses the term hermeneutic in a very broad sense to cover the entire spectrum of the human and social sciences (including the philosophy of science) from the early and middle part of the nineteenth century in so far as they reflected an antipositivistic stance in their theoretical and practical orientation. Since the term idealism seemed inadequate to do justice to the diversity among the antipositivistic authors — among them Droysen, Dilthey, Simmel, Weber, Rickert, and Windelband— von Wright uses the designation hermeneutic for the entire movement. Ibid., p. 3ff.

45. "Jedes Begreifen einer Sache setzt, als Bedingung seiner Möglichkeit, in dem Begreifenden schon ein Analogon des nachher wirklich Begriffenen voraus, eine *vorhergängige, ursprüngliche Übereinstimmung* zwischen dem Subject und Object." *Gesammelte Schriften,* vol. IV, p. 48 (my italics).

46. In his extensive review essay of the historical-critical edition of Droysen's *Historik* (1977) (Sect. A, Bibl.) in the journal *History and Theory,* vol. XIX (1980), I, p. 73.

47. Since its first publication by R. Hüber in 1937, Droysen's *Historik* has been reissued seven times (8th ed. in 1977).

48. G. P. Gooch, *History and Historians in the Nineteenth Century* (1959), pp. 125–31 (Sect. A, Bibl.). However, Droysen's theoretical work did not go entirely unnoticed in the

50                                      *Introduction*

United States during his lifetime. An English translation of the *Outline of the Historik* by
E. Benjamin Andrews, president of Brown University, appeared in Boston in 1897 (Sect.
A, Bibl.).

49. For a discussion of the *Historik,* see the references given by Hüber in his edition.
Droysen himself explains the nature of his undertaking in his introduction, op. cit., p. 3ff.

50. See p. 123 below.

51. *Einleitung zum Kawiwerk— Über die Verschiedenheit des menschlichen Sprachbaus
und ihren Einfluss auf die Entwicklung des Menschengeschlechts. Gesammelte Schriften,*
vol. VII, pp. 1–349. Eng. trans.: *Linguistic Variability and Intellectual Development*
(1971) (Sect. A, Bibl.).

52. Whereas the close resemblance between Vico's and Dilthey's epistemology of the
human sciences has caught the attention of modern commentators, the startling kinship
between the Italian philosopher's and Droysen's hermeneutic conception of the world of
culture and history still remains to be explored. On the affinity between Vico and Dilthey,
see L. Rubinoff, "Vico and the Verification of Historical Interpretation," in *Vico and Contemporary Thought* (1976), pp. 94–121 (Sect. B, Bibl.), and H. N. Tuttle, "The Epistemological Status of the Cultural World in Vico and Dilthey," in *Giambattista Vico's Science
of Humanity* (1976), pp. 241–50 (Sect. B, Bibl.).

53. *Historik,* op. cit., p. 26. My translation.

54. *Outline,* # 9, see below 121.

55. *Historik,* op. cit., p. 35. My translation.

56. Ibid.

57. The German terms are: Die pragmatische Interpretation, Die Interpretation der
Bedingungen, Die psychologische Interpretation, Die Interpretation nach den sittlichen
Mächten oder Ideen.

58. Droysen distinguishes between four modes of historical representation: the analytical
or investigative, the narrative, the didactic, and the discussive mode.

59. For a general treatment of Boeckh, see the works by J. Wach (1926) (Sect. B, Bibl.)
and Steinthal (Sect. A, Bibl.).

60. Boeckh's role within the tradition of nineteenth century classical scholarship is examined by several of the contributors to the recent volume *Philologie und Hermeneutik im
19. Jahrhundert* (Sect. C, Bibl.). See also nn. 61 and 64 below.

61. *Enzyklopaedie und Methodologie der philologischen Wissenschaften* (1886) (Sect.
B, Bibl.). For particulars regarding this work, see the headnote, p. 132 below.

62. *Enzyklopaedie,* p. 10. My translation. For an excellent analysis of Boeckh's definition of philology, see F. Rodi, "'Erkenntnis des Erkannten'—August Boeckh's Grundformel der hermeneutischen Wissenschaften," in *Philologie und Hermeneutik* (1979), pp.
68–83 (Sect. C, Bibl.).

63. *Enzyklopaedie,* p. 75; see also p. 133 below.

64. E. D. Hirsch (1967) (Sect. B, Bibl.).

65. A persuasive reexamination of Boeckh's theory of interpretation was offered by
Ingrid Strohschneider-Kohr, "Textauslegung und hermeneutischer Zirkel—Zur Innovation des Interpretationsbegriffs von August Boeckh," in *Philologie und Hermeneutik*
(1979), pp. 84–102 (Sect. C, Bibl.).

66. On Dilthey's achievements, see the works by Ermarth (1978), Hodges (1952), Makkreel (1975) (Sect. A, Bibl.).

67. *Einleitung in die Geisteswissenschaften. Versuch einer Grundlegung für das Studium der Gesellschaft und der Geschichte. Gesammelte Schriften*, vol. I (Sect. A, Bibl.).

68. Droysen wrote a lengthy review of Buckle's *History of Civilization in England* in which he took issue with the assumptions of the nineteenth-century positivistic school of history: "Erhebung der Geschichte zum Rang einer Wissenschaft," reprinted in *Historik* (1977), pp. 386–405.

69. See, in particular, his "Ideas concerning a descriptive and analytic psychology" (Ideen über eine beschreibende und zergliedernde Psychologie) from 1894. *Gesammelte Schriften*, vol. V, pp. 139–240 (Sect. A, Bibl.).

70. He had made some important headway, however, in his studies on literature and literary theory. See Mueller-Vollmer (1963) (Sect. A, Bibl.).

71. In this context, see Dilthey's statements in *Gesammelte Schriften*, vol. VII, pp. 10, 14, 39ff., and G. Misch's *Lebensphilosophie und Phänomenologie* (1931) (Sect. A, Bibl.).

72. *Der Aufbau der Geschichtlichen Welt in den Geisteswissenschaften. Gesammelte Schriften*, vol. VII, pp. 79–188 (Sect. A, Bibl.).

73. Cf. n. 9 above.

74. L. Wittgenstein, *Philosophische Untersuchungen*, in *Schriften*, I (1960), p. 296: "Und eine Sprache verstehen, heisst, sich eine Lebensform vorstellen." (Sect. B, Bibl.).

75. On this question, see Bollnow (1955), Ermarth (1978), Hodges (1952), Makkreel (1975), Mueller-Vollmer (1963) (Sect. A, Bibl.).

76. *The German Ideology* (1970), p. 42 (Sect. B, Bibl.). In holding with our own philological findings, Marx uses "äussern" for "to express": "Wie die Individuen ihr Leben äussern, so sind so." *Marx-Engels Studienausgabe*, vol. I, p. 86 (Sect. B, Bibl.).

77. *Gesammelte Schriften*, vol. VII, p. 217 (Sect. A, Bibl.). See also p. 161 below.

78. Paul Ricoeur (1976) (1977) (Sect. B, Bibl.).

79. In an essay entitled "Transzendentale Hermeneutik?" published in *Wissenschaftstheorie der Geisteswissenschaften* (1975) (Sect. C, Bibl.).

80. *Logical Investigations* I and II (1976) (Sect. A, Bibl.).

81. Roman Ingarden (Sect. A, Bibl.); E. D. Hirsch (1967) and M. Leibfried (1970) (Sect. B, Bibl.).

82. *The Phenomenology of Internal Time Consciousness* (1964), *The Crisis of European Sciences* (1970), *Husserliana* (1950 ff.) (Sect. A, Bibl.).

83. A. Schutz (1967) (Sect. B, Bibl.).

84. I am particularly referring to Husserl's detailed studies of the "acts of passive synthesis" and of the constitution of intersubjectivity and of the processes of mental representations found in vols. XI–XV, XXII of the collected works, *Husserliana* (Sect. A, Bibl.).

85. J. N. Findlay in his preface to *Logical Investigations* I, p. 3 (Sect. A, Bibl.).

86. This basic hermeneutic element in Husserl's phenomenology was recently pointed out by G. Buck in *New Literary History* X (1978) (Sect. A, Bibl.).

87. See, for example, Chomsky's *Aspects of the Theory of Syntax* (1965) for his discussion of what is considered "acceptable" and what is taken as "grammatical" in a given language (see pp. 11, 19, 75–79) (Sect. B, Bibl.).

88. Stanley Fish (1970) (Sect. B, Bibl.).

89. *Logical Investigations* I, p. 295.

90. Sect. A, Bibl.

91. See Ingarden's "Preface" to *The Literary Work of Art*.

92. "Das Verstehen ist nur ein Ineinandersein [lit., "an existing-in-and-through-each other"] dieser beiden Momente. . . ." *Schleiermacher: Hermeneutik und Kritik* (1977), p. 79 (Sect. A, Bibl.).

93. Sect. A, Bibl.

94. This is sect. 7: "The phenomenological method of investigation."

95. P. 37. (Ger. ed.), p. 61f. (Eng. ed.). Translations of quotations have been slightly revised by the present writer.

96. *Die Aussage* is the term Heidegger uses.

97. The Eng. trans. uses somewhat misleadingly "idle talk" for Heidegger's term *das Gerede*.

98. Emil Staiger (1946) (Sect. B, Bibl.).

99. Ludwig Binswanger (1942) (Sect. B, Bibl.).

100. Concerning this movement, see J. Robinson's *The New Hermeneutic* (1964) (Sect. B, Bibl.); on Heidegger's impact on recent theology, the works by Noller (1967) and Robinson (1963) (Sect. A, Bibl.).

101. Quoted by Schubert Ogden in his anthology *Existence and Faith: Shorter Writings of Rudolf Bultmann* (1960), p. 14 (Sect. A, Bibl.) from Bultmann's essay, "Das Problem einer theologischen Exegese des Neuen Testaments" (1925).

102. "The Historicity of Man and Faith," in *Existence and Faith* (1960), p. 94 (Sect. A, Bibl.).

103. "The Problem of Hermeneutics," in *Essays, Philosophical and Theological* (1955), pp. 252–53 (Sect. A, Bibl.).

104. Ibid., p. 254.

105. Sect. A, Bibl.

106. *The Positivist Dispute in German Sociology* (1976) (Sect. A, Bibl.: "Habermas").

107. Evidenced by the contributions to the *Gadamer Festschrift Hermeneutik und Dialektik* (1970) (Sect. C, Bibl.) and to the volume *Theorie-Diskussion: Hermeneutik und Ideologiekritik* (1971) (Sect. C, Bibl.). H. J. Sandkühler in *Praxis und Geschichtsbewusstsein* (1973) (Sect. B, Bibl.) has advanced a harsh criticism of Gadamer's philosophical hermeneutic from an orthodox Marxian point of view.

108. Jürgen Habermas, *Zur Logik der Sozialwissenschaften*, 2nd ed. (1975), p. 87 (Sect. A, Bibl.). All quotes—including the motto of this section—are my translations.

109. D. C. Hoy, *The Critical Circle* (1978), p. 5f. (Sect. B, Bibl.).

110. For example, in his essay, "The Problem of Language in Schleiermacher's Hermeneutics," in *Schleiermacher as Contemporary*, pp. 68–84 (Sect. A, Bibl.).

111. *Wahrheit und Methode*, p. 366. These and the following quotes are my translations.

112. Ibid., p. 376.

113. Ibid.

114. Zimmerli in Simon-Schaefer-Zimmerli, *Theorie zwischen Kritik und Praxis* (1975), p. 97 (Sect. B, Bibl.).

115. *Zur Logik der Sozialwissenschaften* (1975) (Sect. A, Bibl.).

116. Max Weber, p. 4 (Sect. B, Bibl.).

117. Habermas, op. cit., p. 281. My translation.

118. Sect. B, Bibl.

119. Sect. B, Bibl.

120. *Das Verstehen* (1955) (Sect. A, Bibl.).

121. Ibid.

122. Sect. A, Bibl.

123. These and some other aspects of the concepts of understanding and interpretation I have treated in a more systematic fashion in my contribution to the *Yearbook of Comparative Criticism,* vol. X (1983), pp. 41–64, entitled "Understanding and Interpretation: Toward a Definition of Literary Hermeneutics."

124. K.-O. Apel, "Scientistics, Hermeneutics, Critique of Ideology," Last selection in this volume.

# 1

# Reason and Understanding: Rational Hermeneutics

## Johann Martin Chladenius

JOHANN MARTIN CHLADENIUS (1710–1759) was born in Wittenberg the son of a theologian, Martin Chladenius. He attended the *Gymnasium* (classical high school) in Coburg until the age of fifteen and studied at the University of Wittenberg where he received a master's degree in 1731. In 1732 he began teaching as a teaching master (Magister legens) in Wittenberg, at first in philosophy and later in theology as well. After habilitating himself with a doctorate in ancient church history in Leipzig, he became a professor at that university in 1742. In 1744 he quit his post in order to become headmaster of the *Gymnasium* at Coburg. He accepted a professorship for "theology, rhetoric, and poetry" at the University of Erlangen in 1748, where his duties required that he obtain an additional doctorate in theology. He stayed at Erlangen until his death. Chladenius was a prolific writer on a great many topics in theology, history, philosophy, and pedagogy. Important for the development of hermeneutics were his *Science of History* (*Allgemeine Geschichtswissenschaft* of 1752 and his *New Definitive Philosophy* (*Nova philosophia definitiva*) of 1750 which contains a chapter on hermeneutic definitions. Among Chladenius's predecessors must be mentioned Konrad Dannhauer (*Idea boni Interpretes— The Idea of the Good Interpreter*, 1630), J. G. Meister (*Dissertatio de interpretatione— Dissertation on Interpretation*, 1698) and above all, Johann Heinrich Ernesti with his work on secular hermeneutics (*De natura et constitutione Hermeneuticae profanae— On the Nature and Constitution of Secular Hermeneutics*, 1699). Chladenius's *Introduction to the Correct Interpretation of Reasonable Discourses and Writings*, published in Leipzig in 1742, was the first systematic treatise on interpretation theory written in German. Even though Chladenius's work was well received and widely discussed among his contemporaries, it did not bring about the establishment of general hermeneutics as an independent branch of philosophy as its author had hoped. The following selections comprise chapters 4 and 8 of the *Introduction*. They deal with Chladenius's concept of interpretation (selection 1) and the interpretation of historical writings (selection 2). It is in the latter that Chladenius develops his famous notion of the point-of-view or perspective (*Sehe-Punkt*). The remaining chapters of the book deal with topics like the classification of discourses and writings, the nature of words and their meaning, the interpretation of discourses and the interpretation of writings, and with the general characteristics of interpretations and the task of the interpreter. For literature on Chladenius, see Bibliography, Section A.

# ON THE CONCEPT OF INTERPRETATION

148. Unless pretense is used, speeches and written works have one intention—that the reader or listener completely understand what is written or spoken. For this reason, it is important that we know what it means to completely understand someone. Here it would be best if we agree only to review certain types of books and speeches which we fully understand so that we may then be able to arrive at a general concept.

149. A history which is told or written to someone assumes that that person will use his knowledge of the prevailing conditions in order to form a reasonable resolution. This aim can also be upheld by virtue of the nature of the account and our own common sense. If, then, we can obtain an idea of the conditions from the account which will allow us to make an appropriate decision, we have completely understood the account.

If, for example, a commander receives an unsigned letter from a good friend which tells of a fortress which is to be taken by surprise, the letter would of course possibly cause the commander to think that it is perhaps his fortress which is meant and that he must therefore be on the alert; assuming that this letter is to be read as a warning. If these thoughts are aroused in the commander and he subsequently examines the necessity of further circumspection, then he has completely understood the message. But if more details are reported to him, then he will have to make a more definitive and determined resolution in correspondence with these. This must also take place, if he is to have thoroughly understood the letter.

150. One can acquire general concepts and moral lessons from histories and the author may, in fact, intend to teach us these concepts and lessons. If we read a story written with such intentions and really learn the concepts and lessons which can and should be extrapolated, then we have completely understood the history and the book.

151. Stories are also told and written in order to amuse the reader and listener. Here there must be something in the story which causes pleasure when we imagine it in our mind. If in reading and hearing a story of this kind I focus my attention on just that which is able to bring about the pleasure and if I consequently experience the pleasure which is intended, then I have understood the book completely. This category includes the many collections of funny stories which one cannot fully understand if one does not sense the intended pleasure himself.

152. One fully understands an order if one can discern the will of the person giving the command, insofar as he wanted to make his will known. One soon sees from this that it is difficult to understand laws and commands; for it is not enough that I— depending on the type of command— discover the nature of the will of the commanding person, but it is essential to understand the extent to which he has expressed his will in words and how much of this he wants to have me know about. For in actuality, the will of the superior is not the concern of the person receiving the order beyond the extent to which it can be perceived in his words. The rest, which is not present in the words of the command, is not considered part of the command.

153. It is another thing to understand a proposition in itself and to understand it as being presented and asserted by someone; the latter only concerns us in the interpretation. From Descartes we have the statement: One should doubt all things once. If I say I understand the statement completely then this means that I am acquainted with Descartes's opinions, which can either be correct or incorrect, founded or unfounded. We can accept this as a sign of complete understanding if the statements deduced or inferred by the author of the proposition are also made understandable by the same.

154. A meaningful oration or written work is presented or written in order to cause a stirring in our souls. These stirrings serve joy, laughter, seriousness, shame, sadness, and other emotions. An obstacle may be present which does not allow these emotions to be awakened at certain times and in certain people. But, if in listening to or reading a meaningful oration or writing one senses the intended emotion, or at least sees that such an emotion could result if there were no obstacles, then one has fully understood that oration or writing.

155. If, drawing from the examples we have cited, one fully understands this or that writing, one can make the following general concept by abstraction. One understands a speech or writing completely if one considers all of the thoughts that the words can awaken in us according to the rules of heart and mind.

156. There should be no difference between fully understanding a speech or writing and understanding the person who is speaking or writing. For they too have the same rules to consider as the reader and the listener. Thus, the speaker or writer can be thinking of the same thing as the reader or listener when he uses certain words. Consequently, it would make no difference whether I imagine what the writer thought by using certain words, or whether I reflect about what one could imagine with these words according to the rules. Because one cannot foresee everything, his or her words, speeches, and writings may mean something which was not intended. Thus in trying to understand these writings, we may think of something which the writer was not conscious of. It can also happen that a person imagines or thinks that he has expressed his opinion in such a way that one would have to understand him. But everything still is not there in his words which would enable us to completely comprehend the sense of what he is

saying. Therefore, we always have two things to consider in speeches and in written works: a comprehension of the author's meaning and the speech or writing itself.

157. A speech or written work is completely understandable if it is constructed so that one can fully understand the intentions of the author according to psychological rules. But if one cannot understand everything which the author intended from his words, or if one is caused with reason to consider more than the author wanted to say, then the writing is not understandable. In keeping with our remarks in 156, all books and speeches produced by people will have something in them which is not understandable.

158. The concept of the intelligible and the unintelligible may be applied to every part or passage in a speech or in a book.

159. We do not understand a word, sentence, speech, or writing at all if we do not retain anything. But it is impossible for us not to understand a book written according to a grammar and lexicon with which we are familiar. It is possible, however, that we do not completely understand it. For full understanding takes place only when one imagines all things which can be thought of with each word according to psychological rules (155). So the complete understanding of a speech or writing must encompass a number of concepts. If we are still lacking some of these concepts which are necessary for this full understanding, then we still have not understood the passage completely.

160. And so one can understand very little of a speech or book if we are still lacking many of the concepts necessary for its comprehension. In everyday life one does not analyze things and certainly not in the manner that is necessary for interpretation. One commonly claims not to have understood a book at all instead of saying, as one should, that we have only understood some of the book.

161. Experience teaches us that we understand a book better the second time when we have only understood very little on the first cursory reading; for in general, the more often we read a book, the more we understand it, which is the same as saying that we think more about the words and so come closer to a full understanding (155). If one thinks more about a book in retrospect and with reason, we say that we are learning to read the book.

162. If we do not entirely comprehend a book, three situations are possible: either we do not understand some passages at all, or we understand all passages incompletely, or both; rather than saying that we do not understand some passages at all or others incompletely.

163. Learning to understand a book, then, means either that one understands a passage which one previously did not understand, or that both happen simultaneously (162), which will more often be the case.

164. If the sense of a passage is certain, it is called a clear passage; if the meaning is uncertain or unknown, it is a dark passage. A passage that is capable of stimulating all sorts of thoughts in us is considered productive. But if it does not

give us any concepts, or fewer than one desires, then we shall call it unproductive.

165. The passages of a speech or written work are often less productive than their creator imagines, because he often puts more into words than he can reasonably expect his reader to perceive (156). And, on the other hand, some passages are often more productive than the author thinks because they inspire many more thoughts than he intended, some of which he would rather have left unthought.

166. If one learns to understand a book, many thoughts arise in us which we had not had before reading it (161). If this happens because we now understand passages which we formerly did not understand at all (163), then a dark passage has become clear and somewhat productive (164). But if we learn to understand certain passages better, then the unproductive passages will have become more productive. Consequently, our learning to understand a text consists of dark passages becoming clear and unproductive ones becoming productive.

167. Time has no influence on this process but on the things themselves which change in time. Therefore, because we learn to understand a book with time (160), it does not mean that the cause must lie in time, but that it was the thoughts which arose and were changed in our mind. If one wants to learn to understand a book a little at a time, then one must acquire the concepts which are necessary for a complete understanding of the book.

168. These concepts, which we slowly acquire and are the cause for our learning to understand a book (167), either originate in us independently of the book, or we have acquired them because we expected to learn to understand the book through them. Imagine that we are reading Cicero's speech before Milo. At first, much will appear which we do not understand. Some things will become understandable to us later only if we read the speech again. We soon realize that a knowledge of Roman history and antiquity would contribute a great deal to our comprehension of the speech. Before we undertake another reading of the speech we take a look at these related works and discover how much our comprehension of this beautiful speech has increased.

169. There is nothing more common than someone, who, in his desire for us to understand a certain book, will teach us those concepts necessary for its understanding. And we say of this person that he has interpreted the book for us. An interpretation is, then, nothing other than teaching someone the concepts which are necessary to learn to understand or to fully understand a speech or a written work.

170. It may just so happen that we ourselves will arrive in time at the concepts necessary for the understanding of a text (168). But this method alone is copious and precarious. We can achieve our goal more quickly if we can learn the concepts we are lacking from someone who fully understands the book and knows which concepts we need to acquire. We could act as interpreters ourselves in the hopes that we would be lucky enough to hit upon the correct and necessary concepts, but it would still be easier, if someone who understands the book were to help us.

171. Since an interpretation only takes place if we are still lacking certain concepts necessary to the complete understanding of the book, the interpreter's duty terminates when we completely understand the work.

172. If we should ask for an interpreter, then we should acknowledge that we have not completely understood the book. The next simple question one might ask is how we know that we still do not completely understand the meaning of a book. This conjecture may have a good many causes, so we shall only take a few of these as examples.

173. If an account which we hold to be true, as the author would have it, seems to contain things which contradict another account also purported to be true, then we still do not understand either one of the two or both of them completely. We will show in the following that a true account can appear to contradict another one. The fault of the apparent contradiction is to be found in the person who feels that the narrative does not present the nature of things the same way as he perceives it. From this one can conclude that we either read too much or too little into the words and, therefore, do not have the correct concepts which the words should call forth. We consequently still do not fully understand the history.

174. If we read a story which is acclaimed for its ingenuity and we know that many people have been inspired by it, yet we still remain unmoved by it, then this is also a sign that we have not yet understood it. This also applies to an ingenious speech. The complete understanding of such a text demands that we be moved by it, or, at least, that we recognize how the text could move certain readers or listeners (154). It follows that if we do not sense any of these things, then we have not completely understood it.

175. If we are certain from specific details that a commanding officer has made his will known to us and things nevertheless occur where we no longer know what his intent is, then we have not completely understood the commands and laws which were given to us. For if a commanding officer has made his will known to us, there must be enough cause contained in the words of the orders and laws for us to understand his will from them. If we perceive this, then we would fully understand the laws and commands (152). But because we do not know his will, regardless of its having been made known to us, then we must not have fully understood the laws and commands in this instance.

176. In this and in other cases where we do not fully understand a text we need an interpretation. The interpretation is different in each instance so that another interpretation must be used for every dark or unproductive passage (169). The interpretation may express itself in an infinite number of ways, but, just as all repeated human actions proceed according to certain laws, an interpretation is also bound by certain principles which may be observed in particular cases. It has also been agreed that a discipline is formed if one explains, proves, and correlates many principles belonging to a type of action. There can be no doubt, then, that a discipline is created when we interpret according to certain rules. For this we

have the Greek name "hermeneutic" and in our language we properly call it the art of interpretation.

177. Very little knowledge of this discipline can be found in the field of philosophy. It consists of a few rules with many exceptions which are only suitable for certain types of books. These rules, which were not allowed to be regarded as a discipline, were given a place among the theories of reason. The theory of reason deals with matters pertaining to general epistemology and cannot go into the area of history, poetry, and other such literature in depth. For this is the place of interpretation and not a theory of reason. Hermeneutics is a discipline in itself, not in part, and can be assigned its place in accordance with the teachings of psychology.

178. Aside from the shortcoming mentioned above, as to the unsuitable placement of this discipline (177), other oversights were made which have distorted its reputation and made it unrecognizable. Philology and criticism, insofar as the latter consists of improving and restoring damaged passages, have almost always been associated with hermeneutics; but when the critic and philologist have done their work on a book, the work of the interpreter is just beginning. One has arrived at the notion that this admixture of philologist and critic could constitute an excellent interpreter. Indeed, we have them to thank for the fact that we receive the book in its entirety and that we can clearly discern the text. All of these are great merits but differ only too greatly from those of interpretation. Many interpretations that were advanced with this belief in mind lacked the necessary prerequisites.

179. Many things were demanded of interpretations which were impossible, either in themselves, or according to the few principles of interpretation which were available. An interpretation can only take place if the reader or listener cannot understand one or more passages (169, 170). On the other hand, it is impossible to find an interpretation if the words in themselves do not contain anything from which the meaning can be conjectured or ascertained with certainty. The interpreter has been called to give meaning to such dark and ambiguous passages, which is of course impossible. To ask him to give even a probable meaning to these passages would be too great a demand, for an interpreter is not in a position to be called to account for passages, even when their meaning is obvious and clear. It cannot be denied that a probable interpretation can be made where a certain one is not possible, but this would be too difficult to put into rules since a rational theory of probability has not yet been sufficiently developed, even though the manner by which we obtain certain truths has been thoroughly ascertained. It is no wonder then that the theory of interpretation has been attacked in its most difficult chapter and that it has not been easy to come away from this.

180. Yet another type of interpretation has come to be grouped with the main type and has also been a considerable hindrance to the progress of the discipline. We express both our perceptions of things and our desires when we speak or

write. In fact, in some speeches and written works, we have no other aim than to explain to someone else what we know or want—as is the case, for example, in contracts and transactions. Here, if one expresses himself ambiguously, unclearly, contradictorily, or indefinitely, then one may at first attempt to find a probable explanation (179). But, if this is insufficient, then it often must be assumed that the statement which has been made cannot be verified by the text itself with the necessary degree of certainty or probability. This mode of giving meaning to someone's words without being made accountable for it may be called a judicial interpretation *(interpretationem judicarem)* because only a judge or someone who claims the duties of a judge can be held responsible for an interpretation of this kind. This is indispensable for court procedure and is therefore highly worthy of a careful investigation. Such interpretations must, however, not be grouped with the main type of interpretation, but treated separately with special rules. We shall say more about this below.

181. The reputation of the art of interpretation is also distorted by the fact that it was initially used to show how a person should interpret a book or passage himself. This envisaged the purpose for the art of interpretation. An interpreter should guide a person (let us say his pupil) who does not understand a text to a true understanding of it. Therefore, the interpreter must understand the work himself. But according to the general concept, one should interpret a work before one knows the meaning, which is impossible.

182. Some people believe that there would not be much left of the discipline or for interpretation if we were to exclude the grammatical ambiguities (178), the ambiguous and unintelligible passages (179), and the judicial decrees (180). And they would subsequently contend that this is an empty and useless endeavor. The following should provide more than enough material to the contrary, and we can say beforehand that there would still be a considerable amount left to interpret for this or that reader even if a book were written with all necessary caution, and even if there were no difficulties with orthography or language such that a philologist or critic needed to supplement it. This is because interpretation consists of teaching the reader or listener certain concepts necessary for a complete understanding of a text (169). In constructing an interpretation, one must consider the insight of the pupil and use this or that interpretation in accordance with the pupil's lack of knowledge. Since there is no one interpretation of a book suitable for all readers, there may be as many as there are classes of readers grouped according to knowledge and insight. To be precise, almost every person needs a special interpretation.

183. In the act of interpreting, one provides certain concepts which the reader lacks (169). This can just be a matter of a few words or an extended speech containing many sentences. We call an interpretation of a book which consists of parts containing single words, scholia, or glosses. But if the parts are long and consist in turn of many smaller parts, then we call this a commentary.

184. The concepts which belong to the complete understanding of a text and which are consequently contained in the glosses and commentaries can appear in written form; as we can see, these make up no small portion of our stock of books. After one knows the rules of interpretation, we will go on to show how one could and should write commentaries.

185. In interpreting a book, one must be sure that the pupil is taught the concepts he is lacking in order to understand the book (169). Because this can be done with many as well as with few words, one needs to keep this in mind and be able to explicate a passage with brevity or at length. It is not sensible to write nothing but glosses, nor is it a good idea to write a commentary which consists solely of long passages. A reasonable interpretation will consist of both glosses and lengthy annotations.

186. Many centuries ago, scholars considered the production of interpretations to be one of the most prestigious endeavors and, because there were no principles which would have enabled these to be done reasonably (177), one cannot be surprised that many interpretations were unsuccessful and that the disciplines which were built up on interpretations were completely devastated. This is proven in the case of philosophy by the unfortunate interpretations made of Aristotle, by the glossaries for jurisprudence, and by the interpretations of the Fathers and the Scholastic teachers. They finally saw no alternative but to toss the interpretations out and to start all over again.

187. In philosophy there is little need for the art of interpretation. Here, every individual must rely on the strength of his own ability to think. A proposition in a philosophical work at which we can only arrive after much interpretation does not do us a particular service because we then ask whether it is true and how one should prove it—which really belongs to the art of philosophy.

188. We need a hermeneutics all the more in the arts, e.g., in rhetoric, poetry, history, and antiquities, from which we generally have more to learn than from the old Roman and Greek scholars. But when we find, as we have seen in (173, 174, 175), that we still only understand little after we have already acquired the general *requisita,* e.g., a knowledge of the words and their relationship (2, 3), then we still need an interpretation (169). A number of the scholia and commentaries which we often find by old scribes have slowly developed this way. We can learn to save and use the rules from hermeneutics and then go on to improve and extend their usage.

189. Theology relies primarily on the interpretation of Holy Scripture. For this reason, much effort has been made over the course of many years to collect rules suitable for its interpretation. Hermeneutics would stand itself in good stead here to acknowledge that it alone does not determine the matter. The Holy Scriptures are a work of God for which many rules might be more certain than for human books. However, many rules which might be useful here cannot be applied at all. Revelation has its own special criticism which goes beyond this—there are secrets

and prophecies which we are led to, not through philosophy, but through revelation. It is a book which is written for the whole world and it has its own special consequences for the interpretation which can only be introduced in a work of God. The usefulness of the general rules for the interpretation of the Holy Scriptures will reveal itself when these have become better known and more precise with time.

190. The books of law which we find among humans are all constituted such that they need some sort of an interpretation (175). The history of scholarship illustrates the disorder which Bartholus and Baldus have brought to the science of law. Just as the lack of knowledge about the principles of interpretation was damaging and troublesome for them, one can assume that we cannot hope to be insured against new confusion unless scholars are in agreement about these rules.

191. If one ignores that hermeneutics is not needed for philosophy (187), but considers how much theology and jurisprudence depend on this discipline (189, 190), then one sees how important it is that a person first thoroughly acquaint himself with hermeneutics before making this discipline his life work. It is not enough for a scholar merely to know the tenets of the theory of reason; these must be so familiar to him that he is never affected by words which are meaningless to him, tautological explanations, circular proofs, or by other mistakes. A person who is well versed in theology and jurisprudence should firmly inculcate himself with the principles of interpretation, so that such words produce no response, rather than a false one. However, one frequently forgets to practice the general rules of hermeneutics—which were formerly presupposed—at the time when they are most appropriate, so that our whims and those of others may become confused with a true interpretation of a dark passage.

192. Clearly, an interpretation has to be correct. It must teach us the kinds of thoughts which will ultimately allow us to come closer to an understanding of a text (169). But one tends to think of things which hinder our perception of the meaning and allow us to misconstrue the words and to mistake wrong interpretations for correct ones. If such similarly wrong interpretations are produced by an oversight, we call them twisted interpretations. For everyone would like to present his ideas to another person as an interpretation when he thinks he has understood a text. However, just as we called a presumed understanding a misunderstanding, we can also use this term to designate a false interpretation.

193. If one misinterprets a passage and is conscious of it, yet still tries to present the interpretation as a correct one, then one willfully misrepresents the meaning of a text. We carefully distinguish misunderstanding from misrepresentation because one is a mistake of understanding and the other is the result of malicious intent. If one wants to convey to someone that he has misrepresented a text, then it is not enough to convince him that he has misunderstood and misinterpreted the passage. It must be demonstrated to him that he did such a thing against his better knowledge and conscience. The misunderstanding has to be

dealt with through instruction and the misrepresentation must be met with measures to keep the maliciousness under control.

194. Hermeneutics teaches us accordingly to discover and avoid misunderstandings and misrepresentations, for these have caused much evil in the world. Admittedly, much harm may have been done by the lack of rules for proper interpretation.

195. Unrefined forms of misrepresentations were used before even a few principles of interpretation had been acknowledged and presented to the various disciplines. Many men of some reputation presented their thoughts as the true opinion and interpretation of the author, taking no interest in being able to account for these interpretations. Introduced in such a manner, they found little applause among the people, not even from those with a limited understanding. An attempt was slowly made to restrict these arbitrary interpretations through rules, and from these grew the principles of hermeneutics, which have been taught up to now. Many people abused the rules to the point of misrepresentation in their attempts to justify various false interpretations. This succeeded quite easily because many of the rules were too general. If more definitive rules are introduced in addition to the general ones, the abundance of these misrepresentations will be increasingly curbed—assuming that they will be properly applied.

# On the Interpretation of Historical Books and Accounts

306. Things which happened and things past are written down in historical books for future generations (46). The things which happen in the world are of both a physical and a moral nature. The former refers to changes of body and is generally perceived by the senses; whereas the latter happens through human will and understanding. The nature of the first is well enough known, but the moral things stand in need of further explication. This category includes offices, titles, rights, grievances, privileges, and all such things which are created and abolished again through man's volition. These moral things, their changes and the histories which evolve from them, must be perceived through reason. But this generally only refers to common reason which all people possess with no particular expertise in the synthetic theories of reason. One can gain an idea of these moral things and the things which came to pass within them, if one pays attention to human activity. At a public place, for example, one sees that all sorts of things are set out for sale on certain days which does not happen at other places. In this way, one arrives at the notion of marketplace. If I later hear or see myself that the same merchants are no longer at this place, but have gathered together at another place,

and I also notice that this happens in response to an order which has been issued, then I know that the marketplace has been moved—which is a type of history. Mere attention, which, in this case, is no greater than is generally found with all people, serves to teach me adequately about the subject and its histories.

307. Histories are accounts of things that have happened (306). If one intends— as is presumed—to speak the truth about an event, he cannot recount it in a way that differs from his perception of it. We arrive, therefore, at the author's conception of the event directly through his account of it; however, our understanding of it is also shaped indirectly both by the account and the conclusions which we ourselves draw from it. If we take exact note of the changes of a thing, we form nothing but judgments; a history thus consists of pure judgments or postulates, which are virtually one and the same. There are two types of judgments: intuitive and discursive judgments (*judicia intuitiva et discursiva*). Because conclusions and deductions are so tenuous in historical accounts and because one wishes to present only truths which are indisputable and avoid even the implication of surreptitious propositions and premature judgments, then such accounts must consist of pure intuitive judgments, so that we only present that which we have perceived through mere attentiveness. Although the reputation of historical insight is largely acquired through the fact that much of this must be brought out through personal experience, evidence given by others, or through speculation, the following still remains certain. Had we been present at the right time, we would have come to know the same historical proposition through mere attentiveness, which we would otherwise have to learn about indirectly. This proposition is then, according to its origin, an intuitive judgment.

The proposition—Charlemagne was born in Germany—is an intuitive judgment, for it can also be correct if stated another way, disregarding the fact that it must also be known through documents, evidence, and conjecture. It is a truth perceived by those who lived at that time and who were at court; a truth conceived by a very general intuitive judgment.

308. Different people perceive that which happens in the world differently, so that if many people describe an event, each would attend to something in particular—if all were to perceive the situation properly. The cause of the difference is due partly to the place and positioning of our body which differs with everyone; partly to various associations with the subject, and partly to individual differences in selecting objects to attend to. It is generally accepted that there can only be one correct representation for each object and that if there are some differences in description, then one must be completely right and the other completely wrong. This principle is not in accordance with other general truths or with the more exact perceptions of our soul. With the following general example we only wish to prove how differently we can conceive of one particular event.

Assume there are three spectators at a battle which is underway: one is on a hill near the right flank of the one army, the other is on a rise near the left flank, and the third person observes the same army from behind the battle. If these three spectators should make an exact catalogue of what has taken place during the battle, then none of the descriptions would be in complete agreement with any of the others. The first person who stood near the right flank might state that his flank suffered a great deal and retreated a little at one point. He might go on to relate various specific conditions which will not have occurred to the person positioned near the left flank. Whereas this person might report dangerous events which are unknown to the first person. Each of the two will claim to have perceived certain happenings that the other person will not concede to have witnessed but will hold instead to something imagined. For the small changes and turns of a throng of soldiers appear quite differently from a distance than from up close. The dispute between the first two might be decided through the third spectator who stood behind the army or he might just add to it with new facts which the others will not want to accept. This is the nature of all histories. A rebellion is perceived one way by a loyal subject, a rebel perceives it another way, a foreigner or a person from court will perceive it still another way, and all of these perceptions will differ from a citizen or farmer, even if they know nothing about it other than that which seems plausible. Surely, certain parts of all true accounts of an event must be in agreement with each other, because we still agree about the principles of human knowledge, even if we find ourselves confronted with different conditions and do not perceive certain parts of the event in the same way. We only wish to claim that true accounts still may differ, even if different people recount the event in correct accordance with their perceptions.

309. We shall designate the term viewpoint to refer to those conditions governed by our mind, body, and entire person which make or cause us to conceive of something in one way and not in another. Because the positioning of our eyes— and especially their distance from the object perceived—causes us to receive one particular image and not another, there is consequently a reason why we should come to know something one particular way and not another in all our perceptions; and this is determined by the viewpoint. A king, for example, has no accounts of events which take place in distant provinces other than those reported to him by the governors whom he has relegated to the different areas. These reports are responsible for the kings being properly, falsely, laboriously, thoroughly, or only slightly informed about the situation in the provinces. They provide, then, the viewpoint according to which a great ruler bases his notions about what is going on in distant provinces. The present designation of the word viewpoint probably originates with Leibnitz; it appears otherwise only in the context of optics. What he was trying to illustrate can best be seen in our definition which clearly explains the same concept. We are making use of the same concept because it is indispensable if one wishes to take into account the numerous changes in a person's conception of a thing.

310. We conclude from this concept that people who see a thing from a different

viewpoint must also have different conceptions about it, and those who see something from the same viewpoint must have the same notion about a thing. Although
it should be noted that the phrase "one and the same" may not be construed as
"completely the same," as it is impossible for two people to perceive something
from one and the same viewpoint, in that innumerous differences can always be
found in the conditions of body, mind, and of the entire person which engender
a multiplicity in their perceptions. It has long been established that no two people
can have one and the same perception of things which is captured in the famous
saying: *quot capita, tot sensus* ("As many heads, as many options").

311. If people perceive a thing from a different viewpoint and they tell each
other about their conceptions and the conclusions they have drawn from them,
then it will appear to each that the other's account has the following characteristics. First, one will come across all sorts of improbable things in the other
person's description. Because sufficient proof of this cannot be presented here
without many subtle metaphysical propositions, we would prefer to confirm this
hypothesis as an observation by example. If, when the Spanish arrived, they had
shown an American the specific parts of a rifle, its structure, and how to load it,
then the American would certainly have had a concept of it. But if he were told
to be careful with the rifle because it might endanger his life, or if he were told
that people had already had bullets shot into their bodies, then the Indian would
not have understood any of this. If a shot were to follow, he would be thoroughly
surprised as he would not have expected such a thing to happen. And so, a private
individual can believe everything to be at peace and hold an attack on his country
for impossible—especially if he is at court where talk centers on the great dangers
which threaten from internal or outside unrest.

312. This is especially true when human actions are related to us from a viewpoint which differs from the one we have previously held. We find the ensuing
qualities unexpected, i.e., that some circumstances come about more easily and
naturally than we had previously imagined: there was more intrigue, artfulness,
or luck, than we had thought; many actions seem more praiseworthy than before
and many seem more shameful. Furthermore, some parts of the story will bring
us pleasure which had not been particularly pleasing before. On the one hand,
we will participate more in the story than before, and on the other, it will seem
to be something which has little to do with us. Not to mention the other unexpected things which will arise when two people with different viewpoints make
their insights known to one another. These will depend on the different types of
history, i.e., whether it be state, church, or natural history.

313. Furthermore, when another person perceives a thing or an event from a
viewpoint which differs from ours, we usually think we have come across something incongruous, contradictory, or paradoxical. For we judge the nature of a
thing according to the concept we have of it. Whatever disagrees with our concept, must in our opinion, also disagree with the nature of the object itself.

Different things may come up in another person's account which seem to contend with ours because we do not know the nature of the ideas precisely enough. It often seems to us as though there were contradictions and inconsistencies in history itself. One often encounters this sort of contradiction when comparing different accounts of the same event, regardless of the fact that the authors composed them with such scrupulosity that they would swear with a clear conscience to the conscientiousness of their work. Clearly, the event itself cannot contain contradictions; it alone may be presented to the observers so differently that the accounts of it contain something contradictory in themselves.

314. The number of these contradictions is not decreased by the fact that a person immediately draws conclusions while watching an event and later considers these to be a part of the event although they do not belong to it and are more probably incorrect. Such a statement, which one believes to have experienced although it is actually concluded from the experience, is called a surreptitious statement. For example, in the evening when the sky is brightly lit, one often sees a light fall downwards in the air or to the side. A completely injudicious person would immediately imagine he had seen a star fall from the sky and burn out in the course of its fall. A more intelligent person would say that a star had flickered or that it had emitted a beam of light. Everyone tends to describe the event according to his own perception; at the same time, however, presenting his imagined or incorrect judgment of the falling heavenly body as the event itself. Such hasty and premature conclusions creep into almost all of our accounts and it would be difficult even for a philosopher to keep from bringing his own conclusions into the event, although he may be scrupulously trained to distinguish between his judgment and the thing itself.

315. Because of the unexpected and incongruous things which we encounter in an event told from a viewpoint which differs from ours (311, 313), it also follows that we have difficulty believing that the event took place. We know that things cannot happen which are contradictory and without sufficient reason and, therefore, that we need not believe them. We find things in this same story which are incongruous or for which there is not sufficient cause and it is difficult for us to believe the story for this reason—even if the narrator were plausible enough otherwise.

316. An account of things which did not happen is called a fiction (66). When (hi)stories, with which we ourselves are familiar, are related to us by someone who perceives them from another viewpoint, we do not believe that they actually took place (315) and they appear therefore to be a fiction to us. Similarly, because of its apparent incredibility, that which actually took place (and thus belongs to historical accounts) acquires the reputation of a fable.

317. If a story is told to us from a viewpoint which seems improbable, then it may appear to us to be a fiction (316) because of its incredibility. But since fables are not appropriate in all cases, the improbability may mean that we push the

blame for the lack of knowledge of the event onto the person telling the story, or it may also mean that we believe he planned to deceive the reader (16). In both cases, the conclusion casts a poor light on the author and it thus becomes necessary to show how the author of an account could unjustly be met with such criticism. We will then go on to show how one might save both these passages and the author himself.

318. The event and the concept of the event are commonly held to be one and the same, which is not always incorrect. Yet one must indicate the difference and clearly make note of it, particularly when one is dealing with the interpretation of an event. For it is not the event in itself, but the concept of the event which is unclear to another person and is in need of an interpretation. The difference is, by the way, very noticeable: the event is one and the same, but the concept of it different and manifold. There is nothing contradictory in an event; the contradictions arise from the different conceptions of the same thing. All things in an event have sufficient reason; in its conception, things can appear which seem to happen without sufficient reason.

319. A history is narrated or written down so that readers and listeners will believe it. If the event is possible in itself and the narrator is worthy of belief, then there exists no reason or cause for us not to believe it. We see, however, that we do not want to believe an account because it seems unexpected, incongruous, and fabulous. Such accounts are then in need of an interpretation (169). In this case it is the responsibility of the interpreter to eliminate the improbable, the incongruous, and the fabulous aspects of the account, or to place his pupil in a position where the account no longer appears to him to have these characteristics. And we must show how an interpreter might practically be able to do this.

320. The reason we do not believe a history presented to us from a strange viewpoint is that we think we find contradictions or fabulous elements in it (319). We will always sense a difficulty in believing such accounts as long as these elements are not done away with. Meanwhile, it is possible for one to gradually stop noticing such contradictory and unexpected elements and allow oneself, in the end, to be persuaded by an account, although the doubts have not been proved unfounded. Accordingly, this is a means of making an account plausible for someone by putting their attentiveness to sleep, so that they no longer experience the doubt which they felt in the beginning.

. . .

324. Therefore, an interpreter must imagine the account which he wishes to interpret from both viewpoints; from the viewpoint of the person who finds it incredible and from the perspective of the scribe who wrote it. But since we are usually lacking such interpreters, we must help ourselves and serve as interpreters. Our concern here nevertheless is that we gradually learn to understand

an account which we did not thoroughly understand in the beginning and which is why we did not believe it (161). This means in this case that we learn the circumstances of the event of which we were previously unaware and that we learn to reflect on those details which are already known to us (323). But we cannot foresee which details we are missing and which details would allow us to comprehend the account if they were known to us.

325. But because each account has its own specific place, particular people, and certain time, and because it is the knowledge of these things which enables us to comprehend it, we can give this rule according to which one must interpret incredible accounts for himself. One must inquire about all details concerning time and place, if and where an event took place. Subsequently, one can generally arrive, in this manner, at a knowledge of those details which will make the entire matter comprehensible and plausible.

326. If an interpreter either cannot interpret a seemingly incongruous and incredible account according to the prescribed method (322, 323), or if he for some reason is unable to make the crucial details clear to his pupil, then he can move him to accept the account if he clearly shows him that there are indeed true accounts in which there are things which will seem implausible or incongruous to this or that reader. Furthermore, he may impress on him that a student of history should place his trust more in the integrity and insight of the writer of the history, rather than to doubt the account itself because of apparent absurdity and contradiction with other truths.

327. Two or more similar accounts are called parallel histories. Just as many types of similarities may be found in accounts, there are also many types of parallel histories to be discovered. An example of a peculiar type of this sort is when both events share the same cause and consequence—as in the case where the very greatness of an empire has afforded the opportunity for its downfall, or where often the most insignificant persons in the republic have undertaken the greatest changes.

328. When a history appears to us to be incredible and there also exist parallel histories of whose truth there is no doubt, then we are easily persuaded that the account in question is not necessarily incredible. Therefore, if a pupil does not believe an account because it seems incongruous and the interpreter of the account wishes to make it plausible to him, then he can make use of this expedient. By bringing in parallel accounts which cannot be called into question, he can demonstrate that accounts of this sort are indeed possible.

329. If the authors of two accounts contradict one another, regardless of whether the issue has been presented correctly or from different viewpoints (312), the reader will generally think the authors were so opposed to each other that one must necessarily be in the right and the other in the wrong. Of course, it could be that this contradiction is only an apparent one (313), and stems from the fact that the reader does not completely understand either one or both of the authors

of the accounts. An interpreter should accordingly reconcile the contradictory elements by presenting the account to the pupil in such a way that he no longer finds a contradiction.

330. When two authors contradict one another— regardless of whether they are both in the right— then the one account will appear to us to be contradictory and incongruous if we assume the other one to be true. If a story seems to be incongruous, then we are lacking certain details. Thus, if an interpreter wants to reconcile the contradictory account (329), he must either teach his pupil the details missing from the narration which are unknown to him (322), or at least bring it home to the pupil that he remember them. In this case, it is the insight of the interpreter which is needed, just as we demanded this from the interpreter of incredible passages (324).

331. However, if one wants to arrive at his own interpretation, then one must carefully note just how each of the authors of the contradictory accounts views the time, place, and the people pertinent to his narration (324). He must also collect all the details and make precise observations, for we often fall upon the details which it is necessary to know by chance (325). Even so, we still cannot promise ourselves the assured success of our efforts. If it happens that there are no more details on the issue recorded elsewhere, then it will remain impossible to find an interpretation which is certain.

# 2

# Foundations: General Theory and Art of Interpretation

## Friedrich D. E. Schleiermacher

FRIEDRICH (DANIEL ERNST) SCHLEIERMACHER (1768–1834), the founder of modern Protestant theology, was also a respected classical philologist (best known through his work on Plato) and an original thinker in his own right. His interest in hermeneutic problems was first kindled when he lived in Berlin in close personal contact with Friedrich Schlegel and the other Romantics (1796–1802). Among his group, Schlegel was the first to apply the principles of transcendental idealism to the realm of literature with his *Philosophy of Philology*. Taking his cues from Schlegel's suggestive insights, Schleiermacher went to work in a consistent and systematic fashion, and thus became the founder of modern hermeneutics. By critically uniting the hermeneutic traditions in Protestant theology and the rhetorical and philological traditions of classical scholarship with the new transcendental approach inherited from Kant and Fichte, Schleiermacher created the "classical" system of Romantic hermeneutics. He wrote down his ideas first in aphoristic form (1805, 1809–10), subsequently elaborated a draft of his system, and finally produced a detailed outline of his ideas in 1819. This so-called *Compendium of 1819* served Schleiermacher as the basis for the lecture course which he taught repeatedly over the years when he held his chair in Protestant theology at the University of Berlin between 1810 and 1834. In 1828 he added additional notes ("Marginal Notes") and comments to the original text. After Schleiermacher's death, his student, F. Lücke, published in 1838 a volume called *Hermeneutics and Criticism* which offered a coherent version of Schleiermacher's hermeneutics, composed of notes taken by students attending his lectures and of Schleiermacher's own notes and outlines. It was only in 1958 that Schleiermacher's manuscripts were published separately and in their entirety by one of Gadamer's students, H. Kimmerle. The text of the Lücke edition has recently been reissued (F. D. E. Schleiermacher, *Hermeneutik und Kritik*, 1977. Sect. A, Bibl.). The selections are from the English translation by J. Duke and J. Forstman of the Kimmerle edition. They comprise the "Introduction," "Part 1: Grammatical Interpretation," and "Part 2: Technical Interpretation" of the *Compendium of 1819*, together with the marginal notes of 1828, which are reproduced here in smaller type following the passages to which they relate. A few short paragraphs which did not directly contribute to the main argument have been omitted from "Part 1."

# [GENERAL HERMENEUTICS]

## *Introduction*

I. 1. At present there is no general hermeneutics as the art of understanding but only a variety of specialized hermeneutics.* Ast's explanation, p. 172; Wolf, p. 37.[1]

*1828
1. Hermeneutics and criticism are related such that the practice of either one presupposes the other.
In both, the relationship to the author is general and varied.
Hermeneutics is presumed to be unimportant because it is necessary where criticism is hardly applicable at all, in general because the task of criticism supposedly ends, whereas the task of hermeneutics is endless. The hermeneutical task moves constantly. My first sentence refers to this movement.
2. With respect to its study of both genre and language, special hermeneutics is only an aggregate of observations and does not meet the requirements to science. To seek understanding without reflection and to resort to the rules of understanding only in special cases is an unbalanced operation. Since one cannot do without either of these two standpoints, one must combine them. This occurs in two ways: (1) Even where we think we can proceed in an inartistic way we often encounter unexpected difficulties, the clues for the solution of which may be found in the materials already passed over. Therefore, we are always forced to pay attention to what may be able to resolve these problems. (2) If we always proceed artistically, we come at the end to an unconscious application of the rules, without ever having been inartistic.

1. Hermeneutics deals only with the art of understanding, not with the presentation of what has been understood. The presentation of what has been understood would be only one special part of the art of speaking and writing, and that part could be done only by relying upon general principles.
2. Nor is hermeneutics concerned exclusively with difficult passages of texts written in foreign languages. To the contrary, it presupposes a familiarity with both the contents and the language of a text. Assuming such familiarity, difficulties with particular passages of a text arise only because the easier ones have not been understood. Only an artistically sound understanding can follow what is being said and written.
3. It is commonly believed that by following general principles one can trust one's common sense. But if that is so, by following special principles, one can trust one's natural instincts.
2. It is very difficult to assign general hermeneutics its proper place among the sciences.

1. For a long time it was treated as an appendix to Logic, but since Logic is no longer seen as dealing with applied matters, this can no longer be done. The philosopher per se has no interest in developing hermeneutical theory. He seldom works at understanding, because he believes that it occurs by necessity.[2]

2. Moreover, philology has become positivistic. Thus its way of treating hermeneutics results in a mere aggregate of observations.

3. Since the art of speaking and the art of understanding stand in relation to each other, speaking being only the outer side of thinking, hermeneutics is a part of the art of thinking, and is therefore philosophical.*

*General hermeneutics is related to criticism as to grammar. And since there can be no communication or even acquisition of knowledge without all three, and since all correct thinking is based on correct speaking, all three are related to dialectics.

1. Yet these two are to be related in such a way that the art of interpretation at once depends upon and presupposes composition. They are parallel in the sense that artless speaking does not require any art to be understood.

II. 4. Speaking is the medium for the communality of thought, and for this reason rhetoric and hermeneutics belong together and both are related to dialectics.

1. Indeed, a person thinks by means of speaking. Thinking matures by means of internal speech, and to that extent speaking is only developed thought. But whenever the thinker finds it necessary to fix what he has thought, there arises the art of speaking, that is, the transformation of original internal speaking, and interpretation becomes necessary.

2. Hermeneutics and rhetoric are intimately related in that every act of understanding is the reverse side of an act of speaking, and one must grasp the thinking that underlies a given statement.

Dialectics relies on hermeneutics and rhetoric because the development of all knowledge depends on both speaking and understanding.

5. Just as every act of speaking is related to both the totality of the language and the totality of the speaker's thoughts, so understanding a speech always involves two moments: to understand what is said in the context of the language with its possibilities, and to understand it as a fact in the thinking of the speaker.*

*3. Explanation of 5 and 6
How grammatical and psychological interpretation are related to dialectical and rhetorical thinking.
Each makes use of the other. Grammatical and psychological remain the main divisions.

1. Every act of speaking presupposes a given language. This statement could also be reversed, not only for the absolutely first act of speaking in

a language, but also for its entire history, because language develops through speaking. In every case commnication presupposes a shared language and therefore some knowledge of the language. Whenever something comes between the internal speaking and its communication, one must turn to the art of speaking. So the art of speaking is due in part to a speaker's anxiety that something in his use of language may be unfamiliar to the hearer.

2. Every act of speaking is based on something having been thought. This statement, too, could be reversed, but with respect to communication the first formulation holds because the art of understanding deals only with an advanced stage of thinking.

3. Accordingly, each person represents one locus where a given language takes shape in a particular way, and his speech can be understood only in the context of the totality of the language. But then too he is a person who is a constantly developing spirit, and his speaking can be understood as only one moment in this development in relation to all others.

6. Understanding takes place only in the coinherence of these two moments.

1. An act of speaking cannot even be understood as a moment in a person's development unless it is also understood in relation to the language. This is because the linguistic heritage [*Angeborenheit der Sprache*] modifies our mind.

2. Nor can an act of speaking be understood as a modification of the language unless it is also understood as a moment in the development of the person (later addition: because an individual is able to influence a language by speaking, which is how a language develops).

III. 7. These two hermeneutical tasks are completely equal, and it would be incorrect to label grammatical interpretation the "lower" and psychological interpretation the "higher" task.*

*On 7. There is no way to distinguish between what is easy or difficult in general terms. Rather, to one person the one task is easier; to another, the other. Consequently, there are two different main approaches and main works, notes on language and introductions.

4. Continuation of 7. Neither task is higher than the other. 6, 8, 9.

1. Psychological interpretation is higher when one regards the language exclusively as a means by which a person communicates his thoughts. Then grammatical interpretation is employed only to clear away initial difficulties.

2. Grammatical interpretation and language, because it conditions the thinking of every person, are higher only when one regards the person and his speaking exclusively as occasions for the language to reveal itself. Then psychological interpretation and the life of the individual become subordinate considerations.

3. From this dual relation it is evident that the two tasks are completely equal.

8. The task is finally resolved when either side could be replaced by the other, though both must be treated, that is to say, when each side is treated in such a way that the treatment of the other side produces no change in the result.

   1. Both grammatical and psychological interpretation must be treated, even though either can substitute for the other, in accordance with II, 6.

   2. Each side is complete only when it makes the other superfluous and contributes to its work. This is because language can be learned only by understanding what is spoken, and because the inner make-up of a person, as well as the way in which external objects affect him, can only be understood from his speaking.

9. Interpretation is an art.

   1. Each side is itself an art. For each side constructs something finite and definite from something infinite and indefinite. Language is infinite because every element is determinable in a special way by the other elements. This statement also applies to psychological interpretation, for every intuition of a person is itself infinite. Moreover, external influences on a person will have ramifications which trail off into infinity. Such a construction, however, cannot be made by means of rules which may be applied with self-evident certainty.

   2. In order to complete the grammatical side of interpretation it would be necessary to have a complete knowledge of the language. In order to complete the psychological side it would be necessary to have a complete knowledge of the person. Since in both cases such complete knowledge is impossible, it is necessary to move back and forth between the grammatical and psychological sides, and no rules can stipulate exactly how to do this.

10. The success of the art of interpretation depends on one's linguistic competence and on one's ability for knowing people.

   1. By "linguistic competence" I am not referring to a facility for learning foreign languages. The distinction between one's mother tongue and a foreign language is not at issue here. Rather, I refer to one's command of language, one's sensitivity to its similarities and differences, etc. — It could be claimed that in this respect rhetoric and hermeneutics must always belong together. But hermeneutics requires one kind of competence, rhetoric requires another, and the two are not the same. To be sure, both hermeneutics and rhetoric require linguistic competence, but hermeneutics makes use of that competence in a different way.

   2. One's ability to know people refers especially to a knowledge of the subjective element determining the composition of thoughts. Thus, just as with hermeneutics and rhetoric, so with hermeneutics and the artful description of persons, there is no permanent connection. Nonetheless, many errors in hermeneutics are due to a lack of this talent or to a flaw in its application.

   3. Insofar as these abilities are universal gifts of nature, hermeneutics is

everybody's concern. To the extent that a person is deficient in one of these talents, he is hampered, and the other gift can do no more than help him choose wisely from the suggestions made by others.

IV. 11. The art of interpretation is not equally interested in every act of speaking. Some instances fail to spark its interest at all, while others engage it completely. Most, however, fall somewhere between these two extremes.*

*Hour 5. 10–11.
On 11. Of minimal worth is such common speech as (a) business discussions [*geschäftliche*] and (b) conversations. Of maximal worth, predominately for language: (a) original [*urbildlich*] for the production of thoughts = too much. Those types of speech between these two extremes lie closer to one extreme or the other—(a) toward common speech, that is, with a relatively important subject matter and a graceful presentation; (b) toward creative [*geniale*] speech, the classical quality of the language need not be original, and the originality in the combination of elements need not be classical.
A great deal of talent is necessary not only to deal with difficult passages, but also in order not to be content with an immediate purpose, and to pursue both directions in order to reach the goal.

1. A statement may be regarded to be of no interest when it is neither important as a human act nor significant for the language. It is said because the language maintains itself only by constant repetition. But that which is only already available and repeated is itself of no significance. Conversations about the weather. But these statements are not absolutely devoid of significance, since they may be said to be "minimally significant," in that they are constructed in the same way as more profound statements.
2. A statement may be of maximum significance for one side of interpretation or the other. It is maximally significant for the grammatical side when it is linguistically creative to an exceptional degree and minimally repetitive: classical texts. A statement is maximally significant for the psychological side when it is highly individualized and minimally commonplace: original texts. The term "absolute" is reserved for statements that achieve a maximum of both linguistic creativity and individuality: works of genius [*das Genialische*].
3. "Classical" and "original" statements cannot be transitory, but must be definitive for later productions. Indeed, even absolute texts are influenced to some degree by earlier and more common ones.
12. Although both sides of interpretation should always be applied, they will always be weighted differently.*

*6. 12 and 13 were begun.

[1]. This is because a statement that is grammatically insignificant is not

necessarily psychologically insignificant and vice versa. Thus, in dealing with a text that is in one respect insignificant, we cannot reach what is significant in it by applying both sides equally.

2. A minimum of psychological interpretation is appropriate when what is to be interpreted is predominately objective. Pure history, especially in its details, whereas the overall viewpoint requires more psychological interpretation since it is always subjectively affected. Epics. Commercial records that can be used as historical sources. Didactic treatments in the strict sense on every subject. In such cases the subjective is not applied as a moment of interpretation, but results from the interpretation. A minimum of grammatical interpretation in conjunction with a maximum of psychological is appropriate in dealing with letters, especially personal letters. There is a point of transition along the continuum from historical and didactic pieces to personal letters. Lyric poetry. Polemics?

13. There are no methods of interpretation other than those discussed above.

1. For example, in the dispute over the historical interpretation of the New Testament there emerged the curious view that there are several different kinds of interpretation. To the contrary, only historical interpretation can do justice to the rootedness of the New Testament authors in their time and place. (Awkward expressions. Concepts of time.) But historical interpretation is wrong when it denies Christianity's power to create new concepts and attempts to explain it in terms of conditions which were already present in the time. It is proper to reject such a one-sided historical interpretation, but it is improper to reject historical interpretation altogether.[3] The crux of the matter, then, lies in the relationship between grammatical and psychological interpretation, since new concepts developed from the distinctive manner in which the authors were affected.

V. 2. Historical interpretation is not to be limited to gathering historical data. That task should be done even before interpretation begins, since it is the means for re-creating the relationship between speaker and the original audience, and interpretation cannot begin until that relationship has been established.

3. Allegorical interpretation does not deal with allegories where the figurative meaning is the only one intended, regardless of whether the stories are based on truth, as in the parable of the sower, or on fiction, as in the parable of the rich man, but to cases where the literal meaning, in its immediate context, gives rise to a second, figurative meaning. Such instances cannot be dismissed by citing the general principle that a given passage can have only one meaning, that is, its usual grammatical one. Allusions always involve a second meaning, and if a reader does not catch this second meaning along with the first, he misses one of the intended meanings, even though he may be able to follow the literal one. At the same time, to claim that there is an

allusion where there actually is none is also an error. An allusion occurs when an additional meaning is so entwined with the main train of thought that the author believes it would be easily recognized by another person. These additional meanings are not merely occasional and unimportant, but just as the whole world is posited ideally in man, it is always considered real, although only as a dark shadow-image. There is a parallelism of different stages [*Reihen*] in the large and the small, and therefore there can occur in any one something from another: parallelism of the physical and the ethical of music and painting. But these parallelisms are to be noted only when figurative expressions indicate them. There is a special reason why parallelism occurs without clues, especially in Homer and in the Bible.*

*Hour 7. Continuation of 13.
In the search for what is rich in meaning and significance, dogmatic and allegorical interpretations share the common assumptions that the result should be as rich as possible for Christian doctrine and that nothing in the Holy Scriptures should be seen to be insignificant or of merely passing significance..
Move from this discussion to the question of inspiration. Given the great variety of ideas of inspiration, it is best, first of all, to test what sort of consequences the strictest idea leads to, i.e., the idea that the power of the spirit extends from the inception of the thought to the act of writing itself. Due to the variants, this no longer helps us. These were, however, already present before the Scriptures were collected. Here, too, then, criticism is necessary. — But even the first readers of the apostles' epistles would have had to abstract from their ideas to the author and from the application of their knowledge of that, and would have become completely confused. If one then asks why the Scriptures did not arise in a totally miraculous way without the involvement of humans, we must answer that the divine spirit can have chosen the method it did only if it wanted everything traced back to the declared author. Therefore, this interpretation must be correct. The same point holds with respect to the grammatical side. But then every element must be treated as purely human, and the action of the Spirit was only to produce the inner impulse.
Other views, ascribing some special trait to the spirit (e.g., protection from error) but not others, are untenable. For example, protection from error means that the process of writing is hedged in, but putting down what insight in a given place devolves on the author.

VI. This accounts for the singularity of Homer as a book for general education and of the Old Testament as a body of literature from which everything is to be drawn. To this it should be added that the mythical contents in both are developed into esoteric [*gnomische*] philosophy on the one hand and into history on the other. But there is no technical interpretation for myth because it cannot be traced back to a single person, and the shifting in ordinary understanding between the literal and figurative meanings draws out the double meaning most clearly. In the case of the New Testament, however, the situation was quite different, and a method based on two principles was developed. First, in keeping with the close connection between the two testaments, the type of explanation used in interpreting the Old Testament was applied to the New Testament as well, and this type of interpretation was carried over into scholarly interpretations. The second principle was the idea, more thoroughly applied to the New Testament than to the Old, that the Holy Spirit was the author. Since the Holy Spirit could not be conceived as an individual consciousness that changed in time, there arose a tendency to find everything in each part. Universal truths or particular instructions satisfy this inclination, but the results which are produced are in the main unconnected and, taken in isolation, insignificant.

4. Incidentally, the question arises whether on account of the Holy Spirit the Scriptures must be treated in a special way. This question cannot be answered by a dogmatic decision about inspiration, because such a decision itself depends upon interpretation.

1. We must not make a distinction between what the apostles spoke and what they wrote, for the church had to be built on their speeches.

2. But for this reason we must not suppose that their writings were addressed to all of Christendom, for in fact each text was addressed to specific people, and their writings could not be properly understood in the future unless these first readers could understand them. But these first readers would have looked for what was specifically related to their own situations, and from this material they had to derive the whole truth of Christianity. Our interpretation must take this fact into account, and we must assume that even if the authors had been merely passive tools of the Holy Spirit, the Holy Spirit could have spoken through them only as they themselves would have spoken.*

*Whether the view that everything in the Scriptures was inspired means that everything must relate to the whole church? No. This view would necessarily entail that the original recipients would interpret them incorrectly, so that it would have been better if the Holy Spirit had not produced the Scriptures as occasional writings. Therefore, grammatical and psychological interpretation always proceed in accord with the general rules. To what extent a specialized hermeneutics is still required cannot be discussed until later.

VII. 5. The worst offender in this respect is cabalistic interpretation which labors to find everything in the particular elements and their signs. —One sees that whatever efforts can be legitimately called interpretation, there are no other types except those based on the different relationships between the two sides we have noted.

14. The distinction between artful and artless interpretation is not based on the difference between what is familiar to us and what is unfamiliar, or between what is spoken and what is written. Rather, it is based on the fact that we want to understand with precision some things and not others.*

*14–16. We stand at the point of total opposition between artless and artful interpretation. If one moves to the latter only when difficulties are encountered, one will come to no more than discrete observations. —Precise understanding means that one grasps the easy parts of the meaning and uses them as a key for interpreting the difficult parts.

1. Were the art of interpretation needed only for foreign and ancient texts, then the original readers would not have required it. Were this the case, then in effect the art of interpretation would be based on the differences between the original readers and us. But historical and linguistic knowledge removes that obstacle, and so only after significant points of comparison between the first readers and us have been reached can interpretation begin. Therefore, the only difference between ancient and foreign texts and contemporary texts in our own language is that the comparisons necessary for interpreting the former cannot be completed prior to the interpretation but begins and is completed with the process of interpretation. As he works the interpreter should keep this fact in mind.

2. Nor do written texts alone call for the art of interpretation. Were that true, the art would be necessary only because of the difference between written and spoken words, that is, because of the loss of the living voice and the absence of supplementary personal impressions. But the latter must themselves be interpreted, and that interpretation is never certain. To be sure, the living voice facilitates understanding, and a writer must take this fact into consideration. Were he to do so, then, on the assumption that the art of interpretation is not necessary for oral statements, the art would not be necessary for the written text. But that simply is not the case. Therefore, even if an author did not consider the effects of the living voice, the necessity for the art of interpretation is not based on the difference between oral and written statements.*

*That the art is necessary more for spoken than written language, because as the speech is spoken one cannot remember the various rules which are to be used.

3. Given this relationship between speaking and writing, the distinction between artful and artless interpretation must be based on nothing else than the principle stated above, and it follows that artistic interpretation has the same aim as we do in ordinary listening.

VIII. 15. There is a less rigorous practice of this art which is based on the assumption that understanding occurs as a matter of course. The aim of this practice may be expressed in negative form as: "misunderstanding should be avoided."

1. This less rigorous practice presupposes that it deals mainly with insignificant matters or that it has a quite specific interest, and so it establishes limited, easily realizable goals.

2. Even here, however, difficulties may necessitate recourse to artful interpretation. In this way hermeneutics originated from artless practice. But because it was applied only to difficult cases, it produced merely a collection of observations. At the same time this practice gave rise to special hermeneutics, since difficult passages could be more easily worked out within a delimited framework. Both theological and juristic hermeneutics arose in this way,[4] and even the philologists have pursued only specialized aims.

3. In short, the less rigorous practice is based on the fact that the speaker and hearer share a common language and a common way of formulating thoughts.

16. There is a more rigorous practice of the art of interpretation that is based on the assumption that misunderstanding occurs as a matter of course, and so understanding must be willed and sought at every point.

1. This more rigorous practice consists in grasping the text precisely with the understanding and in viewing it from the standpoint of both grammatical and psychological interpretation.

(Note: It is common experience that one notices no distinction until . . . [the] beginning of a misunderstanding.)

2. Therefore, this more rigorous practice presupposes that the speaker and hearer differ in their use of language and in their ways of formulating thoughts, although to be sure there is an underlying unity between them. This is one of the less significant matters overlooked by artless interpretation.*

*9. Discuss the difference (*pistis*) between the subjective interpretation and the objective as such.

17. Both qualitative misunderstanding of the contents of a work and quantitative misunderstanding of its tone are to be avoided.*

*17. Negative formulation of the task: to avoid misunderstanding the material and formal elements.

1. Objective qualitative misunderstanding occurs when one part of speech in the language is confused with another, as for example, when the meanings of two words are confused. Subjective qualitative misunderstanding occurs when the reference of an expression is confused.

2. Subjective quantitative misunderstanding occurs when one misses the potential power of development of a part of speech or the value given it by the speaker. Analogous to this, objective quantitative misunderstanding occurs when one mistakes the degree of importance which a part of speech has.

3. From quantitative misunderstanding, which usually receives less consideration, qualitative always develops.

4. This thesis (17) encompasses the full task of interpretation, but because it is stated negatively we cannot develop rules from it. In order to develop rules we must work from a positive thesis, but we must constantly be oriented to this negative formulation.

5. We must also distinguish between passive and active misunderstanding. The latter occurs when one reads something into a text because of one's own bias. In such a case the author's meaning cannot possibly emerge.*

*Hour 10. 17,5. This represents the maximum, because it is caused by completely false presuppositions. — 18. 19.

IX. 18. The rules for the art of interpretation must be developed from a positive formula, and this is: "the historical and divinatory, objective and subjective reconstruction of a given statement."

1. "Objective-historical" means to consider the statement in [its] relation to the language as a whole, and to consider the knowledge it contains as a product of the language. — "Objective-prophetic" means to sense how the statement itself will stimulate further developments in the language. Only by taking both of these aspects into account can qualitative and quantitative misunderstanding be avoided.

2. "Subjective-historical" means to know how the statement, as a fact in the person's mind, has emerged. "Subjective-prophetic" means to sense how the thoughts contained in the statement will exercise further influence on and in the author. Here, again, unless both of these aspects are taken into account, qualitative and quantitative misunderstandings are unavoidable.

3. The task is to be formulated as follows: "To understand the text at first as well as and then even better than its author." Since we have no direct knowledge of what was in the author's mind, we must try to become aware of many things of which he himself may have been unconscious, except insofar as he reflects on his own work and becomes his own reader. Moreover, with respect to the objective aspects, the author had no data other than we have.

4. So formulated, the task is infinite, because in a statement we want to trace a past and a future which stretch into infinity. Consequently, inspiration is as much a part of this art as of any other. Inasmuch as a text does not evoke such inspiration, it is insignificant. — The question of how far and in which directions interpretation will be pressed must be decided in each case on practical grounds. Specialized hermeneutics and not general hermeneutics must deal with these questions.

19. Before the art of hermeneutics can be practiced, the interpreter must put himself both objectively and subjectively in the position of the author.

1. On the objective side this requires knowing the language as the author

knew it. But this is a more specific task than putting oneself in the position of the original readers, for they, too, had to identify with the author. On the subjective side this requires knowing the inner and the outer aspects of the author's life.

2. These two sides can be completed only in the interpretation itself. For only from a person's writings can one learn his vocabulary, and so, too, his character and his circumstances.

20. The vocabulary and the history of an author's age together form a whole from which his writings must be understood as a part, and vice versa.

1. Complete knowledge always involves an apparent circle, that each part can be understood only out of the whole to which it belongs, and vice versa. All knowledge which is scientific must be constructed in this way.

2. To put oneself in the position of an author means to follow through with this relationship between the whole and the parts. Thus it follows, first, that the more we learn about an author, the better equipped we are for interpretation, but, second, that a text can never be understood right away. On the contrary, every reading puts us in a better position to understand because it increases our knowledge. Only in the case of insignificant texts are we satisfied with what we understand on first reading.

X. 21. An interpreter who gains all his knowledge of an author's vocabulary from lexical aids and disconnected observations can never reach an independent interpretation.*

*Hour 11. 19, 20, 21, 22. I only began 22. Neither 21 nor 22 were applied to the New Testament.
Hour 12. Apply 21 and 22 to the New Testament.

1. The only source independent of interpretation for knowing an author's vocabulary is the immediate, living heritage of the language. With Greek and Latin that source is incomplete. That is why the first lexicographical works, which searched the whole literature in order to learn about the language, were put together. Consequently, these dictionaries must be constantly emended by interpretation itself, and every artful interpretation must contribute to that end.

2. By the "vocabulary" of an author I include the dialect, sentence structure, and type of language characteristic of a given genre, the latter beginning with the distinction between poetry and prose.

3. Various aids may be indispensable for a beginner's first steps, but an independent interpretation demands that the interpreter acquire his background knowledge through independent research. All of the information about a language which dictionaries and other resource works supply represents the product of particular and often questionable interpretations.

4. In New Testament studies, especially, it can be said that the questionableness and arbitrariness of interpretation is due in large measure to this failure. For references to particular observations can lead to contradictory results. — The road to comprehending the language of the New Testament leads one from classical antiquity through (a) Macedonian Greek, (b) the Jewish secular writers (Josephus and Philo), (c) the deuterocanonical writings, and (d) the Septuagint, which is closest to Hebrew.

22. An interpreter who gains his historical knowledge solely from prolegomena cannot reach an independent interpretation.

1. Any editor who wants to be helpful should provide such prolegomena, in addition to the usual critical aids. Preparing such prolegomena requires a knowledge of the whole circle of literature to which a writing belongs and of everything that has been written about a given author. For this reason these prolegomena themselves depend on interpretation, and . . . at the same time how they were compiled may be irrelevant to the aim of the reader. The precise interpreter, however, must gradually derive all of his conclusions from the sources themselves. Thus he must proceed from the easier to the more difficult passages. A dependence on prolegomena is most damaging when one takes conclusions from them that should have been derived from the original sources.

2. In New Testament studies a separate discipline has been created to deal with this background information, the Introduction. The Introduction is not truly an organic part of the theological sciences, but it does serve a practical purpose for both the beginner and the master, because it is helpful to have all the previous research on a given topic collected in one place. But the interpreter must contribute to extending and verifying this information.

---

The various ways of arranging and using this fragmentary background information have given rise to different, but also one-sided, schools of interpretation, which can easily be branded as fads [*als Manier*].

XI. 23. Also within each given text, its parts can only be understood in terms of the whole, and so the interpreter must gain an overview of the work by a cursory reading before undertaking a more careful interpretation.

1. Here, too, there seems to be a circle. This provisional understanding requires only that knowledge of the particulars which comes from a general knowledge of the language.

2. Synopses provided by the author are too sparse to serve the purpose of even technical interpretation, and the summaries which editors customarily give in prolegomena bring the reader under the power of their own interpretations.

3. The interpreter should seek to identify the leading ideas by which all the

others are to be assessed. Likewise, in technical interpretation, one should try to identify the basic train of thought by reference to which particular ideas may be more readily recognized. That these tasks are indispensable for both technical and grammatical interpretation can be easily seen from the various types of misunderstanding.

4. It is not necessary to gain an overview of insignificant texts, and although an overview seems to offer little help in dealing with difficult texts, it is nonetheless indispensable. It is characteristic of difficult authors that an overview is of little help.*

*13. 23. General rule for the method: (a) Begin with a general overview of the text. (b) Comprehend it by moving in both directions simultaneously. (c) Only when the two coincide for one passage does one proceed to another passage. (d) When the two do not agree, it is necessary to go back until the error in calculation is found.

---

Whenever we are actually engaged in the interpretation of a particular text, we must always hold the two sides of interpretation together. But in setting forth the theory of hermeneutics we must separate them and discuss the two separately. Nonetheless, each side of interpretation must be developed so thoroughly that the other becomes indispensable, or better, that the results of the two coincide. Grammatical interpretation comes first.

# [GRAMMATICAL AND TECHNICAL INTERPRETATION]

## *Part I: Grammatical Interpretation*

XII. 1. First canon: A more precise determination of any point in a given text must be decided on the basis of the use of language common to the author and his original public.

1. Every point needs to be more precisely defined, and that determination is first of all provided by the context. Considered in isolation, every element of language, both formal and material, is indefinite. For any given word or linguistic form we can conceive a certain range [*Cyclus*] of usages.

2. Some term what a word is thought to mean "in and of itself" its meaning [*Bedeutung*] and what the word is thought to mean in a given context its "sense" [*Sinn*]. Others argue that a word can have only a single meaning

[*Bedeutung*] and not a sense [*Sinn*]; that a sentence regarded in isolation has a sense [*Sinn*], but not a purport [*Verstand*], for only a complete text has a purport. Of course, it could be claimed that even a whole text would be more completely understood in the context of its entire world, but this consideration leads us beyond the sphere of interpretation altogether. — The latter terminology is certainly preferable inasmuch as a sentence is an inseparable unity and as such its sense [*Sinn*] is also a unity, that is, there is a mutual co-determination of its subject and predicate. Nonetheless, this terminology is not adequate to linguistic usage. For with reference to the purport [*Verstand*] of a text, meaning and sense are identical. The truth is that in interpretation the task of clarifying what is vague, is never-ending. — When a given sentence is a self-enclosed whole, the distinction between sense and purport seems to disappear, as in the case of epigrams and maxims. This whole, however, must be determined by the reader: each reader has to puzzle through such statements as best he can. The meaning is decided by reference to the particular subject matter.

3. The era in which an author lives, his development, his involvements, his way of speaking—whenever these factors make a difference in a finished text—constitute his "sphere." But this sphere cannot be found *in toto* in every text, for it varies according to the kind of reader the author had in mind. But how do we determine who these readers were? Only by a cursory reading of the entire text. But determining the sphere common to the author and the readers is only the first step. It must be continued throughout the process of interpretation, and it is completed only when the interpretation itself is concluded.

4. There are several apparent exceptions to the rule.

a. Archaic expressions lie beyond the immediate linguistic sphere of the author and his readers. They serve the purpose of making the past contemporaneous with the present; they are used in writing more than in speaking, in poetry more than in prose.

b. Technical expressions occur in even the most common forms of speaking, as, for example, in legal proceedings, even though not everyone understands them. This fact leads us to observe that an author does not always have his entire public in mind, but only certain sectors of it. Consequently, the application of this rule requires a certain amount of art, since it depends on the interpreter's sensitivity [*richtige Gefühle*].

XIV. 5. The statement that we must consciously grasp an author's linguistic sphere, in contrast to other organic aspects of his language, implies that we understand the author better than he understood himself. Both in our general survey and in our work on particular passages difficulties arise, and we must become aware of many things of which the author himself was unaware.

6. By drawing on our general survey of the work, interpretation may

continue smoothly for some time without actually being artless, because everything is held together in a general picture. But as soon as some detail causes us difficulty, we begin to wonder whether the problem lies with the author or with us. We may assume that the author is at fault only when our overview of the text uncovers evidence that the author is careless and imprecise, or confused and without talent. Our own errors may be caused in two ways. We may have made an early mistake in understanding that had continued unnoticed, or our knowledge of the language might be inadequate. In either case, the correct word usage does not occur to us. I will discuss the former later, because it is related to the use of parallel passages. I want to discuss the latter now.

7. Dictionaries, which are the normal resources for supplementing our knowledge of a language, view the various usages of a word as a many-faceted, loosely-bound aggregate. They do not trace the meaning [*Bedeutung*] back to its original unity, because to do so would require that the material be arranged according to the system of concepts, and this is impossible. The multiplicity of meanings, then, is to be analyzed into a series of distinctions. The first is the distinction between the literal and the figurative. Upon closer scrutiny this distinction disappears. In similes two parallel series of thoughts are connected. Each word stands in its own series and should be determined only in those terms. Therefore, it retains its own meaning. In metaphors this connection is only suggested, and often only a single aspect of the concept is emphasized. For example, *coma arborum* is foliage, but *coma* still means hair. And we speak of the lion as the king of the animals. But a lion does not govern, and kings are not entitled to devour others on the principle that "might makes right." Such a single usage of the word has no meaning, and usually the entire phrase must be given. This distinction may be ultimately traced to the belief that not all non-literal [*geistliche*] meanings are original, but that they are imagistic usages of words that had sense-referents. XV. But this question lies beyond the sphere of hermeneutics. Even if *theos* (God) is derived from *theō*, this fact would not be immediately evident in the language because it arose in the primitive history of the language, with which hermeneutics does not deal. The question is whether non-literal ideas [*geistliche Vorstellungen*] are a second shape of development that does not begin until after the language has been formed, and there does not seem to be any answer to that question. It is undeniable that there are non-literal words which at the same time signify sense-objects, but a parallelism governs these cases in that both, as they present themselves to us, are included in the idea of one living whole. This accounts, too, for the use of the same words for matters relating to space and time. The two meanings are essentially the same because we can determine space only by reference to time, and vice versa. Terms for form and

movement are also interchangeable, and so a "creeping plant" is not a figurative expression. There are just as many problems with the distinction between original and derived meanings. In Latin *hostis* originally meant "stranger," but it came to mean "enemy." Originally all strangers were enemies. Later it became possible to be friendly with foreigners, and people instinctively decided that the word had referred more to a difference of disposition than to a distance of space. One could therefore speak of certain fellow citizens as *hostes* [enemies], but perhaps only those who had been exiled. People also make a distinction between general and specific meanings, the former occurring in ordinary conversation and the latter in special areas of discussion. Often these meanings are basically the same, or elliptical. Thus, the word "foot" stands for a measurement of length or a unit of poetry, or for a step, or a step forward. The difference between general and particular meanings, then, develops because the terminology used in a special discipline takes on a more general meaning when used by groups of people who do not understand it precisely. Frequently, too, foreign words become garbled and remolded until they seem to be native words. All of the other distinctions about word-meanings arise in similar ways.

8. The basic task, even for dictionaries designed specifically for interpreters, is to identify the true and complete unity of a given word. Of course, the occurrence of a word in a given passage involves an infinite, indeterminate multiplicity. The only way to grasp the unity of a word within such a multiplicity of usages is to consider the multiplicity as a clearly circumscribed grouping with a unity of its own. Such a unity in turn must break up into distinctions. But a word is never isolated, even when it occurs by itself, for its determination is not derived from itself, but from its context. We need only to relate this contextual use to this original unity in order to discover the correct meaning in each case. But to find the complete unity of a word would be to explain it, and that is as difficult as completely explaining objects. The elements of dead languages cannot be fully explained because we are not yet in a position to trace their whole development, and those of living languages cannot be explained because they are still developing.

XVI. 9. Granting that a multiplicity of usages is possible with an existing unity, then a multiplicity must already be present in the unity: several major points are bound together as variables within certain limits. One's linguistic sense must be attentive to this, and when uncertainties arise, reference to a dictionary can help orient us to what is known about the word. The various instances cited in the dictionary should be regarded merely as a reasonable selection. One must connect the various citations in order to bring into view the full range of the word and to determine the meaning of a given usage.

10. The same holds for the formal element. The rules of grammar are just like the meanings cited in a dictionary. Thus, in dealing with particles, a

grammar serves as a dictionary. It is even more difficult, however, to deal with the formal elements of the language.

11. To use these aids is in effect to make use of another author, and so all of the rules of interpretation apply here as well. These two resources represent only a certain segment of our knowledge of a language, and usually each is written from a definite point of view. Therefore, in the use of these aids a scholar will make corrections and additions in order to reach a better understanding. All of his work should contribute to this end.

3. Second Canon. The meaning of each word of a passage must be determined by the context in which it occurs.

1. The first canon serves only to exclude certain possibilities. This second canon, however, seems to be determinative, a "jump" which must be justified.

a. One moves from the first canon to the second. Each word has a determinative linguistic sphere. In explaining a word we use only what we believe can be expected to occur within that linguistic sphere. Similarly, the whole text more or less forms the context and surroundings of each passage.

b. Likewise, one moves from the second canon to the first. When the given connection of subject, predicate, and supplementary words is not sufficient to explain the meaning, one must turn to other passages where these same words occur and under certain conditions, to other works of the author or even to works written by others in which these words appear. But one must always remain within the same linguistic sphere.

2. Consequently, the distinction we have made between the two canons, that the first is exclusive and the second determinative, is more apparent than real. In each particular case this second canon, too, only excludes certain possibilities. Every modifier excludes a certain number of otherwise possible meanings, and the determination of the word emerges by a process of elimination. Since the application of this canon, carried to its farthest extent, involves the entire theory of parallel passages, these two canons comprise the whole of grammatical interpretation.

XXI. 3. We must now discuss how to determine the formal and material elements, and we must deal with both in a way that draws on the immediate context and on parallels, and aims at both qualitative and quantitative understanding. Either set of divisions may be made the major basis for organizing the discussion. But the first is the most natural, because it is a two-way road that runs through the entire operation.

4. The use of parallel passages as a resource is only an apparent extension of the canon, and the use of parallel passages is limited by the canon. For a passage is "parallel" only when it can be considered, with respect to the

point in question, as identical with the sentence itself, and so can be considered part of a unified context.

5. Granting that the formal and material elements constitute the major divisions of our discussion, it is best to begin by considering how to determine the formal element, because our understanding of a given passage is related to our preliminary understanding of the whole, and the sentence is recognized as a unity only through the formal element.

4. On determining the formal element.*

*1828. I have already dealt with the material element.

We must divide formal elements into those that combine sentences and those that combine parts of speech to form a sentence.

1. At this point we must begin with the simple sentence, because combining individual statements into clauses and combining clauses to construct sentences are the same, whereas combining the parts of speech into a simple sentence is quite different. Included in the first are conjunctions and their rules, and whatever substitutes for them. Included in the second are prepositions.

The crux of the matter concerns the type of combination, its degree, and how much has been combined. In speech, as in everything else, there are only two types of combination, organic and mechanical, i.e., an inner fusion and an external adjoining of parts. This distinction, however, is not absolute, since one often seems to shade off into the other. Often a causal or adversative particle seems merely additive. In such cases it has lost or even abandoned its true content. But often an additive term becomes decisive, and it may then be said to have been enhanced or made emphatic. In this way a qualitative difference becomes quantitative. Often, however, this transposition is only apparent, and the interpreter must always refer back to the original meaning. Often, too, apparent transpositions are due to the fact that the extent or the object of the connection have not been correctly identified. Thus one should not decide about a given case until all other questions have been considered.

XXII. a. An organic connection may be more or less cohesive, but one should never suppose that it has lost all its meaning, as is sometimes done when statements which have been combined do not seem to belong together. But ($\alpha$) the last clause before the particle can be a mere addition, and therefore the connective terms refer back to the main clause. Or the first clause after the connective term may be merely introductory, such that the connection refers to the major thoughts which follow. Of course, in order to specify the extent of a given connection, these dependent clauses should be changed into parenthetical statements

(*Zwischensätze*). The degree to which this procedure can be applied varies according to the style of the work. The more free the style, the more the author must rely on the reader. (β) Often, however, the connection does not refer to the last major thought but to a whole series of thoughts. Otherwise entire sections could not be connected. In writings with well-defined divisions, the points made in one section may be recapitulated in the course of moving to another, and the connection becomes an entire sentence which includes as well the main contents of the section which is to follow. More ponderous constructions may contain additions and repetitions, as well as elements that ought not to have been carried over. But even in more flowing constructions the reader must pay attention to the transitions. Therefore, a general overview of the text is doubly necessary before a given point can be understood.

b. That simply adjoining two statements can, as it were, become emphatic is due to the fact that all our organic connective terms (*denn; weil; wenn*) have evolved from particles that originally related solely to space and time. Thus it becomes possible that even today particles can be enhanced in their meanings. The canon, then, is based on the fact that one ought never presuppose that an author has merely tacked the whole together. Mere connection predominates in descriptions and narratives, but even there not completely, for this would make the writer nothing more than a transcriber. When the author is not a mere transcriber, mere additions can only be in the service of organic connections, that is, they are enclosed in them, follow from them, or lead to them. Therefore, even if no organic connection is evident, it must be implicit.[5]

XXIII. 5. Application to the New Testament

1. Even when a writer thinks in the language he uses, he frequently relies on his mother tongue in conceiving the work. Moreover, the combination of thoughts is already included in this initial conception, and so special attention is to be directed to the mixture of Hebrew and Greek.

2. This is all the more important because the two languages are so different.

   a. Due to their lack of education, the New Testament writers could not appropriate the richness of the Greek language, nor could they by casual listening catch the significance of the different types of connectives. Nonetheless, they sometimes used these along with those they knew well.

   b. Consequently, Greek signs which correspond in certain respects were readily considered fully equivalent.

3. It is therefore necessary to construct a whole from the Greek meanings of a sign and from the corresponding Hebraic ones and to make his judgment on this basis.

4. A loose style of writing permits extensive latitude in the use of these elements because the sentences themselves are joined together with little art.

5. The great differences among the New Testament writers in this respect are not to be overlooked. Paul works from the Greek most of all; John the least.

6. The reference works are poorly constructed for these purposes. It is especially important to refer to New Testament dictionaries in conjunction with dictionaries for the Septuagint. Above all, it is important to pay close attention ever to those passages that present no difficulties, for otherwise there is no way to assess the range of usages that are allowable. Failure to do this frequently causes errors.

7. Here I especially want to mention (for I forgot to include it under 4. a., above) that there are also subjective connections, namely, those that give reasons why something has previously been asserted. Since these combinations are indistinguishable in form from objective ones, they are often taken as a restriction of the meaning of a mere transition.

6. The problem of determining what parts of speech hold a sentence together is resolved by the interplay of several considerations.

1. In referring back to the general content, the leading ideas are of primary importance. In considering how the statements are put together, the subjects and predicates, in short, the material element, are the key.

2. In the immediate context the way in which the formal elements have been put together is the key; that is, the construction explains the particles, and vice versa.

3. In the succeeding material one must pay attention to coordinating and subordinating forms of combination.

4. The application must make good sense. The final determination must always be based on a more impartial reconstruction.

7. With respect to combinations within the sentence itself, the most difficult elements are the prepositions and the parts of speech immediately dependent upon them.

1. It makes no difference whether the sentence consists of only a subject and predicate or has a copula as well. In either case the immediate combination should not be mistaken. Even when a sentence is expanded by means of adjectives and adverbs, it forms a whole centered on its subject and predicate. The preposition, however, gives the verb a more precise determination, that is, it indicates how the object is related to the verb. The genitive, *status constructus,* provides a more precise determination of the subject. The meaning [*Sinn*] of a preposition is easily determined by reference to the subject and object. The material element is decisive.

2. In the New Testament Hebraicizing tendencies predominate. Therefore, the interpreter must always have in mind the corresponding Hebrew forms.

## Part 2: Technical Interpretation

1. Both technical and grammatical interpretation begin with a general overview of a text designed to grasp its unity and the major features of its composition. But in technical interpretation the unity of the work, its theme, is viewed as the dynamic principle impelling the author, and the basic features of the composition are viewed as his distinctive nature, revealing itself in that movement.

(Note: Unity of the work. — Its organization is often merely external and vague. Can be destroyed. At other times the organization is deliberately obscured. The more unified the work, the more artistic it is, and vice versa. The artistic quality of a work is not to be judged solely by its language, for example, in dialogues and letters. — Extremely loose and extremely tight writing are outside the scope of interpretation. — Preliminary task: to know in advance the aim of a work, its circle, and its ideas.)

The unity of the work is to be found in the way the sphere of language has been grammatically constructed. The chief features of composition are to be found in the way the connections between the thoughts have been constructed. Technical interpretation attempts to identify what has moved the author to communicate. Objective differences, such as whether the treatment is popular or scientific, are functions of this motivating principle. Nonetheless, an author organizes his thought in his own peculiar way, and this peculiar way is reflected in the arrangement he chooses. Likewise, an author always has secondary ideas which are determined by his special character. Thus the distinctiveness of an author may be recognized by the secondary ideas that distinguish him from others. To recognize an author in this way is to recognize him as he has worked with language. To some extent he initiates something new in the language by combining subjects and predicates in new ways. Yet to some extent he merely repeats and transmits the language he has received. Likewise, when I know his language, I recognize how the author is a product of the language and stands under its potency. These two views, then, are only two ways of looking at the same thing.

2. The ultimate goal of technical interpretation is nothing other than a development of the beginning, that is, to consider the whole of the author's work in terms of its parts and in every part to consider the content as what moved the author and the form as his nature moved by that content.

When I have exhausted the meaning of every part of the text, there is nothing left to be understood. Moreover, it is self-evident that the relative distinction between understanding the parts and understanding the whole is mediated by the fact that each part is to be treated in the same way as the whole. The aim, however, can be achieved only by holding these two considerations together. Although much of a text can be understood by grammatical interpretation alone, grammatical interpretation cannot grasp how the work is a necessary undertaking of the author, since a sense for this necessity emerges only if the genesis of the text is never lost from view.

3. The goal of technical interpretation should be formulated as the complete understanding of style.

We are accustomed to restrict the term "style" to the way language is handled. But thoughts and language are intertwined, and an author's distinctive way of treating the subject is manifested by his organization of his material and by his use of language.

Since a person always has numerous ideas, the development of any specific one involves accepting something and excluding something else. — Yet when an idea does not develop from the distinctive character of the author, but is acquired by study or by custom, or is cultivated for its effect, then there is mannerism, and mannerism is always poor style.

4. The goal of technical interpretation can only be approximated.

Despite all our progress we are still far from the goal. There are still conflicts over Homer, and the three tragedians still cannot be perfectly distinguished.[6] — Not only do we never understand an individual view [*Anschauung*] exhaustively, but what we do understand is always subject to correction. This becomes evident when we consider that, beyond doubt, the best test is the attempt to imitate an author. But since imitation is so rarely successful and since higher criticism is still embroiled in disputes, we know we are quite far from our goal.

5. Before technical interpretation can begin, one must learn the way the author received his subject matter and the language, and whatever else can be known about the author's distinctive manner [*Art und Weise*] of writing.

This first task includes learning about the state of a given genre when the author began to write. The second includes learning about the use of language current in this area and related areas. Consequently, exact understanding in this regard requires knowing about related literature current in that era as well as earlier models of style. In technical interpretation there is no substitute for such comprehensive and systematic research.

Learning about the author's manner of writing is a laborious task, and the easiest way to gain such knowledge is to turn to secondary sources. These works, however, make judgments which must be assessed by acts of interpretation. Consequently, reliance on such distant works is to be avoided. As aids for understanding, biographical sketches of authors were originally included in editions of their works, but they usually neglected discussing the question of literary models. Certainly a useful prolegomenon will give the most necessary information about the other two points.

On the basis of this background knowledge and the initial overview of the work, the interpreter develops a provisional conception in terms of which the distinctiveness of the author is to be sought.

6. From the moment it begins, technical interpretation involves two methods: a divinatory and a comparative. Since each method refers back to the other, the two should never be separated.

By leading the interpreter to transform himself, so to speak, into the author, the divinatory method seeks to gain an immediate comprehension of the author as an individual. The comparative method proceeds by subsuming the author under a general type. It then tries to find his distinctive traits by comparing him with the others of the same general type. Divinatory knowledge is the feminine strength in knowing people; comparative knowledge, the masculine.

Each method refers back to the other. The divinatory is based on the assumption that each person is not only a unique individual in his own right, but that he has a receptivity to the uniqueness of every other person.

This assumption in turn seems to presuppose that each person contains a minimum of everyone else, and so divination is aroused by comparison with oneself. But how is it possible for the comparative method to subsume a person under a general type? Obviously, either by another act of comparison (and this continues into infinity) or by divination.

The two methods should never be separated. Divination becomes certain only when it is corroborated by comparisons. Without this confirmation, it always tends to be fanatical. But comparison does not provide a distinctive unity. The general and the particular must interpenetrate, and only divination allows this to happen.

7. The idea of the work, as the will which leads to the actual composition, can be understood only by the joint consideration of two factors: the content of the text and its range of effects.

The content itself does not dictate how it must be treated. As a rule the theme of the work is easy to identify, even if it is not explicitly stated. But for that very reason we can be misled. — What is usually called the "aim" of the work in the strict sense of the word is a different matter entirely. It is often quite external, and it exercises only a limited influence on a few passages. This influence can usually be accounted for from the character of the people who were being addressed. But if one knows who these people were and what effect these passages were to have on them, then, since these factors determine the composition of the work, the interpreter knows everything that is necessary.

## Notes

1. The two classical philologists with whose work Schleiermacher takes issue here and elsewhere. In 1829 he delivered two addresses before the Royal Prussian Academy: "On the Concept of Hermeneutics, with reference to F. A. Wolf's Instruction and Ast's Textbook." Cf. Friedrich Ast, *Grundlinien der Grammatik: Hermeneutik und Kritik* (Landshut, 1808); Friedrich August Wolf, *Darstellung der Altertumswissenschaft nach Begriff, Umfang, Zweck und Wert* (Berlin, 1807).

2. Cf. Christian Wolff in his *Vernünftige Gedanken von den Kräften des menschlichen Verstandes* (see bibl.), chs. 10, 11, 12, offered a brief treatment of the problems of textual understanding within the framework of logic. Since philosophical texts were believed not to offer any special hermeneutical problems, they were excluded from consideration by the Enlightenment theoreticians. Thus Chladenius (see bibl.) insists (§ 187) that in philosophy we do not need the art of interpretation, since we can rely immediately on our power of thinking in order to judge whether a philosophical statement is true or false. For Schleiermacher, on the other hand, all understanding is in need of critical examination and reconstructing.

3. Historical and philological methods of interpreting the Holy Scriptures were applied in the eighteenth century by J. A. Turrentinus (*De sacra scripturae interpretandae methodo tractatus bipartitus*, 1728) and by J. S. Semler (*Abhandlung von freier Untersuchung des Canon*, 1771–75). Orthodox and pietistic theologians opposed such historical interpretation on principle and advanced instead the notion of an immediate illumination while interpreting the Scriptures.

4. On the history of theological and juristic hermeneutics, see H.-G. Gadamer's article in *Historisches Wörterbuch der Philosophie*, ed. by J. Ritter (Darmstadt: Wissenschaftliche Buchgesellschaft, 1974) vol. 3, and the literature cited therein (1061–73).

5. Schleiermacher's outline here is unclear, and the text has been outlined by the translators. (Translator's note)

6. The conflict over Homer was sparked by F. A. Wolf's *Prolegomena ad Homerum* (Halle, 1794). In this piece Wolf advances the thesis that the works traditionally ascribed to Homer (the *Iliad* and the *Odyssey*) originated in six different eras and represent the work of several authors. Schleiermacher is referring to the three ancient tragedians, Aeschylus, Sophocles, and Euripedes. (Translator's note)

# 3

# Foundations:
# Language, Understanding,
# and the Historical World

================= Wilhelm von Humboldt =================

WILHELM VON HUMBOLDT (1767–1835) was born and raised on an estate in Tegel (near Berlin). He was of North German and French Huguenot extraction and was educated together with his younger brother Alexander (the scientist) by private tutors. He then studied law, classics, and philosophy first at Frankfurt-on-the-Oder and later in Göttingen. In 1791 he resigned from a post in the Prussian judiciary in Berlin in order to dedicate himself to his studies. For several years he resided in Jena in close association with the poets Schiller and Goethe and concentrated his efforts on studying classical languages and culture, philosophy, anthropology, political theory, aesthetics, and literature. He composed essays and treatises in all of these areas. While in Paris (1797–1801) and later in Rome (1802–1808), Humboldt focused his interests more and more on his linguistic studies. His work on the Basque language (based on actual field work in the Basque country) was influential for the development of linguistics in the United States. During the Napoleonic Wars Humboldt pursued an active political career as a liberal reformer. He was largely responsible for the reform of the Prussian school system and was the founder of the University of Berlin in 1810. He also served as Prussian ambassador in Vienna and in London. In 1820, during the era of Metternich, his political career came to an abrupt end, and Humboldt was now able to devote his remaining years to his linguistic studies. Besides the major European (ancient and modern) tongues, he mastered Sanskrit, Chinese, Japanese, and Arabic, and did extensive work on the American Indian languages and the languages of Malaysia. Hermeneutic ideas and principles pervade many of Humboldt's writings on history, language, and poetry. The first selection illustrates Humboldt's concept of understanding which he saw as an outgrowth of man's linguistic nature. It is taken from his *Introduction to the Kawi Language* (published posthumously in 1836). For Humboldt, "understanding" is a basic characteristic of human behavior which is linked with man's capacity for speech and with the nature of language itself. Humboldt defines language in energetic terms as an activity both intellectual and social. Humboldt's argumentation, which typically is complex and multifaceted, permits the reader to perceive one and the same phenomenon from different perspectives. The second selection consists of an address Humboldt delivered before the Berlin Academy of Sciences in 1821. It was first published in the proceedings of the Academy in 1822. There Humboldt develops a theory of understanding as an integral part of a theory of history and historical investigation. There was for him an essential affinity between the creativity of the poet and artist and the activity of the historian who tried to understand what is only partially accessible to him. Ideas in history were forces in Humboldt's eyes, pervading both the object of historical knowledge and the subjective conceptualization performed by the historian. Humboldt's essay points out to us many of the problems which have dominated hermeneutic debates in the human sciences until today.

# THE NATURE AND CONFORMATION
# OF LANGUAGE

Since the variation in languages is based upon their form, and since the latter is most closely associated with the intellectual capacities of nations together with the forces permeating them at the instant of their creation or new formation we must now develop this concept in detail.

The discrete principles of morphology come to light when we reflect on language in general and when we dissect individual idioms. They include the phonetic form (*Lautform*) and the usage to which the phonetic form is put to designate objects and to associate ideas. Usage is founded upon the requirements that thinking imposes upon language, whence the general laws governing language originate. This component is identical in all human beings as such in its original direction to the point of the peculiarity of their natural endowments or subsequent developments. In contrast, the phonetic form is the actual constitutive and guiding principle respective to the variability of languages, both inherently and in the retarding force which it opposes to the innate speech tendency involved. As a component of the complete human organism related intimately to its inherent intellectual power, it is associated naturally with the total disposition of the nation. However, the manner and reasons underlying this association are cloaked in an obscurity scarcely permitting any clarification. The individual morphology of every language is derived from these two intellectually interdependent principles. They constitute the points which linguistic research and analysis must accept to investigate in their relationships. The most indispensable factor is that, with respect to this undertaking, a proper and worthy consideration of language, attentive to the depths of its origins and the extent of its scope, be used as a basis of operation. For the present, then, we shall be content to examine these parameters.

At this point, I shall discuss the process of language in its broadest sense. I shall consider it not merely in its relationship to speech and the stock of its word components as its direct product, but also in its relationship to the human capacity for thought and perception. The entire course of operation, starting from its emanation from the intellect to its counteraction upon the latter, will be considered.

Language is the formative organ of thought. Intellectual activity—completely intellectual, completely inward, and to a certain extent passing without a trace—becomes externalized in speech and perceptible to the senses. It and the language, therefore, form a unity and are indivisible from one another. Intellectual activity is inherently tied to the necessity of entering into a combination with the phoneme (*Sprachlaut*). Otherwise thought cannot attain distinctness, the image cannot become a concept. The indissoluble bond connecting thought, vocal apparatus, and hearing [auditory perception] to language is an invariable part of the original constitution of human nature, and defies further explanation. The coincidence of the sound with the idea thus becomes clear. Just as the idea, comparable to a flash of lightning, collects the total power of imagination into a single point and excludes everything that is simultaneous, the phonetic sound resounds in abrupt sharpness and unity. Just as the thought engages the entire disposition, the phonetic sound is endowed with a penetrating power that arouses the whole nervous system. This feature, distinguishing it from all other sensory impressions, is visibly based upon the fact that the ear is receptive to the impression of a motion, especially to the sound of a true action produced by the voice (which is not always the case for the remaining senses). Furthermore, this action proceeds from the interior of a living creature; as an articulated sound from a thinking being and as an unarticulated sound from a merely sensing creature.

Inasmuch as thought in its most typically human relationships is a longing to escape from darkness into light, from limitation into infinity, sound streams from the depths of the breast to the external ambient. There it finds in the air, this most subtle and motile of all elements whose apparent incorporeality significantly corresponds to the intellect, a marvelously appropriate intermediary substance. The incisive sharpness of the phoneme is indispensable to our understanding of physical and other objects, for objects in external nature, as well as in the internally excited activity, exert a compulsion upon man, penetrating his being with a mass of characteristics. He, however, strives to compare, distinguish, and combine. Furthermore, he aims at the formation of an ever more comprehensive unity. He demands, therefore, to be able to comprehend objects in terms of a definite unity and requires the unit of sound to represent them appropriately. The sound, however, does not displace any of the other impressions which the objects are capable of producing upon the external or internal senses, but instead becomes their bearer. Moreover, it adds, in its individual association with the object, a new designative impression according to the manner in which the individual sensitivity of the speaker conceives it. The sharpness of the sound permits an indeterminable number of modifications, absolutely distinct from each other in conception and not mixing together in combination. This is not true to the same extent of any other sensory effect. Inasmuch as intellectual striving does not merely occupy human understanding but stimulates the entire human being, it is especially promoted by the sound of the human voice. For, as living sound, it proceeds, as does respiration itself, from the breast; it accompanies—even without speech—pain and joy, aversion and avidity, breathing life from which it streams forth into the mind which receives it. In this respect it resembles language. The latter reproduces the evoked sensation simultaneously with the object represented. Thus it connects man with the universe or, to express it differently, associates his independent activity with his sensory receptivity. To the phoneme, finally, is appropriate the erect posture of humans, which is denied to animals and by which man is, so to speak, called upright. For speech does not want to resound dully along the ground; it desires to pour forth freely from the lips toward the person at whom it is directed, accompanied by the facial expression of the speaker, as well as by the gestures of his hand; speech thus wishes to be associated with everything that designates the humanity of man.

After this provisional consideration of the suitability of the sound to the operations of the intellect, we may now proceed to examine in greater detail the relationship of cogitation to language. Subjective activity in thought produces an object, for no idea may be considered a mere receptive contemplation of an already present object. The activity of the senses must be synthetically combined with the intimate operation of the intellect, and from this association the idea is liberated. With respect to the subjective force involved, it then becomes the object, which is perceived anew, and which then reverts to the subjective force. For this purpose language is indispensable, for when in its intellectual striving it makes its way past the lips, its product wends its way back to the speaker's own ear. The concept is thus shifted over into a state of objectivity, without losing its subjectivity. Only language is capable of this. Without this feature, that is, without this continuous regression of objectivity to the subject, in which language collaborates, the formation of concepts (and consequently all true thinking) is impossible. Apart from the communication between one human and another, speech is a necessary condition for reflection in solitude. As a phenomenon, however, language develops only in social intercourse, and humans understand themselves only by having tested the comprehensibility of their words on others. For objectivity is increased whenever a word coined by oneself resounds from a stranger's lips. However, subjectivity suffers no loss, since humans always feel a bond with their fellows; indeed, it is intensified, since the idea transformed into speech no longer pertains exclusively to a single subject. By being transmitted to others, it becomes associated with the common heritage of the entire human race, each of whose members possesses an innate quality demanding fulfillment from the other members. The broader and more active this social intercourse in its effect upon a language, the more the language profits, other conditions remaining constant. What language makes necessary in the simple act of production of ideas is incessantly repeated in the intellectual life of man. Communication through language furnishes him conviction and stimulation. The power to think requires something equal to yet differentiated from itself. It is fired up by its equivalent; from its counterpart it acquires a touchstone for its innermost products. Although the basis for the perception of truth reposes in man's inner recesses, his intellectual striving toward truth is always surrounded by the danger of deception. With an immediate and clear sense only for his varying limitations, he is forced to regard truth as something external to himself. One of the most powerful media to approach veracity, and to measure one's remoteness from it, is the social exchange of ideas. All speech, starting from the very simplest, consists of an association of the individual perception with the common denominator of human nature.

The situation is no different as far as understanding is concerned. Nothing can be present in the mind (*Seele*) that has not originated from one's own activity. Moreover understanding and speaking are but different effects of the selfsame power of speech. Speaking is never comparable to the transmission of mere matter (*Stoff*). In the person comprehending as well as in the speaker, the subject matter must be developed by the individual's own innate power. What the listener receives is merely the harmonious vocal stimulus. It is, therefore, natural for man to enunciate immediately what he has just comprehended. In this way language is native to every human being in its entire scope; this signifies that everyone possesses a drive, controlled by a modified regulatory power, that is directed toward bringing forth little by little his entire language and understanding it when produced, as the internal or external occasion requires.

Understanding then, as we have come to understand it, could not be based upon man's spontaneous mental activity and his social discourse would have to be something other than the mutual arousing of the speech impulse in the listener—if the unity of human nature did not underlie the variation of the individual—splitting itself up, as it were, into distinct individualities. The comprehension of words is something completely different from the understanding of unarticulated sounds and includes much more than the mere reciprocal production of sounds and of the indicated object. The word can also be taken as an indivisible entity, just as we recognize the significance of a written word group without being sure of its alphabetic composition. It might be possible that the mind of the child operates in this way during the very beginnings of linguistic comprehension. Whenever his animal sensory capacity, along with his human power of speech, is excited (and it is probable that even in children there is no instant when this—no matter how feebly attested—would not be the case), the word is perceived as articulated. Now, however, the factor which articulation adds to the simple evocation of its meaning (an evocation which naturally takes place more completely as a result of the articulation) is that it represents the word with no intermediate solely through its form as a part of an infinite whole, of a language. Because of articulation, therefore, even in individual words the possibility is present of constructing from the elements of language a number of other words actually running to an indeterminately high number, according to definite feelings and rules, and to establish thereby a relationship between all words, corresponding to the relationship of the concepts. The spirit would not, however, get any idea of this artificial mechanism, nor would it comprehend articulation any more than the blind man does colors, were there not a power residing in it that permits attainment of such a possibility. Indeed, language may be regarded not as a passive entity, capable of being surveyed in its entirety, nor as something impartable bit by bit, but rather as an eternally productive medium; one for which, furthermore, the laws of its genetic processes are defined, but for which the scope and to some extent the character of its products remain completely undetermined. The speech learning of children is not an apportioning of words, a depositing in the files of memory, and a subsequent repetitive babbling through the lips, but a growth of speech capacity via maturation and practice. What one has heard does more than merely report information to oneself. It also prepares the mind to understand more easily what has not yet been heard and clarifies that which has been long-since heard though only half or not at all understood at the time. This is because the similarity between what has been heard long ago and what has just been perceived suddenly becomes obvious to the perceptive power, which has become more acute in the interim. This sharpens the urge and the capacity to channel material heard into the memory more rapidly, and it permits increasingly less thereof to pass by as mere sound. Progress hence accelerates in steadily increasing proportions, since the heightening of technique and the accumulation of information reciprocally intensify and expand. The fact that there is a development of the power to create speech taking place among children, rather than a mechanical learning, also proves that, since a certain period during one's life is allotted to the development of the most important human powers, all children speak and understand under the most varied circumstances at approximately the same age, varying only within a short time span. But how could the hearer gain control over himself simply by the growth of his own power over the spoken word, developing in isolated fashion within him, if the same essence were not in the speaker and the listener, separated individually and mutually appropriate, so that a signal, created out of the deepest and most personal nature, and as fine as the articulated sound, is a sufficient mediator to stimulate both of them identically?

Against this the objection could be raised that before they learn to speak children of every people, when displaced from their native linguistic ambient, will develop their speech proclivity in the foreign tongue. This incontrovertible fact, it could be averred, proves distinctly that speech is merely a reproduction of what has been heard and, without consideration of the uniformity or variability of the being, depends entirely upon social intercourse. In cases of this kind, it has been hard to observe with sufficient exactitude how difficult it was to overcome the inherited structure, and how the latter nevertheless persisted unconquered in its most delicate nuances. Disregarding the foregoing, we can explain this phenomenon sufficiently by the fact that man is everywhere one with his kind, and development of speech capacity may proceed with the aid of any given individual. It does not for this reason evolve any the less from the intimate self; only because it simultaneously requires external stimulation must it prove analogous to that which it is experiencing, and it is capable of so doing via the coincident features of all human tongues. Even disregarding this, however, we can say that the power of genealogy over languages lies clearly enough before our eyes in their distribution according to nations. In itself, this is easily comprehensible, inasmuch as descent acts so powerfully, in fact predominantly on the entire individuality with which each particular language is most intimately associated. If language were not to enter by its very origin from the recesses of human nature into an actual association with physical descent, why would the parental idiom, for the educated and the uncultured as well, possess a so much greater power and intimacy than a foreign tongue? Does not one's native tongue capture the ear with a kind of sudden enchantment after a long absence, and does it not awaken nostalgia when heard on foreign soil? This certainly is based not upon its intellectual attributes, nor upon the idea or emotion expressed, but precisely upon its most inexplicable and most individual features, its phonemes and sounds. It seems to us as if we are perceiving a part of our very selves through our native tongue.

In a consideration of the factor produced by language, the manner of conception cannot be substantiated; it is as if it merely designated the objects perceived in themselves. Moreover, one would never exhaust the deep and full content of language by means of these objects. Just as no concept is possible without language, at the same time language cannot be an object for the mind since, indeed, every external object attains complete substantiality only through the medium of a concept. However, the entire manner of subjective perception of objects is transmitted necessarily into the structure and into the usage of language. For the word originates precisely from this perception; it is an offprint not of the object per se, but of the image of the latter produced in the mind. Inasmuch as subjectivity is unavoidably admixed with all objective perception, we can consider each individual, quite independently from his language, as possessing his own standpoint for viewing the world. However, the fact that it may be regarded thus is greatly enhanced by language, since the word, as will be shown subsequently, with an accretion of self-significance (*Selbstbedeutung*), becomes the object and obtains a new property. This property being of a phonemic kind is necessarily analogous to that of the language as a whole; since a homogeneous subjectivity operates on the language of a nation, each language embodies a view of the world peculiarly its own. Just as the individual sound intervenes between object and man, the entire language does so between him and nature acting upon him both externally and internally. He surrounds himself with an ambient of sounds in order to assimilate and process the world of objects. These expressions do not in any way exceed the measure of simple truth. Man lives principally, or even exclusively with objects, since his feelings and actions depend upon his concepts as language presents them to his attention. By the same act through which he spins out the thread of language he weaves himself into its tissues. Each tongue draws a circle about the people to whom it belongs, and it is possible to leave this circle only by simultaneously entering that of another people. Learning a foreign language ought hence to be the conquest of a new standpoint for the previously prevailing world-view of the individual. In fact, it is so to a certain extent, inasmuch as every language contains the entire fabric of concepts and the conceptual approach of a portion of humanity. But this achievement is never complete, because one always carries over into a foreign tongue to a greater or lesser degree one's own viewpoint and that of one's mother tongue.

# ON THE TASK OF THE HISTORIAN

The task of the historian is the depiction of what has taken place. The more purely and completely he succeeds at this depiction, the more perfectly will he have resolved his task. This straightforward depiction is both a primary and indispensable requirement of his enterprise and the highest achievement to which he can attain. Considered from this perspective, he appears to be only reproducing what he has taken in, not spontaneous and creative.

What has taken place, however, is only partially visible in the world of the senses; the remainder must be added through feeling, deduction, and conjecture. What is apparent is scattered, disconnected, isolated; that which connects this piecework, places the single fact in its true light, and gives shape to the whole remains concealed from direct observation. By means of the latter we can perceive only the circumstances which accompany and succeed one another, not the inner causal connection itself, however, upon which alone the inner truth rests. If one attempts to relate the most insignificant factual event and to say strictly only that which has really occurred, one soon notices how, without the most extreme caution in the selection and weighing of expressions, small specifications, extending beyond that which has occurred, intrude throughout and give rise to untruths or uncertainties. Even language itself contributes to this process, because, springing from the entire fullness of the spirit, it often lacks expressions which are free from all auxiliary meanings. Thus there is nothing as rare as a literally true story and nothing as much the proof of a healthy, well-ordered, discerning spirit and of a free and objective state of mind; thus to a certain extent the historical truth resembles the clouds, which take shape before our eyes only in the distance; and thus the facts of history in their particular connecting circumstances are little more than the results of tradition and research which have been accepted as true because they are the most probable in themselves and also fit best into the context of the whole.

With the bare discernment of what has really taken place, however, the skeleton of the event has still scarcely been won. What we obtain from it is the necessary foundation for history, its material, but not history itself. To stop at this point would mean to sacrifice the essential inner truth founded in the causal relationships for one that is external, literal, only apparent, to choose certain error in order to avoid a still uncertain danger of error. The truth of all that has taken place depends upon the addition of that invisible part of each fact mentioned above, and which the historian therefore must contribute. Considered from this perspective, he *is* spontaneous and even creative; not in that he brings forth that which is not present, but in that he forms, of his own ability, that which he could not have perceived in its true reality by receptivity alone. Like the poet, but in a different manner, he must take the scattered pieces he has gathered into himself and work them into a whole.

It may seem questionable to allow the domains of the historian and the poet to overlap, if even at only one point, but the activities of both are undeniably related. For if, in accordance with what has been said above, the historian in his depiction is able to attain to the truth of what has taken place only by supplementing and connecting what was incomplete and fragmented in his direct observation, he can do so, like the poet, only through the imagination. But there exists a crucial difference between the historian and the poet which eliminates all danger, in that the historian subordinates his imagination to experience and to the exploration of reality. In this subordination the imagination does not function as pure imagination and is therefore more properly called faculty of presentiment *[Ahndungs-vermögen]* and talent for combination *[Verknüpfungsgabe]*. With this alone, however, history would still be assigned too low a standing. The truth of what has taken place may seem simple, but is in fact the highest achievement that can be conceived. For if it were fully attained, it would reveal that which conditions all real things as a necessary chain. The historian must therefore strive for the necessary—not to give his material necessity through the domination of form, like the poet, but to keep fixed in his mind the ideas which are its laws, because only insofar as he is filled by them is he able to find their trace in his pure investigation of real events in their reality.

The historian gathers in all strands of earthly activity and all imprints of supernatural ideas; the sum of all being is more or less directly the object of his work and he must therefore pursue all directions of the human spirit. Speculation, experience, and poetic composition are not, however, isolated, mutually opposed and mutually limiting activities of the spirit, but rather different radiant facets of it. Two paths must therefore be followed simultaneously in order to approach the historical truth: the exact, impartial, critical determination of what has taken place and the connection of the results of this investigation, the intuitive conjecture of that which is not attainable by the former means. Whoever follows only the first of these paths will miss the essence of the truth itself; on the other hand, whoever neglects this path in favor of the second risks the danger of misrepresenting it in its details. Even the simple and straightforward description of nature cannot make do with the enumeration and portrayal of parts and the measurement of sides and angles, for there still remains a living breath which animates the whole and an inner character which speaks from it, neither of which can be measured or merely described. The description of nature is also driven to utilizing the second of these means, namely to represent the form of the general and individual being of natural bodies. In history too, nothing isolated or individual is to be found by this second path, much less anything fictively invented and added. Rather, by assimilating into itself the form of all that takes place, the spirit will understand better the material which can actually be investigated, and learn to recognize more in it than the mere operation of reason is able to do. It is exactly upon this assimilation of the investigative capability and the object under investigation that all depends. The more deeply the historian is able to comprehend humanity and its activity through his genius and study, or the more humanly he is disposed by nature and circumstance, and the more purely he allows his humanity to reign, the more completely will he resolve the task of his enterprise. The chronicles are proof of this. Despite many distorted facts and a number of obvious fictions, the good ones among them cannot be denied a basis in the most genuine historical truth. The older of the so-called memoirs follow these, although the close reference to the individual in them is often detrimental to the general reference to humanity which history requires, even in the treatment of a single point.

Although history, like every scientific occupation, serves many subordinate purposes, its work is no less than that of philosophy and poetry a free art, complete in itself. The immense throng of ceaselessly pressing world events—in part arising from the physical constitution of the earth, the nature of humanity, the character of nations and individuals, in part springing forth as if from nothing, and as if sown by a wonder, dependent upon dimly sensed forces, and obviously ruled by eternal ideas rooted deep in the heart of man—is an infinity, which the mind will never be able to bring into a single form, but which constantly provokes it to try and gives it the strength to partially succeed. As philosophy strives toward the first principles of things, and art toward the ideal of beauty, history strives toward the picture of human destiny in full truth, living fullness, and pure clarity, perceived by a spirit directed toward its object in such a way that the attitudes, feelings, and demands of personality are lost and dissolved in it. To bring forth and nourish this state of mind is the ultimate goal of the historian, one which he is able to achieve only when he pursues his immediate goal with conscientious faithfulness—the straightforward depiction of what has taken place.

For it is the sense of reality which he is called upon to awaken and to enliven, and his enterprise is circumscribed subjectively by the development of this notion, as objectively by that of depiction. Every intellectual endeavor which exercises an effect upon the whole man possesses something which can be called its element, its effective force, the secret of its influence upon the spirit, and which is so obviously distinct from the objects which it draws into its sphere that these often serve only to bring it before the mind in a new and different way. In mathematics this is the reduction to number and line, in metaphysics the abstraction from all experience, in art the marvelous treatment of nature in which everything appears to be taken from nature and yet nothing can be found existing in it in the same way. The element in which history moves is the sense of reality, and in this lies not only the feeling of the transitoriness of being in time and its dependence on preceding and accompanying causes but also, on the other hand, the consciousness of inner spiritual freedom, and the recognition on the part of reason that reality, despite its seemingly accidental nature, is nevertheless bound by an inner necessity. If one mentally scans even only one human life, one is seized by the various moments through which history stimulates and captivates, and in order to resolve the task of his enterprise the historian must assemble events in such a manner that they move the spirit in a way similar to that of reality itself.

In this aspect, history is related to the active life. It does not serve primarily through individual examples of what is to be followed or avoided, which are often misleading and seldom instructive. Rather, its true and inestimable use—arising more through the form which adheres to events rather than through the events themselves—is to enliven and refine our sense for the treatment of reality, to prevent its dissipation in the realm of mere ideas and yet to govern it by ideas, and, on this narrow middle path, to keep present in the mind the fact that there can be no successful intervening in the press of events other than by recognizing that which is true in each given dominant trend of ideas and adhering to this truth with determination.

History must always bring forth this inner effect, whatever its object may be, whether the narration of a coherent network of events or a single event. The historian who is worthy of the name must depict each event as part of a whole, or, in other words, on the basis of a single event depict the form of history itself.

This leads us to a more precise exposition of the notion of the depiction required of him. The network of events lies before him in apparent confusion, ordered only chronologically and geographically. He must separate the necessary from the accidental, uncover the inner succession, and make visible the truly effective forces in order to give his depiction a shape upon which not an imaginary or dispensable philosophical value or a poetic attractiveness rests, but rather its primary and most essential requisite, its truth and faithfulness. For one only half recognizes events or recognizes them in a distorted way, if one stops at their superficial appearance; indeed, the ordinary observer constantly intermixes them with errors and untruths. These are dispelled only by the true shape which reveals itself only to the historian's naturally gifted vision, a vision which has been further sharpened by study and practice. How then should he begin in order to be successful here?

Historical depiction, like artistic depiction, is an imitation of nature. The basis of each is the recognition of true shape, the discovery of the necessary, and the separation of the accidental. We must therefore not be reluctant to compare the more easily recognizable procedure of the artist to that of the historian, which has been subject to greater doubts.

The imitation of organic shape can occur in two ways: through a direct copying of external outlines, as exactly as hand and eye are able to do, or from the inside outwards, through the previous study of the way in which these external outlines arise from the idea and the form of the whole, through the abstraction of their relationships, through a process by means of which the shape first is recognized completely differently from the way in which it is perceived by the unskilled eye and then is born anew by the imagination in such a manner that in addition to its literal conformity with nature it bears in itself another, higher truth. For the greatest merit of the work of art is the revelation of the inner truth of shapes which is obscured in their appearance in reality. The two ways mentioned above have been the criteria of false and genuine art in all periods and genres. There are two people, greatly separated in time and place, both of whom, however, signify for us starting points of culture, with whom this distinction is exceedingly obvious— the Egyptians and the Mexicans. Numerous similarities between the two have been shown, and indeed correctly. Both had to overcome that dangerous obstacle to all art, their use of the iconic image as a written sign. In the drawings of the latter a correct view of shape is nowhere to be found, while in the case of the former there is style in the most insignificant hieroglyphic.* Quite understandably. In the Mexican drawings there is scarcely a trace of the notion of inner form or

---

*I wish only to illustrate what was said on art with an example; it is thus far from my intention to pass a definitive judgment on the Mexicans. There are even sculptures of theirs, like the head here in the Königliches Museum, which was brought back by my brother, which bear a more favorable witness to their artistic accomplishment. If one considers how small the extent of our knowledge of the Mexicans is and how recent the paintings which we know are, it would be very risky to judge their art according to what could very well stem from the period of its sharpest decline. The fact that degenerate forms of art can exist even at the stage of its highest development became especially apparent to me in the case of the small bronze figures which are found in Sardinia and which obviously seem to stem from the Greeks or Romans, but which by no means lag behind the Mexican ones in incorrectness of proportion. A collection of this sort is found in the Collegium Romanum in Rome. It is also probable, for other reasons, that at an earlier time and in another region the Mexicans stood at a much higher level of culture. The historical traces of their migrations which are carefully collected and compared with one another in the works of my brother are indications of this.

knowledge of organic structure; everything is directed toward the imitation of the outer shape. Now, for such an imperfect art, however, the attempt to pursue the external outlines must fail completely and thus lead to distortion, although the search for proportion and symmetry is evident despite the helplessness of the hand and tools.

In order to understand the outline of the shape from the inside outwards, we must go back to form itself and to the essential nature of the organism, thus to mathematics and natural history. The latter gives us the concept of shape, the former its idea. A third factor must be added to these two as a unifying element— the expression of the soul, of the spiritual life. Pure form, however, as it manifests itself in the symmetry of parts and the equilibrium of proportions is the most essential element, and also the earliest, since the still fresh, youthful spirit is more attracted by pure science and is able to penetrate it more readily than experimental science, which requires various preparations. This is evident in Egyptian and Greek sculpture. A purity and severity of form, scarcely fearful of harshness, stands out in all: the regularity of circles and semicircles, the sharpness of angles, and the distinctness of lines. The remainder of the external outline rests upon this sure basis. Where the more exact knowledge of organic structure is still lacking, this is already present in brilliant clarity, and when the artist had become master of this structure too, when he had learned to lend his work a flowing grace, to breath into it a divine expression, it still would never have occurred to him to stimulate and attract by means of these without having first provided for the form. That which was essential remained for him the first and highest concern.

All the variety and beauty of life, therefore, does not help the artist, if in the solitude of his imagination they are not accompanied by the inspiring love of pure form. Thus, it becomes comprehensible that art should arise in a people whose life was certainly not the most mobile or graceful, who hardly excelled in beauty, but whose mind had turned to mathematics and mechanics at an early time, a people who had a taste for huge, very simple, but severely regular buildings and transferred this architectonics of proportion to the imitation of the human figure, while contesting with a hard material the elements of every line. The situation of the Greek was different in all aspects. He was surrounded by a charming beauty, a richly active, sometimes even disorderly life, a rich and diverse mythology; and his chisel was easily able to win every shape from a receptive marble or indeed, in the earliest times, from wood. The depth and the seriousness of his artistic sense is all the more to be admired insofar as despite all these temptations toward a superficial grace he elevated the Egyptian severity of form still further by a more thorough knowledge of organic structure.

It may seem strange to consider as the basis of art not exclusively the richness of life, but also the dryness of mathematical intuition, but it is nonetheless true; and the artist would not need the inspiring force of genius if he were not called upon to transform the deep seriousness of rigorously dominating ideas into the appearance of free play. There is also a captivating magic in the bare intuition of mathematical truths, of the eternal relationships of space and time, whether they reveal themselves in musical tones, numbers, or lines. Their contemplation imparts in itself an eternally new satisfaction in the discovery of constantly new relationships and of problems which always allow for a complete solution. The sense for the beauty of the form of pure science can be weakened in us only by too early and too frequent an application.

The artist's imitation thus proceeds from ideas, and the truth of shape appears to him only by means of these. The same must also be true of historical imitation, since in both cases it is nature which is to be imitated. The question is then only whether there are such ideas which are able to guide the historian and what they might be.

Further progress along these lines, however, requires great caution in order that even the mere mention of ideas does not harm the purity of historical accuracy. For although both the artist and the historian depict and imitate, their goals are completely different. The artist skims off from reality only fleeting appearances and touches reality only to swing himself away from it; the historian seeks it and it alone and must absorb himself in it. For this reason and because he cannot be content with a loose external connection of individual events, but rather must attain to the central point from which their true concatenation can be understood, the historian must seek the truth of the event in a way similar to that in which the artist seeks the truth of shape. The events of history lie even less open to us than the appearances of the world of the senses and do not allow us to merely read them off. Our understanding of them is only the combined result of their own constitution and the meaning which we bring to them. Here too, as with art, we cannot by the mere operation of reason deduce them all logically one from the other and dissect them into concepts. What is right, fine, hidden can be grasped only because the mind is properly attuned to grasp it. The historian too, like the artist, brings forth only distorted images, if he sketches merely the isolated individual circumstances of events as they appear to present themselves, arraying one next to the other, if he does not rigorously account for their inner connection, gain an intuition of the effective forces, recognize the direction which they take at a given moment, and investigate their connections both with concurrent states of affairs and with preceding changes. In order to be able to do so, he must be familiar with the constitution, the effect, and the reciprocal dependency of these forces, since the complete penetration of the particular always presupposes the knowledge of the general under which it is subsumed. In this sense, the comprehension of what has taken place must be guided by ideas.

It goes without saying, of course, that these ideas arise from the profusion of events itself, or, to be more precise, arise in the mind through a consideration of these events which is undertaken with a true historical sense. They must not be lent to history as an alien addition, a mistake which is easily committed by so-called philosophical history. Historical accuracy is threatened much more by the danger of a philosophical treatment than by that of a poetic one, since the latter is at least accustomed to giving its material a certain degree of freedom. Philosophy prescribes a goal for events; this search for final causes, even if one wishes to derive them from the essence of man and of nature itself, disturbs and distorts any free view of the characteristic effect of historical forces. Teleological history, therefore, never attains to the living truth of world destinies, because the individual must always find the peak of his development within the span of his own fleeting existence. It therefore is not able to locate the ultimate purpose of events in that which is living, but rather seeks it in lifeless institutions and in the notion of an ideal whole, whether in the generally developing cultivation and population of the earth, in the rising culture of peoples, in the closer ties among them all, in the final attainment of a state of perfection of civil society, or in some idea of this sort. The activity and happiness of individuals are indeed immediately dependent upon all of these, but what each generation receives from that which has been achieved by all previous generations is neither a proof of its capability, nor even an instructive practice material for it. For that which is the fruit of the spirit and the character—science, art, moral institutions—loses its spiritual element and becomes material, if it is not constantly revitalized by the spirit. All of these things carry in themselves the nature of thought, which can only be preserved insofar as it is thought.

It is thus to the effective and productive forces that the historian must turn. Here he is in his own characteristic domain. What he can do in order to bring to the consideration of the labyrinthinely entwined events of world history which are fixed in his mind that particular form through which alone their true connection becomes apparent is to draw this form from the events themselves. The contradiction which appears to lie here disappears upon closer examination. Every act of comprehension of a subject matter presupposes, as a condition of its possibility, the existence of an analogue in the person who comprehends of that which is subsequently actually comprehended—a preceding original correspondence between subject and object. Comprehension is by no means merely a developing out of the subject, nor a drawing from the object, but rather both at once, for it always consists of the application of a previously present general idea to a new particular instance. Where two beings are separated by a total gap, no bridge of understanding extends from one to the other; in order to understand one another, they must have, in another sense, already understood one another. In the case of history, this preliminary basis of comprehension is very clear, for everything which is effective in world history is also active within man himself. Thus, the deeper the sensitivity of a nation's spirit for all that is human, the more delicately, diversely, and purely it is affected by this, the greater will be its tendency to possess historians in the true sense of the word. The historian must add to this preparation a critical practice through which he attempts to correct his preliminary impressions of the object until, through repeated reciprocal action, clarity as well as certainty emerge.

In this way, through the study of the productive forces of world history, the historian sketches for himself a general picture of the form of the connection of all events; and within this sphere lie the ideas discussed above. They are not brought to history from without, but rather constitute the essence of history itself. For every dead and every living force acts according to the laws of its nature, and everything that happens stands in an inseparable connection in time and space.

In this aspect, history seems like a dead clockwork, following immutable laws and driven by mechanical forces, no matter how manifold and lively its movement before our eyes might be. For one event gives rise to another; the extent and the constitutive nature of each effect are prescribed by its cause; and even the apparently free will of the individual finds its determination in circumstances which were immutably laid out long before his birth, indeed long before the formation of the nation to which he belongs. Thus to be able to calculate from each single moment the whole series of the past, and even of the future, seems to be impossible not in itself, but rather only because of a deficient knowledge of a set of intermediate links. It has long been known, however, that the exclusive pursuit of this path would lead away from the insight into the truly productive forces, that in every activity involving living beings it is precisely the main element itself which defies all calculation, and that this apparently mechanical determination does in fact fundamentally obey free-working impulses.

Thus, in addition to the mechanical determination of one event by another, we must pay particular attention to the characteristic nature of the forces involved; and the first step here is their physiological activity. All living forces—man like plants, nations like individuals, the human race like individual peoples—indeed even the products of the human spirit, such as literature, art, customs, the external form of bourgeois society, have characteristic features, developments, and laws in common, insofar as they depend upon a certain sequence of continued activity. Thus the progressive attainment of a culmination point, and the gradual falling away from it, the transition of certain perfections into degenerate forms, and so forth. A mass of historical information undeniably lies here, but the productive principle itself does not become visible through it; rather, only a form is recognizable to which that principle must submit if it does not find in it an elevating and supporting carrier.

The psychological forces of the multiply interpenetrating human capabilities, sensations, inclinations, and passions are even less calculable in their course and are not so much subject to recognizable laws as rather graspable only through certain analogies. As the direct mainsprings of actions and the most immediate causes of the occurrences arising from them, they are of preeminent concern to the historian and are most frequently employed by him in the explanation of events. But it is particularly this approach which demands the greatest degree of caution. It is the least world historical: it degrades the tragedy of world history to the melodrama of everyday life and all too easily misleads one into tearing the individual event out of the context of the whole and into setting a petty machinery of personal motivations in the place of world destiny. In this approach, everything is centered in the individual, but the individual is not recognized in his unity and depth, in his essential being. For this being cannot be split open in such a way, analyzed, or judged according to experiences which are drawn from many individuals and are therefore also supposed to apply to many. Its particular force penetrates all human emotions and passions and also impresses upon all its stamp and its character.

One could make an attempt to classify historians according to these three approaches, but the characterization of the truly gifted ones among them would not be exhausted by any of these, nor indeed by all of them taken together. For these approaches do not even exhaust the causes of the connection of events, and the fundamental idea which alone makes possible an understanding of events in their full truth does not lie in their sphere. They encompass only the phenomena of dead, living, and spiritual nature which are easily graspable in their regularly self-reproducing order, but none of the free and independent impulses of an original force. These phenomena give account only of regular developments which reoccur according to a recognized law or certain experience; but that which arises like a wonder and which may be accompanied by mechanical, physiological, and psychological explanations but is not really deducible from any of them remains not only unexplained within such a framework but also unrecognized.

No matter how one might begin, the phenomenal realm can only be comprehended from a point external to it, and the reflective stepping out from it is as free of danger as a blind withdrawal into it is certain of error. World history is not understandable without a world order.

An adherence to this point of view also gives us the considerable advantage of not regarding the comprehension of events as closed by explanations drawn from the natural sphere. To be sure, this hardly makes the last, most difficult, and most important part of the historian's task any easier for him, since he is not provided with any special organ of perception by means of which he can directly investigate the plans of this world order, and any attempt to do so, like the search for final causes, might well only lead him astray. But the directing principle of events which lies external to natural development nonetheless reveals itself in these events themselves through means which, while if not themselves phenomenal objects, nevertheless cling to them and can be recognized in them, like incorporeal beings which cannot be perceived unless one steps out of the phenomenal realm and mentally enters into that realm in which they have their origin. The last condition of the resolution of the task of the historian is thus linked to their investigation.

The number of productive forces in history is not exhausted by those which directly manifest themselves in events. Even if the historian has investigated all of these both singly and in combination—the shape and the transformations of the earth's surface, the changes of climate, the intellectual ability and the character of nations and, more particularly, of individuals, the influences of art and science, the deeply penetrating and widespread influences of social institutions—remains an even more powerfully effective principle, not immediately visible, but lending these forces impetus and direction—namely, ideas, which, in accordance with their very nature, lie beyond the finite realm, but rule and control world history in all its aspects.

There can be no doubt that such ideas reveal themselves, that certain phenomena which cannot be explained by a mere action in accordance with natural laws owe their existence to their animating breath, and, likewise, that there is consequently a certain point at which the historian is referred to a realm beyond that of phenomenal events in order to recognize them in their true shape.

Such an idea expresses itself in a dual way: both as a directing tendency, which is initially not apparent, but gradually becomes visible and finally irresistible, seizing many particulars in various places and under various circumstances; and also as a generative force which in its scope and prominence cannot be derived from any of its accompanying circumstances.

Examples of the former can be found without difficulty; they have scarcely ever been misunderstood. But it is very likely that many events which are currently explained in a more material and mechanical way must be regarded in this manner.

Examples of generative forces, phenomena for whose explanation accompanying circumstances are not sufficient, are the eruption of art in its pure form in Egypt, as we mentioned above, and, perhaps even more striking, the sudden development in Greece of the free and yet self-regulating individuality with which language, poetry, and art suddenly stand at a state of perfection, the gradual way to which has been sought in vain. For what is admirable in Greek culture and what above all holds the key to it appears to me to be the fact that while the Greeks received all the important things which they assimilated from nations that were divided into castes, they themselves remained free from this constraint. They always retained forms analogous to castes, but moderated this strict notion into the freer one of schools and free associations, and through both a division of the original national spirit into tribes, nations, and individual cities—a more manifold division than had ever before existed in a people—and an ever increasing unification, they brought the diversity of individuality into a most lively interaction. Greece thus established an idea of national individuality which neither existed before that time nor has existed since; and since the secret of all being lies in individuality, the world-historical progress of mankind is dependent upon the extent, the freedom, and the particular character of the reciprocal actions of individual beings.

Indeed, an idea can appear only in a natural context, and thus in the case of these phenomena too we can demonstrate a number of favorable causes, a transition from less perfect to more perfect forms, and justifiably assume them to exist where there are enormous gaps in our knowledge. But the wonderful element lies nonetheless in the seizing of the initial direction, in the first spark. Without this, the favorable circumstances could have no effect, nor could practice or gradual progress, even for centuries, lead to the goal. The idea can entrust itself only to a spiritually individual force, but the seed which the idea plants in this force develops in its own way, this way remains the same when it passes on into other individuals, and the plant which sprouts from it attains flower and fruition and afterwards wilts and disappears no matter how the circumstances and individuals involved might be structured—all these facts show that it is the autonomous nature of the idea which completes its course in the phenomenal realm. In this manner, forms attain reality in all the various species of physical being and spiritual creation, forms in which some aspect of infinity is reflected and through whose intervention in life new phenomena are brought forth.

While a sure approach to the investigation of the spiritual world has always been the pursuit of analogies in the physical world, one cannot expect to find in the latter the development of such significantly new forms. The varieties of organization have at one time or another found their set forms and although they never exhaust themselves in their organic individuality within these forms, fine nuances are not directly visible, nor hardly even visible in their effect on spiritual development. Creation in the physical world occurs suddenly in space, creation in the spiritual world occurs gradually in time, or, rather, at least the former more readily finds the resting point upon which creation loses itself in a uniform reproduction. Organic life, however, stands much closer to spiritual life than do form and physical structure, and the laws of each find more ready application in the realm of the other. In a state of healthy vigor this is less visible, although it is very likely that even here changes in accordance with hidden causes occur in relationships and tendencies and, with the ages, gradually alter the disposition of organic life. But in an abnormal state of life, in diseased forms, there is undeniably an analogue to be found in tendencies which arise suddenly or gradually without explainable causes and seem to follow their own particular laws and thus point to a hidden connection of things. This has been confirmed by repeated observations, even though they may not be historically useful for a long time.

Every human individuality is an idea rooted in the phenomenal realm, and sometimes this idea shines forth so brightly that it seems to have taken on the form of the individual only in order to reveal itself in it. If one pursues the development of human activity, there remains, after the subtraction of all its determining causes, something fundamental which, instead of being stifled by such influences, transforms them; and in this element there lies an incessant active striving to provide an external existence for its own particular inner nature. The same is true for the individuality of nations and in many periods of history is much more apparent in their case than in the case of individuals, since in certain epochs and under certain conditions man has developed in a herdlike manner as it were. In the midst of the history of peoples directed by needs, passions, and apparent chance, the spiritual principle of individuality continues to exercise an effect stronger than that of such elements; it seeks to create room for the idea which inhabits it and it succeeds like a delicate plant which, through the organic swelling of its vessels, is able to crack walls which have otherwise defied the effects of centuries.

In addition to the direction which peoples and individuals lend to the human race by their deeds, they also pass down forms of spiritual individuality more lasting and more effective than occurrences and events.

There are, however, also ideal forms, which while not constitutive of human individuality itself, are related to it indirectly. Among these is language. For although each language reflects the spirit of a nation, it has an earlier and more independent basis. Its own essential being and its internal coherence are also so strong and so influential that its independent nature exercises a greater effect than that which is exercised upon it, and each important language appears to be a unique form for the production and communication of ideas.

In an even purer and more complete way the eternal fundamental ideas of all that is conceivable obtain for themselves being and power; beauty in all physical and spiritual forms; truth in the immutable activity of each force according to its innate law; and justice in the inexorable course of events which eternally judge and punish themselves.

From our human perspective, we cannot directly detect the plans of world order, but can only guess at them through the ideas by means of which they reveal themselves, and therefore all history is only the realization of an idea. In this idea lies both its force and its goal. Thus by immersing ourselves in the study of the generative forces, we arrive at a more correct path to the final causes toward which the spirit naturally strives. The goal of history can only be the realization of the idea which is to be represented through humanity, in all aspects and in all the shapes in which finite form is able to combine with the idea. The course of events can only break off when both are no longer capable of a full interpretation.

Thus we have succeeded in locating the ideas which must guide the historian and can return to the comparison between him and the artist. For the historian, the investigation of the active and passive forces occurring in life plays a role comparable to that of the knowledge of nature and the study of organic structure for the artist; and the ideas which unfold silently and magnificently in the context of world events and yet do not belong to them are for him what proportion, symmetry, and the notion of pure form are for the artist. The enterprise of the historian in its final but most simple solution is the depiction of the striving of an idea to achieve existence in reality. For it does not always succeed in its initial attempt, and not seldom does it degenerate when it is not able to gain pure mastery over the opposing material. There are two things to which we have to hold in the course of this investigation: that an idea which is itself not directly perceptible rules in all that takes place, but that this idea can only be recognized in the events themselves. The historian therefore cannot exclude the power of the idea from his depiction and seek all solely in the material; he must at least leave room open for its effect; he must further keep his spirit receptive for it; but above all, he must guard against attributing to reality ideas which he has himself created, or sacrificing the living richness of the individual in his search for the relationships of the whole. This freedom and delicacy of perspective must become his very own nature to such an extent that he brings it to the consideration of each event, for no one event is fully separable from the whole, and, as we have shown above, a part of everything that happens lies beyond the realm of direct perception. If the historian is lacking in this freedom of perspective, he does not recognize the events in their scope and their depth; if he is lacking in delicacy of perspective, then he damages their simple and living truth.

# Johann Gustav Droysen

JOHANN GUSTAV DROYSEN (1808–1884) was born in Treptow, Pomerania, and attended the classical high school (*Gymnasium*) in Stettin before enrolling at the University of Berlin as a student. He taught high school in that city for several years and began to teach history at the university in 1833 as an instructor (*Privatdozent*). During these years, his main interest lay in the field of classics. He published translations of Aeschylus and Aristophanes. In 1833 he published his *History of Alexander the Great* which was to become a standard work and established Droysen's reputation as a historian. The sequel volumes, *History of Hellenism* (1836–1843), dealt with the fate of Greek civilization after Alexander's death. In 1840 Droysen received a professorship at the University of Kiel where he became involved in the political conflict between Denmark and Germany regarding the status of Schleswig-Holstein. He was elected a member of the revolutionary Frankfurt Parliament in 1848 and served as secretary for the committee in charge of drafting an all-German constitution. After the failure of the revolution, Droysen moved to Jena and finally (1859) to Berlin where he remained until his death. His major scholarly interest was now centered around the history of Prussia. He published a biography of Count Yorck von Wartenburg (1851–52) and then embarked on his intended magnum opus, a *History of Prussian Politics* (1855–1884), of which he completed seven volumes. During his entire career Droysen displayed a strong sense for the theoretical and methodological problems of the historical discipline vis-à-vis the rapidly growing influence of the natural sciences. He was the most outspoken critic of the positivist approach to history as practiced by Taine and Buckle. Beginning in 1857 Droysen regularly taught a course at the University of Berlin which he called *Encyclopedia and Methodology of History*. He taught this course eighteen times before his death. An outline of the course for his students was published in 1858 (3rd edition, 1882) under the title *Historik*.

In 1937 R. Hübner published an integral text of Droysen's course (together with the *Outline*). An historical-critical edition of all of Droysen's theoretical writings has begun to appear (Sect. A, Bibl.). The selection "On Interpretation" is taken from the Hübner edition of the *Historik* and comprises sections 37 (The Investigation of Origins) and 38 (The Modes of Interpretation) of the full version of the text (*Enzyklopädie*), as well as sections 39–44 (The Four Kinds of Interpretation) from the *Grundriss* (*Outline*). The selection on "The Historical Method" was reprinted from the English edition of the *Outline* published in Boston in 1897. It is characteristic for Droysen's approach that he brings the tools and the insights of the new philological hermeneutics to bear upon the study of history and society.

# HISTORY AND
# THE HISTORICAL METHOD

## 1

Nature and History are the widest conceptions under which the human mind apprehends the world of phenomena. And it apprehends them thus, according to the intuitions of time and space, which present themselves to it as, in order to comprehend them, it analyzes for itself in its own way the restless movement of shifting phenomena.

Objectively, phenomena do not separate themselves according to space and time; it is our apprehension that thus distinguishes them, according as they appear to relate themselves more to space or to time.

The conceptions of time and space increase in definiteness and content in the measure in which the side-by-side character of that which is and the successive character of that which has become, are perceived, investigated and understood.

## 2

The restless movement in the world of phenomena causes us to apprehend things as in a constant development, this transition on the part of some seeming merely to repeat itself periodically, in case of others to supplement the repetition with ascent, addition, ceaseless growth, the system continually making, so to speak, "a contribution to itself."[1] In those phenomena in which we discover an advance of this kind, we take the successive character, the element of time, as the determining thing. These we grasp and bring together as History.

## 3

To the human eye, only what pertains to man appears to partake of this constant upward and onward motion, and of this, such motion appears to be the essence and the business. The *ensemble* of this restless progress upward is the moral world. Only to this does the expression "History" find its full application.

## 4

The science of History is the result of empirical perception, experience and investigation (*historia*). All empirical knowledge depends upon the "specific energy" of the nerves of sense, through the excitation of which the mind receives not "images" but signs of things without, which signs this excitation has brought before it. Thus it develops for itself systems of signs, in which the corresponding external things present themselves to it, constituting a world of ideas. In these the mind, continually correcting, enlarging and building up *its* world, finds itself in possession of the external world, that is, so far as it can and must possess this in order to grasp it, and, by knowledge, will and formative power, rule it.

## 5

All empirical investigation governs itself according to the data to which it is directed, and it can only direct itself to such data as are immediately present to it and susceptible of being cognized through the senses. The data for historical investigation are not past things, for these have disappeared, but things which are still present here and now, whether recollections of what was done, or remnants of things that have existed and of events that have occurred.

## 6

Every point in the present is one which has come to be. That which it was and the manner whereby it came to be—these have passed away. Still, ideally, its past character is yet present in it. Only ideally, however, as faded traces and suppressed gleams. Apart from knowledge these are as if they existed not. Only searching vision, the insight of investigation, is able to resuscitate them to a new life, and thus cause light to shine back into the empty darkness of the past. Yet what becomes clear is not past events as past. These exist no longer. It is so much of those past things as still abides in the now and the here. These quickened traces of past things stand to us in the stead of their originals, mentally constituting the "present" of those originals.

The finite mind possesses only the now and the here. But it enlarges for itself this poverty-stricken narrowness of its existence, forward by means of its willing and its hopes, backward through the fullness of its memories. Thus, ideally locking in itself both the future and the past, it possesses an experience analogous to eternity. The mind illuminates its present with the vision and knowledge of past events, which yet have neither existence nor duration save in and through the mind itself. "Memory, that mother of Muses, who shapes all things,"² creates for it the forms and the materials for a world which is in the truest sense the mind's own.

## 7

It is only the traces which *man* has left, only what man's hand and man's mind has touched, formed, stamped, that thus lights up before us afresh. As he goes on fixing imprints and creating form and order, in every such utterance the human being brings into existence an expression of his individual nature, of his "I." Whatever residue o ˙ such human expressions and imprints is anywise, anywhere, present to us, that speaks to us and we can understand it.

## *The Historical Method*

## 8

The method of historical investigation is determined by the morphological character of its material. The essence of historical method is *understanding* by means of *investigation*.

## 9

The possibility of this understanding arises from the kinship of our nature with that of the utterances lying before us as historical material. A further condition of this possibility is the fact that man's nature, at once sensuous and spiritual, speaks forth every one of its inner processes in some form apprehensible by the senses, mirrors these inner processes, indeed, in every utterance. On being perceived, the utterance, by projecting itself into the inner experience of the percipient, calls forth the same inner process.³ Thus, on hearing the cry of anguish we have a sense of the anguish felt by him who cries. Animals, plants and the things of the inorganic world are understood by us only in part, only in a certain way, in certain relations, namely those wherein these things seem to us to correspond to categories of our thinking. Those things have for us no individual, at least no personal, existence. Inasmuch as we seize and understand them only in the relations named, we do not scruple to set them at naught as to their individual existences, to dismember and destroy them, to use and consume them. With human beings, on the other hand, with human utterances and creations, we have and feel that we have an essential kinship and reciprocity of nature: every "I" enclosed in itself, yet each in its utterances disclosing itself to every other.

## 10

The individual utterance is understood as a simple speaking forth of the inner nature, involving possibility of inference backward to that inner nature. This inner nature, offering this utterance in the way of a specimen, is understood as a central force, in itself one and the same, yet declaring its nature in this single voice, as in every one of its external efforts and expressions. The individual is understood in the total, and the total from the individual.

The person who understands, because he, like him whom he has to understand, is an "I," a totality in himself, fills out for himself the other's totality from the individual utterance and the individual utterance from the other's totality. The process of understanding is as truly synthetic as analytic, as truly inductive as deductive.

## 11

From the logical mechanism of the understanding process there is to be distinguished the act of the faculty of understanding. This act results, under the conditions above explained, as an immediate intuition, wherein soul blends with soul, creatively, after the manner of conception in coition.

## 12

The human being is, in essential nature, a totality in himself, but realizes this character only in understanding others and being understood by them, in the moral partnerships of family, people, state, religion, etc.

The individual is only relatively a totality. He understands and is understood only as a specimen and expression of the partnerships whose member he is and in whose essence and development he has part, himself being but an expression of this essence and development.

The combined influence of times, peoples, states, religions, etc., is only a sort of an expression of the absolute totality, whose reality we instinctively surmise and believe in because it comes before us in our "*Cogito ergo sum,*"[4] that is, as the certainty of our own personal being, and as the most indubitable fact which we can know.

## 13

The false alternative between the materialistic and the idealistic view of the world reconciles itself in the historical, namely in the view to which the moral world leads us; for the essence of the moral world resides in the fact that in it at every moment the contrast spoken of reconciles itself in order to its own renewal, renews itself in order to its own reconciliation.

## 14

According to the objects and according to the nature of human thinking, the three possible scientific methods are: the speculative, philosophically or theologically, the physical, and the historical. Their essence is to find out, to explain, to understand. Hence the old canon of the sciences: Logic, Physics, Ethics, which are not three ways to one goal, but the three sides of a prism, through which the human eye, if it will, may, in colored reflection, catch foregleams of the eternal light whose direct splendor it would not be able to bear.

## 15

The moral world, ceaselessly moved by many ends, and finally, so we instinctively surmise and believe, by the supreme end, is in a state of restless development and of internal elevation and growth, "on and on, as man eternalizes himself."⁵ Considered in the successive character of these its movements the moral world presents itself to us as History. With every advancing step in this development and growth, the historical understanding becomes wider and deeper. History, that is, is better understood and itself understands better. The knowledge of History is History itself. Restlessly working on, it cannot but deepen its investigations and broaden its circle of vision.

Historical things have their truth in the moral forces, as natural things have theirs in the natural "laws," mechanical, physical, chemical, etc. Historical things are the perpetual actualization of these moral forces. To *think* historically, means to see their truth in the actualities resulting from that moral energy.

### Notes

1. Aristotle *De anima* 2.5.7.
2. Aeschylus *Prometheus* 466.
3. This passage clearly echoes Humboldt's famous characterization of language and speech from his *Introduction to the Kawi Language.* See the first selection by Humboldt above, p. 100.
4. Descartes's dictum from the *Discourse* "I think, therefore, I am."
5. Dante *Inferno* 15.84.

# The Investigation of Origins

First, some preliminary remarks. We concluded the chapter on criticism without finding a rubric which would do justice to the investigation of origins. Should we not determine and establish a point as the genetic beginning of an historical phenomenon such as Christianity? Or is this a matter for interpretation?

I must acknowledge that this task is made impossible by the method set forth by myself and would like to add that herein also lies what seems to me to be a good indication of the correctness of my method.

Indeed, it is the nature of the narrative to portray historical events as a process and to allow these to present themselves genetically to the ear of the hearer, thus allowing them virtually to unfold before him. However, it is equally clear that we, in so narrating, are only seeking to imitate the sequence as it appears to us to be "becoming" and that we reconstruct this sequence by inquiry. It is sheer abstraction and fallacious to believe that we can find the origin of that which has become through inquiry; this would be the same as to trace the true origin of the illustrious history of the Romans back to Romulus and Remus.

Both founders are preceded by a long line of influences. It would be even more illusory to search for the origin of something with the belief that it is possible to find the true essence of that from which this development proceeded. The studies on this question conducted by the Baur school have become a model for the field of theology. Here the true core of archetypal Christianity is sought. As with an onion, layer after layer is peeled away in order to come at last to the innermost center. But what is "last and innermost"? Is it Christ, his eminent person and biography? Does it consist in the teachings and creeds, or is there one doctrine which is the sum of all others? Perhaps the Word of the filial relationship to God or Love, which is valued above all else, will be found at the center. Perhaps this is the grain of seed, which, having been cast out, sprouted and grew to become a tree which overshadowed the world. The seed first became a tree by growing and it was first through this tremendous growth that the seed came into its true "being." It is of no use to deny the existence of the tree because the original seed can no longer be traced or because one is uncertain whether this, that, or a third point is the actual beginning. If one were to dig down to the roots from which this tree has grown in order to find the original germ seed, it would no longer be there. Its beginning only repeats itself through its fruit; if the tree no longer bears fruit, then its life and moving force are at an end and it withers away.

This is true of all historical phenomena. To arrive at a point which is the origin, in its complete and eminent sense, it must be sought exclusively outside the realm of historical research. We cannot go beyond relative origins which are posited by us as a beginning in relation to what has evolved from them. We can only find and posit the origin in relation to that which has already become. For if we speculate, we can certainly construct an unmitigated and absolute beginning in which we could devoutly believe; but we could not prove it historically. He who wishes to establish such an origin would not do so using a historical method as he might run the risk of being drawn into the tedious discussion over whether the chicken came before the egg, or the even more uninteresting theory on the *generatio aequivoca* of the primeval protoplasm put forth by the followers of Darwin. It is essential to have a clear understanding of the fact that our empirical research can only proceed from current materials. Furthermore, if the results are presented in the form of narration, they will have been assigned an origin ad hoc which, therefore, can only be a relative one. This is important to note because, in explaining the origin of that which has become, the genetic mode of narration consistently leads one to the misconception that it is possible to verify historically why things had to come into being and why they had to become what they became.

But this issue has yet another aspect worthy of note which also wants clarification.

It goes without saying that we can only completely understand something after we understand how this thing has come to be what it is. But we can only know something if we investigate and understand what it is like in the most precise way. The fact that we conceive of the present and the existing as "having become" is only a form and a mode of expressing this understanding. And, on the other hand, we develop our concept of becoming and having become from the existing which we analyze and conceptualize chronologically in order to understand it.

As one can see, we are moving in a circle; however, one which brings *us* further, but not the issue at hand. One moment we have an object before us which we observe as existing, and in the next moment, we conceive of it as having become. Here we have a dual formula for the way in which we see and conceive of the object; it is not the object, but our understanding of the object which we control and enhance by viewing it stereoscopically from two sides at once, or, more accurately, from two points of vision.

One must know this in order to realize just how far the limits of our discipline can and want to be extended. It [our discipline] proceeds empirically in that the material used for investigation is both given and existing; it is precise because it obtains its results by drawing proper syllogisms for such material and not from hypothesized origins. This accuracy is strengthened by its attempt to explain phenomena that are empirically available without using nonempirical primary origins.

For if one were to accept that our discipline sets itself the task of explaining the present from the past through deductive reasoning, then one would acknowledge that the conditions for that which follows are already present in the preceding, whether these were established by inquiry or not. Such a discipline would exclude one of the most intrinsic properties of the historical world, that is, the moral world: the freedom of will, the responsibility for one's own action and the right of every individual to be a new beginning and totality unto himself. To this discipline the moral world would become an uninteresting analogy for the perpetuity of matter and the mechanics of atoms. For the future would already have been preconceived in the past. It would already have to have been present in embryo form in the beginning; events would need only to reveal and interpret themselves in order to be able to evolve logically from the preceding. This mechanism is not even experienced by plants since it is not yet contained in its seed, but requires nourishment from the earth, air, or light, and with this it is nourished and enhanced to become that which it has not yet become in its seed.

These observations suffice to refute the false doctrine of organic preformation or history's so-called "organic" development. That which is generally extolled as organically preformed is, admittedly, a factor, a condition of historical life—but I might add that this is the least historical as it belongs to the natural substratum. If taken seriously, the truly organic development would exclude progress, the *epidosis eis auto.*[1]

This preface was necessary to prevent the concept of interpretation which we are about to discuss from being misconstrued. We are not interpreting historical facts such as the Revolution of 1789 or the Battle of Leipzig in order to infer situations and conditions whose necessary results these events would be. On the contrary, we are interpreting existing materials in order to find out—by explicating and interpreting—what can be perceived as going beyond the facts to which they attest. This we are doing on the basis of explication, interpretation, and the best possible understanding of these facts. Our interpretation intends to enliven and analyze these dry, lifeless materials in the hopes of returning them to life and allowing them to speak again through the art of interpretation.

# THE MODES OF INTERPRETATION

I understand the speech of a person standing before me by hearing his words and taking in the tone and accent of his voice, the expression of his eyes and face and the gesticulation of his hands. For it is the full expression of excitement and mood which manifests itself and which allows me to comprehend this person's innermost being, what he feels, and to have compassion for what is going on inside him.

It is already a different matter when the same person writes to me when I am not present. In reading, I instinctively complete his letter by imagining the tone of his voice and the expression of his face as I know them otherwise to be. I imagine that I hear and see him.

If I do not know the author of the letter personally, the impression I have of the letter is much flatter. Unless the statement is particularly emphatic or skillfully written, it will require much effort to imagine the personality behind such a letter.

If someone tells me of a conversation with someone or of a letter from someone with whom I am befriended, I am able to correct and control the narrator's portrayal with my own additional knowledge. I might even be acquainted with the narrator and be aware of his nature, his aspirations, and his relationship to my friend. I will correct his story with this information in mind and will know just how much to believe. According at least to my knowledge and opinion of my friend, he would not have spoken in such a way nor would he have meant such a thing. I shall correct the facts, make my decision, or form my opinion on the basis of this.

And if I should learn through third or fourth hand what my friend said or wrote, I shall be all the more cautious. And still more so, if I am to learn from this source what someone has said whom I do not know. I shall first try to learn more about this person in order to gain an idea of his personality.

These are roughly the same variances we find in historical materials which are presented to us and also the same procedures which we must subject them to.

Criticism has done away with all sorts of imperfections and impurities which the material initially had. Not only has it purified and verified them, but it has organized them so that they may lie well ordered before us.

The rest of our task is now clear to us. We are now concerned with understanding the things before us; that is, to comprehend them as an expression of that element within them which wanted to express itself.

If we were to continue schematically, we would have to go back to what we said earlier and say: that which lies before us as historical material is the expression and imprint of acts of volition and we must try to understand them in these manifestations.

But the matter is not so simple. We are not so much concerned with the particular voluntary acts of those who acted; we are more interested in gaining an idea and understanding of the events and the conditions (i.e., the facts) which were evoked by the acts of volition. Each of these facts arises as a rule from interaction with many other facts and some were formed in such a way that they opposed and acted against one another. And how should we react to facts, that is, to evidence or remains of facts, in which (as with the remains of the Old Roman Wall, or the *leges barborum,* or the founding of Knights' Orders in Jerusalem) there are no longer any traces of a personal will and what is left to speak to us is merely something general, like the genius of a race, the insight of an age, the same uniform attitude of countless believers?

The task of historic interpretation, then, is not as simple as our understanding of someone who is speaking to us.

But we do take our essential foundation from there. First of all, it is important to find the viewpoints around which we will focus our historic understanding and interpretation. These encompass everything which one can understand.

1. In keeping with the nature of the subject, we turn first to the basic historical material as it has been organized by criticism; this order almost provides us with a sketch of the factual context which we complete through the pragmatic interpretation.

2. The facts for which these materials serve as proof took place at such and such a time and in such and such a country; they were part of that present and were under the influence of all of the conditioning factors present at the time. All of these factors worked together and exercised an inhibiting or a stimulating influence on the situation which constituted that period of time. Each factor also stood under the local, economic, religious, and technical conditions. The traces of these effects present in the historic material must be found and reestablished in terms of their impact and range. This is the interpretation of the conditions.

3. Our material will not always be constituted such that we can still state the voluntary actions of the people concerned; and even where we can recognize the leaders, or the productive individuals, the body of spectators and people being lead will evade our scrutiny. But if these masses seem here to lack significance and effectiveness, if they seem to be receptive and passive, this is only so when seen beside the unfolding of some great event. The leading figures do not just guide and determine the masses, they also represent them. We will have to understand the opinions and perceptions of these leading figures, their inclinations, behavior, and purpose; and we shall have to try to imagine ourselves in their place in order that we may recognize the facts attested to by the material, keeping in mind not only their actual course of development, but, more importantly, the conditions under which they evolved and their unfolding through the will and passions of those actively involved. This is the psychological interpretation.

4. Our understanding is still incomplete. One factor still remains which is not easily categorized under these three points. This is of no special significance, although seemingly imperceptible, for it always carries the entire action and often suddenly bursts forth with tremendous energy. Over and above all particular interests, individual talents, and personal intentions, there is a common factor which is more powerful than all of the factors taken together. It is under the effect of this factor that the conditions become active and begin to focus themselves. The entire pragmatic process is ruled and moved solely by this factor. These are the common and moral forces from which man derives his expression, his unity, and his strength; these are alive in the feelings and the conscience of every person. They elevate him above his small self and draw him as a participator into the great creations which offer him more than an individual and ephemeral existence. This is what is meant by the expression "interpretation of ideas." Perhaps we should reformulate this as the interpretation according to moral forces.

Still another observation should be made at this point. We saw that, according to Böhmer, the only method of an historian is to lay out the materials he has gathered. One often hears—most notably in philological circles—the opinion that any step beyond this is an arbitrary product of the imagination. But it is precisely this imagination which is immediately active in producing a picture of the events past—be they recorded or not—and the saga illustrates to us just how historic necessity is forced to proceed in such a manner. This also applies to the dilettantism of today. The main objective is to find norms which produce an adequate and secure procedure and one which also yields assured results.

Consequently, the second and greatest danger is that we involuntarily bring in the views and presuppositions of our own time and the present interferes with our understanding of the past. As mentioned in the criticism of correctness and validity.[2] Shakespeare's dramatic works (*Troilus and Cressida* and *Midsummer Night's Dream*) present that heroic people, the Greeks, according to the courtly customs of the author's own times. It is only through cautious, methodical interpretation that we can gain concrete and assured results and so correct our notions about the past. This will enable us to measure the past according to its own standards.

## 39

(a) The *pragmatic interpretation* takes up the critical state of affairs; that is, the critically verified remnants and ordered interpretations which are left from the actual course of events. It examines the causal nature of that course in order to reconstruct it.

The simple *demonstrative* method is sufficient when the material is plentiful. When there is a lack of material, we are lead to analogy, a comparison of this X with the unknown.

The analogy between two Xs, in as much as they supplement one another, becomes the *comparative* method.

The *hypothesis* is the postulation of a correlation in which the fragmentary evidence conforms to its conjectured direction and is thus confirmed by evidence.

## 40

(b) The *interpretation of the conditions* bases itself on the fact that the conditions were already potentially contained in the once actual state of affairs. At the same time, these conditions make this situation possible and will, for that matter, always be partially present in its residuum and interpretations.

(An example can be seen in the aesthetically unpleasing position of the Borghesian gladiator with respect to the line of the tympanum, for which the statue was created.)

The conditions of *space*—aside from the countless minor relationships—can be illuminated through geography: the theater of war, the battlefield, natural boundaries, the formation of valleys in Egypt, and the formation of the marshland by the North Sea.

The conditions of *time* which govern a situation can be broken down into a development of facts and into concurrent events which were more or less determining forces of the same.

A third group of conditions comprises the material and moral means which enabled the course of the event to become an actuality.

In the area of material means lies the multiplicity of matter and tools which constitute the vast field of *technological* interpretation—an area which has remained virtually unexplored. The passions, moods, prejudices, and opinions which rule the masses lie in the realm of morals. The statesman, the general, and the artist are all similarly determined by these aspects, as they all depend on the same for their own effectiveness.

# 41

(c) The *psychological interpretation* attempts to determine the acts of will which elicited the event. This method concerns itself with the person who willed the act, the forcefulness of that person's will, his intellect, and the extent to which all these things had an effect on the event. The person who wills the act is neither consumed by the event nor can the event be considered the sole product of that person's will and intelligence; it is neither the pure nor the entire expression of his personality.

The personality as such does not find the measure of its value in history, or in what it accomplishes, does, or endures. The personality is reserved its own realm in which it communes with itself and God alone—regardless of how many or how few its talents, how great or how small its influence and success. This intimate realm is the source of willing and being, the realm in which all things are justified or damned either before the historic individual or before God. Each individual gains the most certitude through his conscience—the essence of his existence. This is a sanctuary which research cannot penetrate.

One person may understand another person well; but this is only superficial; he apprehends his deeds, speech, and gestures as separate moments, never truly, never completely. It is true, however, that one friend can believe in another friend and that in the love of the one for the other, his self is held secure through the other's image: "You must be this way, for it is so that I understand you." This is the secret of all upbringing.

Writers such as Shakespeare create the course of events based on the nature of the people they are portraying; they tailor their psychological interpretation to the event. In reality, other forces beside personality are at work here.

Things take their course despite the evil or benevolent will of the individual who carries them out.

History's continuity, its work and progress, is located in the moral forces, where every individual, poor and small, has his place and share in them.

But even the most brilliant, the strongest and most powerful of wills, is only one impulse in this movement of moral forces. It is nonetheless a distinctive and effective one in its place. Historical research perceives the individual only as such; it is not his individual person which is significant here, but his position and work as part of this or that moral force and as transmitter of the idea.

## 42

(d) *The interpretation of the ideas* fills the gap left by the psychological interpretation.

For the individual constructs his own world to the same extent to which he shares in the ethical forces of his age. And insofar as he assiduously and prosperously builds on his spot for the short duration of his life, will he have furthered the common possessions in and for which he has lived. And he will, for his part, have served the ethical forces which outlive him.

A person would not be a person without these forces. However, these will only grow and intensify through the common work between people, races, times, and in the movement of history, whose evolution and growth is their unfolding.

The ethical system of any period is only the speculative form and the recapitulation of the unfolding to that point, only an attempt to sum it up according to its theoretical content and to articulate it.

Every age is a complex manifestation of all moral forces. This is true no matter how advanced its stage of development and it is true regardless of the degree to which the higher might still be encapsulated in the lower forms, i.e., the state within the family.

### Notes

1. Greek: enlargement, growth out of itself.
2. Reference to section 32—not included in this selection—which deals with the critical methods for testing the validity and correctness of alleged facts or events which have come down to us.

# 4

# Philological Hermeneutics

===================== Philip August Boeckh =====================

PHILIP AUGUST BOECKH (1785–1867) was born in Karlsruhe where he attended the *Gymnasium* or classical high school. He went to Halle to study with Schleiermacher and with F. A. Wolf, the classical philologist and famous author of the *Prolegomena ad Homerem*. In 1809 he began teaching at Heidelberg and subsequently moved to the newly founded University of Berlin (1811), where he also served as the director of the philological and pedagogical seminar for a number of years. Boeckh made substantial contributions to classical scholarship and covered many aspects of ancient and Greek civilization from Athenian political economy to Greek philosophy (Plato and the Pythagoreans) to Athenian tragedy and the poetry of Pindar and others. The collection of his minor writings comprises seven volumes. In his approach to hermeneutics Boeckh combined the ideas of Schleiermacher with the exacting methods of classical philology taught to him by Wolf and Ast. As early as 1809 he designed a special course, entitled *Encyclopedia and Methodology of the Philological Sciences,* which was to serve as a scholarly introduction to the entire field of classical philology. This course was revised and amplified over the years by Boeckh until 1866 (two years before his death), when he offered it for the twenty-sixth time. His student, Bratuschek, produced an integral text from Boeckh's notes and from student notebooks (including his own) which appeared in 1877. A revised edition (edited by Klussmann) of the *Encyclopedia* was published in 1866. The book contains a special section, "Theory of Hermeneutics," and one entitled "Theory of Criticism." Boeckh considered hermeneutics the basis for all philological studies, and philology the universal discipline concerned with all aspects of human culture in its historical manifestations. Our selections are taken from the (partial) English translation of the *Encyclopedia* by J. Prichard (Sect. A, Bibl.).

## FORMAL THEORY OF PHILOLOGY

A formal theory of philological knowing is as superfluous as logic, the formal theory of philosophical understanding, is unnecessary. Men thought logically before logic was discovered, and understood unfamiliar thoughts without any theory of understanding—as they do every day. . . . Correct understanding, like logical thinking, is an art, and therefore rests partly on a half-unconscious preparation. And yet the many mistakes made daily in interpretation of unfamiliar thoughts teach us that special skill and talent are needed for understanding as much as for any art. Both religion and philosophy, for example, are directed like poetry entirely toward inner contemplation, and both work by a priori reasoning. Since understanding requires a directly opposite mode of thinking, it is no wonder that religious men and philosophers, like poets, have only the slightest knowledge of interpretation—especially if they subscribe to mysticism. The Orient, on account of its suppression of the understanding, has on the whole little talent for interpretation.

Understanding is essentially ability to judge, aided of necessity by imagination. It demands objectivity and receptiveness; the more subjective a man is, the less has he the gift of understanding.

For philosophy, the Neoplatonists in their exposition of Plato furnish a shining illustration how exposition can be practiced counter to all understanding. Of the New Testament there is neither beginning nor end of false exposition. And yet among its expositors are gifted, well-informed men whose understanding is wide, but not for this kind of interpretation. Celebrated philologists, too, often misunderstand their own understanding; even the best of them frequently go astray. If there is an art of understanding, it must have its theory, which must comprehend the scientific development of the laws of understanding, not merely practical rules such as are generally found in most treatments of interpretation and criticism. These rules, though good in themselves, are first clarified in theory and then better learned in their application, just as the philological art is best learned through practice. From practice the laws of the theory can be inductively derived.

The value of theory consists not in any ability it has to make a man a good exegete or critic, any more than knowledge of logic makes one a philosophical thinker, but in its capacity to bring unconscious activity to the level of consciousness. The goal toward which interpretation and criticism strive, and the point of view by which they must be guided, are much the same as that which philology practices dimly and vaguely by mere empiricism, until it is elevated by theory to scientific clarity. Theory, then, rules practical philological activity. It sharpens the vision and guards against errors by showing their causes and the boundaries of sure knowledge. Theory makes philology an art, though many philologists regard mere empirical dexterity in interpretation and criticism as art.

According to our definition of understanding, we distinguish interpretation and criticism as separate but essential elements in it. . . . The two are obviously different functions. When we assign to hermeneutics the task of understanding the subjects themselves, we surely do not imply that anything can be understood without reference to much besides. For interpretation many auxiliaries must be used. The aim of hermeneutics is to understand the essential nature of the subject.

When criticism establishes whether a manuscript reading is correct, or whether a work belongs to a specific author, decision is reached through investigating the relation of that reading to its context or the relation in which the peculiar characteristics of the work stand to the specific author. This research shows the agreement or difference of the two compared objects, and therefrom further conclusions are drawn.

Such a procedure is followed in every critical project. In order, for example, to form an opinion concerning a historical transaction, the critic investigates whether it agrees or not with the end sought from it, or with the law, etc. In aesthetic criticism of a poem, the investigation considers whether it conforms to the artistic principles of the genre to which it belongs. The task of criticism is, in fine, not to understand a subject in itself, but to discover the relation of several subjects. It will later be shown that the hermeneutic and critical functions act reciprocally.

Both interpretation and criticism are always busied with something handed down or at least communicated. This thing communicated is either a symbol of the thing known, differing from it in form, e.g., in the shape of letters, musical notation, etc.; or it is a picture agreeing in form with the object expressed in it, as in works of art or craft. Recent kinds of intellectual expression are to some extent hieroglyphics, which must be interpreted through hermeneutics and criticism in order that one may proceed from right understanding of the forms to their significance in the works of human activity, or rather to their content and meaning. This is a special aspect, still little considered.

# THEORY OF HERMENEUTICS

The term hermeneutics is derived from *hermeneia,* which obviously related to the name of the god Hermes. . . . From the original significance of Hermes, who clearly is one of the deities of earth, there developed the concept of him as the messenger of the gods, the go-between of gods and men. He makes manifest the divine thoughts, translates the infinite into the finite, the divine spirit into sensory phenomena, and therefore he denotes analysis, measure, and particularizing. The discovery of everything that becomes understood is ascribed to him, especially language and literature. The essence of *hermeneia* consists in that which the Romans called *elocutio:* the expression of thought—not the understanding, but the rendering intelligible. Consequently, *hermeneia* has long signified the rendering of one person's language intelligible to another, the work of the interpreter. As such it is not essentially different from *exegesis,* and the two words may be used as synonyms. They are concerned not so much with interpreting as with actually understanding, which becomes possible only through interpretation.

This understanding is the re-forming process of *hermeneia* as *elocutio*.

As the actions of the understanding, or the principles according to which one will understand, are everywhere the same, no specific distinction of interpretation can be made with respect to the subjects to be interpreted. Such distinctions as sacred and secular interpretation are accordingly untenable. If a sacred book is of human origin, it must be understood according to human rules in the usual treatment applied to books. If it is of divine origin, it stands on a level above all human interpretation, and can be apprehended only through divine inspiration. Obviously, every truly sacred book, like every highly gifted man's work that is the product of inspiration, may become fully intelligible only through both human and divine means at once. The human spirit, which gives shape to all ideas after its own laws, is itself of divine origin.

There is notwithstanding a special application of general interpretative principles with reference to specific areas. We have a special hermeneutics of the New Testament, of Roman law, of Homer, etc. Here belongs the branch of artistic interpretation, which has to explain works of plastic art as one explains works of literature. Archaeological interpretation is not treated here.

Since the great mass of verbal tradition is fixed through written record, the business of the philologist is with the text, in which he must gain understanding of three things:

1. The writing, the symbol of the thing signifying.
2. Language, the thing signifying.
3. The thing signified, the knowledge contained in language. The palaeographer stops with the proof of the symbol. The mere grammarian confines himself to the symbol of the thing signified, language. Only when one presses on to the thing signified, the thought, does genuine knowledge arise. We shall now presume the comprehension of the letters and shall not busy ourselves with the art of deciphering them, which, when there is no key to it, is itself an interpretation of infinite, unknown areas. Nor are we concerned with the difference between notation for oral speech and for thought, since we treat not the audible aspect of language but only the concepts bound up with the words as objects for interpretation. And though we restrict ourselves here to speech as the most general instrument of communication, the principles we arrive at must be valid for expression by other means than language.

Effective divisions of interpretation may be drawn only from the essential nature of interpretative activity. Essentially as regards understanding and its expression, interpretation is consciousness of that through which the meaning and significance of the thing communicated are conditioned and defined. Here belongs first the objective significance of the means of communication, language in its most widely significant sense. The meaning is first conditioned by the literal meaning of the words and thus can be understood only when the common expression is fully understood. But every speaker or writer employs language in a special, personal way, modifying it according to his own individuality. To understand anyone, therefore, his subjective qualities must be taken into account.

Exposition from that common, objective aspect of language, we denote by the term *grammatical* interpretation; from the subjective standpoint, *individual* interpretation.

The sense of each communication is further conditioned by the actual circumstances in which it came into being, the knowledge of which is presumed in those to whom it was addressed. To understand it, one must transplant himself into these circumstances. A book derives its true significance first from ideas current at the time when it was written. This exposition from the aspect of its actual milieu we call *historical* interpretation. This is not what one usually means by explanation of the subject, i.e., an amassing of historical notes; these can be dispensed with for understanding the work, for exegesis needs to supply only as much as conditions this understanding. Historical interpretation, in this sense closely allied to grammatical interpretation, investigates how the literal meaning of the words is modified through objective conditions.

The individual aspect of the communication is moreover modified through the subjective conditions under whose influence it was composed, which determine the purpose and direction of the work. In communication goals exist that are common to many writers. Out of these arise well-defined species of communication, the literary genres. The characteristics of poetry and prose, and of their varieties, lie in the subjective aim and goal of the literary performance. Under these general differences are classed the individual aims of the several authors, which constitute varieties in the genres. The goal is the ideal, higher unity of the communication; this, established as a norm, is the standard of art and as such is always imprinted in a particular form or genre. Exegesis of the work of art from this aspect is best named *generic* interpretation. It is as closely related to individual interpretation as historical interpretation is to grammatical.

The following outline indicates that in these four kinds of interpretation all requirements for understanding are comprehended; the list is complete. Interpretation is:

I. Understanding from the objective conditions of the thing communicated:
   a. from the literal meaning of the words—*grammatical interpretation;*
   b. from the meaning of the words in reference to the material relations and context of the work—*historical interpretation.*
II. Understanding from the subjective conditions of the thing communicated:
   a. from the subject itself—*individual interpretation;*
   b. from the subject in reference to subjective relations which lie in the aim and direction of the work—*generic interpretation.*

How are these different kinds of interpretation interrelated? We have made our analysis on the basis of the concept given above; in practice, the kinds constantly intermingle. Without individual interpretation the literal meaning is unintelligible, for each word spoken by anyone is drawn from the common vocabulary but invested with an additional, peculiar meaning. To obtain this latter meaning, one must know the individuality of the speaker. Likewise the general sense of words is modified by their actual relations in discourse and by the kinds of discourse. To interpret these modifications, one needs historical and generic interpretation, the bases of which are in turn to be found only through grammatical interpretation, from which all interpretation starts.

We have here a circle of reasoning that points backward to the aforementioned problem, in which the formal and material functions in philology were mutually dependent. For example, grammatical interpretation requires knowledge of the historical development of grammar; historical interpretation is impossible without special knowledge of general history; individual interpretation requires knowledge of matters pertaining to individual man; and generic interpretation rests upon historical knowledge. In fine, the various kinds of interpretation presume substantial amounts of factual knowledge, and yet these different bodies of knowledge become known first through interpretation of all the sources. This circle can, however, be broken in the following way. Grammatical interpretation provides the literal meaning of the word, treats it under various conditions, and relates it to the language as a whole. The history of language is established; grammars and lexica are made, which in turn serve grammatical interpretation and are themselves perfected with the progressing interpretative activity. This work provides a basis for the other sorts of interpretation and at the same time for constituting the material disciplines. The further these disciplines are developed, the more nearly complete becomes the interpretation.

For instance, New Testament interpretation must lag behind interpretation of the Greek classics because its grammar, stylistic theory, and historical conditioning forces are far less perfectly known. The grammatical usage of Attic writers is far more accurately formulated than is the grammar of New Testament discourse, which is the product of a bad mixture of Greek and oriental usage, an inferior jargon. The New Testament writers, moreover, were unlettered men, with no concept of such highly developed art as is found in Attic writing. To understand their way of writing, one must become familiar with the religious enthusiasm and oriental warmth of their ideas. A mythical darkness also cloaks the circumstances in which these works came into being.

As another example, for the classical period in Greece lyric poetical form is the least known, and consequently interpretation of the lyrics is especially difficult. The style of the poet is to be discovered through interpretation from his works themselves, and yet the interpretation depends in its most significant points upon the concept which one has derived from his literary style. To shun the *petitio principii* here requires particular skill.

The fact that while the kinds of interpretation always co-operate, they are not always equally applicable, lightens the task of interpretation. Grammatical interpretation applies at its maximum where individual interpretation is at its minimum. Writers like Cicero, who expresses the general spirit and usage of his time, are above all to be grammatically interpreted—a characteristic which simplifies the exposition. The more original, on the other hand, a writer is, the more subjective his views and his linguistic expression, the greater is the preponderance of individual interpretation. For this reason Tacitus is harder to interpret than Cicero. Entire literary types differ in like manner. The more objective the presentation, the more does the task devolve upon grammatical interpretation. In epic and history, one must abandon extensively not only individual, but also historical interpretation when the subjective quality of the author does not relieve the need. In like manner, the most complicated interpretation occurs in prose in such works as private letters, in poetry in the lyric.

The circle which embraces the interpretative task cannot be resolved in all cases, and can never be resolved completely. From this fact come the limits which are placed upon interpretation. First, it is obviously impossible to establish the meaning of an expression or a trope through comparison with other instances of its use if it appears nowhere else. When precisely the same specimen is at once the sole basis for grammatical and individual interpretation, or for individual and generic, or for historical and generic, the problem is insoluble. Besides this, every single utterance is conditioned by an infinite number of circumstances, and it is therefore impossible to bring to clear communication. Gorgias stated in his work on nature, in which he declares that nobody thinks like another man, that the speaker and his auditor do not have the same idea; and not even the individual views a subject always in the same light, for which reason he fails to understand himself completely. Thus the task of interpretation is to reach as close an approximation as possible by gradual, step-by-step progression; it cannot hope to reach the limit.

In certain instances complete understanding is reached in response to a feeling, and the interpreter will approach completeness accordingly as he becomes more in possession of such a feeling. It can cut the Gordian knot of uncertainty, but can proceed no further. Thanks to this feeling, he re-cognizes what another has previously known; without it, there could exist no capacity for communication. Though individuals of course differ, they yet correspond in many respects. One can, therefore, understand an alien individuality to a certain degree through reasoned calculation; but in many utterances one can apprehend completely through vivifying contemplation what is intuitively conveyed to him. To the above-quoted statement by Gorgias another stands opposed: like knows like. This is the only means through which understanding becomes possible; kindred spirits are requisite. He who thus practices exposition can alone be termed a kindred interpreter, for the intuition which proceeds from the interpreter's identification with the work to be interpreted brings out what lies within. Here imagination takes the place of understanding as hermeneutic activity.

Hence it also comes to pass that, aside from quality of training, not everyone can be equally good as an expositor; and above all an original talent belongs to interpretation. What Ruhnken says of the critic—*Criticus non fit, sed nascitur* ("the critic is born, not made")—is valid also for interpretation: *interpres non fit, sed nascitur.* This means that one can generally acquire no knowledge, but can only develop and discipline what is innate in him. Character is shaped through discipline; through speculation the penetration is sharpened; but clearly character itself must first be present. Some naturally have penetration into understanding, and conversely many expositions are fundamentally perverted, because man can be born to misunderstanding as well as to understanding.

Interpretative talent is not developed by mechanical practice of hermeneutical precepts; these must rather, after they become vividly alive through actual interpreting, become so familiar through practice that one unconsciously observes them. They must at the same time combine to form a conscious theory, which alone guarantees the trustworthiness of the clarifying interpretation. In genuine interpreters, this theory is itself elevated into intuition; and so arises correct taste, which guards against sophistical, strained interpretations.

The author composes according to the laws of grammar and style, but is as a rule unconscious of them. The interpreter, however, cannot fully explain without consciousness of these laws. The man who understands must reflect on the work; the author brings it into being, and reflects upon his work only when he becomes as it were an expositor of it. The interpreter consequently understands the author better than the author understands himself.

The interpreter must bring to clear awareness what the author has unconsciously created, and in so doing many things will be opened to him, many windows will be unlocked which have been closed to the author himself. But though he must come to know what lies objectively in the work alien to the author's awareness of it, the interpreter must keep it separate from the author's subjective knowledge of the work. If he does not so separate them, he follows the practice of the allegorical interpretation in Plato, of ancient exposition of Homer, and of the New Testament. The result is quantitative error; he understands too much. This is as faulty as its opposite, quantitative lack of understanding, which occurs when the sense of the author is not fully understood.

One can also misunderstand qualitatively, which occurs when something other is understood than the author had in mind and is put in its place. This takes place especially in allegorical interpretation, as in incorrect interpretation of an allegory already there.

Here we draw nearer to allegorical interpretation, which many view as a separate kind. The Middle Ages derived from Alexandrian philosophy and theology the controlling view that a fourfold sense could be distinguished in literature: literal, allegorical, moral, and anagogical or mystical. Here are four sorts of interpretation, which may be reduced to two: literal interpretation on the one

hand, and on the other the remaining three, which are all allegorical, i.e., showing a sense different from the literal. Moral and anagogical interpretation are only
subdivisions of the allegorical. The sense which is substituted for the literal is
moral when, as in a parable or fable, one finds a moral idea in the actual picture
presented. In anagogical signification the allegorical meaning is on the speculative level; for example, a concept in a fable is comprehended supersensually: it
is elevated from the aesthetic to the noetic. The literal interpretation can also
signify an ideal picture or a sensory object, for which allegorical interpretation
substitutes another sensory object. Such an allegory may be called simple or
historical.

Allegory has by its very nature extended application for it is a kind of representation founded deep in the nature of speech and thought. Myths, as sensory symbols of the suprasensible, must first be allegorically explained, for they include
another than the meaning expressed in the words. Accordingly it is justifiable to
interpret Holy Writ allegorically, for its basic principle is that of myth; only it
is a debatable question to what extent its writers were conscious of its allegorical
sense. All classical poetry is full of myth, and art as a whole generally proceeds
symbolically, so that all branches of ancient art require allegorical interpretation.
All epic is mythical narrative; the ancients have therefore already interpreted
Homer allegorically. Here, however, this kind of interpretation goes beyond the
poet's meaning; he knows nothing of the myth's primitive meaning. The expositor
must carefully distinguish where he interprets Homer and where the myth itself.
Quite otherwise is the case with Dante; in the *Divina Commedia* he uses the myth
throughout with full awareness. Allegorical interpretation is quite at home with
him; we have from his own words in his remarkable *Convivio* authentic allegorical expositions. It contains a philosophy of love like that in Plato's *Symposium.*
He explains there how every work can be understood in a fourfold sense, and how
he himself in his own poems had always in view the other, higher kinds besides
the literal. So Beatrice, for example, in the *Divina Commedia* is at the same time
an allegorical representation of the highest science, speculative theology. In
Dante's allegories there is a noble, exalted aspiration, which was in keeping with
the spirit of his time, yet in many peculiar and wondrous concepts also draws to
itself the weaknesses of that time.

In lyric poetry, there is the most conscious employment of allegory. In Pindar,
allegory appears only in a specific sense, as application of the myth or history
which he treats to the circumstances of his contemporaries whom he celebrates
in his idea. He uses myths not for their own sake; they are means of setting in
an ideal light something actual and nonmythical. They are idealized pictures of
human life, and consequently may have a moral thought as their meaning. Although in many lyric forms no consciously intentional allegory has a place, yet
all forms have the symbolic character peculiar to the art as a whole. In all of them
the problem is to understand the thought, which reveals itself even in the slightest

play of imagination. Here, indeed, the understanding is transmitted chiefly through a delicate intuitive feeling.

The most difficult allegorical interpretation occurs in drama. Drama is essentially the presentation of an action, but the kernel of the action, its soul, is the thought which is made evident through it. The symbolic character is especially evident in plays like the *Prometheus* of Aeschylus; but in all tragedies a general, governing idea hovered before the eyes of the ancient poet. This symbolic quality in Sophocles is most deeply imprinted in the *Antigone,* where the ethical idea is vividly embodied in the *dramatis personae* that moderation is best and that even in righteous activity no one may be overweening or give way to passion.

Comedy expresses not merely a general, but often a particularized, thought, referring to events and circumstances of the times. Of this second sort is Aristophanes. He is symbolic through and through, as the names of his choruses indicate: wasps, clouds, frogs, etc. *The Birds* contains a thoroughgoing allegory: the founding of the state of the birds satirizes the Athenian political situation at the time of the Sicilian enterprise. This comedy is an example of historical allegory, as *Antigone* exemplifies the moral sort, and *Prometheus* the speculative.

In prose, too, allegorical interpretation is applicable, so far as the mythical element reaches, for instance in religious prose and in philosophy. The myths of Plato must be allegorically explained. On account of their artistic structure, it is necessary on the one hand to explain the philosophical thought in them, and on the other to investigate whence the picture is derived and how its form and essence are conditioned. In *Phaedrus,* for example, they derive from the concept of the universe held by Philolaus. But Plato has clothed his thoughts in allegorical garb not merely in his myths, and allegorical interpretation is not to be denied him. In all the realms of prose allegorical parts are found.

The criterion for the applicability of allegorical interpretation can obviously lie only in the decision whether the literal meaning does not suffice for understanding. It becomes necessary when the grammatical interpretation gives a sense not consonant with the situations imparted through individual, historical, and generic interpretation. When, for example, the literal sense of a Pindaric ode fails to correspond to its purpose and to the historical references that lie at its base, one is obliged to go beyond its literal meaning. The allegorical sense will always have that metaphorical significance of the literal words which corresponds equally to the character of the language and to the other conditions. In order then to ascertain the proper metaphorical meaning, it is necessary to choose that one among the several possible meanings which the spirit of the whole work and the relations of all its parts require. This can be found only through individual and generic interpretation; at the same time historical interpretation brings the actual conditions under consideration. The allegorical sense must not be sought beyond the point of the motivation, and it is not at all easy to keep within the proper bounds. In a pedantic writer, generally speaking, the allegory must be sought in details only. In a truly classical work it will be always on a grand scale. Playful or meticulous interpretation is allowable only in the case of a playful or meticulous writer.

If one fails to recognize an expressed allegory, he has made a quantitative error, since he has understood too little though he may have understood the rest correctly. Thus in a relief or a painting it is possible to understand all the separate parts and the significance of the whole without learning its allegorical meaning. If one understands an allegory where none is intended, he has also made a quantitative error, which is, however, qualitative as well; for he has read a false meaning into it. While allegory is a particular and very important kind of representation, understanding it is by no means a separate kind of interpretation. It consists rather, like every other work, in the co-operation of the four kinds of hermeneutic activity: grammatical, historical, individual, and generic.

# THEORY OF CRITICISM

Criticism is, according to our definition given above, that philological performance through which an object becomes understood not by itself nor for its own sake, but for the establishment of a relation and a reference to something else, so that the recognition of this relation is itself the end in view. This performance is signified in the name criticism. The basic meaning of *krinein* is analysis and separation; every analysis and separation is, moreover, determination of definite relation between two objects. The expression of such a relation is a judgment; to judge signifies also to separate and is a synonym of passing sentence.

For the concept of criticism the kind of judgment that is passed is quite immaterial. However, the unbounded possible scope of judgments is limited by the goal of critical activity. It can concern itself only with understanding the relation of what is communicated to its conditioning circumstances. Since interpretation explains the communication itself out of these conditioning circumstances, criticism must subdivide into the same classes into which interpretation is divided. There are accordingly grammatical, historical, individual, and generic criticism, and these four kinds of critical activity must naturally be internally connected just like the corresponding interpretative performances. As what is communicated arises from the conditioning circumstances of the communication, these are its measure. What is communicated may conform to its conditioning circumstance or not, that is, it may conform to the measuring principle inherent in them or it may deviate from that principle. If also a communication is handed down through tradition, as in the ancient authors, criticism has to investigate its relation to this tradition. What is communicated can be dimmed through destructive natural influences or through error and oversight of the transmitters, or it can be deliberately changed by them. It is therefore necessary to establish whether the form of the work before us agrees with the original or deviates from it.

Criticism has consequently a threefold task. First, it must investigate whether a literary work, or its parts, are in keeping with the grammatical, literal sense of the language, with its historical basis, with the individuality of the author, and with the characteristics of its genre. In order not to follow a merely negative course, it must secondly establish, when something seems not in keeping, how it may be made more conformable. Thirdly, it has to investigate whether the form handed down is original or not. It will be seen that with this all specifically critical efforts are exhausted. I shall demonstrate this fact through detailed development of the theory which runs parallel to the statement of interpretation that is my personal theory. I shall first, however, present several general remarks about the value of criticism, the critical talent, the levels of critical truth, and the relation of criticism to interpretation.

The essence of criticism is not the tracking of all possible meanings. It must, to be sure, ponder which forms of a document may be possible under the given terms, but it does so only to select from these possibilities what is effective and appropriate. In this, then, lies its value. When it falls foul of all tradition, criticism is a destructively annihilating force. But it negates only error, and since error is denial of truth, in this negation it works positively. If one were to remove criticism and permit erroneous tradition to survive unchallenged, both knowledge and life, in so far as they rest upon historical footing, would soon fall into extreme error, as they did in the Middle Ages, which were hampered most of all by lack of criticism. Without criticism, all historical truth founders. Furthermore, critical activity disciplines through discovery of what is out of keeping with the subject. Thereby, it destroys all hollow phantasy and chimera in relation to historical data. At the same time it works effectually upon one's own development when it becomes self-criticism.

For every science it is the balance of truth which weighs the import of the basic data, teaches discernment between the probable and the merely plausible, the true and the untrue, the merely subtle and the intuitively evident. If there were more criticism in the world, the literary granaries would not be filled with chaff instead of wheat, chaff served by uncritical minds, which very frequently carries the name of criticism; nothing is less truly critical than the disgraceful conjectures of many so-called critics.

It has been wisely said that every genuine scholar in a science must be *ipso facto* a critic. Since critical examination and comparison together establish correctness in the tradition, they refer all scientific progress as it advances to the ideal of knowledge; thus they become on this positive side a necessary instrument of all scientific investigation; they form judgment and taste.

One should not, however, over-value criticism as the characteristic task of philology. It was once thought that the salvation of the world lay in investigating syllables and punctuating words; and with that vanity which is often characteristic of the philologists this grammatical labor was described as the peak of all knowledge, so that it was called *diva critica* ("the goddess criticism"). A rare divinity indeed! Many a man might with Faust in such a case become fearful of his godlikeness. It was a biased, false criticism which became thus over-valued; true criticism keeps on guard against excessive self-esteem. Overweening criticism can only act destructively, since it rejects the self-effacing exposition which is the only sure basis of judgment.

Genuine criticism is unassuming, and its beneficial effects are unpretentious, because it produces no creations of its own. Its value is shown only in the devastation which enters as soon as it is absent. When an age is hostile to criticism, because it is viewed as either pedantic or destructive, either false criticism prevails or true criticism is unrecognized. There must always be a counterweight to criticism to keep it from curtailing productivity and weakening the power of the idea. It has been well said: "Criticism is a very cunning guide, always negative; like the *daimon* of Socrates, it halts you, but does not make you proceed."

Few men practice genuine criticism; it belongs to a higher endowment than does interpretation. If it is to reproduce the original or what is in conformity to that, it demands more spontaneity than does interpretation, in which the subject's contribution predominates. This ratio varies, however, when one takes into consideration the corresponding kinds of both activities. Individual interpretation, for instance, possesses far more spontaneity than criticism of words, but less than belongs to individual criticism.

The nature of the critic's talent parallels the problems which the critic has to solve. In order to distinguish the inappropriate from the appropriate in the tradition, he must unite objectivity with delicate judgment. Acuteness and sagacity are requisite for the restoration of the original, but in addition the critic, as Bentley demands in the preface to his edition of Horace, must have a suspicious mind (*animus suspicax*) to prevent his accepting as appropriate and genuine whatever is presented. Finally, for all three tasks of criticism the greatest exactness is requisite. Specious critical talent consists in subtlety and impertinence; it substitutes for the demands of the subject its own subjective concepts and starts to criticize without entering interpretatively into understanding.

One must never suppose that the critic has the power to solve his problem with his understanding alone, or that the critical talent consists merely in a higher level of acuteness, a gift of discrimination. Obviously, criticism shares in the logical circle which arises in the interpretative task: the single part must be judged on the basis of the including whole, and this whole in turn on the basis of the single part. The final decision must here lie for criticism in the immediate awareness which arises from an incorruptible sense for historical truth. To bring this awareness to its inner strength and clarity must be the critic's highest ambition. It is developed into an artistic driving force, which intuitively hits the target. This power, however, is the product of great interpretative practice.

The true critic will accordingly be always a good interpreter. The reverse is not always the case. As there are many grammatical interpreters who comprehend nothing of individual interpretation, many interpreters likewise know nothing about criticism. This lack occurs especially in expositors of factual knowledge, whom their material at times so overwhelms that they forget judgment, the sifting process. An uncritical interpreter can accomplish nothing with a work until a good critic has blazed the trail for him. As a rule, however, exceptional interpretative talent is also critical.

The true divining power of criticism lies only in its inner union with the interpretative sense; it becomes capable of divination when by means of its creative imaginative power is supplies what is lacking in the tradition. That is generative criticism; it wells up from its own power, not from the page. It arises in varying form: in some it shows clarity and cheer; in others it is obscure, deep, but supremely excellent in its inner quality. This difference lies not merely in the performance, but in the sort of critical perception of the idea itself. This divining power must always be united with a wise prudence. His suspicious mind easily leads the critic astray, unless it is restrained through an objective point of view. One can in general assert that of one hundred conjectures made by critics, not five are correct. The best critic is swift to conjecture but slow to express judgment.

Criticism, in union with interpretation, should impart historical truth. Historical truth is based upon the same logical conditions as truth in general, specifically: (1) on the correctness of the premises; (2) on the correctness of the procedure toward the conclusion. The premises may be immediately recognized as true, like the mathematical principles or indeed all such clear, simple intuitions of the human intellect; or they may be recognized only through inference from other true principles which need no further special attention. In so far now as a critical-exegetical assertion rests upon immediately certain or surely proved premises, and in so far as the conclusion based on these premises is correct, we have discovered the actual historical truth.

Akin to the truth are the plausible (*verisimile*), the presumable (*probabile*), and the credible. These are demonstrable levels of truth. We call plausible that which approximates the whole truth without being thoroughly proved to be true. We call presumable that which agrees with other truths without being itself confirmed. We call credible that which agrees with our ideas without objective proof of its truth. All this depends on following inferential statements from the premises; for if the conclusion is false, one cannot speak of any level of scientific truth at all. The essence of the credible lies, to be sure, in the uncertainty of the premises to an otherwise certain conclusion. Since its premises rest upon and agree only with our presumption, but are otherwise unproven ideas, all that is logically concluded from them is merely possible.

In the case of the plausible, the premises are objectively capable of demonstration. The essence of truth lies in the fact that if one thing exists, the other is necessary; the essence of the plausible, however, depends on the fact that if the one thing exists, the other is not indeed necessary but possibly and indeed usually is so. The level of probability is arranged, therefore, according to the completeness of the induction upon which one or both premises of the conclusion are based. But since in actual experience no such induction can be complete, interpretation and criticism cannot attain to the full degree of truth unless the premises are immediately certain.

The presumable is obviously only a lower level of the plausible. The measuring scale for the certainty of the premises is of course very subjective and depends heavily upon the level of one's intuitive capability. One who is steeped in the lore of the past looks upon something as immediately certain which to another is thoroughly uncertain. Yet the greater knowledge conceals a danger of error if the person making the decision thinks he has in his view a complete induction. Anyone whose areas of knowledge are incomplete, that is, anyone who lacks adequate perception of antiquity, overlooks innumerable relations, and can believe his premises to be true, nearly true, or in harmony with the truth, whereas they are directly opposed to it.

No fruitful critical or exegetical undertaking is to be thought of without a basis on the greatest possible fullness of observation of the past. The scope of these observations lies in one's erudition, their depth in one's native talent; premises are to be validated only according to the measure of these two. The credible, as it merely agrees with one's idea, is therefore a doubtful and almost entirely useless category. What is credible to one man, who has fullness of learning and natural talent, the unlearned and dull man finds incredible; and what is credible to the latter, the former frequently sees as quite impossible.

The levels of certainty are extremely subjective not only by reason of their premises, but frequently also by reason of demonstration. By the term "form of demonstration" I understand here not the general logical meaning. Philological demonstration has a form which is not given through ordinary logic alone. No one can demand that a man write in syllogisms. Leibnitz, who often expressed his teaching syllogistically in appendices, says: "Just as it is improper to be always making verses, so also it is improper always to fling about syllogisms." It is a question of the correct dialectic method, for dialectic is possible with or without syllogisms; it is possible without syllogisms, in so far as the deduction may be abbreviated without any incorrectness resulting from the brief statement. It is enough that the conclusion stand up under the test of syllogistic form.

An investigator of greater mental acuteness may find finer distinctions in the same object than those seen by another; he is in a position to bring to even greater certainty what the other may have presented as only plausible. He defines more exactly through more accurate analyses and draws conclusions through synthesis of these which the other has been unable to draw. This is philological critical dialectic. Fruitful synthesis allows the premises to be brought into such a position and union that more emerges from them than one usually sees. But the greatest acuteness falls into error if certainty of perception deserts it; the most acute investigations become a web of mistakes if the premises are false. One must accordingly be more on his guard against nothing than against a vain acuteness and against merely subjective decisions. As far as in him lies, he must seek to arrive at a sort of mathematical objectivity; and however much active synthesis is required, holding to this objectivity he must never abandon clear vision, at which as alpha and omega everything culminates.

Paramount for criticism is the synthesis of every fragment where the whole must be made up of individual pieces. Here a high level of attentiveness is requisite, and often, as one fails to hold fast to this level, as he does at times in uninteresting matters, a successful outcome is attainable only step by step.

Historical truth is ascertained through co-operation of interpretation and criticism. We must accordingly investigate more closely how this co-operation proceeds. Interpretation always culminates, as we have seen, in the observation of contradictions and relations; but it considers them only in order to understand the separate situations in themselves. On the contrary, criticism must everywhere presuppose the interpretative activity, the explanation of separate items, in order to proceed thence to solve its specific problem, which is to comprehend into an inclusive whole the relation of these details. One cannot judge without understanding the thing in itself; criticism accordingly presupposes the interpretative problem to have been solved. Frequently, however, it is impossible to understand the subject to be interpreted without first having reached a decision about its nature; interpretation accordingly presupposes the solution of the critical problem. From this arises again a circle in reasoning, which limits our activity for each difficult interpretative or critical problem and can be solved only through approximation. Since in these circumstances one must continually pass from the one to the other, in practice criticism and interpretation cannot be separated. Neither of them can precede the other in time. But for the expression of what is comprehended this combination can be preserved only when clarity does not suffer from it. For difficult and extensive problems the critical notes must be separated from the interpretative commentary.

In the great circle of reasoning which the relation of interpretation to criticism presents, there lie then new and ever new circles, since every kind of interpretation and criticism presupposes the completion of all the other interpretative and critical problems. We shall consider this situation through more precise inspection of the four kinds of critical activity, to which we now turn.

# 5

# The Hermeneutics
# of the Human Sciences

=================================== Wilhelm Dilthey ===================================

WILHELM DILTHEY (1833–1911) was born at Biebrich in the Rhineland (near the city of Mainz) into the family of a Protestant minister of the Reformed Evangelical church. After having attended the *Gymnasium* (classical high school) in Wiesbaden, he studied theology first at Heidelberg but, like so many of the nineteenth-century German intellectuals, changed over to philosophy. Dilthey received his doctorate in that discipline in Berlin in 1864. Subsequently, he taught at Basel as a colleague of Jakob Burckhardt, at Kiel and at Breslau, and finally in Berlin (1882) where he remained until his death. Dilthey's interests and writings ranged over a multitude of subjects from practically all areas of the humanities and social sciences. Since he conceived of these as fundamentally interpretive disciplines, practically all of his writings are of interest to the student of hermeneutics. His hermeneutics proper derived inspiration from several sources: Schleiermacher's *Hermeneutik*, the approaches to history developed by the nineteenth-century German historical school (Savigny, Raumer, Niebuhr, Welcker, among others), and the desire to develop a sound methodological basis for the humanities and human sciences at large, which was necessitated by the rise of the natural sciences. His contribution to twentieth-century hermeneutics is twofold. Through his interpretation of Schleiermacher and the hermeneutic tradition, he has largely determined the way Schleiermacher and the task of hermeneutics itself were viewed for many decades. Of greater significance for twentieth-century hermeneutics are his pioneering contributions toward a new foundation of the theory and methodology of the human sciences. In his later studies, intended as a comprehensive *Critique of Historical Reason,* he advanced a new type of analysis of the processes of understanding and explication, an analysis which Heidegger would take up again and radicalize in *Being and Time.* The selections are taken from studies and drafts which Dilthey produced during the last decades of his life and which were published for the first time in volume 7 of his collected works in 1926. They document how, according to Dilthey, the formal methods of interpretation in the human and social sciences are derived from those ordinary forms of understanding that are characteristic of human life and social interaction.

# AWARENESS, REALITY: TIME

## From "Draft for a Critique of Historical Reason"

I am presupposing what I have said before about life and lived experience. We must now demonstrate the reality of what is apprehended in such experience: as we are concerned here with the objective value of the categories of the mind-constructed world which emerge from experience, I shall first indicate the sense in which the term "category" is to be used. The predicates which we attribute to objects contain forms of apprehension. The concepts which designate such forms I call categories. Each form contains one rule of the relationship. The categories are systematically related to each other and the highest categories represent the highest points of view for apprehending reality. Each category designates its own universe of predications. The formal categories are forms of all factual assertions. Among the real categories there are those which originate in the apprehension of the mind-constructed world even though they are then transferred to apply to the whole of reality. General predicates about a particular individual's pattern of lived experience arise in that experience. Once they are applied to the understanding of the objectifications of life and all the subjects dealt with by the human studies the range of their validity is increased until it becomes clear that the life of the mind can be characterized in terms of systems of interactions, power, value, etc. Thus these general predicates achieve the dignity of categories of the mind-constructed world.

The categorial characterization of life is temporality which forms the basis for all the others. The expression "passsage of life" indicates this already. Time is there for us through the synthesizing unity of consciousness. Life, and the outer objects cropping up in it share the conditions of simultaneity, sequence, interval, duration and change. The mathematical sciences derived from them the abstract relationships on which Kant based his doctrine of the phenomenal nature of time.

This framework of relationships embraces, but does not exhaust, the lived experience of time[1] through which the concept of time receives its ultimate meaning. Here time is experienced as the restless progression, in which the present constantly becomes the past and the future the present. The present is the filling of a moment of time with reality; it is experience, in contrast to memory or ideas of the future occurring in wishes, expectations, hopes, fears and strivings. This filling with reality constantly exists while the content of experience constantly changes. Ideas, through which we know the past and the future, exist only for those who are alive in the present. The present is always there and nothing exists except what emerges in it. The ship of our life is, as it were, carried forward on a constantly moving stream, and the present is always wherever we are on these waves—suffering, remembering or hoping, in short, living in the fullness of our reality. But we constantly sail along this stream and the moment the future becomes the present it is already sinking into the past. So the parts of filled time are not only qualitatively different from each other but, quite apart from their content, have a different character according to whether we look from the present back to the past or forward to the future. Looking back we have a series of memory pictures graded according to their value for our consciousness and feelings: like a row of houses or trees receding into the distance and becoming smaller the line of memories becomes fainter until the images are lost in the darkness of the horizon. And the more links, such as moods, outer events, means and goals, there are between the filled present and a moment of the future the greater is the number of possible outcomes, the more indefinite and nebulous the picture of the future becomes. When we look back at the past we are passive; it cannot be changed; in vain does the man already determined by it batter it with dreams of how it could have been different. In our attitude to the future we are active and free. Here the category of reality which emerges from the present is joined by that of possibility. We feel that we have infinite possibilities. Thus the experience of time in all its dimensions determines the content of our lives. This is why the doctrine that time is merely ideal is meaningless in the human studies. We recollect past events because of time and temporality; we turn, demanding, active and free, towards the future. We despair of the inevitable, strive, work and plan for the future, mature and develop in the course of time. All this makes up life, but, according to the doctrine of the ideality of time, it is based on a shadowy realm of timelessness, something which is not experienced. But it is in the life actually lived that the reality known in the human studies lies.

The antinomies which thought discovers in the lived experience of time spring from its cognitive impenetrability. Even the smallest part of temporal progress involves the passing of time. There never *is* a present: what we experience as present always contains memory of what has just been present. In other cases the past has a direct affect on, and meaning for, the present and this gives to memories a peculiar character of being present through which they become included in the present. Whatever presents itself as a unit in the flow of time because it has a unitary meaning, is the smallest unit which can be called a lived experience. Any more comprehensive unit which is made up of parts of a life, linked by a common meaning, is also called an experience, even where the parts are separated by interrupting events.

Experience is a temporal flow in which every state changes before it is clearly objectified because the subsequent moment always builds on the previous one and each is past before it is grasped. It then appears as a memory which is free to expand. But observation destroys the experience. So there is nothing more peculiar than the form of composition which we know as a part of a life: the only thing that remains invariable is that the structural relationship is its form.

We can try to envisage the flow of life in terms of the changing environment or see it, with Heracleitus, as seeming, but not being, the same, as seeming both many and one. But, however much we try—by some special effort—to experience the flow and strengthen our awareness of it, we are subject to the law of life itself according to which every observed moment of life is a remembered moment and not a flow; *it is fixed by attention which arrests what is essentially flow.* So we cannot grasp the essence of this life. What the youth of Sais unveils is form and not life.[2] We must be aware of this if we are to grasp the categories which emerge in life itself.

Because of this characteristic of real time, temporal succession cannot, strictly speaking, be experienced. The recalling of the past replaces immediate experience. When we want to observe time the very observation destroys it because it fixes our attention; it halts the flow and stays what is in the process of becoming. We experience changes of what has just been and the fact that these changes have occurred. But we do not experience the flow itself. We experience persistence when we return to what we have just seen or heard and find it still there. We experience change when particular qualities of the composite whole have been replaced. The same applies when we look into ourselves, become aware of the self which experiences duration and change, and observe our inner life.

Life consists of parts, of lived experiences which are inwardly related to each other. Every particular experience refers to a self of which it is a part; it is structurally interrelated to other parts. Everything which pertains to mind is interrelated: interconnectedness is, therefore, a category originating from life. We apprehend connectedness through the unity of consciousness which is the condition on all apprehension. However, connectedness clearly does not follow from the fact of a manifold of experiences being presented to a unitary consciousness. Only because life is itself a structural connection of experiences—i.e. experienceable relations—is the connectedness of life given. This connectedness is apprehended in terms of a more comprehensive category which is a form of judgment about all reality—the relation between whole and part.

The life of the mind is based on the physical and represents the highest evolutionary stage on earth. Science, by discovering the laws of physical phenomena, unravels the conditions under which mind occurs. Among observable bodies we find that of man: experience is related to man in a way which cannot be further explained. But with experience we step from the world of physical phenomena into the realm of mental reality. This is the subject-matter of the human studies on which we must reflect: the value of knowledge in them is quite independent of the study of their physical conditions.

Knowledge of the mind-constructed world originates from the interaction between lived experience, understanding of other people, the historical comprehension of communities as the subject of historical activity and insight into objective mind.[3] All this ultimately presupposes experience, so we must ask what it can achieve.

Experience includes elementary acts of thought. I have described this as its intellectuality. These acts occur when consciousness is intensified. A change in a state of mind thus becomes conscious of itself. We grasp an isolated aspect of what changes. Experience is followed by judgments about what has been experienced in which this becomes objectified. It is hardly necessary to describe how our knowledge of every mental fact derives entirely from experience. We cannot recognize in another person a feeling we have not experienced. But for the development of the human studies it is decisive that we attribute general predicates, derived from experience and providing the point of departure for the categories of the human studies, to the subject who contains the possibilities of experience in the confines of his body. The formal categories spring, as we saw, from the elementary acts of thought. They are concepts which stand for what becomes comprehensible through these acts of thought. Such concepts are unity, multiplicity, identity, difference, grade and relation. They are attributes of the whole of reality.

## Notes

1. [Editor's note] *Erlebnis der Zeit*. Throughout this selection Dilthey uses the terms *erleben, Erlebnis, das Erleben*.
2. [Translator's note] Sais is the name of an ancient Egyptian city. The reference is to a poem by Schiller about a youth there who unveiled the statue of truth.
3. See p. 164 n. 3.

# THE UNDERSTANDING OF OTHER PERSONS AND THEIR LIFE-EXPRESSIONS

Understanding and interpretation is the method used throughout the human sciences. It unites all their functions and contains all their truths. At each instance understanding opens up a world.

Understanding of other people and their life-expressions is developed on the basis of experience (*Erlebnis*) and self-understanding and the constant interaction between them. Here, too, it is not a matter of logical construction or psychological dissection but of an epistemological analysis. We must now establish what understanding can contribute to historical knowledge.

## (1) *Life-Expressions*

What is given always consists of life-expressions. Occurring in the world of the senses they are manifestations of mental content which they enable us to know. By "life-expressions" I mean not only expressions which intend something or seek to signify something but also those which make a mental content intelligible for us without having that purpose.

The mode and accomplishment of the understanding differs according to the various classes of life-expressions.

Concepts, judgments and larger thought-structures form the first of these classes. As constituent parts of knowledge, separated from the experience in which they occurred, what they have in common is conformity to logic. They retain their identity, therefore, independently of their position in the context of thought. Judgment asserts the validity of a thought independently of the varied situations in which it occurs, the difference of time and people involved. This is the meaning of the law of identity. Thus the judgment is the same for the man who makes it and the one who understands it; it passes, as if transported, from the speaker to the one who understands it. This determines how we understand any logically perfect system of thought. Understanding, focusing entirely on the content which remains identical in every context, is, here, more complete than in relation to any other life-expression. At the same time such an expression does not reveal to the one who understands it anything about its relation to the obscure and rich life of the mind. There is no hint of the particular life from which it arose; it follows from its nature that it does not require us to go back to its psychological context.

Actions form another class of life-expressions. An action does not spring from the intention to communicate; however, the purpose to which it is related is contained in it. There is a regular relation between an action and some mental content which allows us to make probable inferences. But it is necessary to distinguish the state of mind which produced the action by which it is expressed from the circumstances of life by which it is conditioned. Action, through the power of a decisive motive, steps from the plenitude of life into one-sidedness. However much it may have been considered it expresses only a part of our nature. It annihilates potentialities which lie in that nature. So action, too, separates itself from the background of the context of life and, unless accompanied by an explanation of how circumstances, purposes, means and context of life are linked together in it, allows no comprehensive account of the inner life from which it arose.

How different it is with the expressions of a "lived experience"! A particular relation exists between it, the life from which it sprang, and the understanding to which it gives rise. For expressions can contain more of the psychological context than any introspection can discover. They lift it from depths which consciousness does not illuminate. But it is characteristic of emotive expressions that their relation to the mental content expressed in them can only provide a limited basis for understanding. They are not to be judged as true or false but as truthful or untruthful. For dissimulation, lie and deception can break the relation between the expression and the mental content which is expressed.

The important distinction which thus emerges is the basis for the highest significance which life-expressions can achieve in the human studies. What springs from the life of the day is subject to the power of its interests. The interpretation of the ephemeral is also determined by the moment. It is terrible that in the struggle of practical interests every expression can be deceptive and its interpretation changed with the change in our situation. But in great works, because some mental content separates itself from its creator, the poet, artist or writer, we enter a sphere where deception ends. No truly great work of art can, according to the conditions which hold good and are to be developed later, wish to give the illusion of a mental content foreign to its author; indeed, it does not want to say anything about its author. Truthful in itself it stands—fixed, visible and permanent; this makes its methodical[1] and certain understanding possible. Thus there arises in the confines between science[2] and action an area in which life discloses itself at a depth inaccessible to observation, reflection and theory.

## (2) *The elementary forms of understanding*

Understanding arises, first of all, in the interests of practical life where people are dependent on dealing with each other. They must communicate with each other. The one must know what the other wants. So first the elementary forms of understanding arise. They are like the letters of the alphabet which, joined together, make higher forms of understanding possible. By such an elementary form I mean the interpretation of a single life-expression. Logically it can be expressed as an argument from analogy, based on the congruence between the analogy and what it expresses. In each of the classes listed individual life-expressions can be interpreted in this way. A series of letters combined into words which form a sentence is the expression of an assertion. A facial expression signifies pleasure or pain. The elementary acts of which continuous activities are composed, such as picking up an object, letting a hammer drop, cutting wood with a saw, indicate the presence of certain purposes. In this elementary understanding we do not go back to the whole context of life which forms the permanent subject of life-expressions. Neither are we conscious of any inference from which this understanding could have arisen.

The fundamental relationship on which the process of elementary understanding rests is that of the expression to what is expressed. Elementary understanding is not an inference from an effect to a cause. Nor must we, more cautiously, conceive it as a procedure which goes back from the given reality to some part of the context of life which made the effect possible. Certainly the latter relation is contained in the circumstances themselves and thus the transition from one to the other is, as it were, always at the door, but it need not enter. What is thus related is linked in a unique way. The relation between life-expressions and the world of mind which governs all understanding, obtains here in its most elementary form; according to this, understanding tends to spell out mental content which becomes its goal; yet the expressions given to the senses are not submerged in this content. How, for instance, both the gesture and the terror are not two separate things but a unity, is based on the fundamental relation of expression to mental content. To this must be added the generic character of all elementary forms of understanding which is to be discussed next.

### (3) *Objective mind and elementary understanding*

I have shown how significant the objective mind[3] is for the possibility of knowledge in the human studies. By this I mean the manifold forms in which what individuals hold in common have objectified themselves in the world of the senses. In this objective mind the past is a permanently enduring present for us. Its realm extends from the style of life and the forms of social intercourse to the system of purposes which society has created for itself and to custom, law, state, religion, art, science and philosophy. For even the work of genius represents ideas, feelings and ideals commonly held in an age and environment. From this world of objective mind the self receives sustenance from earliest childhood. It is the medium in which the understanding of other persons and their life-expressions takes place. For everything in which the mind has objectified itself contains something held in common by the I and the Thou. Every square planted with trees, every room in which seats are arranged, is intelligible to us from our infancy because human planning, arranging and valuing—common to all of us—have assigned a place to every square and every object in the room. The child grows up within the order and customs of the family which it shares with other members and its mother's orders are accepted in this context. Before it learns to talk it is already wholly immersed in that common medium. It learns to understand the gestures and facial expressions, movements and exclamations, words and sentences, only because it encounters them always in the same form and in the same relation to what they mean and express. Thus the individual orientates himself in the world of objective mind.

This has an important consequence for the process of understanding. Individuals do not usually apprehend life-expressions in isolation but against a background of knowledge about common features and a relation to some mental content.

This placing of individual life-expressions into a common context is facilitated by the articulated order in the objective mind. It embraces particular homogeneous systems like law or religion, which have a firm, regular structure. Thus, in civil law, the imperatives enunciated in legal clauses designed to secure the highest possible degree of perfection in the conduct of human affairs, are related to judicial procedures, law courts and the machinery for carrying out what they decide. Within such a context many kinds of typical differences exist. Thus, the individual life-expressions which confront the understanding subject can be considered as belonging to a common sphere, to a type. The resulting relationship between the life-expression and the world of mind not only places the expression into its context but also supplements its mental content. A sentence is intelligible because a language, the meaning of words and of inflections, as well as the significance of syntactical arrangements, is common to a community. The fixed order of behaviour within a culture makes it possible for greetings or bows to signify, by their nuances, a certain mental attitude to other people and to be understood as doing so. In different countries the crafts developed particular procedures and particular instruments for special purposes; when, therefore, the craftsman uses a hammer or saw, his purpose is intelligible to us. In this sphere the relation between life-expressions and mental content is always fixed by a common order. This explains why this relation is present in the apprehension of an individual expression and why—without conscious inference based on the relation between expression and what is expressed—both parts of the process are welded into a unity in the understanding.

In elementary understanding the connection between expression and what is expressed in a particular case is, logically speaking, inferred from the way the two are commonly connected; by means of this common connection we can say of the expression that it expresses some mental content. So we have an argument from analogy; a finite number of similar cases makes it probable that a subject has a particular attribute.

The doctrine of the difference between elementary and higher forms of understanding here put forward justifies the traditional distinction between pragmatic and historical interpretation by basing the difference on the relation—inherent in understanding—between its elementary and higher forms.

## (4) *The higher forms of understanding*

The transition from elementary to higher forms of understanding is already prepared for in the former. The greater the inner distance between a particular, given life-expression and the person who tries to understand it, the more often uncertainties arise. An attempt is made to overcome them. A first transition to higher forms of understanding is made when understanding takes the normal context of a life-expression and the mental content expressed in it for its point of departure. When a person encounters, as a result of his understanding, an inner difficulty or a contradiction of what he already knows, he is forced to re-examine the matter. He recalls cases in which the normal relation between life-expression and inner content did not hold. Such a deviation occurs when we withdraw our inner states, ideas or intentions from observation, by an inscrutable attitude or by silence. Here the mere absence of a visible expression is misinterpreted by the observer. But, beyond this, we must frequently reckon on an intention to deceive. Facial expressions, gestures and words contradict the mental content. So, for different reasons, we must consider other expressions or go back to the whole context of life in order to still our doubts.

The interactions of practical life also require judgments about the character and capacities of individuals. We constantly take account of interpretations of individual gestures, facial expressions, actions or combinations of these; they take place in arguments from analogy but our understanding takes us further; trade and commerce, social life, profession and family point to the need to gain insight into the people surrounding us so that we can make sure how far we can count on them. Here the relation between expression and what is expressed becomes that between the multiplicity of expressions of another person and the inner context behind them. This leads us to take account of changing circumstances. Here we have an induction from individual life-expressions to the whole context of a life. Its presupposition is knowledge of mental life and its relation to environment and circumstances. As the series of available life-expressions is limited and the underlying context uncertain, only probable conclusions are possible. If we can infer how a person we have understood would act in new circumstances, the deduction from an inductively arrived insight into a mental context can only achieve expectations and possibilities. The transition from an, only probable, mental context to its reaction in new circumstances can be anticipated but not forecast with certainty. As we shall soon see, the presupposition can be infinitely elaborated but cannot be made certain.

But not all higher forms of understanding rest on the relations between product and producer. It is clear that such an assumption is not even true in the elementary forms of understanding; but a very important part of the higher ones is also based on the relation between expression and what is expressed. In many cases the understanding of a mental creation is merely directed to the context in which the individual, successively apprehended, parts form a whole. If understanding is to produce knowledge of the world of mind as efficiently as possible, it is most important that its independent forms should be appreciated. If a play is performed, it is not only the naive spectator who is wholly absorbed in the plot without thinking of the author; even the cognoscenti can be wholly captivated by the action. Their understanding is directed towards the plot, the characters and the fateful interplay of different factors. Only so will they enjoy the full reality of the cross-section of life presented and understand and relive the action as the poet intended. All this understanding of mental creations is dominated by the relation between expressions and the world of mind expressed in them. Only when the spectator notices that what he has just accepted as a piece of reality is the poet's artistically planned creation does understanding pass from being governed by the relation between expression and what is expressed to being dominated by that between creation and creator.

The common characteristic of the forms of higher understanding mentioned is that by means of an induction from the expressions given they make the whole context comprehensible. The basic relation determining the progress from outer manifestations to inner content is either, in the first instance, that of expression to what is expressed or, frequently, that of product to producer. The procedure rests on elementary understanding which, as it were, makes the elements for reconstruction available. But higher understanding is distinguishable from elementary by a further feature which completely reveals its character.

The subject-matter of understanding is always something individual. In its higher forms it draws its conclusions about the pattern within a work, a person, or a situation, from what is given in the book or person and combined by induction. It was shown previously in our analysis of lived experience (*Erlebnis*) and of our understanding of self that the individual constitutes an intrinsic value in the world of the mind; indeed it is the only intrinsic value we can ascertain without doubt. Thus we are concerned with the individual not merely as an example of man in general but as a totality in himself. Quite independently of the practical interest which constantly forces us to reckon with other people, this concern, be it noble or wicked, vulgar or foolish, occupies a considerable place in our lives. The secret of personality lures us on to new attempts at deeper understanding for its own sake. In such understanding, the realm of individuals, embracing men and their creations, opens up. The unique contribution of understanding in the human studies lies in this; the objective mind and the power of the individual together determine the mind-constructed world. History rests on the understanding of these two.

But we understand individuals by virtue of their kinship, by the features they have in common. This process presupposes the connection between what is common to man and the differentiation of these common features into a variety of individual mental existences; through it we constantly accomplish the practical task of mentally living through, as it were, the unfolding of individuality. The material for accomplishing this task is formed by the facts combined by induction. Each fact has an individual character and is grasped as such; it, therefore, contains something which makes possible the comprehension of the individual features of the whole. But the presupposition on which this procedure is based assumes more and more developed forms as we become absorbed in the particular and the comparison of it with other things; thus the business of understanding takes us into ever greater depths of the mind-constructed world. Just as the objective mind contains a structural order of types, so does mankind, and this leads from the regularity and structure of general human nature to the types through which understanding grasps individuals. If we assume that these are not distinguished qualitatively, but, as it were, through emphasis on particular elements—however one may express this psychologically—then this represents the inner principle of the rise of individuality. And, if it were possible, in the act of understanding, both to grasp the changes brought about by circumstances in the life and state of the mind, as the outer principle of the rise of individuality, and the varied emphasis on the structural elements as the inner principle, then the understanding of human beings and of poetic and literary works would be a way of approaching the greatest mystery of life. And this, in fact, is the case. To appreciate this we must focus on what cannot be represented by logical formulae (i.e. schematic and symbolic representations which alone are at issue here).

## (5) *Empathy, re-creating and re-living*[4]

The approach of higher understanding to its object is determined by its task of discovering a vital connection in what is given. This is only possible if the context which exists in one's own experience and has been encountered in innumerable cases is always—and with all the potentialities contained in it—present and ready. This state of mind involved in the task of understanding we call empathy, be it with a man or a work. Thus every line of a poem is re-transformed into life through the inner context of lived experience from which the poem arose. Potentialities of the soul are evoked by the comprehension—by means of elementary understanding—of physically presented words. The soul follows the accustomed paths in which it enjoyed and suffered, desired and acted in similar situations. Innumerable roads are open, leading to the past and dreams of the future; innumerable lines of thought emerge from reading. Even by indicating the external situation the poem makes it easier for the poet's words to evoke the appropriate mood. Relevant here is what I have mentioned before, namely that expressions may contain more than the poet or artist is conscious of and, therefore, may recall more. If, therefore, understanding requires the presence of the vital coherence of our mental life this can be described as a projection of the self into some given expression.

On the basis of this empathy or transposition there arises the highest form of understanding in which the totality of mental life is active—re-creating or re-living. Understanding as such moves in the reverse order to the sequence of events. But full empathy depends on understanding moving with the order of events so that it keeps step with the course of life. It is in this way that empathy or transposition expands. Re-experiencing follows the line of events. We progress with the history of a period, with an event abroad or with the mental processes of a person close to us. Re-experiencing is perfected when the event has been filtered through the consciousness of a poet, artist or historian and lies before us in a fixed and permanent work.

In a lyrical poem we can follow the pattern of lived experiences in the sequence of lines, not the real one which inspired the poet, but the one, which, on the basis of this inspiration, he places in the mouth of an ideal person. The sequence of scenes in a play allows us to re-live the fragments from the life of the person on the stage. The narrative of the novelist or historian, which follows the historical course of events, makes us re-experience it. It is the triumph of re-experiencing that it supplements the fragments of a course of events in such a way that we believe ourselves to be confronted by continuity.

But what does this re-experiencing consist of? We are only interested in what the process accomplishes; there is no question of giving a psychological explanation. So we shall not discuss the relation of this concept to those of sympathy and empathy, though their relevance is clear from the fact that sympathy strengthens the energy of re-living. We must focus on the significance of re-living for grasping the world of mind. It rests on two factors; envisaging an environment or situation vividly always stimulates re-experiencing; imagination can strengthen or diminish the emphasis on attitudes, powers, feelings, aspirations and ideas contained in our own lives and this enables us to re-produce the mental life of another person. The curtain goes up and Richard appears. A flexible mind, following his words, facial expressions and movements, can now experience something which lies outside any possibility in its real life. The fantastic forest of *As You Like It* transposes us into a mood which allows us to re-produce all eccentricities.

This re-living plays a significant part in the acquisition of mental facts, which we owe to the historian and the poet. Life progressively limits a man's inherent potentialities. The shaping of each man's nature determines his further development. In short, he always discovers, whether he considers what determines his situation or the acquired characteristics of his personality, that the range of new perspectives on life and inner turns of personal existence is limited. But understanding opens for him a wide realm of possibilities which do not exist within the limitations of his real life. The possibility of experiencing religious states in one's own life is narrowly limited for me as for most of my contemporaries. But, when I read through the letters and writings of Luther, the reports of his contemporaries, the records of religious disputes and councils, and those of his dealings with officials, I experience a religious process, in which life and death are at issue, of such eruptive power and energy as is beyond the possibility of direct experience for a man of our time. But I can re-live it. I transpose myself into the circumstances; everything in them makes for an extraordinary development of religious feelings. I observe in the monasteries a technique of dealing with the invisible world which directs the monk's soul constantly towards transcendent matters; theological controversies become matters of inner life. I observe how what is thus formed in the monasteries *is spread* through innumerable channels — sermons, confessions, teaching and writings—to the laity; and then *I notice* how councils and religious movements *have spread* the doctrine of the invisible church and universal priesthood everywhere and how it comes to be related to the liberation of personality in the secular sphere. Finally, I see that what has been achieved by such struggles in lonely cells can survive, in spite of the church's opposition. Christianity as a force for shaping family, professional and political life converges with the spirit of the Age in the cities and wherever sophisticated work is done as by Hans Sachs or Dürer. As Luther leads this movement we can understand his development through the links between common human features, the religious sphere, this historical setting and his personality. Thus this process reveals a religious world in him and his companions of the first period of the Reformation which widens our horizon of the possibilities of human existence. Only in this way do they become accessible to us. Thus the inner-directed man can experience many other existences in his imagination. Limited by circumstances he can yet glimpse alien beauty in the world and areas of life beyond his reach. Put generally: man, tied and limited by the reality of life is liberated not only by art—as has often been explained—but also by historical understanding. This effect of history, which its modern detractors have not noticed, is widened and deepened in the further stages of historical consciousness.

## (6) *Explication or interpretation*

Re-creating and re-living what is alien and past shows clearly how understanding rests on special, personal talent. But, as this is a significant and permanent condition of historical science, personal talent becomes a technique which develops with the development of historical consciousness. It is dependent on permanently fixed life-expressions being available so that understanding can always return to them. The methodological understanding of permanently fixed life-expressions we call explication. As the life of the mind only finds its complete, exhaustive and therefore, objectively comprehensible expression in language, explication culminates in the interpretation of the written records of human existence. This art is the basis of philology. The science of this art is hermeneutics.

The explication of surviving remnants [from the human past] is inherently and necessarily linked to their critical examination. This arises from difficulties of explication and leads to the purification of texts, and the rejection of documents, works and traditions. Explication and critical examination have, in the course of history, developed new methodological tools, just as science has constantly refined its experiments. Their transmission from one generation of philologists and historians to another rests predominantly on personal contact with the great virtuosi and the tradition of their achievements. Nothing in the sphere of scholarship appears so personally conditioned and tied to personal contact as this philological art. Its reduction to rules by hermeneutics was characteristic of a stage in history when attempts were made to introduce rules into every sphere; this hermeneutic systematization corresponded to theories of artistic creation which considered it as production governed by rules. In the great period when historical consciousness dawned in Germany, Friedrich Schlegel, Schleiermacher and Boeckh replaced this hermeneutic systematization by a doctrine of ideals which based the new deeper understanding on a conception of mental creation; Fichte had laid its foundations and Schlegel had intended to develop it in his sketch of a science of criticism. On this new conception of creation rests Schleiermacher's bold assertion that one has to understand an author better then he understood himself. In this paradox there is an element of truth which can be psychologically explained.

Today hermeneutics enters a context in which the human studies acquire a new, important task. It has always defended the certainty of understanding against historical scepticism and wilful subjectivity; first when it contested allegorical interpretation, again when it justified the great Protestant doctrine of the intrinsic comprehensibility of the Bible against the scepticism of the Council of Trent, and then when, in the face of all doubts, it provided theoretical foundations for the confident progress of philology and history by Schlegel, Schleiermacher and Boeckh. Now we must relate hermeneutics to the epistemological task of showing the possibility of historical knowledge and finding the means for acquiring it. The basic significance of understanding has been explained; we must now, starting from the logical forms of understanding, ascertain to what degree it can achieve validity.

We found the starting-point for ascertaining how far assertions in the human studies correspond to reality in the character of lived experience which is a becoming aware of reality.

When lived experience is raised to conscious attention in elementary acts of thought, these merely reveal relations which are contained in the experience. Discursive thought represents what is contained in lived experience. Understanding rests primarily on the relationship, contained in any experience which can be characterized as an act of understanding, of expression to what is expressed. This relation can be experienced in its uniqueness. As we can only transcend the narrow sphere of our experience by interpreting other life-expressions, understanding achieves central significance for the construction of the human studies. But it was also clear that it could not be considered simply as an act of thought; transposition, re-creation, re-living—these facts pointed towards the totality of mental life which was active in it. In this respect it is connected with lived experience which, after all, is merely a becoming aware of the whole mental reality in a particular situation. So all understanding contains something irrational because life is irrational; it cannot be represented by a logical formula. The final, but quite subjective, certainty derived from this re-living cannot be replaced by an examination of the cognitive value of the inferences by which understanding can be represented. These are the limits set to the logical treatment of understanding by its own nature.

Though laws and forms of thought are clearly valid in every part of science and scholarship and even the methods of research are extensively inter-related, understanding introduces procedures which have no analogy in the methods of science. For they rest on the relation between expressions and the inner states expressed in them.

We must distinguish understanding from those preliminary grammatical and historical procedures which merely serve to place the student of a written document (*fixiert Vorliegenden*) from the past or a distant place and linguistically foreign, in the position of a reader from the author's own time and environment.

In the elementary forms of understanding we infer from a number of cases in which a series of similar life-expressions reflects similar mental content that the same relation will hold in other similar cases. From the recurrence of the same meaning of a word, a gesture, an overt action, we infer their meaning in a fresh case. One notices immediately, however, how little this form of inference achieves. In fact, as we saw, expressions are also reflections of something general; we make inferences by assigning them to a type of gesture or action or range of usage. The reference from the particular to the particular contains a reference to the general which is always represented. The relation becomes even clearer when, instead of inferring the relation between a series of particular, similar, expressions and the mental life expressed, we argue from analogy about some composite, individual, facts. Thus from the regular connection between particular features in a composite character we infer that this combination will reveal an, as yet unobserved, trait in a new situation. By this kind of inference we assign a mystical writing which has been newly discovered, or has to be chronologically re-classified, to a particular circle of mystics at a particular time. Such an argument always tends to infer the structure of such products from individual cases and thus to justify the new case more profoundly. So, in fact, the argument from analogy when applied to a new case becomes an induction. These two forms of inference can only be relatively distinguished in understanding. As a result, our expectations of a successful inference in a new case are invariably limited—how much no general rule can determine but only an evaluation of the varying circumstances. A logic of the human studies would have to discover rules for such evaluation.

So understanding itself, because it is based on all this, has to be considered as induction. This induction is not of the type in which a general law is inferred from an incomplete series of cases; it is rather one which co-ordinates these cases into a structure or orderly system by treating them as parts of a whole. The sciences and the human studies share this type of induction. Kepler discovered the elliptical path of the planet Mars by such an induction. Just as he inferred a simple mathematical regularity from observations and calculations by means of a geometrical intuition, so understanding must try to link words into meaning and the meaning of the parts into the structure of the whole given in the sequence of words. Every word is both determined and undetermined. It contains a range of meanings. The means of syntactically relating these words are, also, within limits, ambiguous; meaning arises when the indeterminate is determined by a construction. In the same way the value of the whole, which is made up of sentences, is ambiguous within limits and must be determined from the whole. This determining of determinate-indeterminate particulars is characteristic. . .⁵

# Notes

1. [Editor's note] *Kunstmäßig* is Dilthey's term which means "in accordance with the rules inherent in the art of hermeneutics."
2. [Editor's note] *Wissen.*
3. [Editor's note] Dilthey employs Hegel's term *objektiver Geist* to denote the inter-subjective products and creations of human culture as constituted by the systems of law or economics, political and social institutions or natural languages. Dilthey introduced the term in his treatise "The Construction of the Historical World in the Human Sciences" of 1910 (*GS,* vol. VII, p. 146)
4. Dilthey uses *Hineinversetzen* (to place oneself mentally into something, hence empathy or transposition); *Nachbilden* (to imitate and reconstruct and thus to re-create something); *Nacherleben* (to re-live something in our inner experience).
5. The text ends in this unfinished sentence.

# 6

# The Phenomenological Theory of Meaning and of Meaning Apprehension

=============================== Edmund Husserl ===============================

EDMUND HUSSERL (1859–1938) was born in Prossnitz, Moravia (now Prostéjov, Czechoslovakia), under the Austro-Hungarian Empire. After graduation from the German high school (*Gymnasium*) in Olmütz (Olomouc), he studied mathematics, physics, astronomy, and philosophy at the Universities of Leipzig, Berlin, and Vienna. He received a doctorate in Vienna in 1882 with a thesis called *Contributions to the Theory of the Calculus of Variation*. He worked first for the mathematician Weierstrass in Berlin as an assistant. In 1883 he transferred to Vienna to study philosophy with Franz Brentano. In 1886 he went to Halle where he received his second doctorate and *venia legendi* (*Habilitation*) with a thesis *On the Concept of Number: A Psychological Analysis,* in which the ground was laid for his further work in philosophy. From 1887 to 1901 Husserl taught at Halle and was occupied mainly with the problems of providing a secure philosophical grounding for mathematics and formal logic. The results of his labors were contained in his epoch making work, *Logical Investigations* (1900–01), which established his reputation as a philosopher and founder of a new philosophical direction—phenomenology. Between the years 1901 and 1916 Husserl taught at Göttingen where he gathered a circle of students and disciples from many countries and backgrounds. They would eventually carry the phenomenological viewpoint into different disciplines and in different directions. After having accepted a call to Freiburg in 1916, Husserl concentrated for the rest of his life on developing his philosophy, teaching and writing almost incessantly. When he died in 1938, he left over 40,000 pages of manuscripts in shorthand, most of which have now been published, or are scheduled for publication, in his collected works (see Sect. A, Bibl.). The impulses which Husserl gave to hermeneutics (its theory and practice) are numerous and far reaching. Best known is the influence of his phenomenological method on Heidegger in *Being and Time*. Of at least equal importance is the impact which his last work, *The Crisis of European Sciences and the Task of Phenomenology,* with its notion of "life-world" (*Lebenswelt*), has enjoyed in the social sciences. (See, for instance, A. Schutz's

*Phenomenology of the Social World.* Sect. B, Bibl.) Yet it is often overlooked that his early work, *Logical Investigations,* constitutes a landmark for hermeneutic theory, because for the first time it brings to bear the phenomenological method on the problems of the constitution and understanding of meaning, problems which clearly transcend the realms of pure mathematics or logic. In a very important sense, *Logical Investigations* must be read also as a theory of hermeneutics, or more accurately, as the establishment of the ground and possibility of hermeneutics. This can be gathered convincingly from the *Investigations* I ("Expression and Meaning"), from which our selections are taken; and from III ("On the Theory of Wholes and Parts"), IV ("The Distinction Between Independent and Nonindependent Meanings, the Idea of Pure Grammar"), and many sections of the remaining *Investigations,* for example, "Sense and Understanding" in VI. The relevance of Husserl's analyses for present-day hermeneutic discussions becomes evident to the reader in the introductory sections to I in which basic distinctions are drawn—a sine qua non without which notions like meaning, sense, expression, and understanding in the human sciences remain largely ambiguous.

# ESSENTIAL DISTINCTIONS

## *An ambiguity in the term "sign"*

The terms "expression" and "sign" are often treated as synonyms, but it will not be amiss to point out that they do not always coincide in application in common usage. Every sign is a sign for something, but not every sign has "meaning," a "sense" that the sign "expresses." In many cases it is not even true that a sign "stands for" that of which we may say it is a sign. And even where this can be said, one has to observe that "standing for" will not count as the "meaning" which characterizes the expression. For signs in the sense of indications (notes, marks, etc.) *do not express* anything, unless they happen to fulfill a significant as well as an indicative function. If, as one unwillingly does, one limits oneself to expressions employed in living discourse, the notion of an indication seems to apply more widely than that of an expression, but this does not mean that its content is the genus of which an expression is the species. To mean is *not a particular way of being a sign in the sense of indicating something.* It has a narrower application only because meaning—in communicative speech — is always bound up with such an indicative relation, and this in its turn leads to a wider concept, since meaning is also capable of occurring without such a connection. *Expressions* function meaningfully even in *isolated mental life, where they no longer serve to indicate anything.* The two notions of sign do not therefore really stand in the relation of more extensive genus to narrower species.

The whole matter requires more thorough discussion.

## The essence of indication

Of the two concepts connected with the word "sign," we shall first deal with that of an *indication*. The relation that here obtains we shall call the *indicative relation*. In this sense a brand is the sign of a slave, a flag the sign of a nation. Here all marks belong, as characteristic qualities suited to help us in recognizing the objects to which they attach.

But the concept of an indication extends more widely than that of a mark. We say the Martian canals are signs of the existence of intelligent beings on Mars, that fossil vertebrae are signs of the existence of prediluvian animals etc. Signs to aid memory, such as the much-used knot in a handkerchief, memorials etc., also have their place here. If suitable things, events or their properties are deliberately produced to serve as such indications, one calls them "signs" whether they exercise this function or not. Only in the case of indications deliberately and artificially brought about, does one speak of standing for, and that both in respect of the action which produces the marking (the branding or chalking etc.), and in the sense of the indication itself, i.e. taken in its relation to the object it stands for or that it is to signify.

These distinctions and others like them do not deprive the concept of indication of its essential unity. A thing is only properly an indication if and where it in fact serves to indicate something to some thinking being. If we wish to seize the pervasively common element here present we must refer back to such cases of "live" functioning. In these we discover as a common circumstance the fact that certain objects or states of affairs *of whose reality someone has actual knowledge* indicate to him *the reality of certain other objects or states of affairs,* in the sense that *his belief in the reality of the one is experienced* (though not at all evidently) *as motivating a belief or surmise in the reality of the other.* This relation of "motivation" represents a *descriptive unity* among our acts of judgement in which indicating and indicated states of affairs become constituted for the thinker. This descriptive unity is not to be conceived as a mere form-quality founded upon our acts of judgement, for it is in their unity that the essence of indication lies. More lucidly put: the "motivational" unity of our acts of judgement has itself the character of a unity of judgement; before it as a whole an objective correlate, a unitary state of affairs, parades itself, is meant in such a judgement, appears to be in and for that judgement. Plainly such a state of affairs amounts to just this: that certain things *may* or *must* exist, *since* other things have been given. This "since," taken as expressing an objective connection, is the objective correlate of "motivation" taken as a descriptively peculiar way of combining acts of judgement into a single act of judgement.

## Two senses of "demonstration" (Hinweis und Beweis)

We have sketched the phenomenological situation so generally that what we have said applies as much to the "demonstration" of genuine inference and proof, as to the "demonstration" of indication. These two notions should, however, be kept apart. their distinctness has already been suggested by our stress on the *lack of insight* in indications. In cases where the existence of one state of affairs is evidently inferred from that of another, we do not in fact speak of the latter as an indication or sign of the former, and, conversely, we only speak of demonstration in the strict logical sense in the case of an inference which is or could be informed by insight. Much, no doubt, that is propounded as demonstrative or, in the simplest case, as syllogistically cogent, is devoid of insight and may even be false. But to propound it is at least to make the claim that a relation of consequence could be seen to hold. This is bound up with the fact that there is an objective syllogism or proof, or an objective relationship between ground and consequent, which corresponds to our subjective acts of inferring and proving. These ideal unities are not the experiences of judging in question, but their ideal "contents," the propositions they involve. The premises prove the conclusion no matter who may affirm the premises and the conclusion, or the unity that both form. An ideal rule is here revealed which extends its sway beyond the judgements here and now united by "motivation"; in supra-empirical generality it comprehends as such all judgements having a like content, all judgements, even, having a like form. Such regularity makes itself subjectively known to us when we conduct proofs with insight, while the precise rule is made known to us through ideative reflection on the contents of the judgements experienced together in the actual context of "motivation," in the actual inference and proof. These contents are the propositions involved.

In the case of an indication there is no question of all this. Here insight and (to put the matter objectively) knowledge regarding the ideal connections among the contents of the judgements concerned, is quite excluded. When one says that the state of affairs *A* indicates the state of affairs *B*, that the existence of the one points to that of the other, one may confidently be expecting to find *B* true, but one's mode of speech implies no objectively necessary connections between *A* and *B*, nothing into which one could have insight. The contents of one's judgements are not here related as premises are to a conclusion. At times no doubt we do speak of "indications" even in cases where there is an objective relation of entailment (a mediate one, in fact). A mathematician may make use (so he says) of the fact that an algebraic equation is of uneven order as a sign that it has at least one real root. To be more exact, we are here only concerned with the possibility that someone who fails to carry out and see the cogency of the relevant thought-chain, may make use of a statement about an equation's uneven order as an immediate, blind motive for asserting the equation to have some necessarily connected property which he needs for his mathematical purposes. In such situations, where certain states of affairs readily serve to indicate others which are, in themselves, their consequences, they do not function in thought as logical grounds of the latter, but work through connections which previous actual demonstration, or blind learning on authority, has established among our convictions, whether as actual mental states or as dispositions for such. Nothing is of course altered in all this by the possible presence of an accompanying merely habitual knowlege of an objectively present rational connection.

If an indication (or the connection of "motivation" in which such a soi-disant objective relation makes its appearance) is without essential relation to a necessary connection, the question arises whether it may not claim to be essentially related to a connection of probability. Where one thing indicates another, where belief in the one's existence furnishes one with an empirical motive or ground— not necessary but contingent— for belief in the existence of the other, must the motivating belief not furnish a *ground of probability* for the belief it motivates? This is not the place for a close discussion of this pressing question. We need only observe that the question may correctly be answered in the affirmative in so far as such empirical "motivations" all fall under an ideal jurisdiction in virtue of which they may be spoken of as "justified" or "unjustified," or, objectively expressed, in which they may be spoken of as real, i.e. valid, motivations which lead to a probability or perhaps to an empirical certainty, or *per contra,* as merely apparent, i.e. invalid, motivations, which do not lead to such a probability. One may, e.g., cite the controversy as to whether volcanic phenomena do or do not indicate that the earth's interior is molten, and so on. One thing is sure, that to talk of an indication is not to presuppose a definite relation to considerations of probability. Usually such talk relates not to mere surmises but to assured judgements. The ideal jurisdiction to which we have here accorded authority must first demand, therefore, that we should scale down our confident judgements to modest surmises.

I shall here observe, further, that we cannot avoid talking about "motivation" in a general sense which covers strict demonstration as much as empirical indication. Here in fact we have a quite undeniable phenomenological affinity, obvious enough to register itself in ordinary discourse. We commonly speak of reasoning and inference, not merely in the sense of logic, but in a sense connected with empirical indications. This affinity plainly extends more widely: it covers the field of emotional, and, in particular, of volitional phenomena, to which talk of "motives" was at first alone confined. Here too "because" has a part to play, covering as wide a linguistic territory as does the most general sense of "motivation." I cannot therefore approve of Meinong's censure of Brentano's terminology, which I have here adopted.[1] But I entirely agree with him that in perceiving something as "motivated" we are not at all perceiving it as caused.

*Digression on the associative origin of indication*
The mental facts in which the notion of indication has its "origin," i.e. in which it can be abstractively apprehended, belong to the wider group of facts which fall

under the historical rubric of the "association of ideas." Under this rubric we do not merely have those facts which concern the "accompaniment" and "reactivation" of ideas stated in the laws of association, but the further facts in which association operates creatively, and produces peculiar descriptive characters and forms of unity.[2] Association does not merely restore contents to consciousness, and then leave it to them to combine with the contents there present, as the essence or generic nature of either may necessarily prescribe. It cannot indeed disturb such unified patterns as depend solely on our mental contents, e.g. the unity of visual contents in the visual field. But it can create additional phenomenological characters and unities which do not have their necessary, law-determined ground in the experienced contents themselves, nor in the generic forms of their abstract aspects.[3] If *A* summons *B* into consciousness, we are not merely simultaneously or successively conscious of both *A* and *B*, but we usually *feel* their connection forcing itself upon us, a connection in which the one points to the other and seems to belong to it. To turn mere coexistence into mutual pertinence, or, more precisely, to build cases of the former into intentional unities of things which seem mutually pertinent, is the constant result of associative functioning. All unity of experience, all empirical unity, whether of a thing, an event or of the order and relation of things, becomes a phenomenal unity through the felt mutual belongingness of the sides and parts that can be made to stand out as units in the apparent object before us. That one thing points to another, in definite arrangement and connection, is itself apparent to us. The single item itself, in these various forward and backward references, is no mere experienced content, but an apparent object (or part, property etc., of the same) that appears only in so far as experience (*Erfahrung*) endows contents with a new phenomenological *character,* so that they no longer count separately, but help to present an object different from themselves. In this field of facts the fact of indication also has its place, in virtue whereof an object or state of affairs not merely recalls another, and so points to it, but also provides evidence for the latter, fosters the presumption that it likewise exists, and makes us immediately feel this in the manner described above.

*Expressions as meaningful signs: Setting aside of a*
*sense of "expression" not relevant for our purpose*

From indicative signs we distinguish *meaningful* signs, i.e. *expressions.* We thereby employ the term "expression" restrictively: we exclude much that ordinary speech would call an "expression" from its range of application. There are other cases in which we have thus to do violence to usage, where concepts for which only ambiguous terms exist call for a fixed terminology. We shall lay down, for provisional intelligibility, that each instance or part of *speech,* as also each sign that is essentially of the same sort, shall count as an expression, whether or not such speech is actually uttered, or addressed with communicative intent to any persons or not. Such a definition excludes facial expression and the various gestures which involuntarily accompany speech without communicative intent, or those in which a man's mental states achieve understandable "expression" for his environment, without the added help of speech. Such "utterances" are not expressions in the sense in which a case of speech is an expression, they are not phenomenally one with the experiences made manifest in them in the consciousness of the man who manifests them, as is the case with speech. In such manifestations one man communicates nothing to another: their utterance involves no intent to put certain "thoughts" on record expressively, whether for the man himself, in his solitary state, or for others. Such "expressions," in short, have properly speaking, *no meaning*. It is not to the point that another person may interpret our involuntary manifestations, e.g. our "expressive movements," and that he may thereby become deeply acquainted with our inner thoughts and emotions. They "mean" something to him in so far as he interprets them, but even for him they are without meaning in the special sense in which verbal signs have meaning: they only mean in the sense of indicating.

In the treatment which follows these distinctions must be raised to complete conceptual clarity.

*Questions as to the phenomenological and intentional distinctions which pertain to expressions as such*

It is usual to distinguish two things in regard to every expression: 1. The expression physically regarded (the sensible sign, the articulate sound-complex, the written sign on paper etc.); 2. A certain sequence of mental states, associatively linked with the expression, which make it be the expression of something. These mental states are generally called the "sense" or the "meaning" of the expression, this being taken to be in accord with what these words ordinarily mean. But we shall see this notion to be mistaken, and that a mere distinction between physical signs and sense-giving experiences is by no means enough, and not at all enough for logical purposes.

The points here made have long been observed in the special case of names. We distinguish, in the case of each name, between what it "shows forth" (i.e. mental states) and what it means. And again between what it means (the sense or "content" of its naming presentation) and what it names (the object of that presentation). We shall need similar distinctions in the case of all expression, and shall have to explore their nature precisely. Such distinctions have led to our distinction between the notions of "expression" and "indication," which is not in conflict with the fact that an expression in living speech also functions as an indication, a point soon to come up for discussion. To these distinctions other important ones will be added which will concern the relations between meaning and the intuition which illustrates meaning and on occasion renders it evident. Only by paying heed to these relations can the concept of meaning be clearly delimited, and can the fundamental opposition between the symbolic and the epistemological function of meanings be worked out.

## Expressions as they function in communication

Expressions were originally framed to fulfil a communicative function: let us, accordingly, first study expressions in this function, so that we may be able to work out their essential logical distinction. The articulate sound-complex, the written sign etc., first becomes a spoken word or communicative bit of speech, when a speaker produces it with the intention of "expressing himself about something" through its means; he must endow it with a sense in certain acts of mind, a sense he desires to share with his auditors. Such sharing becomes a possibility if the auditor also understands the speaker's intention. He does this inasmuch as he takes the speaker to be a person, who is not merely uttering sounds but *speaking to him*, who is accompanying those sounds with certain sense-giving acts, which the sounds reveal to the hearer, or whose sense they seek to communicate to him. What first makes mental commerce possible, and turns connected speech into discourse, lies in the correlation among the corresponding physical and mental experiences of communicating persons which is effected by the physical side of speech. Speaking and hearing, intimation of mental states through speaking and reception thereof in hearing, are mutually correlated.

If one surveys these interconnections, one sees at once that all expressions in *communicative* speech function as *indications*. They serve the hearer as signs of the "thoughts" of the speaker, i.e. of his sense-giving inner experiences, as well as of the other inner experiences which are part of his communicative intention. This function of verbal expressions we shall call their *intimating function*. The content of such intimation consists in the inner experiences intimated. The sense of the predicate "intimated" can be understood more narrowly or more widely. The *narrower* sense we may restrict to *acts which impart sense*, while the *wider* sense will cover *all* acts that a hearer may introject into a speaker on the basis of what he says (possibly because he tells us of such acts). If, e.g., we state a wish, our judgement concerning that wish is what we intimate in the narrower sense of the word, whereas the wish itself is intimated in the wider sense. The same holds of an ordinary statement of perception, which the hearer forthwith takes to belong to some actual perception. The act of perception is there intimated in the wider sense, the judgement built upon it in the narrower sense. We at once see that ordinary speech permits us to call an experience which is intimated an experience which is *expressed*.

To understand an intimation is not to have conceptual knowledge of it, not to judge in the sense of asserting anything about it: it consists simply in the fact that the hearer *intuitively* takes the speaker to be a person who is expressing this or that, or as we certainly can say, *perceives* him as such. When I listen to someone, I perceive him as a speaker, I hear him recounting, demonstrating, doubting, wishing etc. The hearer perceives the intimation in the same sense in which he perceives the intimating person—even though the mental phenomena which make him a person cannot fall, for what they are, in the intuitive grasp of another. Common speech credits us with percepts even of other people's inner experiences; we "see" their anger, their pain etc. Such talk is quite correct, as long as, e.g., we allow outward bodily things likewise to count as perceived, and as long as, in general, the notion of perception is not restricted to the adequate, the strictly intuitive percept. If the essential mark of perception lies in the intuitive persuasion that a thing or event is itself before us for our grasping—such a persuasion is possible, and in the main mass of cases actual, without verbalized, conceptual apprehension—then the receipt of such an intimation is the mere perceiving of it. The essential distinction just touched on is of course present here. The hearer perceives the speaker as manifesting certain inner experiences, and to that extent he also perceives these experiences themselves: he does not, however, himself experience them, he has not an "inner" but an "outer" percept of them. Here we have the big difference between the real grasp of what is in adequate intuition, and the putative grasp of what is on a basis of inadequate, though intuitive, presentation. In the former case we have to do with an experienced, in the latter case with a presumed being, to which no truth corresponds at all. Mutual understanding demands a certain correlation among the mental acts mutually unfolded in intimation and in the receipt of such intimation, but not at all their exact resemblance.

## Expressions in solitary life

So far we have considered expressions as used in communication, which last depends essentially on the fact that they operate indicatively. But expressions also play a great part in uncommunicated, interior mental life. This change in function plainly has nothing to do with whatever makes an expression an expression. Expressions continue to have meanings as they had before, and the same meanings as in dialogue. A word only ceases to be a word when our interest stops at its sensory contour, when it becomes a mere sound-pattern. But when we live in the understanding of a word, it expresses something and the same thing, whether we address it to anyone or not.

It seems clear, therefore, that an expression's meaning, and whatever else pertains to it essentially, cannot coincide with its feats of intimation. Or shall we say that, even in solitary mental life, one still uses expressions to intimate something, though not to a second person? Shall one say that in soliloquy one speaks to oneself, and employs words as signs, i.e. as indications, of one's own inner experiences? I cannot think such a view acceptable. Words function as signs here as they do everywhere else: everywhere they can be said to point to something. But if we reflect on the relation of expression to meaning, and to this end break up our complex, intimately unified experience of the sense-filled expression, into the

two factors of word and sense, the word comes before us as intrinsically indifferent, whereas the sense seems the thing aimed at by the verbal sign and meant
by its means: the expression seems to direct interest away from itself towards its
sense, and to point to the latter. But this pointing is not an indication in the sense
previously discussed. The existence of the sign neither "motivates" the existence
of the meaning, nor, properly expressed, our belief in the meaning's existence.
What we are to use as an indication must be perceived by us as existent. This holds
also of expressions used in communication, but not for expressions used in soliloquy, where we are in general content with imagined rather than with actual
words. In imagination a spoken or printed word floats before us, though in reality
it has no existence. We should not, however, confuse imaginative presentations,
and the image-contents they rest on, with their imagined objects. The imagined
verbal sound, or the imagined printed word, does not exist, only its imaginative
presentation does so. The difference is the difference between imagined centaurs
and the imagination of such beings. The word's nonexistence neither disturbs nor
interests us, since it leaves the word's expressive function unaffected. Where it
*does* make a difference is where intimation is linked with meaning. Here thought
must not be merely expressed as meaning, but must be communicated and intimated. We can only do the latter where we actually speak and hear.

One of course speaks, in a certain sense, even in soliloquy, and it is certainly
possible to think of oneself as speaking, and even as speaking to oneself, as, e.g.,
when someone says to himself: "You have gone wrong, you can't go on like that."
But in the genuine sense of communication, there is no speech in such cases, nor
does one tell oneself anything: one merely conceives of oneself as speaking and
communicating. In a monologue words can perform no function of indicating the
existence of mental acts, since such indication would there be quite purposeless.
For the acts in question are themselves experienced by us at that very moment.

*Phenomenological distinctions between the phenomena of*
*physical expression and the sense-giving and sense-fulfilling act*
If we now turn from experiences specially concerned with intimation, and consider expressions in respect of distinctions that pertain to them equally whether
they occur in dialogue or soliloquy, two things seem to be left over: the expressions themselves, and what they express as their meaning or sense. Several
relations are, however, intertwined at this point, and talk about "meaning," or
about "what is expressed," is correspondingly ambiguous. If we seek a foothold
in pure description, the concrete phenomenon of the sense-informed expression
breaks up, on the one hand, into the *physical phenomenon* forming the physical
side of the expression, and, on the other hand, into the *acts* which give it *meaning*
and possibly also *intuitive fullness,* in which its relation to an expressed object
is constituted. In virtue of such acts, the expression is more than a merely sounded
word. It *means* something, and in so far as it means something, it relates to what

is objective. This objective somewhat can either be actually present through accompanying intuitions, or may at least appear in representation, e.g. in a mental image, and where this happens the relation to an object is realized. Alternatively this need not occur: the expression functions significantly, it remains more than mere sound of words, but it lacks any basic intuition that will give it its object. The relation of expression to object is now unrealized as being confined to a mere meaning-intention. A *name*, e.g., names its object whatever the circumstances, in so far as it *means* that object. But if the object is not intuitively before one, and so not before one as a named or meant object, mere meaning is all there is to it. If the originally *empty* meaning-intention is now fulfilled, the relation to an object is realized, the naming becomes an actual, conscious relation between name and object named.

Let us take our stand on this fundamental distinction between meaning-intentions void of intuition and those which are intuitively fulfilled: if we leave aside the sensuous acts in which the expression, *qua* mere sound of words, makes its appearance, we shall have to distinguish between two acts or sets of acts. We shall, on the one hand, have acts essential to the expression if it is to be an expression at all, i.e. a verbal sound infused with sense. These acts we shall call the *meaning-conferring acts* or the *meaning-intentions*. But we shall, on the other hand, have acts, not essential to the expression as such, which stand to it in the logically basic relation of *fulfilling* (confirming, illustrating) it more or less adequately, and so actualizing its relation to its object. These acts, which become fused with the meaning-conferring acts in the unity of knowledge or fulfillment, we call the *meaning-fulfilling* acts. The briefer expression "meaning-fulfillment" can only be used in cases where there is no risk of the ready confusion with the *whole* experience in which a meaning-intention finds fulfillment in its correlated intuition. In the realized relation of the expression to its objective correlate,[4] the sense-informed expression becomes one with the act of meaning-fulfillment. The sounded word is first made one with the meaning-intention, and this in its turn is made one (as intentions in general are made one with their fulfillments) with its corresponding meaning-fulfillment. The word "expression" is normally understood—wherever, that is, we do not speak of a "mere" expression—as the *sense-informed* expression. One should not, therefore, properly say (as one often does) that an expression *expresses its meaning* (its intention). One might more properly adopt the alternative way of speaking according to which the *fulfilling act* appears as *the act expressed by the complete expression:* we may, e.g., say, that a statement "gives expression" to an act of perceiving or imagining. We need not here point out that both meaning-conferring and meaning-fulfilling acts have a part to play in intimation in the case of communicative discourse. The former in fact constitute the inmost core of intimation. To make them known to the hearer is the prime aim of our communicative intention, for only in so far as the hearer attributes them to the speaker will he understand the latter.

*The phenomenological unity of these acts*

The above distinguished acts involving the expression's appearance, on the one hand, and the meaning-intention and possible meaning-fulfillment, on the other, do not constitute a mere aggregate of simultaneously given items in consciousness. They rather form an intimately fused unity of peculiar character. Everyone's personal experience bears witness to the differing weight of the two constituents, which reflects the asymmetry of the relation between an expression and the object which (through its meaning) it expresses or names. Both are "lived through," the presentation of the word and the sense-giving act: but, while we experience the former, we do not live *in* such a presentation at all, but solely in enacting its sense, its meaning. And in so far as we do this, and yield ourselves to enacting the meaning-intention and its further fulfillment, our whole interest centres upon the object intended in our intention, and named by its means. (These two ways of speaking have in fact the same meaning.) The function of a word (or rather of an intuitive word-presentation) is to awaken a sense-conferring act in ourselves, to point to what is intended, or perhaps given intuitive fulfillment in this act, and to guide our interest exclusively in this direction.

Such pointing is not to be described as the mere objective fact of a regular diversion of interest form one thing to another. The fact that two presented objects *A* and *B* are so linked by some secret psychological coordination that the presentation of *A* regularly arouses the presentation of *B,* and that interest is thereby shifted from *A* to *B*—such a fact does not make *A* the expression of the presentation of *B*. To be an expression is rather a descriptive aspect of the *experienced unity* of sign and thing signified.

What is involved in the descriptive difference between the physical sign-phenomenon and the meaning-intention which makes it into an expression, becomes most clear when we turn our attention to the sign *qua* sign, e.g., to the printed word as such. If we do this, we have an external percept (or external intuitive idea) just like any other, whose object loses its verbal character. If this object again functions as a word, its presentation is wholly altered in character. The word (*qua* external singular) remains intuitively present, maintains its appearance, but we no longer intend it, it no longer properly is the object of our "mental activity." Our interest, our intention, our thought—mere synonyms if taken in sufficiently wide senses—point exclusively to the thing meant in the sense-giving act. This means, phenomenologically speaking, that the intuitive presentation, in which the physical world-phenomenon is constituted, undergoes an essential phenomenal modification when its object begins to count as an *expression*. While what constitutes the object's appearing remains unchanged, the intentional character of the experience alters. There is constituted (without need of a fulfilling or illustrative intuition) an act of meaning which finds support in the verbal presentation's intuitive content, but which differs in essence from the intuitive intention directed upon the word itself. With this act, the new acts or act-complexes that we call "fulfilling" acts or act-complexes are often peculiarly blended, acts whose object coincides with the object meant in the meaning, or named through this meaning.

## Notes

1. A. V. Meinong, *Göttinger gel. Anz.* (1892), p. 446.
2. To use personification and to talk of association as "creating" something, and to employ other similar figurative expressions in common use, is too convenient to be abandoned. Important as a scientifically exact but circumlocutory description of the relevant facts may be, ready understanding absolutely requires that we talk figuratively wherever ultimate exactness is not needed.
3. I talk above of "experienced contents," not of meant, apparent objects or events. Everything that really helps to constitute the individual, "experiencing" consciousness is an experienced content. What it perceives, remembers, inwardly presents etc., is a meant or intentional object. This point will be further discussed in Investigation V.
4. I often make use of the vaguer expression "objective correlate" (*Gegenständlichkeit*) since we are here never limited to objects in the narrower sense, but have also to do with states of affairs, properties, and non-independent forms, etc., whether real or categorical.

# TOWARDS A CHARACTERIZATION OF THE ACTS WHICH CONFER MEANING

*Illustrative mental pictures as putative meanings*
We have oriented our concept of meaning, or meaning-intention, towards the phenomenological character essential to an expression as such, which distinguishes it descriptively in consciousness from a merely sounded word. Such a character is, in our view, possible, and quite often actual, though the expression does not help us to know anything, does not stand in the loosest, remotest relation to sensualizing intuitions. It is now time to take up our stance towards a widely held, perhaps almost dominant conception, which, as against our own, sees the whole role of the expression, with all its living meaning, in the arousal of certain images which regularly accompany it.

To understand an expression means, on this view, to meet with pertinent mental pictures. Where these are absent, an expression is void of sense. These mental pictures are themselves often said to be the meanings of words, and those who say so, claim to be getting at what ordinary speech means by the "meaning of an expression."

It shows the retarded state of descriptive psychology that such speciously obvious doctrines should be entertained, and entertained despite long-standing objections urged against them by unprejudiced thinkers. Verbal expressions are no doubt often accompanied by images, which may stand in an intimate or a distant relation to their meanings, but to treat such accompaniments as necessary conditions for understanding runs counter to the plainest facts. Thereby we know that the meaningfulness of an expression—let alone its meaning—cannot consist in the existence of such images, and cannot be disturbed by their absence. A comparison of a few casually observed imaginative accompaniments will soon show how vastly they vary while the meanings of words stay constant, and how they often are only very distantly related to the latter, whereas true illustrations, which genuinely carry out or confirm the meaning-intention of our expression, can often only be evoked with difficulty or not at all. Let a man read a work in an abstract field of knowledge, and understand the author's assertions perfectly, and let him then try to see what *more* there is to such reading than the words he understands. The circumstances of observation are most favourable to the view we reject, since an interest in finding images tends psychologically to evoke images, while the tendency to read back the findings of reflection into the original situation, makes us include all new images which stream in during the observation in the psychological content of our expression. Despite these favouring circumstances, the view we oppose, which sees the essence of the meaningful in accompanying imagery, must at least cease to look for introspective confirmation in the sort of case in question. Take, e.g., well-understood algebraical signs, or complete formulae, or verbal propositions such as "Every algebraical equation of uneven grade has at least one real root," and carry out the needful observations. To report my own findings in the last case: I see an open book which I recognize as Serret's *Algebra,* I see the sensory pattern of an algebraical equation in Teubnerian type, while accompanying the word "root," I see the familiar $\sqrt{\phantom{x}}$. I have however read the sentence very many times and have understood it perfectly, without experiencing the slightest trace of accompanying images that have anything to do with its presented object. The same happens when expressions like "culture," "religion," "science," "art," "differential calculus" etc., are intuitively illustrated.

We may further point out that what we have said applies not only to expressions which stand for highly abstract objects, mediated by complex relations, but to names of individual objects, well-known persons, cities, landscapes. A readiness for intuitive representation may be present, but it remains unfulfilled at the moment in question.

*Continuation of the above. Arguments and counter-arguments*

Should someone object that there are highly evanescent images even in such cases, that a mental picture emerges only to disappear forthwith, we reply that the full understanding of the words, their complete living sense, persists after such an image has vanished, and cannot therefore consist in its presence.

If the objector shifts to saying that the mental image has become unobservable, perhaps always was so, but that, whether observable or not, it still exists, and makes continued understanding possible, we need not be in doubt as to our answer. We reply that whether or not such an assumption is necessary or plausible on grounds of genetic psychology, this is not anything that need be gone into here. It is quite irrelevant to our essentially descriptive question. Let us grant that there often are unobservable images. Despite this, however, an expression can quite often be understood, and quite observably so. But surely it is absurd to suppose that an abstract, sense-making aspect of an image should be observable, while the whole complete, concrete image-experience remains unobservable? How does the matter stand, further, in cases where our meaning is absurd? Unobservability can here not depend on the contingent limits of mental capacity, since such an image cannot exist at all: if it could, it would provide us with a self-evident guarantee of the possibility, the semantic consistency, of the thought in question.

It can, of course, be pointed out that we do, after a fashion, illustrate even absurdities, such as a straight line enclosing a space, or triangles the sum of whose angles is greater or less than two right angles. In metageometric treatises there are even drawings of such forms. No one would, however, dream of taking intuitions of this sort as truly illustrating the concepts in question, or of letting them pass as owning such verbal meanings. Only in cases where the image of a thing meant is really adequate to it, are we tempted to seek the sense of our expression in such an image. But if we rule out absurd expressions— which none the less have their sense— are images normally adequate? Even Descartes cited his "chiliagon" to shed light on his distinction between *imaginatio* and *intellectio*. Our imaginative idea of a chiliagon is no more adequate than are our images of space-enclosing straight lines or intersecting parallels: in both cases we have rough, merely partial illustrations of a thing thought of, not complete exemplifications. We speak of a closed straight line, and draw a closed curve, thereby only illustrating the curvature. In the same fashion we think of a chiliagon, while we imagine any polygon with "many" sides.

We need not look for recondite geometrical illustrations to prove the inadequacy of illustration even in the case of consistent meanings. It is a well-known fact that no geometric concept whatsoever can be adequately illustrated. We imagine or draw a stroke, and speak or think of a straight line, and so in the case of all figures. The image everywhere provides only a foothold for *intellectio*. It offers no genuine instance of our intended pattern, only an instance of the sort of sensuous form which is the natural starting-point for geometrical "idealization."

In these intellectual thought-processes of geometry, the idea of a geometrical figure is constituted, which is then expressed in the fixed meaning of the definitory expression. Actually to perform this intellectual process may be presupposed by our first formation of primitive geometrical expressions and by our application of them in knowledge, but not for their revived understanding and their continued significant use. Elusive sensuous pictures function, however, in a phenomenologically graspable and describable manner, as mere aids to understanding, and not as themselves meanings or carriers of meaning.

Our conception will perhaps be censured for its extreme nominalism, for identifying word and thought. To many it will seem quite absurd that a symbol, a word, a sentence, a formula should be understood, while in our view nothing intuitive is present beyond the mindless sensible body of thought, the sensible stroke on paper etc. But we are far from identifying words and thoughts, as our statements in the previous chapter show. We do not at all think that, where symbols are understood without the aid of accompanying images, the mere symbol alone is present: we think rather that an understanding, a peculiar act-experience relating to the expression, is present, that it shines through the expression, that it lends it meaning and thereby a relation to objects. What distinguishes the mere word, as a sense-complex, from the meaningful word, is something we know full well from our own experience. We can indeed ignore meaning and pay attention only to a word's sensuous character. It may also be the case that some sensible feature first arouses interest on its own account, and that its verbal or other symbolic character is only then noted. The sensuous habit of an object does not change when it assumes the status of a symbol for us, nor, conversely, does it do so when we ignore the meaning of what normally functions as a symbol. No new, independent content is here added to the old: we do not merely have a sum or association of contents of equal status before us. One and the same content has rather altered its psychic habit: we are differently minded in respect of it, it no longer seems a mere sensuous mark on paper, the physical phenomenon counts as an *understood* sign. Living thus understandingly, we perform no act of presentation or judgement directed upon the sign as a sensible object, but another act, quite different in kind, which relates to the thing designated. It is in this sense-giving act-character—which differs entirely according as our interest plays on the sensible sign or the object presented through it, with or without representative imagery—that meaning consists.

### Understanding without intuition

In the light of our conception it becomes wholly understandable that an expression should be able to function significantly without illustrative intuition. Those who locate the meaning-aspect of symbols in intuition, must find purely symbolic thinking insolubly enigmatic. Speech without intuition must likewise be senseless to them. But truly senseless speech would be no speech at all: it would be like the rattle of machinery. This we of course meet with in the case of verses or prayers learnt by rote and repeated unthinkingly, but not in the cases which here require explanation. Popular comparisons with the squawking of parrots or the cackling of geese, the well-known adage "Where ideas fail us, words come up at the right moment" and so on, are not, soberly considered, to be taken literally. Expressions such as "talk without judgement" or "senseless talk" may and should certainly not be otherwise interpreted than such expressions as "a heartless," "brainless," "empty-headed man" etc. "Talk without judgement" plainly does not mean talk unbacked by judgements, but talk backed by judgements not based on independent, intelligent consideration. Even "senselessness," understood as absurdity or nonsense, is significantly constituted: the sense of an absurd expression is such as to refer to what cannot be objectively put together.

The opposite view can now only take refuge in the strained hypothesis of unconscious, unnoticed intuitions. How little this helps becomes plain if we consider what basic intuition achieves in cases where it is noticeably present. In the vast majority of cases it is by no means adequate to our meaning-intention, a fact, which, in our conception, presents no problem. If the meaningful is not to be found in intuition, speech without intuition need not be speech deprived of thought. If intuition lapses, an act like that which otherwise hangs about intuition, and perhaps mediates the knowledge of its object, continues to cling to the sense-given expression. The act in which meaning is effective is therefore present in either case.

*Thought without intuition and the*
*"surrogative function" of signs*

It should be quite clear that over most of the range both of ordinary, relaxed thought and the strict thought of science, illustrative imagery plays a small part or no part at all, and that we may, in the fullest sense, judge, reason, reflect upon and refute positions, without recourse to more than symbolic presentations. This situation is quite inadequately described if one talks of the "surrogative function of signs," as if the signs themselves did duty for something, and as if our interest in symbolic thinking were directed to the signs themselves. Signs are in fact not objects of our thought at all, even surrogatively; we rather live entirely in the consciousness of meaning, of understanding, which does not lapse when accompanying imagery does so. One must bear in mind that symbolic thinking is only thinking in virtue of a new, intentional act-character: this distinguishes the meaningful sign from the mere sign, i.e. the sounded word set up as a physical object in our mere presentations of sense. This act-character is a *descriptive* trait in the sign-experience which, stripped of intuition, yet understands the sign.

It will perhaps be objected to our present interpretation of symbolic thinking that it conflicts with quite certain facts involved in the analysis of *arithmetical symbolic thought,* facts that I myself have stressed elsewhere (in my *Philosophy of Arithmetic*). In arithmetical thought mere signs genuinely do duty for concepts. "The reduction of the theory of things to the theory of signs" (to quote Lambert) is what all calculation achieves. Arithmetical signs are "so selected and perfected, that the theory, combination, transformation etc. of signs can do what would otherwise have to be done by concepts."[1]

Looked at more closely, however, it is not signs, in the mere sense of *physical* objects, whose theory, combination etc., would be of the slightest use. Such things would belong to the sphere of physical science and practice, and not to that of arithmetic. The true meaning of the signs in question emerges if we glance at the much favoured comparison of mathematical operations to rule-governed games, e.g. chess. Chessmen are not part of the chess-game as bits of ivory and wood having such and such shapes and colours. Their phenomenal and physical constitution is quite indifferent, and can be varied at will. They become chessmen, counters in the chess-game, through the game's rules which give them their fixed *games-meaning.* And so arithmetical signs have, besides their original meaning, their so-to-say games-meaning, a meaning oriented towards the game of calculation and its well-known rules. If one treats arithmetical signs as mere counters in the rule-sense, to solve the tasks of the reckoning game leads to numerical signs or formulae whose interpretation in their original, truly arithmetical senses also represents the solution of corresponding arithmetical problems.

We do not therefore operate with *meaningless signs* in the fields of symbolic-arithmetical thought and calculation. For mere signs, in the sense of *physical* signs bereft of all meaning, do duty for the same signs alive with arithmetical meaning: it is rather that signs taken in a certain *operational or games-sense* do duty for the same signs in full *arithmetical meaningfulness.* A system of natural, and, as it were, unconscious equivocations bears endless fruit, and the much greater mental work which our original array of concepts demanded is eased by "symbolic" operations employing a parallel array of games-concepts.

Naturally such a procedure must be logically justified and its boundaries reliably fixed: here we were only concerned to remove confusions readily caused by misunderstanding of the nature of such "merely symbolical" mathematical thought. If one grasps the sense, set out above, in which the "mere signs" of arithmetic do duty for arithmetical concepts (or for signs in their full arithmetical meaning) it is clear that talk of the surrogative function of arithmetical signs is irrelevant to our present question, the question whether an expression of thought is or is not possible without an accompaniment of illustrative, instantiating or demonstrative intuitions. Non-intuitive symbolic thought in the sense just mentioned, and symbolical thought in the sense of thought which employs surrogative operational concepts, are two quite different things.

*A difficulty regarding our necessary recourse to*
*corresponding intuitions in order to clarify meanings*
*or to know truths resting on them*

One might here ask: If the sense of expressions functioning purely symbolically lies in an act-character which distinguishes the understanding grasp of a verbal sign from the grasp of a sign stripped of meaning, why is it that we have recourse to intuition when we want to establish differences of meaning, to expose ambiguities, or to limit shifts in our meaning-intention?

Again one might ask: Why, if our conception of meaning is right, do we employ corresponding intuitions in order to know purely conceptual truths, i.e. truths known through an analysis of meanings? One can say in general, that in order to be quite clear as to the sense of an expression (or as to the content of a concept) one must construct a corresponding intuition: in this intuition one sees what the expression "really means."

But an expression functioning symbolically also means something, and means the same thing as an expression intuitively clarified. Meaning cannot first have been acquired through intuition: otherwise we should have to say that much the greater part of our experience in speaking and reading is merely an external perceiving or imagining of optic and auditory complexes. We need not again stress that this plainly conflicts with the phenomenological data, that we *mean* this or that with our spoken or written signs, and that this meaning is a *descriptive character* of intelligent speech and hearing, even when these are purely symbolic. Our first question is answered by observing that purely symbolic meaning-intentions often do not clearly keep themselves apart, and do not permit of the easy, sure distinctions and identifications which are needed for practically useful judgements, even if these are not self-evident. To recognize differences of meaning such as that between "moth" and "elephant," requires no special procedures. But where meanings shade unbrokenly into one another, and unnoticed shifts blur boundaries needed for firm judgement, intuitive illustration naturally promotes lucidity. Where an expression's meaning-intention is fulfilled by divergent, conceptually disparate intuitions, the sharp difference in the direction of fulfillment shows up the cleavage of meaning-intentions.

Answering our second question, we recall that all self-evidence of judgement (all realized knowledge in the strong sense of the word) presupposes meanings that are intuitively fulfilled. Where there is talk of a knowledge "springing from the analysis of the mere meanings of words," more is meant than these words suggest. The knowledge meant is one whose self-evidence calls only for pure representation of the "conceptual essences," in which the general word-meanings find their perfect fulfillments: all question as to the existence of objects corresponding to such concepts, or falling under such conceptual essences, is ruled out. But these "conceptual essences" are not the verbal meanings themselves, so that the phrases "based purely on the concepts (essences)," and "springing from a mere analysis of word-meanings," are only by equivocation equivalent. Conceptual essences are rather the fulfilling sense which is "given" when the word-meanings (i.e. the meaning-intentions of the words) terminate in corresponding, directly intuitive presentations, and in certain cogitative elaborations and formations of the same. Such analysis is not therefore concerned with empty thought-intentions, but with the objects and forms by which they are fulfilled. What it therefore offers us are not mere statements concerning elements or relations of meanings, but evident necessities concerning the *objects* thought of in these meanings, and thought of as thus and thus determined.

These discussions point to a field of phenomenological analyses which we have already repeatedly seen to be unavoidable, analyses which bring self-evidence into the *a priori* relations between meaning and knowing, or between meaning and clarifying intuition. They will therefore also have to bring complete clarity into our concept of meaning, both by distinguishing meaning from *fulfilling* sense, and by investigating the sense of such fulfillment.

*Varying marks of understanding and the "quality of familiarity"*

Our conception presupposes a certain separation, even if not quite a sharp one, among the act-characters which confer meaning even in cases which lack intuitive illustration. One cannot indeed think that the "symbolic presentations" which govern the grasp or the significant application of signs, are descriptively equivalent, that they consist in one *undifferentiated* character, the same for all expressions, as if only the sound of the words, the chance sensuous carriers of meaning, made all the difference. Examples of equivocal expressions readily show that we can effect and can recognize sudden changes of meaning, without in the least needing accompanying illustrations. The descriptive difference, here evidently apparent, cannot be the sensuous sign, which remains the same: it must concern the act-character, which is specifically altered. One can likewise point to cases where meaning remains identical while a word changes, in the case, e.g., of mere differences of idiom. Sensuously different signs here count as equivalent (we perhaps even speak of the "same" word, only occurring in different languages), they at once greet us as the same, even before reproductive fancy can furnish images that illustrate their meaning.

Such examples reveal the untenability of the view, plausible at first, that the note of understanding is no more ultimately than what Riehl[2] called the "character of familiarity," and what Höffding,[3] not so suitably, called the "quality of familiarity."[4] Words not understood are just as capable of coming before us in the form of old acquaintances: well-memorized Greek verses stick in our memories longer than our understanding of their sense, they appear familiar but are no longer understood. The missing grasp often comes in a flash afterwards, possibly some time before mother-tongue translations or other aids come up in memory, and the note of understanding now adds its obvious novelty to the note of familiarity, not altering the content sensuously, yet giving it a new mental character. One may similarly recall the way in which the reading or recitation of familiar poetry, unthinking at first, suddenly becomes charged with understanding. There are countless other examples which make evident the peculiar character of understanding.

*Apperception as connected with expression*
*and with intuitive presentations*

The grasp of understanding,[5] in which the meaning of a word becomes effective, is, in so far as *any* grasp is in a sense an understanding and an interpretation, akin to the divergently carried out "objective interpretations" in which, by way of an experienced sense-complex, the intuitive presentation, whether percept, imagination, representation etc., of an object, e.g. an external thing, arises. The phenomenological structure of the two sorts of "grasp" is, however, somewhat different. If we imagine a consciousness prior to all experience, it may very well have the same *sensations* as we have. But it will intuit no things, and no events pertaining to things, it will perceive no trees and no houses, no flight of birds nor any barking of dogs. One is at once tempted to express the situation by saying that its sensations *mean* nothing to such a consciousness, that they do not *count as signs* of the properties of an object, that their combination does not count as a sign of the object itself. They are merely lived through, without an objectifying *interpretation* derived from experience. Here, therefore, we talk of signs and meanings just as we do in the case of expressions and cognate signs.

To simplify comparison by restricting ourselves to the case of perception, the above talk should not be misread as implying that consciousness first looks at its sensations, then turns them into perceptual objects, and then bases an interpretation upon them, which is what really happens when we are objectively conscious of physical objects, e.g. sounded words, which function as signs in the strict sense. Sensations plainly only become presented objects in psychological reflection: in naïve, intuitive presentations they may be *components* of our presentative experience, parts of its descriptive content, but are not at all its objects. The perceptual presentation arises in so far as an experienced complex of sensations gets informed by a certain act-character, one of conceiving or meaning. To the extent that this happens, the perceived *object* appears, while the sensational complex is as little perceived as is the act in which the perceived object is as such constituted. Phenomenological analysis teaches us, further, that sense-contents provide, as it were, the analogical building-stuff for the content of the object presented by their means. Hence talk of colours, extensions, intensities etc., as, on the one hand, sensed, and as, on the other hand, perceived or imagined. Examples readily show that what corresponds in the two cases is in no sense the same, but only generically allied. The *uniform* colouring of a sphere as *seen* by us (i.e. perceived, imagined etc.), was never *sensed* by us.

Signs in the sense of expressions rest on a similar "interpretation," but only in their first conception. In the simpler case where an expression is understood, but is not as yet given life by intuitive illustrations, this first conception makes the *mere sign* appear before us as a physical object, e.g. as a sounded word, given here and now. On this first conception, however, a second is built, which goes entirely beyond the experienced sense-material, which it no longer uses as analogical building-material, to the quite new object of its present meaning. The latter is meant in the act of meaning, but is not presented in sensation. Meaning, the characteristic function of the expressive sign, presupposes the sign whose function it is. Or to talk pure phenomenology: meaning is a variously tinctured act-character, presupposing an act of intuitive presentation as its necessary foundation. In the latter act, the expression becomes constituted as a physical object. It becomes an expression, in the full, proper sense, only through an act founded upon this former act.

What is true in this simplest case of an expression understood and not as yet intuitively illustrated, must also hold in the more complex case where an expression is bound up with a *corresponding* intuition. One and the same expression, significantly used with or without illustrative intuition, cannot derive its meaningfulness from different sorts of acts.

It is certainly not easy to analyse the descriptive situation in certain finer gradations and ramifications that have been passed over here. It is extremely hard to achieve a right conception of the part played by illustrative presentations in confirming meaning-intentions or in conferring self-evidence on them, as well as their relation to the characteristic note of understanding or meaning, the experience which lends sense to an expression even in default of intuition. Here we have a broad field for phenomenological analysis, a field not to be by-passed by the logician who wants to bring clarity into the relations between meaning and object, between judgement and truth, between vague opinion and confirmatory evidence. The analysis in question will receive a thoroughgoing treatment later.[6]

### Notes

1. Lambert, *Neues Organon* (1764), Vol. II, §§ 23–4, p. 16. (Lambert is not referring expressly to arithmetic.)
2. A. Riehl, *Der philosophische Kritizismus,* Vol. II, p. 399.
3. H. Höffding, "Über Wiedererkennen, Assoziation und psychische Aktivität," *Vierteljahrschrift f. wiss. Philos.* Vol. XIII, p. 425.
4. As against this cf. Volkelt, *Erfahrung und Denken,* p. 362.
5. I am not here restricting the use of the word "understanding" to the hearer-speaker relation. The soliloquizing thinker "understands" his words, and this understanding is simply his act of meaning them.
6. See Investigation VI.

## Roman Ingarden

ROMAN INGARDEN (1895-1970) was born in Cracow, Poland, and studied philosophy in Lvov under Twardowski. Later he went to Göttingen to study phenomenology with Husserl and his circle. He followed Husserl's move to Freiburg in 1916 and obtained his doctorate there with a thesis on the philosophy of Henri Bergson (1918). After his return to Poland he completed his second doctorate (*Habilitation*) with a dissertation on the problem of essences, *Essential Questions*, which was published by Husserl in his *Yearbook for Philosophy and Phenomenological Research* in 1925. In 1933 Ingarden became professor of philosophy at Lvov. In 1931 he published in German *The Literary Work of Art: An Investigation on the Borderline of Ontology, Logic and Theory of Literature* (Eng. trans., 1973). This was followed in 1937 in Polish by *The Cognition of the Literary Work of Art* (Eng. trans., 1973). These two works constitute the major contribution of Husserlian strict phenomenology to aesthetics and literary theory until today. From 1939 to 1944 when Polish universities were shut down under the German occupation, Ingarden taught mathematics in a high school in Lvov. During these years he completed in two volumes his major work, *The Controversy Over the Existence of the World* (1947-48). A German edition appeared in three volumes from 1964 to 1966. When eastern Poland and Lvov were annexed by the Soviet Union in 1945, Ingarden was able to obtain a chair in philosophy in Cracow. He was barred from teaching, however, from 1949 until 1956 for his alleged idealist position. Meanwhile, his work gained growing recognition in Europe and America and left its imprint on different schools of criticism. Our selections are taken from the first section of *The Cognition of the Literary Work of Art*, a phenomenological study of the manner and the way by which literary texts assume their meaning for us, and of the nature of the acts through which this meaning is actualized. It is the attitude which the reader assumes—as consumer-recipient or active critic and literary scholar—which decides how a text is understood and explicated. Nevertheless, there are certain structural givens which, although they are actualized by the reader, are not dependent upon him for their essential qualities. The importance of Ingarden's work for present-day hermeneutics derives from his ability to develop a new set of distinctions together with a new manner of viewing the problems of classical interpretation theory.

# ON THE COGNITION OF THE
# LITERARY WORK OF ART

## Preliminary Sketch of the Problem

The main question which I am trying to answer is: How do we cognize the completed literary work set down in writing (or by other means, e.g., in tape recording)? Cognition is, however, only one kind of intercourse a reader can have with the literary work. To be sure, we will not completely ignore the other ways of experiencing the work, but neither will we pay particular attention to them at the moment. Even "cognition" itself can take place in many different ways, which can bring about various results. The type of work read also plays an essential role in determining how cognition takes place.

I use the word "cognition" here for want of a better.[1] It should be taken for the moment in a rather vague and broad sense, beginning with a primarily passive, receptive "experience," in which we, as literary consumers, "become acquainted with" a given work, "get to know" it somehow, and thereby possibly relate to it in a more or less emotional way, and continuing on to the kind of attitude toward the work which leads to the acquisition of effective knowledge about the work. All these extremely diverse attitudes lead to some kind of knowledge about a work, whether it be a novel (for instance, Thomas Mann's *Buddenbrooks*) or a lyric poem (like "Shall I compare thee to a summer's day") or a drama (for instance, Ibsen's *Rosmersholm*). We shall not exclude from consideration other written works, either, such as newspaper articles, essays, and scientific works. On the contrary, one of the matters we are extremely concerned with is becoming aware of how we "understand" scientific works and how we apprehend cognitively the works themselves as well as what is portrayed in them. "Cognition" should thus be taken to mean a kind of intercourse with literary works which includes a certain cognizance of the work and does not necessarily exclude emotional factors. Of course, we take into account from the outset that acquaintance with a work, as well as its cognition, can take place in different ways and lead to various results, according to the peculiar character of the work in question. However, I hope to be able to show in the following that despite this considerable diversity every "cognition" of a literary work has a stock of operations which are always the same for the experiencing subject and that the process of "cognition" follows a course which is characteristically the same in all these diverse cases, provided it is not disturbed or interrupted by external circumstances. And the concluding investigations will show that in certain specific cases one can achieve genuine knowledge of the literary work and even of the literary work of art. We can remove the dangers arising from uncritical use of an unexplicated and possibly much too narrow idea "cognition" as a basis for our investigation only in this way of gradual progress, which does not lead to a delimitation of the ideas involved until its last stage. The exact notion of the cognition of a literary work, and in particular of a literary work of art, will thus be determined only as a result of our investigations. At the same time, we shall consider under what conditions this cognition can be accomplished. But on the way to such a result there are many difficulties to be overcome which are connected with the problem of "objective" knowledge and which can be solved only in a general epistemological investigation. We shall have to content ourselves here with preparing the way to this goal.

By "literary work" I mean primarily a work of belles-lettres, although in the following the term will also apply to other linguistic works, including scientific works. Works of belles-lettres lay claim, by virtue of their characteristic basic structure and particular attainments, to being "works of art" and enabling the reader to apprehend an aesthetic object of a particular kind. But not every work of art is "successful" and thus in a specific sense a "genuine," "valuable" work of art. And not every object of an aesthetic experience is the object of an experience culminating in pleasure or admiration or in a positive value judgment. This is especially true of works of belles-lettres. They can be "genuine" and "beautiful"; generally speaking, they can be of artistic or aesthetic value; but they can just as well be "bad," "not genuine," "ugly"—in short, of negative value. We can experience all these works aesthetically; we can also apprehend them in a preaesthetic cognition or in a cognition which is itself not aesthetic but which builds upon the aesthetic experience. Only the results of the latter cognitive apprehension of the work can give us valid information about the value of the work.[2] Our investigations must therefore encompass both groups of works, those of positive and those of negative value; but we will take into consideration from the outset that the cognition, especially the aesthetic cognition, of a work of positive value follows a different course and can have different properties than that of "bad" works, works of negative value.[3]

## Adaptation of Cognition to the
## Basic Structure of the Object of Cognition

Before we proceed to the description of the "cognition," in our broad sense, of the literary work, we must first consider what is to constitute the object of this "cognition." The epistemological investigations which have been carried out by the phenomenologists since Husserl's *Logical Investigations* show that between the mode of cognition and the object of cognition there is a special correlation; there is perhaps even an adaptation of the cognition to its object. This correlation is especially evident in which attitudes or cognitive operations enter into the process of cognition, in the order of sequence or of simultaneity they follow, in how they reciprocally condition and possibly modify one another, and in the total result to which they all lead, the cognitive value of which depends on the course they take and on their cooperation. For all the basic types of objects of cognition, there are corresponding basic kinds and modes of cognition. For instance: one can gain knowledge of a physical object only by beginning the cognitive process with a sensory perception of the object. Sometimes, of course, we learn about an object through information from another person, but even then this information must be based on a perception. We must use different kinds of perception to gain knowledge of different kinds of attributes of the object. We cannot hear colors or see or touch tones. When we wish to gain knowledge of our own psychological states or processes, we must employ acts of inner perception which are differently structured and proceed differently from those of outer perception; we can neither smell nor taste these processes and states. The situation is analogous in other cases: one must understand and prove mathematical propositions through their meaning; sensory perception plays no part in understanding them. In every case there is a strong correlation between the structure and qualitative constitution of the object of cognition, on the one hand, and the kind of cognition, on the other.[4] In view of this correlation, analysis of a cognitive process is made easier if we examine the basic formation of the object of cognition. Thus it will be useful in our case to begin by calling to mind the basic attributes and structures of the literary work.

But before we do this, we must first consider a possible reproach against our procedure. Are we not becoming involved in a vicious circle when we refer to the basic attributes and structures of literary works in order to explain the way in which we learn about a literary work? Is such reference not tantamount to presupposing the validity and effectiveness of the cognition which informs us about those basic attributes? At the outset of our investigation we do not yet have any positive knowledge about the cognition of a literary work and cannot assume anything about the value and effectiveness of this cognition. Nor do we make such assumptions. It is merely a question of directing our attention to certain processes of consciousness which take place during the reading of an individual work, not in order to apprehend their individual course and individual function, but rather to apprehend what is essentially necessary in that course and function. We refer not to the individual peculiarities of a specific literary work but rather to the essentially necessary structure of the literary work of art as such. We merely use the individual cognition of a work performed during a reading as an example which allows us to look for the essentially necessary structural elements and interconnections among the cooperating functions. These *correspond* in an intelligible way to the essentially necessary structural properties of the literary work in general and can be correlated with individual factors in the work; in fact, they help us to discover and apprehend such factors.

Thus, when we describe the cognitive processes involved in reading a text in their unfolding and their specific character and judge whether they are positively effective—that is, whether they can lead to objectively valid knowledge of the literary work—we presuppose neither the validity of the results of an individual reading nor the effectiveness of the cognitive functions involved in it. We must distinguish here between two different procedures: first, the reading of a specific literary work, or the cognition of that work which takes place during such reading, and, second, that cognitive attitude which leads to an apprehension of the essential structure and peculiar character of the literary work of art as such. These are two different modes of cognition and yield two quite different kinds of knowledge. The first is accomplished in an individual reading of an individual work.

It is a particular kind of experience in which we establish the actuality of this work and its details. The second is not accomplished in a reading at all and does not give us an experience of the actual qualitative constitution of a particular work, say of the *Magic Mountain,* by Thomas Mann. The second kind of cognition differs from an individual reading to such an extent that, even if we completely described the course and functions of an individual reading in our investigation, we would still be merely at the threshold of the difficult problem: What constitutes the general nature (to use the inappropriate but common term) of the literary work of art? Phenomenologists would say that in this case it is a question of an a priori analysis of the substance of the general idea "the literary work of art." This analysis, even if accomplished on the example of a particular literary work of art, or rather on various appropriately chosen examples, is not carried out in reading and understanding the successive sentences of these examples. It is rather a question of the essential differences among various basic elements of the literary work (and the literary work of art) as such: e.g., the difference between the phonetic patterns and phenomena and the sentence meanings (or, more generally, the different types of semantic units) or between the sentence meanings and the intentional sentence correlates projected by them (especially the states of affairs). It is a question of apprehending the constitutive formal and material factors of such elements and the essential differences among the elements which follow from those factors, as well as the various interrelations and connections among the elements. None of this can be discovered in the ordinary reading of a literary work, since the necessary possibilities which must be comprehended in the idea of "the literary work of art" far surpass the individual determinations of any particular work of art. On the other hand, the reading of a particular work can reveal far more about the individual work with respect to the details of the work than the a priori analysis, which is oriented toward the substance of the general idea of the literary work of art. The a priori analysis establishes only the "skeleton" of that which forms the full body of the individual work. It does not, for instance, apprehend the full meaning of the whole sequence of sentences in a work, which is indispensable for the reading of a work; but it attends to the general form of any possible sentence and to other things which cannot be specially heeded and analyzed in a specific reading. To be sure, it cannot be said that there is no relation at all between a general "eidetic" analysis (as Husserl calls it) of the idea of the literary work of art as such and the reading of a particular work. For example, an empirically oriented person might deny the existence or even the possibility of an a priori analysis of the substance of a general idea and yet still be inclined to recognize the possibility of general knowledge about literary works. He would then perhaps say that, on the basis of reading many individual works, one compares the results obtained and establishes the "common" characteristics of the individual works in an "act of generalization." This act of comparison and generalization goes beyond any individual reading; but it is presupposed in this empiricist view of "general" knowledge that the facts found in an individual reading really do exist and, thus, that the knowledge gained in such a reading has its validity. But an "eidetic" analysis of the "general nature" of the literary work of art (that is, of the substance of the general idea) in a phenomenological sense makes no such presupposition. The individual readings only give us a supply of phenomena which can be apprehended in their essential content; we need not presuppose the individual, real existence of the objects which come to givenness in these phenomena. Through these eidetically apprehended phenomena we can establish essential relations among the perceived phenomena and thus determine the essential, necessary structure of the literary work of art as such.

In other words, when in the following we adduce some characteristics of the general structure of the work, we presuppose neither the validity of the cognition of the works accomplished in the individual reading nor their real qualitative constitution. We use the data about the general structure of the literary work of art as such as a heuristic device which allows us to direct our attention to the process of consciousness wherein the cognition of the individual works is accomplished. At the same time it allows us to prepare ourselves for what we can find in the analysis of this process of consciousness, if we remember that the experiences making up this process should lead to, or help in, disclosure of the form and qualitative constitution of individual literary works. The confrontation of the analysis of the experiences in which the reading is accomplished with the essential, necessary structural elements of the literary work of art will, however, give us a better understanding of why those experiences are so complex in themselves and why they proceed in just this essential, typical way.

## Basic Assertions about the
## Essential Structure of the Literary Work of Art

The following general assertions about the essential structure of the literary work of art will be helpful in our further investigations.

1. The literary work is a many-layered formation. It contains (*a*) the stratum of verbal sounds and phonetic formations and phenomena of a higher order; (*b*) the stratum of semantic units: of sentence meanings and the meanings of whole groups of sentences; (*c*) the stratum of schematized aspects, in which objects of various kinds portrayed in the work come to appearance; and (*d*) the stratum of the objectivities portrayed in the intentional states of affairs projected by the sentences.

2. From the material and form of the individual strata results an essential inner connection of all the strata with one another and thus the formal unity of the whole work.

3. In addition to its stratified structure, the literary work is distinguished by an ordered sequence of its parts, which consist of sentences, groups of sentences,

chapters, etc. Consequently, the work possesses a peculiar quasi-temporal "extension" from beginning to end, as well as certain properties of composition which arise from this "extension," such as various characteristics of dynamic development, etc.

The literary work actually has "two dimensions": the one in which the total stock of all the strata extends simultaneously and the second, in which the parts succeed one another.

4. In contrast to the preponderant majority of the sentences in a scientific work, which are genuine judgments, the declarative sentences in a literary work of art are not genuine judgments but only quasi-judgments, the function of which consists in lending the objects portrayed a mere aspect of reality without stamping them as genuine realities. Even sentences of other types—for example, interrogative sentences—undergo a corresponding modification of their function in the literary work of art. Depending on the type of work—e.g., in a historical novel—still other varities of these modifications are possible.[5]

The presence of quasi-judgments in literary works of art constitutes only one feature which distinguishes them from scientific works. Other characteristic features are attached to this one, namely:

5. If a literary work is a work of art having positive value, each of its strata contains special qualities. These are valuable qualities of two kinds: those of artistic and those of aesthetic value. The latter are present in the work of art itself in a peculiar potential state. In their whole multiplicity they lead to a peculiar polyphony of aesthetically valent qualities which determines the quality of the value constituted in the work.

Even in a scientific work, literary artistic qualities can appear which determine certain aesthetically valuable qualities. In a scientific work, however, this is only an ornamentation which has little or no connection with the essential function of the work and which cannot of itself make it a work of art.[6]

6. The literary work of art (like every literary work in general) must be distinguished from its concretizations, which arise from individual readings of the work (or, for instance, from the production of a work in the theater and its apprehension by the spectator).

7. In contrast to its concretizations, the literary work itself is a schematic formation. That is: several of its strata, especially the stratum of portrayed objectivities and the stratum of aspects, contain "places of indeterminacy." These are partially removed in the concretizations. The concretization of the literary work is thus still schematic, but less so than the work itself.

8. The places of indeterminacy are removed in the individual concretizations in such a way that a more or less close determination takes their place and, so to speak, "fills them out." This "filling-out" is, however, not sufficiently determined by the determinate features of the object and can thus vary with different concretizations.

9. The literary work as such is a purely intentional formation which has the source of its being in the creative acts of consciousness of its author and its physical foundation in the text set down in writing or through other physical means of possible reproduction (for instance, the tape recorder). By virtue of the dual stratum of its language, the work is both intersubjectively accessible and reproducible, so that it becomes an intersubjective intentional object, related to a community of readers. As such it is not a psychological phenomenon and is transcendent to all experiences of consciousness, those of the author as well as those of the reader.

## Apprehension of the Written Signs and Verbal Sounds

Until recently, the usual way of becoming acquainted with a literary work of art was to read a printed text; it was rather seldom that we encountered orally presented works. What happens when we prepare to read? At the beginning of our reading, we find ourselves confronted with a book, a volume in the real world consisting of a collection of pages covered with written or printed signs. Thus the first thing we experience is the visual perception of these "signs." However, as soon as we "see" printed signs and not drawings, we perform something more than, or rather something different from, a mere visual perception. In the perception which takes place during reading, we do not attend to the unique and individual features but rather to the typical: the general physical form of the letters as determined by the rules of the written language or, in the case of "fluent" reading, the form of the verbal signs. The individual features do not, of course, vanish entirely from the reader's awareness; the apprehension of the typical form of the verbal signs is thus not the pure apprehension of a species. We do see, for instance, how one letter is repeated in successive verbal signs. But the individual features here are subsumed only under the aspect of their typical form, and in general the quality of individuality recedes unless for some reason it becomes especially important; but it never disappears completely from awareness.[7] In fluent, fast reading we do not perceive the individual letters themselves, although they do not disappear from our consciousness. We read "whole words" and thus easily overlook typographical errors. There are also other details about the printed paper of which one is not completely unaware but to which one does not attend for their own sake. And if we did attend to them, that would prove to be a distraction in reading, because our main attention in visual reading is directed at the apprehension of the typical verbal forms. The same thing happens in hearing a speech or a "recited" literary work, where we do not attend to the details of the concrete sound as such but rather to the verbal sounds as typical forms. If for some reason we do not succeed in apprehending the typical forms, even though the speaker's voice is loud enough, we often say we "didn't hear" the speaker and consequently didn't understand him.

The first basic process of reading a literary work is thus not a simple and purely sensory perception but goes beyond such a perception by concentrating attention on the typical features in the physical or phonetic form of the words.[8] There is still another way in which the basic process of reading goes beyond simple sensory seeing. First, it takes the writing (printing) to be "expression," that is, the carrier of a meaning;[9] second, the verbal sound, which seems to be interwoven in a peculiar way with the written sign of the word, is immediately apprehended, again in its typical form, along with the written sign.

When we read a text "silently" (without speaking the words aloud, even softly), our apprehension is normally not limited to simply seeing the graphic form of the writing, as is the case with Chinese characters when we do not know Chinese,[10] or when we see a drawing (for instance, an arabesque) without any idea that it might be a written message. A normal reader who knows the phonetic form of the language well will combine silent reading with an imaginary hearing of the corresponding verbal sounds and the speech melody as well, without paying particular attention to this hearing. When the verbal sound is relatively important, the reader might even pronounce the sound involuntarily and quietly; this can be accompanied by certain motor phenomena. The auditory apprehension of the phonetic form of the words is so closely related to the visual apprehension of the written form that the intentional correlates of these experiences also seem to be in especially close relation. The phonetic and visual forms of the word seem almost to be merely two aspects of the same "verbal body."

As already mentioned, the verbal body is simultaneously grasped as an "expression" of something other than itself, that is, of the meaning of the word, which refers to something or exercises a particular function of meaning (for instance, a syntactical function).[11] When we know the language in question well and use it daily, we apprehend the verbal sounds not as pure sound patterns but as something which, in addition to its sound, conveys or can convey a certain emotional quality.[12] As I tried to show in my book *The Literary Work of Art,* this quality, which is intuitively felt, can either be determined by the meaning of the word (or the emotional aspect of the object meant) or can be related to the function of the "expression" of the speaker's emotional processes (fear, anger, desire, etc.). The latter possibility refers primarily to words and phrases quoted in a literary text and spoken by a character in the work, and it is brought about not through the phonetic form of the verbal sound but through the tone in which the words are spoken. This emotional quality often aids in the recognition of the typical phonetic form of the verbal sound when recognition is otherwise difficult.

Simultaneous with and inseparable from the described apprehension of the verbal sounds is the understanding of the meaning of the word; the complete word is constituted for the reader in just this experience, which, although compound, still forms a unity. One does not apprehend the verbal sound first and then the verbal meaning. Both things occur at once: in apprehending the verbal sound, one understands the meaning of the word and at the same time intends this meaning actively.[13] Only in exceptional cases, as when the word is, or seems to be, foreign to us, is the apprehension of the verbal sound not automatically connected with understanding the verbal meaning. Then we notice a natural tendency in us to complete the act of understanding. If we cannot grasp the meaning immediately, we notice a characteristic slowing-down or even a halt in the process of reading. We feel a certain helplessness and try to guess the meaning. Usually it is only in such a case that we have a clear thematic apprehension of the verbal sound in its phonetic and visual form; at the same time, we are puzzled about not finding the meaning, which should be immediately apparent and nonetheless does not come to mind. If the meaning occurs to us, then the obstacle is overcome and the act of understanding flows into a new understanding of the following words. But when we know the words well, it is typical that the verbal sound is noted only fleetingly, quickly and without hesitation; it represents only a quick transition to the understanding of the words or sentences. The verbal sound is then heard superficially and almost unconsciously. It appears on the periphery of the field of awareness, and only incidentally does it sound "in our ears," provided, of course, that nothing out of the ordinary draws our attention to it. It is precisely this fleeting way of apprehending the verbal sounds which is the only correct way for the apprehension of the literary work as a whole. This is the reason one often hears the demand for a "discreet" declamation, to prevent the phonetic side of the language from encroaching too much on the hearer, from coming to the fore.

In the literary work, as we have already mentioned, words do not appear in isolation; rather, they join together in a certain arrangement to form whole linguistic patterns of various kinds and orders. In many cases, especially in verse, words are arranged with primary concern not for the context of meaning which they constitute but instead with regard to their phonetic form, so that a unified pattern arises from the sequence of sounds, such as a line of verse or a stanza. Concern for the phonetic form in arrangement also brings about such phenomena as rhythm, rhyme, and various "melodies" of the line, the sentence, or the speech in general, as well as intuitive qualities of linguistic expression, such as "softness" or "hardness" or "sharpness." We usually note these phonetic formations and phenomena even when we read silently; even if we pay no particular attention to them, our notice of them still plays an important role in the aesthetic perception of at least a good number of literary works of art. Not only do they themselves constitute an aesthetically important element of the work; they are often, at the same time, a means of disclosing other aspects and qualities of the work, for instance, a mood which hovers over the situations portrayed in the work. Thus the reader must have an "ear" for the phonetic stratum of the work (for its "music"), although one cannot say that he should concentrate on this stratum particularly. The phonetic qualities of the work must be heard "incidentally" and add their voice to the entirety of the work.

However, because the disclosure of phonetic phenomena of higher order is connected with the individual phases of becoming acquainted with the literary work of art, it will be necessary to return to the phonetic phenomena in later investigations.

## Understanding Verbal and Sentence Meanings

But how do we know that we "understand" words or sentences? In which particular experiences does this "understanding" take place, and when have we really "understood" the text of a work? Who can guarantee that we have correctly understood and not misinterpreted sentences appearing in various contexts and interconnections? The last question comes to mind immediately, but we cannot answer it until much later.

It is a difficult task to describe or simply to indicate the experiences in which we understand words and sentences, because we normally pay no attention to these experiences. Not all scholars are aware of the difficulties which one encounters here.[14] Thus we will have to limit ourselves in our investigation to rudimentary comments; but even a superficial consideration of the experience of understanding demands an explanation of what the meaning of a word or the sense of a phrase is. Unfortunately, this problem, too, is connected with difficulties and is related to various philosophical problems. Without being able to discuss here the numerous theories which have been advanced since Husserl's pioneering *Logical Investigations,*[15] I want to recapitulate the main points of the concept of the meaning of a linguistic entity which I set forth in my book *The Literary Work of Art.*

The meaning of a word can be considered in two different ways: as part of a sentence or a higher semantic unit or as an isolated single word, taken by itself. Although the latter case hardly occurs in practice, still it is wise to consider it.

Contrary to common assertions, the verbal meaning is neither a psychological phenomenon (in particular, an element or feature of a mental experience) nor an ideal object. The former view, held by the psychologistic school, was criticized by E. Husserl and G. Frege. In his *Logical Investigations,* Husserl advanced the second view under Bernard Bolzano's influence, but he relinquished it in his *Formal and Transcendental Logic,* although he retained the terms "ideal meaning" [*ideale Bedeutung*] and "ideal object" [*idealer Gegenstand*]. In my book *The Literary Work of Art* I tried to work out a conception of meaning analogous to Husserl's. The verbal meaning, and with it the meaning of a sentence, is on the one hand something objective which—assuming, of course, that the word has just one meaning—remains identical in its core, however it is used, and is thus transcendent to all mental experiences. On the other hand, the verbal meaning is an intentional configuration of appropriately structured mental experiences. It is either creatively constituted in a mental act, often on the basis of an originary experience; or else it is reconstituted or intended again in mental acts after this constitution has already taken place. To use Husserl's apt expression, the meaning is "conferred on" [*verliehen*] the word. What is "conferred" in an intentional mental experience is itself a "derived intention" [*abgeleitete Intention*], as I have expressed it, which is supported by a verbal sound and which, together with the verbal sound, constitutes the word. The word is recognized and used according to what kind of intention it has. The intention can refer denominatively to objects, characteristics, relations, and pure qualities, but it can also exercise various syntactical and logical functions when various meanings enter into relation with one another or when various objects intended by the meanings are brought into relation with one another.[16]

In a living language it is relatively seldom that we consciously confer meaning on a given word. It happens, for example, when new scientific words are formed by means of a definition or by supplying appropriate examples of objects which are to be grasped and named conceptually.[17] Normally one finds complete words (that is, verbal sounds, together with their meanings) already existing in the languages and simply applies them to the appropriate objectivities.

But when and how do we succeed in finding and thereby actualizing just that meaning which a word has in a given language and in a certain place in the text?[18] Of course it is not seldom that one makes mistakes and *mis*understands this or that word in the text of the work, that is, gives it a meaning other than the one it actually has in that language. This danger in fact exists; but it should be neither exaggerated nor considered unavoidable. Many scholars tend to do just that; they hold a view of the nature of the verbal meaning whereby its correct understanding becomes purely a matter of coincidence. They identify the verbal meaning with the so-called content of a mental act, considering this "content" as a component, a "real part" [*reeller Teil*], in Husserl's sense, of the act. According to this theory, there are in the real external world only so-called physical signs the mental idea of which "combines" with a psychological content through "convention" or random "association." The psychological content, which is naturally always "my own," is supposed to be the meaning of the word, so that the reader of a literary work or the hearer of someone else's speech cannot go beyond the "contents" of his own mental acts. Thus, when two people use the same word, each of them has his own "private" meaning for the (supposedly) identical word, and only the "identity" of the contents they experience accounts for the fact that both use this word with the "same" meaning. From this point of view, the word itself (actually, only the verbal sound—but in this theory the word is equated with the verbal sound) has no meaning at all. To understand in which sense a certain word is being used, one must simply guess what constitutes the content of the speaker's mental act. But the great majority of psychologists maintain that experiences are accessible as objects of cognition only to the experiencing subject. In that case, the correct understanding of the meaning of a word (in short, the understanding of a word) used by another is almost a miracle. Since, according to this theory, understanding is based on a completely random association of exactly the same content with the mere verbal sign, it does not consist in knowing the appropriate verbal meaning. Under these conditions, the correct understanding of literary texts, the authors of which are in many cases unknown and often no longer living, seems to be quite impossible. Each literary text would then have to be understood in each reader's own way, and there would be as many ways of understanding the text as there are readers or readings. It would be impossible to achieve real communication through a literary text. But then, how would "intersubjective" science, as it is called, be possible?[19]

Moreover, this theory does not correspond to the actual situation when two people converse in the same language. For example, if I speak with someone about an external state of affairs and he points out to me another feature of this state of affairs, then he is not interested in the concrete contents of my mental acts, just as I am not interested in the contents of his mental experiences. We are both directing our attention to a state of affairs which is external for both of us; by its characteristics and details we orient ourselves as to whether we are speaking about the same thing and saying the same thing about it. If something does not tally, we can correct our understanding of the other's speech by reference to the state of affairs; we can then "agree" linguistically that we have established and learned this or that. I take an interest in what the other person is thinking at the moment only if he speaks a language I cannot understand or if he cannot speak at all but I see that he wants to communicate something to me. But even then I do not try to discover the concrete flow of the contents of his mental acts but rather the linguistic sense which he is trying to constitute and communicate to me. I go beyond the concrete contents of his experience in order to grasp the not yet understood sense of the linguistic entity. And trying to grasp the concrete contents of the other person's mental experience would hardly be to the point, since these contents are constantly changing in their transition from the continuously flowing present into the past. Once fixed, however, the meaning of a linguistic entity does not undergo such changes; it remains identical as a quasi-static unity until a new meaning is possibly conferred on it.

The source of this psychologistic view of the meaning of linguistic entities lies partly in an incorrect view of how word formation comes about and in a failure to recognize the social nature of every language. It is simply not true that each of us forms the meanings of words for himself alone, in complete isolation, "privately." On the contrary, almost every instance of forming words or conferring meaning represents the common work of two or more people who find themselves confronted with the same object (a thing or a concrete process) or in a common situation. The two people attempt not only to gain knowledge about the nature and properties of the object or situation but also to give it an identical name, with an appropriately constituted meaning, or to describe it in a sentence. The name or sentence becomes intelligible for the two persons with reference to the commonly observed object.[20] Suppose that, in a scientific investigation, it becomes necessary to find a new expression for a new concept. The new meaning will become intelligible to others only if it is either brought into relation with or reduced to other, already intelligible meanings. Or it may be placed in an indirect cognitive relation to appropriate objects, thus giving others the possibility of attaining an immediate apprehension (in particular, a perception) of the object in question and of constituting or reconstituting the word meaning relating to the object in view of this object—of constituting, that is, the meaning already intended by the investigator. Then there are means of checking the correctness of the reconstituted meaning and of discovering and removing possible misunderstandings. However great the practical difficulties may be, it is still beyond doubt that the meaning of a new word is always constituted through the intellectual cooperation of several subjects of consciousness in common and direct cognitive contact with the corresponding objects. The meaning-carrying word originating in this way is thus from the outset an intersubjective entity, intersubjectively accessible in its meaning, and not something with a "private" meaning which must be guessed at through observation of another's behavior. Then, too, words are not fully isolated entities but are always members of a linguistic system,[21] however loose this system may be in an individual case. At any rate, such a linguistic system has certain characteristic qualities and regularities which apply both phonetically and semantically and which are decisive in guaranteeing the identity of individual verbal meanings as well as in determining them. After reference to the direct experience of the same objects, such a linguistic system is the second most effective means for reaching agreement about the identical meanings of words belonging to the same language. Knowledge of a language is not restricted to knowledge of a great many verbal meanings but also pertains to the manifold regularities which govern the language. A word which is at first unintelligible appears together with a sequence of other words, with which it is connected by various syntactic functions or relations established through content. These relations often make it possible to guess the meaning of the word "from context," not only in isolation, as it appears in a dictionary entry, but also in the full form, with the nuances appropriate to this context. All these expedients, well known in philological practice, show that the discovery of the meaning which the word has in context is not impossible when one knows the language relatively well; nor is it so difficult as the psychological theory sometimes maintains.

A living language forms a structured system of meanings which stand in definite formal and material relations to one another and which also exercise various functions in semantic units of greater complexity, particularly in sentences. The structured system of meanings is made possible by the presence of several basic types of words, distinguished from one another by formal elements (form in the grammatical sense) as well as by a different composition of their meaning. We can distinguish three different basic types of words: (1) nouns, (2) finite verbs, and (3) function words.[22] The most important function of the meaning of nouns is the intentional projection of the objects they name. The noun determines its object as to its form (whether it is a thing, a process, or an event, e.g., a tree, a movement, or a blow), as to its qualitative constitution (what kind of object it is and what qualities it has), and finally as to its mode of being (whether it is intended as a real or an ideal or perhaps as a possible object). For instance, the noun "tree" designates a thing in the ontic mode of reality; a phrase like "the similarity of mathematical triangles" designates an ideal relationship among certain mathematical objects; the noun "perceptibility" designates a certain possibility, etc. To each noun belongs a definite purely intentional object which is dependent on the meaning of the noun for its existence, its form, and the stock of material determinations attributed to it. We must distinguish between the purely intentional object and the object, ontically independent of the meaning of the noun, to which the noun can be applied and which, if it exists at all, is real or ideal or what have you in a genuine sense. Of course, there are nouns which do have a purely intentional object without any ontically autonomous object as its correlate, as with the noun "centaur." The purely intentional character of the object is evident.

In contrast to nouns, the function words—such as "is" (as a copula in cognizing something, in a declarative sentence), "or," "and," "to," "each," "by"—do not constitute an intentional object through their meaning; rather, they merely serve to perform various functions in relation to the meanings of other words with which they appear or in relation to the objects of the nouns which they connect. Thus the word "and" between two nouns (dog and cat) joins these nouns together into a semantic unit of a higher order, and as a correlate to this function it creates a certain intentional interdependence of the objects of these nouns. The "and" can also join two sentences, which then cease to be independent and become parts of a compound sentence. Along with the syntactic functions performed by other words—nouns and verbs—through their grammatical forms and their arrangement in the sentence, the functions exercised by the function words play an important role in constituting both sentences and groups of sentences.

The finite verbs, as the most important sentence-forming or coforming element in the language, are just as important in this respect. They determine—although not alone—the states of affairs as purely intentional sentence correlates. In their various forms, in conjunction with the manifold syntactic functions of the function words, they produce a great multiplicity of sentence structures and sentence complexes and, corresponding to them, a multiplicity of sentence correlates, especially states of affairs and their interconnections. Sentences join in diverse ways to form semantic units of a higher order which exhibit quite varied structures; from these structures arise such entities as a story, a novel, a conversation, a drama, a scientific theory.[23] By the same token, finite verbs constitute not only states of affairs which correspond to the individual sentences, but also whole systems of very diverse types of states of affairs, such as concrete situations, complex processes involving several objects, conflicts and agreements among them, etc. Finally, a whole world is created with variously determined elements and the changes taking place in them, all as the purely intentional correlate of a sentence complex. If this sentence complex finally constitutes a literary work, then I call the whole stock of interconnected intentional sentence correlates the "portrayed world" of the work.

But let us return to our investigation of the process of understanding.

When we apprehend a verbal sound or multiplicity of verbal sounds, the first step in understanding it is finding[24] the precise meaning intention which the word has in its language. This meaning intention can appear in two different ways, either in a way characteristic of the word in isolation or in another way, when the word is part of a more complex semantic unit. The meaning of a word undergoes a change, in many cases a regular one, according to the context in which it appears.[25] In particular, it is enriched by specially operative intentions which are performed by the syntactic functions determined by the structure of the corresponding semantic unit of higher order and by the place where the word stands in this semantic unit. In the understanding of a text, the meaning intentions are present in one of these two forms. But whenever the word functions only as part of a sentence, discovering that form of the meaning which the word has in isolation would be neither advisable nor faithful to the text. It is remarkable, however, that in such cases one immediately apprehends the meanings of the individual words in the form they have in context. Usually this apprehension occurs without special effort or resistance; it does not, however, always occur with the same ease. Only in exceptional cases are we oriented toward the discovery of the lexical meaning of words.[26]

The successful immediate discovery of the meaning intention is basically an actualization of this intention. That is: when I understand a text, I think the meaning of the text. I extract the meaning from the text, so to speak, and change it into the actual intention of my mental act of understanding,[27] into an intention identical with the word or sentence intention of the text. Then I really "understand" the text. Of course, this applies only when the work is written in one's so-called native language or at least in a language completely familiar to the reader. Then the text need not be translated into the reader's own language but is immediately thought in the language of the text.[28]

Only when the language of a work is not immediately intelligible to the reader does he have to search for the meanings of individual words separately, find them (sometimes with a dictionary), and only then, after an appropriate interpretation of the sense, "join" them to form a whole sentence. Thus one sometimes reads old Latin texts without having the ability to think in Latin (in which case the fact that Latin is a "dead" language plays an important role). Basically we then understand the text by translating it into our own language, and we check back only to see whether this translation is correct. Disregarding the fact that a translation of a work is never completely adequate (a problem in itself), the course the reading itself follows is quite different in the two cases compared. In the first case we assimilate the meanings of the individual words in such a way that we immediately think whole sentences. This "immediately" should not, of course, be taken to mean that we think the complete sentences all at once, in one moment, or that thinking the individual words is not necessary to the understanding of the whole sentence. Each time we think a sentence explicitly formulated in words, we need a short stretch of time to complete our thought; and it is also necessary when we think a sentence to traverse in mental acts the verbal meanings which form it. In reading a sentence, the opening words which we understand stimulate us to the unfolding of a sentence-generating operation,[29] a special mental flow in which the sentence unfolds. Once we begin to move with the course of thought which the sentence follows, we think it as a separate whole; and the individual verbal meanings are automatically accommodated into the sentence flow as phases of it which are not separately delimited. The verbal meanings can be so accommodated only if they are immediately thought in those nuances of meaning which they have as parts of that sentence. This is possible only because the sentence-generating operation consists in filling out a special kind of system of syntactic functions. The functions are filled by the words which make up the sentence. Once we are transposed into the flow of thinking the sentence, we are prepared, after having completed the thought of one sentence, to think its "continuation" in the form of another sentence, specifically, a sentence which has a connection with the first sentence. In this way the process of reading a text advances effortlessly. But when it happens that the second sentence has no perceptible connection whatever with the first, the flow of thought is checked. A more or less vivid surprise or vexation is associated with the resulting hiatus. The block must be overcome if we are to renew the flow of our reading. If we succeed, each following sentence will be understood as a continuation of preceding sentences. Just what is "continued" or developed is a separate problem, the solution of which depends on the structure of the given work. All that is important just now is that there is such a thing as an expectation for new sentences. And the advancing reading simply actualizes and makes present to us what we are expecting. In our orientation toward what is coming and our attempt to actualize it, we still do not lose sight of what we have just read. To be sure, we do not continue to think vividly the sentences we have already read at the same time that we are thinking the immediately following sentence. Nevertheless, the meaning of the sentence we have just read (and, to a limited degree also, that of several preceding sentences), as well as the sound of the words just pronounced, is still peripherally experienced in the form of a "reverberation." This "reverberation" has, among other things, the consequence that the sentence we are now reading is concretized in its meaning, that is, it receives precisely that nuance of meaning which it should have as a continuation of the sentences preceding it. For, as closer analysis shows, the sentences, too, are only to a certain degree independent of other semantic units in the text and receive their full meaning, with its proper nuances, only as parts of a multiplicity of sentences. The meaning of the sentence completes itself and adapts itself to the meaning of the sentences preceding it, but not only to those preceding it. The meaning of sentences which are yet to come can also share in determining the meaning of the sentence we have just read, can supplement or modify it. During the reading this occurs more distinctly when we know from the start the later parts of the work (for example, through a previous reading). On a first reading this is not so noticeable unless the sentences we have already read are of a kind which enable us to foresee in general outline the meaning of the sentences following. Usually, however, this modification of previous sentences by those which follow displays itself only after reading a series of consecutive sentences. In this case we quickly make a mental survey of the sentences we have already read, the actual meaning of which is disclosed only at this moment, and we think them explicitly again in a new and expanded or connected meaning. Sometimes, however, this occurs automatically, without a special act of explicitly rethinking the sentences. This fact can serve as an argument that the meaning of at least some of the sentences already read does not completely vanish for the reader; rather, he is still peripherally aware of it in the form of a "reverberation" as he reads the succeeding sentences.

In a reading which is properly carried out, the content of the work is organized quasi-automatically into an internally coherent, meaningful whole of a higher order and is not merely a random conglomeration of separate sentence meanings which are completely independent of one another. The various functions of function words, such as "because," "thus," or "consequently," play a significant role in organizing the content of a work into a whole. Interconnections of meaning among several sentences can also be constituted implicitly without the use of such words, through the material content of nouns and verbs. We really understand the content of a work only when we succeed in making use of, and actualizing, all the constitutive elements the text provides and in constituting the organized, meaningful whole of the work in accordance with the meaning intentions contained in the semantic stratum of the text.[30] Of course, we do not always succeed, especially when we do not pay special attention to the meaning of individual sentences which we did not understand immediately, and when we do not return to sentences which we have already read and whose meaning must perhaps be corrected. The connections between sentences are also sometimes unclear and hence require special attention. But if even our special attention is of little avail, then, despite all our efforts, we do not understand the text; it contains, as blank spots, a series of incomprehensible sentences, which we do not know how to integrate properly with the rest. But even if we finally overcome all difficulties, so that we can maintain that we understand the whole text, still, this laborious sort of reading hardly reproduces the original form peculiar to the work. The natural flow of successively developing sentence meanings is interrupted by this mode of reading; the dynamic unfolding of meaning in the natural succession of its parts which is proper to the work is affected or even destroyed, and it is almost totally obscured. In a scientific work this often need have no great significance; in a literary work of art, however, at least the aesthetic effect of the work on the reader is seriously modified. And if the work, as a result of its own unclarities and disorder, cannot be read in any other way, then its aesthetic aspect will be seriously impaired. It makes no difference whether the unclarities are accidental flaws or intended features of the work.

One further comment in closing. The declarative sentences in the literary work of art can theoretically be read in either of two ways: as judgments about a reality ontically independent of the work or as sentences which only appear to be assertions. In the first case we refer in our thoughts immediately (directly) to objects (things, states of affairs, processes, events) which do not belong to the work itself and which, in accordance with this understanding of the declarative sentences, exist in reality and are supposed to be in reality just the way they are intended. When we refer in thought to real objects, we go beyond the realm of being of the literary work, while the objectivities portrayed in the work itself vanish in some measure from the reader's attention. They become "transparent," so that the "ray of vision" of the reader's intention is not arrested by them. In the second case, however, we turn with the intentional act in which the sentence is thought to the objectivities portrayed in the work itself. Thus we remain in the realm of the work itself, without taking an interest in extraliterary reality. This second interpretation of the declarative sentences appearing in the literary work of art is the one proper to it. I shall discuss this subject later. In the following, I shall attempt to describe the experiences of becoming acquainted with, and of apprehending, the literary work of art as these occur when the reader assumes the attitude that the declarative sentences are merely apparent assertions.

## Passive and Active Reading

The activities performed during reading which we have described thus far do not yet exhaust the complex process which we call the cognition of the literary work. Rather, they merely constitute the indispensable means for the performance of a new cognitive operation which is much more important for the cognition of the literary work than the activities previously discussed. This new operation is the intentional reconstruction and then the cognition of the objectivities portrayed in the work.

Any understanding of the semantic units in the literary work (words, sentences, and complexes or structures of sentences) consists in performing the appropriate signitive acts and leads thereby to the intentional projection of the objects of these acts, or the intentional objects of the semantic units. Hence it appears, at first glance, that the understanding in ordinary reading suffices to constitute for the reader the objectivities portrayed in the work. But a closer look shows that this is not the case.

Provisionally, we shall distinguish two different ways of reading the literary work: ordinary, purely passive (receptive) reading and active reading.

Every reading, of course, is an activity consciously undertaken by the reader and not a mere experience or reception of something. Nevertheless, in many cases the whole effort of the reader consists in thinking the meanings of the sentences he reads without making the meanings into objects and in remaining, so to speak, in the sphere of meaning. There is no intellectual attempt to progress from the sentences read to the objects appropriate to them and projected by them. Of course, these objects are always an automatic intentional projection of the sentence meanings. In purely passive reading, however, one does not attempt to apprehend them or, in particular, to constitute them synthetically. Consequently, in passive reading there is no kind of intercourse with the fictional objects.

This purely passive, receptive manner of reading, which is often mechanical as well, occurs relatively often in the reading of both literary works of art and scientific works. One still knows what one is reading, although the scope of understanding is often limited to the sentence which is being read. But one does not become clearly aware of what one is reading about and what its qualitative constitution is. One is occupied with the realization of the sentence meaning itself and does not absorb the meaning in such a way that one can transpose oneself by means of it into the world of the objects in a work; one is too constrained by the meaning of the individual sentences. One reads "sentence by sentence," and each of these sentences is understood separately, in isolation; a synthetic combination of the sentence just read with other sentences, sometimes widely separated from it, is not achieved. If the passive reader were required to make a short summary of the content of what he has read, he would be unable to do it. With a good enough memory, he could perhaps repeat the text within certain limits, but that is all. A good knowledge of the language of the work, a certain amount of practice in reading, a stereotyped sentence structure—all this often results in the reading's running its course quite "mechanically," without the personal and active participation of the reader, although he is the one doing the reading.

It is hard to describe the difference between passive, purely receptive reading and "active" reading because in passive reading we do, after all, think the sentences as we think them also in "active" reading. Thus there seems to be an activity involved in both cases. It would perhaps be easier to contrast these two ways of reading if we could say that, when one reads receptively, one does not think the meanings of the sentences by performing the corresponding signitive acts; rather, one only experiences or feels that they are being performed. By contrast, it is only in active reading that we actually perform the signitive acts. But the matter is not so simple, because in both kinds of reading mental acts are performed. The difference between the two kinds of reading consists merely in the way in which they are performed. It is, however, extremely difficult to describe these modes of performance.

Suppose we assert that in "active" reading one not only understands the sentence meanings but also apprehends their objects and has a sort of intercourse with them. A theory arising from naïve empiricist or positivist realism renders agreement with this assertion more difficult. These realists hold that we can have intercourse with objects only (*a*) when the objects are real and (*b*) when we simply find them present before us without our contribution, thus when we need do nothing but gape at what is before us. It is assumed without further ado in this theory that we are presented with objects only through sense perception or, at most, through inner perception. Thus, if we learn about an object exclusively through understanding a few sentences, then it follows that we cannot have immediate intercourse with that object. This contention appears to exclude all cases in which (as in the preponderant majority of literary works of art) we have to do with objects and events which have never existed or occurred in reality.

However, the realist theory is wrong, primarily in asserting that in sense perception we gain knowledge of the things and events of the real world around us only by passive "gaping." On the contrary, in order really to cognize these things, we must perform a series of often complicated and interconnected acts, which demand of us a considerable degree of activity and attentiveness and which, on the basis of the material provided us through a multiplicity of perceptions, finally lead us to the real object we perceive. And only when the object is thus made accessible to us do we have direct intercourse with it as with something which is truly given and self-present. This theory is also wrong in asserting that, beyond the area of sensory or internal perception, we can gain no direct or even quasi-direct knowledge of objects such as those we know only through the understanding of certain sentences. When we are dealing with the objects of a geometrical investigation, for instance, we sometimes gain a direct apprehension of certain states of affairs pertaining in the geometrical objects, as well as of necessary relationships among them, through understanding certain sentences and with the help of specially modified acts of imagination. When we are unable to succeed at this, we say that we certainly understand the sentences linguistically but that, even when the proof is provided, we are not genuinely convinced that it is really as the proposition in question maintains, nor can we come to clear and distinct awareness of what is "really" being dealt with. Some people express this differently by saying that they certainly "know" what the proposition is about but do not truly understand the sentence, since they obviously derive genuine understanding only from a direct, intuitive apprehension of the corresponding geometrical state of affairs.

Something similar happens when objects are simulated in creative artistic imagination with the help of special acts of consciousness. Such objects are, to be sure, purely intentional or, if we prefer, "fictive"; but, precisely as a result of the particular activity of the creative acts producing them, they attain the character of an independent reality. Once the creative intentionality has thus been actualized, it becomes to a certain degree binding for us. The objects corresponding to the intentional acts are projected in the later phases of the creative process as a quasi-reality to some extent independent of these acts. We take this quasi-reality into account; we must adjust ourselves to it; or, if for some reason it does not satisfy us, we must transform it, or further develop and supplement it, by means of a new creative act.

The reading of a literary work of art can thus be accomplished "actively," in the sense that we think with a peculiar originality and activity the meaning of the sentences we have read; we project ourselves in a cocreative attitude into the realm of the objects determined by the sentence meanings. The meaning in this case creates an approach to the objects which are treated in the work. The meaning, as Husserl says, is only a passageway [*ein Durchgangsobjekt*] which one traverses in order to reach the object meant. In a strict sense the meaning is not an object at all. For, if we think a sentence actively, we attend, not to the meaning, but to what is determined or thought through it or in it. We can say, although not quite precisely, that in actively thinking a sentence we constitute or carry out its meaning and, in so doing, arrive at the objects of the sentence, that is, the states of affairs or other intentional sentence correlates. From this point we can grasp the things themselves which are indicated in the sentence correlates.

Besides its two linguistic strata, the literary work also contains the stream of portrayed objectivities. Thus, in order to apprehend the whole work,[31] it is necessary above all to reach all of its strata, and especially the stratum of portrayed objectivities. Even a purely receptive reading discloses this stratum to the reader, at least distantly and obscurely. Only an active reading, however, permits the reader to discover it in its peculiar, characteristic structure and in its full detail. But this cannot be accomplished through a mere apprehension of the individual intentional states of affairs belonging to the sentences. We must progress from these states of affairs to their diverse interconnections and then to the objects (things, events) which are portrayed in the states of affairs. But in order to achieve an aesthetic apprehension of the stratum of objects in its often complex structure, the active reader, after he has discovered and reconstructed this stratum, must, as we shall see, go beyond it, especially beyond various details explicitly indicated by the sentence meanings, and must supplement in many directions what is portrayed. And in so doing, the reader to some extent proves to be the cocreator of the literary work of art. Let us discuss this in greater detail.

# Notes

1. In particular, it does not correspond to the word used in the Polish version, *poznawać*, which clearly indicates an activity, not necessarily completed, and which can be opposed to the Polish *poznać*, which designates a successful cognitive activity leading to effective knowledge.

2. The word "value" and the word "work" are both used here with a certain double meaning, which will become clear later. We cannot say everything at once.

3. I assumed an analogous standpoint as to method in the investigation of the basic structure of the literary work of art in my book *The Literary Work of Art* [*Das literarische Kunstwerk* (Halle: Max Niemeyer, 1931; 2d ed., Tübingen: Max Niemeyer, 1960; 3d ed., 1965); English translation by George Grabowicz (Evanston, Ill.: Northwestern University Press, 1973)]. This method has been misunderstood from many sides. It does not mean at all that I exclude the artistic or aesthetic value of the literary work of art from consideration.

4. Even when we use artificial apparatus (e.g., a microscope, electron microscope, radar, various electrical measuring devices, etc.) to observe objects (or processes), the structure of the apparatus is designed to function in a certain way which is adapted to the type of object or process which is to be "observed."

5. It is a special problem whether the declarative sentences which are only quoted in the text, for example the sentences spoken by the persons portrayed, also undergo such a modification. This is of particular importance for the drama. The question as to which linguistic and perhaps also extralinguistic means produce the character of quasi-judgments constitutes another problem, which has been investigated by Käte Hamburger. I shall return to this problem in connection with the question of how the reader recognizes that he is dealing only with quasi-judgments and not with genuine judgments, for instance in a novel.

6. I shall later have occasion to speak of the further differences between scientific works and literary works of art.

7. An attentive, purely sensory perception (or, better, a series of continual perceptions of the same thing, in sequence) gives us an object which is in every sense individual. In a fleeting perception we tend to see clearly only a general aspect of the object; we then say: "I see a mountain" or "a table." These words are general nouns and are applied to the object of perception, which is indeed before us in its individuality without every detail being strictly individualized. Only a further, more attentive perception leads to a more exact apprehension of the uniqueness of many details, so that we understand its difference from other "similar" objects. In reading a printed text, the individual letters and verbal signs do not have individual qualities for us; they simply do not matter to us. On the contrary, it would disturb us in our reading if we noted individual differences in letters too much. This becomes especially evident in reading manuscripts, where we purposely ignore individual deviations in the physical form of the letters and direct ourselves to the "character" of the person's handwriting—that is, to what is typical in his handwriting. If we are unsuccessful in apprehending the character of the writing, we will be unable to "decipher" the text at all.

8. I would not place such emphasis on this essentially trivial fact were it not for the

neopositivists, who once tried to reduce sentences to mere writing and this writing, as a linguistic formation, to physical objects: spots of ink on paper, or particles of chalk on a blackboard (see, in this connection, *Erkenntnis*, Vol. III [1933]). But even linguists consider the verbal sound the physical side of the word (see, for example, Emile Benvéniste's newest book, *Problèmes de linguistique générale* [Paris: Gallimard, 1966]).

9. This is the case even when we do not know the meaning (as, for instance, in a foreign language of which we have imperfect knowledge) and thus do not understand the word. The phenomenon of not understanding can occur only where we are dealing from the outset with a written sign and not with a mere drawing.

10. This is the case with all languages whose "pronunciation" we do not know.

11. I use the word "expression' [*Ausdruck*] as Edmund Husserl did in his *Logische Untersuchungen*, 2 vols. (Halle: Max Niemeyer, 1900; 2d ed., 1913); [English translation by J. N. Findlay, *Logical Investigations*, 2 vols. (New York: Humanities Press, 1970)]. Bühler used the same word later in another sense, in which what is expressed is not the meaning of the word in a given language but rather a phenomenon of consciousness or an emotional state of the speaker. In a literary work, words or entire phrases can exercise this new expressive function if they are spoken by the characters in a work, e.g., in a drama. The verbal sounds then gain a new, primarily emotional character, which adheres to them without itself being any physical (visual or acoustic) quality.

12. Julius Stenzel once called attention to this possibility. The often-used word "expression" refers here only to the phonetic or written form of the word and is to be differentiated from "word," which encompasses both the phonetic form and the meaning.

13. When we speak about the "word," we are using an artificial abstraction, because in normal reading or understanding of a foreign language we do not concentrate on individual, isolated words; rather, words form for us from the outset only part of a linguistic structure of greater complexity, usually of a sentence. More about this later.

14. Danute Gierulanka furnished a good analysis of "understanding" in the various possible meanings of the word in her book *Zagadnienie swoistosci poznania matematycznego* (*The Character of Mathematical Knowledge*) (Warsaw: Panstwowe Wydawn. Naukowe, 1962).

15. The neopositivists caused great confusion in the investigation of the meaning of linguistic formations when they tried to eliminate the entire problem by preaching a physicalistic theory of language. Since the Prague Congress (1934), where I was forced to take a stand against the thesis that the meaning of a sentence is its verifiability, and since the appearance of Alfred Tarski's "Der Wahrheitsbegriff in den formalisierten Sprachen," *Studia Philosophica*, Vol. I (1935), the neopositivists have tried to adopt another viewpoint with regard to the problem of meaning. The "later" Wittgenstein, especially in his *Philosophical Investigations*, was aware of these problems but was unable to find a real solution.

16. It is usually said (especially in neopositivist circles) that the words which have a syntactic function designate other "signs." This is false, primarily because the function of such a word is entirely different from the designative function (the word "and" in the phrase "the dog and his master" does not name these two nouns). In the second place, this explanation completely overlooks the much more important function of such words with regard to what is designated by other words, especially nouns.

17. In connection with this kind of naming, it has become popular in the past few years to speak of "deictic" definitions.

18. As I have mentioned, I am considering here only those cases of the cognition of a literary work, and in particular of its semantic stratum, in which the reader really knows the language of the work. This restriction obviates the question as to how one learns a language—that is, the sense and the usage of individual words in larger linguistic formations. This latter case should not be confused with the situation of someone who reads a work in an language he fully understands.

19. Oddly enough, those scholars, like the neopositivists, who postulate the intersubjectivity of science as a *conditio sine qua non* are the same ones who, on the one hand, interpret the meaning or sense of utterances psychologically (or interpret them according to their so-called verifiability) and, on the other hand, maintain the impossibility of knowing another's experiences.

20. The language teachers who have developed the so-called direct method of learning a foreign language have long been aware of this and have devised very subtle methods for teaching their students the meanings of even abstract words without recourse to explicit definitions.

Of course, one must examine further how one comes to the conviction that several perceive the same object and are able to assure themselves of its identity. But these are the last important questions in the clarification of the possibility of "objective" knowledge, questions which have not yet been satisfactorily answered. The lack of satisfactory answers cannot, however, make us doubt the intuitive possession of the identical and common world. But the answers would be impossible if we did not have at our disposal a common language, intelligible to all members of the same speech community.

21. That any given language is a structured system of definite meanings with definite regularities and relationships is the basic assertion of Karl Bühler. Kasimir Ajdukiewicz, the Polish logician, also treated this problem (see "Sprache und Sinn," *Erkenntnis*, Vol. IV, no. 2 [1934]). His concern, however, was not spoken language but the artificial languages of deductive systems. He did not discuss what determines the possibility of an intersubjectively intelligible language. He merely developed the idea of a closed linguistic system, which certainly does not hold for all "languages."

22. See *The Literary Work of Art*, § 15. [*Das literarische Kunstwerk* (Halle: Max Niemeyer, 1931; 2d ed., Tübingen: Max Niemeyer, 1960; 3d ed., 1965; English translation by George Grabowicz (Evanston, Ill.: Northwestern University Press, 1973).] One should remember that both nouns and finite verbs exercise various syntactic and logical functions when they are parts of larger formations. These functions are exercised by the grammatical "forms" of the nouns and the verbs.

23. In my book *The Literary Work of Art* I discussed in somewhat greater detail what I merely sketch here. The matter is very complex and demands a comprehensive investigation. I restrict myself here to a very rudimentary indication. If adequately developed, it would lead, on the one hand, to a theory of language and, on the other, to regional ontologies.

24. Normally one should not take the discovery of the verbal meaning to be the object of a separate investigation. Such a thing is possible, of course, but usually occurs only when we are dealing with a completely unfamiliar word or when we consider the verbal

meaning from a theoretical point of view, analyze it, or compare it with other meanings. But such a consideration is not necessary in an ordinary reading and understanding of a text; it simply does not occur. When we are dealing with a language we know, we apprehend the appropriate meaning immediately, without making it an object of special consideration. We shall soon explain how this immediate apprehension comes about.

25. See *The Literary Work of Art,* § 17.

26. This lexical form of the verbal meaning is, by the way, only an artificial construct of linguistic analysis and not the original form of the verbal meaning, which in living languages is always part of a linguistic unity. In its lexical form the word almost always has many meanings; it becomes unambiguous when it is used concretely in a larger linguistic unit.

27. Husserl would call this a "signitive act" [*signitiver Akt*]. See his *Logical Investigations,* Vol. II, Fifth Investigation, *passim.*

28. This distinction is usually ignored or insufficiently considered, but it is essential for an apprehension of the work which is faithful to the text. Only when one reads a work in its original language can one apprehend the original emotional character of the words and phrases, the peculiar language melody, and all the subtle nuances of meaning of the text, which often have no equivalent in another language.

29. I first discussed the sentence-generating operation in my book *The Literary Work of Art.* The peculiar course of this operation and its possible variations have to be worked out more closely. But, even in the rudimentary fashion in which I treated it at that time, the indication of its existence is of great importance for the understanding of the unity of the sentence and for the possibility of the apprehension of states of affairs. Precisely because Franz Brenano, in his *Von der Klassifikation der psychischen Phänomene* (Leipzig: Duncker & Humblot, 1911), found no place for unified operations extending beyond the phase of the immediate present, he was unable to recognize the existence of states of affairs, which then led to his confused theory of "reism."

30. The concept of "content" in contrast to "form" has, of course, a great many meanings. I have also tried to compare the different concepts and, as far as possible, to define them more precisely. (See, among others, "The General Question of the Essence of Form and Content," *Journal of Philosophy,* Vol. LVII, no. 7 [1960].) In the text I make use of one of these concepts, which seems to me the only justified and useful one for the purpose of analyzing a literary work. The "content" of the literary work will be construed as the organized structure of meaning in the work, which is constituted by the semantic stratum. Of course, the "form" in which it is cast also belongs to this "content." The form is merely the way in which the content of the work is organized into a whole. The form of the semantic stratum must be distinguished, on the one hand, from the forms of the other strata and, on the other, from the form of the whole work, i.e., the totality of strata in the structure of the succession of the parts of the work. Each of these concepts can be determined unambiguously. But we must not contrast these various "forms" with the "content" of the work as a whole; rather, we must reserve the concept of "content" for the organized whole of the semantic stratum. The determination of the various "forms" which can be distinguished in the literary work and the explication of their diverse interrelations require a special investigation, which cannot be carried out here. Such an investigation is the only remedy for the hopeless confusion which currently reigns in discussions of the "form-content

problem." See my investigation in the second volume of the *Studia z estetyki* under the title "O formie i treści dziela sztuki literackiej" (On Form and Content in the Literary Work of Art), pp. 343–473. [Also published as "Das Form-Inhalt-Problem im literarischen Kunstwerk," in Roman Ingarden, *Erlebnis, Kunstwerk und Wert* (Tübingen: Max Niemeyer, 1969), pp. 31–50.—Trans.]

31. As we shall see, this is only possible in a perspectival foreshortening or distortion. I shall have more to say about this later.

# 7

# Phenomenology and Fundamental Ontology: The Disclosure of Meaning

================= Martin Heidegger =================

MARTIN HEIDEGGER (1889–1976). The external and internal facts of Heidegger's life seem scarce, and he has sometimes been called a man without a biography. Born in Messkirch, a small town in the Black Forest, he attended a Jesuit school for several years and subsequently the *Gymnasium* (classical high school) in Freiburg. From 1913 to 1916 he studied at the university in that town, theology at first and then philosophy together with some science and history. He received his doctorate in 1913 and acquired his second doctorate and *venia legendi* (*Habilitation*) three years later under the directorship of the Neokantian philosopher Heinrich Rickert, with a thesis on Duns Scotus's theory of categories. He began teaching that same year. He served in the German army from 1917 to 1919. In 1923 he became professor extraordinary at Marburg where he taught with great success. In 1928 he was appointed to the chair of philosophy at Freiburg which Husserl had vacated. Twice (in 1930 and 1933) Heidegger declined a call to Berlin. After a brief interlude at the beginning of the Third Reich (1933–1934), during which he assumed the rectorship of the university, Heidegger concentrated exclusively on his teaching until 1944 when he was drafted again, this time to dig trenches and foxholes for the army. From 1945 to 1951 he was suspended from the university by the French military government. He became emeritus in 1952, but continued teaching and lecturing until 1966 to 1967. In the years before 1927 Heidegger published essays and articles on various philosophical problems. While teaching at Freiburg, he came increasingly under the influence of Edmund Husserl and his phenomenology. In Marburg he worked in close contact with the theologian Rudolf Bultmann. After *Being and Time* (1927), Heidegger published mainly essays and articles and relinquished his plans for a second part of *Being and Time*. He was highly influential as a teacher, and many of his courses were delivered from booklike manuscripts. His unpublished work is immense and will comprise a good portion of the planned fifty-six volume edition of his writings (see Sect. A, Bibl.). The significance of *Being and Time* for hermeneutics stems from the fact that Heidegger radicalized the Diltheyan notion of understanding as a "category of life" into an "existentiale" (existential category), and thereby undercut the previous methodological discussions in the human sciences. In addition, his newly transformed hermeneutic notions served Heidegger as a basis for his own philosophy which he conceived as a new kind of hermeneutic enterprise itself. Because *Being and Time* represents Heidegger's most systematic effort, it should be studied in its entirety. Nevertheless, the sections 31–34 which we have selected for this *Reader* are relatively self-contained in their argumentation. Furthermore, reading them within the context of other hermeneutic texts may shed some new light on Heidegger's argument as it arises out of the hermeneutic tradition which he intends to overcome and surpass.

# BEING-THERE AS UNDERSTANDING

State-of-mind is *one* of the existential structures in which the Being of the 'there' maintains itself. Equiprimordial with it in constituting this Being is *understanding*. A state-of-mind always has its understanding, even if it merely keeps it suppressed. Understanding always has its mood. If we Interpret understanding as a fundamental *existentiale*, this indicates that this phenomenon is conceived as a basic mode of Dasein's *Being*. On the other hand, 'understanding' in the sense of *one* possible kind of cognizing among others (as distinguished, for instance, from 'explaining'), must, like explaining, be Interpreted as an existential derivative of that primary understanding which is one of the constituents of the Being of the "there" in general.

We have, after all, already come up against this primordial understanding in our previous investigations, though we did not allow it to be included explicitly in the theme under discussion. To say that in existing, Dasein is its "there," is equivalent to saying that the world is 'there'; its *Being-there* is Being-in. And the latter is likewise 'there,' as that for the sake of which Dasein is. In the "for-the-sake-of-which," existing Being-in-the-world is disclosed as such, and this disclosedness we have called "understanding." In the understanding of the "for-the-sake-of-which," the significance which is grounded therein, is disclosed along with it. The disclosedness of understanding, as the disclosedness of the "for-the-sake-of-which" and of significance equiprimordially, pertains to the entirety of Being-in-the-world. Significance is that on the basis of which the world is disclosed as such. To say that the "for-the-sake-of-which" *and* significance are both disclosed in Dasein, means that Dasein is that entity which, as Being-in-the-world, is an issue for itself.

When we are talking ontically we sometimes use the expression 'understanding something' with the signification of 'being able to manage something,' 'being a match for it,' 'being competent to do something.'[1] In understanding, as an *existentiale,* that which we have such competence over is not a "what," but Being as existing. The kind of Being which Dasein has, as potentiality-for-Being, lies existentially in understanding. Dasein is not something present-at-hand which possesses its competence for something by way of an extra; it is primarily Being-possible. Dasein is in every case what it can be, and in the way in which it is its possibility. The Being-possible which is essential for Dasein, pertains to the ways of its solicitude for Others and of its concern with the 'world,' as we have characterized them; and in all these, and always, it pertains to Dasein's potentiality-for-Being towards itself, for the sake of itself. The Being-possible which Dasein is existentially in every case, is to be sharply distinguished both from empty logical possibility and from the contingency of something present-at-hand, so far as with the present-at-hand this or that can 'come to pass.'² As a modal category of presence-at-hand, possibility signifies what is *not yet* actual and what is *not at any time* necessary. It characterizes the *merely* possible. Ontologically it is on a lower level than actuality and necessity. On the other hand, possibility as an *existentiale* is the most primordial and ultimate positive way in which Dasein is characterized ontologically. As with existentiality in general, we can, in the first instance, only prepare for the problem of possibility. The phenomenal basis for seeing it at all is provided by the understanding as a disclosive potentiality-for-Being.

Possibility, as an *existentiale,* does not signify a free-floating potentiality-for-Being in the sense of the 'liberty of indifference' *(libertas indifferentiae).* In every case Dasein, as essentially having a state-of-mind, has already got itself into definite possibilities. As the potentiality-for-Being which it *is,* it has let such possibilities pass by; it is constantly waiving the possibilities of its Being, or else it seizes upon them and makes mistakes.³ But this means that Dasein is Being-possible which has been delivered over to itself—*thrown possibility* through and through. Dasein is the possibility of Being-free *for* its ownmost potentiality-for-Being. Its Being-possible is transparent to itself in different possible ways and degrees.

Understanding is the Being of such potentiality-for-Being, which is never something still outstanding as not yet present-at-hand, but which, as something, which is essentially never present-at-hand, '*is*' with the Being of Dasein, in the sense of existence. Dasein is such that in every case it has understood (or alternatively, not understood) that it is to be thus or thus. As such understanding it 'knows' *what* it is capable of—that is, what its potentiality-for-Being is capable of.⁴ This 'knowing' does not first arise from an immanent self-perception, but belongs to the Being of the "there," which is essentially understanding. And only *because* Dasein, in understanding, is its "there," *can* it go astray and fail to recognize itself. And in so far as understanding is *accompanied by* state-of-mind and as such is existentially surrendered to thrownness, Dasein has in every case already gone astray and failed to recognize itself. In its potentiality-for-Being it is therefore delivered over to the possibility of first finding itself again in its possibilities.

*Understanding is the existential Being of Dasein's own potentiality-for-Being; and it is so in such a way that this Being discloses in itself what its Being is capable of.*[5] We must grasp the structure of this *existentiale* more precisely.

As a disclosure, understanding always pertains to the whole basic state of Being-in-the-world. As a potentiality-for-Being, any Being-in is a potentiality-for-Being-in-the-world. Not only is the world, *qua* world, disclosed as possible significance, but when that which is within-the-world is itself freed, this entity is freed for *its own* possibilities. That which is ready-to-hand is discovered as such in its service*ability*, its us*ability*, and its detriment*ality*. The totality of involvements is revealed as the categorial whole of a *possible* interconnection of the ready-to-hand. But even the 'unity' of the manifold present-at-hand, of Nature, can be discovered only if a *possibility* of it has been disclosed. Is it accidental that the question about the *Being* of Nature aims at the 'conditions of its *possibility*'? On what is such an inquiry based? When confronted with this inquiry, we cannot leave aside the question: *why* are entities which are not of the character of Dasein understood in their Being, if they are disclosed in accordance with the conditions of their possibility? Kant presupposes something of the sort, perhaps rightly. But this presupposition itself is something that cannot be left without demonstrating how it is justified.

Why does the understanding—whatever may be the essential dimensions of that which can be disclosed in it—always press forward into possibilities? It is because the understanding has in itself the existential structure which we call "*projection*."[6] With equal primordiality the understanding projects Dasein's Being both upon its "for-the-sake-of-which" and upon significance, as the worldhood of its current world. The character of understanding as projection is constitutive for Being-in-the-world with regard to the disclosedness of its existentially constitutive state-of-Being by which the factical potentiality-for-Being gets its leeway [Spielraum]. And as thrown, Dasein is thrown into the kind of Being which we call "projecting." Projecting has nothing to do with comporting oneself towards a plan that has been thought out, and in accordance with which Dasein arranges its Being. On the contrary, any Dasein has, as Dasein, already projected itself; and as long as it is, it is projecting. As long as it is, Dasein always has understood itself and always will understand itself in terms of possibilities. Furthermore, the character of understanding as projection is such that the understanding does not grasp thematically that upon which it projects—that is to say, possibilities. Grasping it in such a manner would take away from what is projected its very character as a possibility, and would reduce it to the given contents which we have in mind; whereas projection, in throwing, throws before itself the possibility as possibility, and lets it *be* as such.[7] As projecting, understanding is the kind of Being of Dasein in which it *is* its possibilities as possibilities.

Because of the kind of Being which is constituted by the *existentiale* of projection, Dasein is constantly 'more' than it factually is, supposing that one might want to make an inventory of it as something-at-hand and list the contents of its Being, and supposing that one were able to do so. But Dasein is never more than it factically is, for to its facticity its potentiality-for-Being belongs essentially. Yet as Being-possible, moreover, Dasein is never anything less; that is to say, it *is* existentially that which, in its potentiality-for-Being, it is *not yet*. Only because the Being of the "there" receives its Constitution through understanding and through the character of understanding as projection, only because it *is* what it becomes (or alternatively, does not become), can it say to itself 'Become what you are,' and say this with understanding.

Projection always pertains to the full disclosedness of Being-in-the-world; as potentiality-for-Being, understanding has itself possibilities, which are sketched out beforehand within the range of what is essentially disclosable in it. Understanding *can* devote itself primarily to the disclosedness of the world; that is, Dasein can, proximally and for the most part, understand itself in terms of its world. Or else understanding throws itself primarily into the "for-the-sake-of-which"; that is, Dasein exists as itself. Understanding is either authentic, arising out of one's own Self as such, or inauthentic. The 'in-' of "inauthentic" does not mean that Dasein cuts itself off from its Self and understands 'only' the world. The world belongs to Being-one's-Self as Being-in-the-world. On the other hand, authentic understanding, no less than that which is inauthentic, *can* be either genuine or not genuine. As potentiality-for-Being, understanding is altogether permeated with possibility. When one is diverted into [Sichverlegen in] one of these basic possibilities of understanding, the other is not laid aside [legt . . . sich ab]. *Because understanding, in every case, pertains rather to Dasein's full disclosedness as Being-in-the-world, this diversion of the understanding is an existential modification of projection as a whole.* In understanding the world, Being-in is always understood along with it, while understanding of existence as such is always an understanding of the world.

As factical Dasein, any Dasein has already diverted its potentiality-for-Being into a possibility of understanding.

In its projective character, understanding goes to make up existentially what we call Dasein's *"sight"* [Sicht]. With the disclosedness of the "there," this sight is existentially [existenzial seiende]; and Dasein *is* this sight equiprimordially in each of those basic ways of its Being which we have already noted: as the circumspection [Umsicht] of concern, as the considerateness [Rücksicht] of solicitude, and as that sight which is directed upon Being as such [Sicht auf das Sein als solches], for the sake of which any Dasein is as it is. The sight which is related primarily and on the whole to existence we call *"transparency"* [*Durchsichtigkeit*]. We choose this term to designate 'knowledge of the Self'[8] in a sense which is well understood, so as to indicate that here it is not a matter of perceptually tracking down and inspecting a point called the "Self," but rather one of seizing upon the full disclosedness of Being-in-the-world *throughout all* the constitutive items which are essential to it, and doing so with understanding. In existing, entities sight 'themselves' [sichtet "sich"] only in so far as they have become transparent to themselves with equal primordiality in those items which are constitutive for their existence: their Being-alongside the world and their Being-with Others.

On the other hand, Dasein's opaqueness [Undurchsichtigkeit] is not rooted primarily and solely in 'egocentric' self-deceptions; it is rooted just as much in lack of acquaintance with the world.

We must, to be sure, guard against a misunderstanding of the expression 'sight.' It corresponds to the "clearedness" [Gelichtetheit] which we took as characterizing the disclosedness of the "there." 'Seeing' does not mean just perceiving with the bodily eyes, but neither does it mean pure non-sensory awareness of something present-at-hand in its presence-at-hand. In giving an existential signification to "sight," we have merely drawn upon the peculiar feature of seeing, that it lets entities which are accessible to it be encountered unconcealedly in themselves. Of course, every 'sense' does this within that domain of discovery which is genuinely its own. But from the beginning onwards the tradition of philosophy has been oriented primarily towards 'seeing' as a way of access to entities *and to Being*. To keep the connection with this tradition, we may formalize "sight" and "seeing" enough to obtain therewith a universal term for characterizing any access to entities or to Being, as access in general.

By showing how all sight is grounded primarily in understanding (the circumspection of concern is understanding as *common sense* [*Verständigkeit*], we have deprived pure intuition [Anschauen] of its priority, which corresponds noetically to the priority of the present-at-hand in traditional ontology. 'Intuition' and 'thinking' are both derivatives of understanding, and already rather remote ones. Even the phenomenological 'intuition of essences' ["Wesensschau"] is grounded in existential understanding. We can decide about this kind of seeing only if we have obtained explicit conceptions of Being and of the structure of Being, such as only phenomena in the phenomenological sense can become.

The disclosedness of the "there" in understanding is itself a way of Dasein's potentiality-for-Being. In the way in which its Being is projected both upon the "for-the-sake-of-which" and upon significance (the world), there lies the disclosedness of Being in general. Understanding of Being has already been taken for granted in projecting upon possibilities. In projection, Being is understood, though not ontologically conceived. An entity whose kind of Being is the essential projection of Being-in-the-world has understanding of Being, and has this as constitutive for its Being. What was posited dogmatically at an earlier stage now gets exhibited in terms of the Constitution of the Being in which Dasein as understanding is its "there." The existential meaning of this understanding of Being cannot be satisfactorily clarified within the limits of this investigation except on the basis of the Temporal Interpretation of Being.

As *existentialia*, states-of-mind and understanding characterize the primordial disclosedness of Being-in-the-world. By way of having a mood, Dasein 'sees' possibilities, in terms of which it is. In the projective disclosure of such possibilities, it already has a mood in every case. The projection of its ownmost potentiality-for-Being has been delivered over to the Fact of its thrownness into the "there." Has not Dasein's Being become more enigmatical now that we have explicated the existential constitution of the Being of the "there" in the sense of thrown projection? It has indeed. We must first let the full enigmatical character of this Being emerge, even if all we can do is to come to a genuine breakdown over its 'solution,' and to formulate anew the question about the Being of thrown projective Being-in-the-world.

But in the first instance, even if we are just to bring into view the everyday kind of Being in which there is understanding with a state-of-mind, and if we are to do so in a way which is phenomenally adequate to the full disclosedness of the "there," we must work out these *existentialia* concretely.[9]

## Translator's Notes

1. '. . . in der Bedeutung von "einer Sache vorstehen können," "ihr gewachsen sein," "etwas können."' The expression 'vorstehen' ('to manage,' 'to be in charge') is here connected with 'verstehen' ('to understand').

2. '. . . von der Kontingenz eines Vorhandenen, sofern mit diesem das und jenes "passieren" kann.'

3. '. . . ergreift sie und vergreift sich.'

4. 'Als solches Verstehen "weiss" es, *woran* es mit ihm selbst, das heisst seinem Seinkönnen ist.'

5. '. . . *so zwar, dass dieses Sein an ihm selbst das Woran des mit ihm selbst Seins erschliesst.*'

6. '*Entwurf.*' The basic meaning of this noun and the cognate verb 'entwerfen' is that of 'throwing' something 'off' or 'away' from one; but in ordinary German usage, and often in Heidegger, they take on the sense of 'designing' or 'sketching' some 'project' which is to be carried through; and they may also be used in the more special sense of 'projection' in which a geometer is said to 'project' a curve 'upon' a plane. The words 'projection' and 'project' accordingly lend themselves rather well to translating these words in many contexts, especially since their root meaings are very similar to those of 'Entwurf' and 'entwerfen'; but while the root meaning of 'throwing off' is still very much alive in Heidegger's German, it has almost entirely died out in the ordinary English usage of 'projection' and 'project,' which in turn have taken on some connotations not felt in the German. Thus when the English translation Dasein is said to 'project' entities, or possibilities, or even its own

Being 'upon' something, the reader should bear in mind that the root meaning of 'throwing' is more strongly felt in the German than in the translation.

7. '. . . zieht es herab zu einem gegebenen, gemeinten Bestand, während der Entwurf im Werfen die Möglichkeit als Möglichkeit sich vorwirft und als solche *sein* lässt.' The expression 'einem etwas vorwerfen' means literally to 'throw something forward to some-one,' but often has the connotation of 'reproaching him with something,' or 'throwing something in his teeth.' Heidegger may have more than one of these significations in mind.

8. '"Selbsterkenntnis."' This should be carefully distinguished from the 'Sichkennen.' Perhaps this distinction can be expressed—though rather crudely—by pointing out that we are here concerned with a full and sophisticated knowledge of the Self in all its implica-tions, while in the earlier passage we were concerned with the kind of 'self-knowledge' which one loses when one 'forgets oneself' or does something so out of character that one 'no longer knows oneself.'

9. 'konkreten.' The earlier editions have 'konkreteren' ('more conceretely').

# UNDERSTANDING AND INTERPRETATION[1]

As understanding, Dasein projects its Being upon possibilities. This *Being-towards-possibilities* which understands is itself a potentiality-for-Being, and it is so because of the way these possibilities, as disclosed, exert their counter-thrust [Rückschlag] upon Dasein. The projecting of the understanding has its own possibility—that of developing itself [sich auszubilden]. This development of the understanding we call "interpretation."[2] In it the understanding appropriates understandingly that which is understood by it. In interpretation, understanding does not become something different. It becomes itself. Such interpretation is grounded existentially in understanding; the latter does not arise from the former. Nor is interpretation the acquiring of information about what is understood; it is rather the working-out of possibilities projected in understanding. In accordance with the trend of these preparatory analyses of everyday Dasein, we shall pursue the phenomenon of interpretation in understanding the world—that is, in in-authentic understanding, and indeed in the mode of its genuineness.

In terms of the significance which is disclosed in understanding the world, con-cernful Being-alongside the ready-to-hand gives itself to understand whatever involvement that which is encountered can have.[3] To say that "circumspection discovers" means that the 'world' which has already been understood comes to be interpreted. The ready-to-hand comes *explicitly* into the sight which understands. All preparing, putting to rights, repairing, improving, rounding-out, are accom-plished in the following way: we take apart[4] in its "in-order-to" that which is circumspectively ready-to-hand, and we concern ourselves with it in accordance with what becomes visible through this process. That which has been circumspectively taken apart with regard to its "in-order-to," and taken apart as such—that which is *explicitly* understood—has the structure of *something as something*. The circumspective question as to what this particular thing that is ready-to-hand may be, receives the circumspectively interpretative answer that it is for such and such a purpose [es ist zum . . .]. If we tell what it is for [des Wozu], we are not simply designating something; but that which is designated is understood *as* that *as* which we are to take the thing in question. That which is disclosed in understanding—that which is understood—is already accessible in such a way that its 'as which' can be made to stand out explicitly. The 'as' makes up the structure of the explicitness of something that is understood. It constitutes the interpretation. In dealing with what is environmentally ready-to-hand by interpreting it circumspectively, we 'see' it *as* a table, a door, a carriage, or a bridge; but what we have thus interpreted [Ausgelegte] need not necessarily be also taken apart [auseinander zu legen] by making an assertion which definitely characterizes it. Any mere pre-predicative seeing of the ready-to-hand is, in itself, something which already understands and interprets. But does not the absence of such an 'as' make up the mereness of any pure perception of something? Whenever we see with this kind of sight, we already do so understandingly and interpretatively. In the mere encountering of something, it is understood in terms of a totality of involvements; and such seeing hides in itself the explicitness of the assignment-relations (of the "in-order-to") which belong to that totality. That which is understood gets Articulated when the entity to be understood is brought close interpretatively by taking as our clue the 'something as something'; and this Articulation lies *before* [liegt vor] our making any thematic assertion about it. In such an assertion the 'as' does not turn up for the first time; it just gets expressed for the first time, and this is possible only in that it lies before us as something expressible.[5] The fact that when we look at something, the explicitness of assertion can be absent, does not justify our denying that there is any Articulative interpretation in such mere seeing, and hence that there is any as-structure in it. When we have to do with anything, the mere seeing of the Things which are closest to us bears in itself the structure of interpretation, and in so primordial a manner that just to grasp something *free,* as it were, *of the "as,"* requires a certain readjustment. When we merely stare at something, our just-having-it-before-us lies before us *as a failure to understand it any more.* This grasping which is free of the "as," is a privation of the kind of seeing in which one *merely* understands. It is not more primordial than that kind of seeing, but is derived from it. If the 'as' is ontically unexpressed, this must not seduce us into overlooking it as a constitutive state for understanding, existential and *a priori*.

But if we never perceive equipment that is ready-to-hand without already understanding and interpreting it, and if such perception lets us circumspectively encounter something as something, does this not mean that in the first instance we have experienced something purely present-at-hand, and then taken it *as* a door, *as* a house? This would be a misunderstanding of the specific way in which interpretation functions as disclosure. In interpreting, we do not, so to speak, throw a 'signification' over some naked thing which is present-at-hand, we do not stick a value on it; but when something within-the-world is encountered as such, the thing in question already has an involvement which is disclosed in our understanding of the world, and this involvement is one which gets laid out by the interpretation.[6]

The ready-to-hand is always understood in terms of a totality of involvements. This totality need not be grasped explicitly by a thematic interpretation. Even if it has undergone such an interpretation, it recedes into an understanding which does not stand out from the background. And this is the very mode in which it is the essential foundation for everyday circumspective interpretation. In every case this interpretation is grounded in *something we have in advance*—in a *fore-having*.[7] As the appropriation of understanding, the interpretation operates in Being towards a totality of involvements which is already understood—a Being which understands. When something is understood but is still veiled, it becomes unveiled by an act of appropriation, and this is always done under the guidance of a point of view, which fixes that with regard to which what is understood is to be interpreted. In every case interpretation is grounded in *something we see in advance*—in a *fore-sight*. This fore-sight 'takes the first cut' out of what has been taken into our fore-having, and it does so with a view to a definite way in which this can be interpreted.[8] Anything understood which is held in our fore-having and towards which we set our sights 'foresightedly,' becomes conceptualizable through the interpretation. In such an interpretation, the way in which the entity we are interpreting is to be conceived can be drawn from the entity itself, or the interpretation can force the entity into concepts to which it is opposed in its manner of Being. In either case, the interpretation has already decided for a definite way of conceiving it, either with finality or with reservations; it is grounded in *something we grasp in advance*—in a *fore-conception*.

Whenever something is interpreted as something, the interpretation will be founded essentially upon fore-having, fore-sight, and fore-conception. An interpretation is never a presuppositionless apprehending of something presented to us.[9] If, when one is engaged in a particular concrete kind of interpretation, in the sense of exact textual Interpretation, one likes to appeal [beruft] to what 'stands there,' then one finds that what 'stands there' in the first instance is nothing other than the obvious undiscussed assumption [Vormeinung] of the person who does the interpreting. In an interpretative approach there lies such an assumption, as that which has been 'taken for granted' ["gesetzt" with the interpretation as such—that is to say, as that which has been presented in our fore-having, our fore-sight, and our fore-conception.

How are we to conceive the character of this 'fore'? Have we done so if we say formally that this is something '*a priori*'? Why does understanding, which we have designated as a fundamental *existentiale* of Dasein, have this structure as its own? Anything interpreted, as something interpreted, has the 'as'-structure as its own; and how is this related to the 'fore' structure? The phenomenon of the 'as'-structure is manifestly not to be dissolved or broken up 'into pieces.' But is a primordial analytic for it thus ruled out? Are we to concede that such phenomena are 'ultimates'? Then there would still remain the question, "why?" Or do the fore-structure of understanding and the as-structure of interpretation show an existential-ontological connection with the phenomenon of projection? And does this phenomenon point back to a primordial state of Dasein's Being?

Before we answer these questions, for which the preparation up till now has been far from sufficient, we must investigate whether what has become visible as the fore-structure of understanding and as the as-structure of interpretation, does not itself already present us with a unitary phenomenon—one of which copious use is made in philosophical problematics, though what is used so universally falls short of the primordiality of ontological explication.

In the projecting of the understanding, entities are disclosed in their possibility. The character of the possibility corresponds, on each occasion, with the kind of Being of the entity which is understood. Entities within-the-world generally are projected upon the world—that is, upon a whole of significance, to whose reference-relations concern, as Being-in-the-world, has been tied up in advance. When entities within-the-world are discovered along with the Being of Dasein— that is, when they have come to be understood—we say that they have meaning [*Sinn*]. But that which is understood, taken strictly, is not the meaning but the entity, or alternatively, Being. Meaning is that wherein the intelligibility [Verständlichkeit] of something maintains itself. That which can be Articulated in a disclosure by which we understand, we call "meaning." The *concept of meaning* embraces the formal existential framework of what necessarily belongs to that which an understanding interpretation Articulates. *Meaning is the "upon-which" of a projection in terms of which something becomes intelligible as something; it gets its structure from a fore-having, a fore-sight, and a fore-conception.*[10] In so far as understanding and interpretation make up the existential state of Being of the "there," "meaning" must be conceived as the formal-existential state of Being of the "there," "meaning" must be conceived as the formal existential framework of the disclosedness which belongs to understanding. Meaning is an *existentiale* of Dasein, not a property attaching to entities, lying 'behind' them, or floating somewhere as an 'intermediate domain.' Dasein only 'has' meaning, so far as the disclosedness of Being-in-the-world can be 'filled in' by the entities discoverable in that disclosedness.[11] *Hence only Dasein can be meaningful [sinnvoll] or meaningless [sinnlos].* That is to say, its own Being and the entities disclosed with its Being can be appropriated in understanding, or can remain relegated to non-understanding.

This Interpretation of the concept of 'meaning' is one which is ontologico-existential in principle; if we adhere to it, then all entities whose kind of Being is of a character other than Dasein's must be conceived as *unmeaning* [*unsinniges*], essentially devoid of any meaning at all. Here 'unmeaning' does not signify that we are saying anything about the value of such entities, but it gives expression to an ontological characteristic. *And only that which is unmeaning can be absurd* [*widersinnig*]. The present-at-hand, as Dasein encounters it, can, as it were, assault Dasein's Being; natural events, for instance, can break in upon us and destroy us.

And if we are inquiring about the meaning of Being, our investigation does not then become a "deep" one [tiefsinnig], nor does it puzzle out what stands behind Being. It asks about Being itself in so far as Being enters into the intelligibility of Dasein. The meaning of Being can never be contrasted with entities, or with Being as the 'ground' which gives entities support; for a 'ground' becomes accessible only as meaning, even if it is itself the abyss of meaninglessness.[12]

As the disclosedness of the "there," understanding always pertains to the whole of Being-in-the-world. In every understanding of the world, existence is understood with it, and *vice versa*. All interpretation, moreover, operates in the fore-structure, which we have already characterized. Any interpretation which is to contribute understanding, must already have understood what is to be interpreted. This is a fact that has always been remarked, even if only in the area of derivative ways of understanding and interpretation, such as philological Interpretation. The latter belongs within the range of scientific knowledge. Such knowledge demands the rigour of a demonstration to provide grounds for it. In a scientific proof, we may not presuppose what it is our task to provide grounds for. But if interpretation must in any case already operate in that which is understood, and if it must draw its nurture from this, how is it to bring any scientific results to maturity without moving in a circle, especially if, moreover, the understanding which is presupposed still operates within our common information about man and the world? Yet according to the most elementary rules of logic, this *circle* is a *circulus vitiosus*. If that be so, however, the business of historiological interpretation is excluded *a priori* from the domain of rigorous knowledge. In so far as the Fact of this circle in understanding is not eliminated, historiology must then be resigned to less rigorous possibilities of knowing. Historiology is permitted to compensate for this defect to some extent through the 'spiritual signification' of its 'objects.' But even in the opinion of the historian himself, it would admittedly be more ideal if the circle could be avoided and if there remained the hope of creating some time a historiology which would be as independent of the standpoint of the observer as our knowledge of Nature is supposed to be.

*But if we see this circle as a vicious one and look out for ways of avoiding it, even if we just 'sense' it as an inevitable imperfection, then the act of understanding has been misunderstood from the ground up.* The assimilation of understanding and interpretation to a definite ideal of knowledge is not the issue here. Such an ideal is itself only a subspecies of understanding—a subspecies which has strayed into the legitimate task of grasping the present-at-hand in its essential unintelligibility [Unverständlichkeit]. If the basic conditions which make interpretation possible are to be fulfilled, this must rather be done by not failing to recognize beforehand the essential conditions under which it can be performed. What is decisive is not to get out of the circle but to come into it in the right way. This circle of understanding is not an orbit in which any random kind of knowledge may move; it is the expression of the existential *fore-structure* of Dasein itself. It is not to be reduced to the level of a vicious circle, or even of a circle which is merely tolerated. In the circle is hidden a positive possibility of the most primordial kind of knowing. To be sure, we genuinely take hold of this possibility only when, in our interpretation, we have understood that our first, last, and constant task is never to allow our fore-having, fore-sight, and fore-conception to be presented to us by fancies and popular conceptions, but rather to make the scientific theme secure by working out these fore-structures in terms of the things themselves. Because understanding, in accordance with its existential meaning, is Dasein's own potentiality-for-Being, the ontological presuppositions of historiological knowledge transcend in principle the idea of rigour held in the most exact sciences. Mathematics is not more rigorous than historiology, but only narrower, because the existential foundations relevant for it lie within a narrower range.

The 'circle' in understanding belongs to the structure of meaning, and the latter phenomenon is rooted in the existential constitution of Dasein—that is, in the understanding which interprets. An entity for which, as Being-in-the-world, its Being is itself an issue, has, ontologically, a circular structure. If, however, we note that 'circularity' belongs ontologically to a kind of Being which is present-at-hand (namely, to subsistence [Bestand]), we must altogether avoid using this phenomenon to characterize anything like Dasein ontologically.

## Translator's Notes

1. Heidegger uses two words which might well be translated as 'interpretation': 'Auslegung' and 'Interpretation.' Though in many cases these may be regarded as synonyms, their connotations are not quite the same. 'Auslegung' seems to be used in a broad sense to cover any activity in which we interpret something 'as' something, whereas 'Interpretation' seems to apply to interpretations which are more theoretical or systematic, as in the exegesis of a text. We shall preserve this distinction by writing 'interpretation' for 'Auslegung,' but 'Interpretation' for Heidegger's 'Interpretation,' following similar conventions for the verbs 'auslegen' and 'interpretieren.'

2. 'Auslegung.' The older editions have 'Auslegung.'

3. '. . . gibt sich . . . zu verstehen, welche Bewandtnis es je mit dem Begegnenden haben kann.'

4. 'auseinandergelegt.' Heidegger is contrasting the verb 'auslegen' (literally, 'lay out') with the cognate 'auseinanderlegen' ('lay asunder' or 'take apart').

5. '. . . was allein so möglich ist, dass es als Aussprechbares vor-liegt.' Here we follow the reading of the earlier editions. The hyphen in 'vor-liegt' comes at the end of the line in the later editions, but is undoubtedly meant to suggest (like the italicization of the 'vor' in the previous sentence) that this verb is to be interpreted with unusual literalness.

This paragraph is noteworthy for an exploitation of the prefix 'aus' ('out'), which fails to show up in our translation. Literally an 'Aussage' ('assertion') is something which is 'said out'; an 'Auslegung' ('interpretation') is a 'laying-out'; that which is 'ausdrücklich' ('explicit') is something that has been 'pressed out'; that which is 'aussprechbar' (our 'expressible') is something that can be 'spoken out.'

The verbs 'ausdrücken' and 'aussprechen' are roughly synonymous; but 'aussprechen' often has the more specific connotations of 'pronunciation,' 'pronouncing oneself,' 'speaking one's mind,' 'finishing what one has to say,' etc. While it would be possible to reserve 'express' for 'ausdrücken' and translate 'aussprechen' by some such phrase as 'speak out,' it is more convenient to use 'express' for both verbs, especially since 'aussprechen' and its derivatives have occurred very seldom before the present chapter, in which 'ausdrücken' rarely appears. On the other hand, we can easily distinguish between the more frequent 'ausdrücklich' and 'ausgesprochen' by translating the latter as 'expressed' or 'expressly,' and reserving 'explicit' for both 'ausdrücklich' and 'explizit.'

6. '. . . die durch die Auslegung herausgelegt wird.'

7. In this paragraph Heidegger introduces the important words 'Vorhabe,' 'Vorsicht,' and 'Vorgriff.' 'Vorhabe' is perhaps best translated by some such expression as 'what we have in advance' or 'what we have before us'; but we shall usually find it more convenient to adopt the shorter term 'fore-having,' occasionally resorting to hendiadys, as in the present sentence, and we shall handle the other terms in the same manner. 'Vorsicht' ('what we see in advance' or 'fore-sight') is the only one of these expressions which occurs in ordinary German usage, and often has the connotation of 'caution' or 'prudence'; Heidegger, however, uses it in a more general sense somewhat more akin to the English 'foresight,' without the connotation of a shrewd and accurate prediction. 'Vorgriff' ('what we grasp in advance' or 'fore-conception') is related to the verb 'vorgreifen' ('to anticipate') as well as to the noun "Begriff."

8. 'Die Auslegung gründet jeweils in einer *Vorsicht,* die das in Vorhabe Genommene auf eine bestimmte Auslegbarkeit hin "anschneidet."' The idea seems to be that just as the person who cuts off the first slice of a loaf of bread gets the loaf 'started,' the fore-sight 'makes a start' on what we have in advance—the fore-having.

9. '. . . eines Vorgegebenen.' Here, as in many other passages, we have translated 'vorgeben' by various forms of the verb 'to present'; but it would perhaps be more in line with Heidegger's discussion of the prefix 'vor-' to write '. . . of something fore-given.'

10. '*Sinn ist das durch Vorhabe, Vorsicht und Vorgriff strukturierte Woraufhin des Entwurfs, aus dem her etwas als etwas verständlich wird.*' (Notice that our usual translation of 'verständlich' and 'Verständlichkeit' as 'intelligible' and 'intelligibility,' fails to show the connection of the words with 'Verständnis,' etc. This connection could have been brought

out effectively by writing 'understandable,' 'understandability,' etc., but only at the cost of awkwardness.)

11. Sinn "hat" nur das Dasein, sofern die Erschlossenheit des In-der-Welt-seins durch das in ihr entdeckbare Seiende "erfüllbar" ist.' The point of this puzzling and ambiguous sentence may become somewhat clearer if the reader recalls that here as elsewhere the verb 'erschliessen' ('disclose') is used in the sense of 'opening something up' so that its contents can be 'discovered.' What thus gets 'opened up' will then be 'filled in' as more and more of its contents get discovered.

12. 'Der Sinn von Sein kann nie in Gegensatz gebracht werden zum Seienden oder zum Sein als tragenden "Grund" des Seienden, weil "Grund" nur als Sinn zugänglich wird, und sei er selbst der Abgrund der Sinnlosigkeit.' Notice the etymological kinship between 'Grund' ('ground') and 'Abgrund' ('abyss').

# ASSERTION AS A DERIVATIVE MODE OF INTERPRETATION

All interpretation is grounded on understanding. That which has been articulated[1] as such in interpretation and sketched out beforehand in the understanding in general as something articulable, is the meaning. In so far as assertion ('judgment')[2] is grounded on understanding and presents us with a derivative form in which an interpretation has been carried out, it *too* 'has' a meaning. Yet this meaning cannot be defined as something which occurs 'in' ["an"] a judgment along with the judging itself. In our present context, we shall give an explicit analysis of assertion, and this analysis will serve several purposes.

For one thing, it can be demonstrated, by considering assertion, in what ways the structure of the 'as,' which is constitutive for understanding and interpretation, can be modified. When this has been done, both understanding and interpretation will be brought more sharply into view. For another thing, the analysis of assertion has a special position in the problematic of fundamental ontology, because in the decisive period when ancient ontology was beginning, the λόγος functioned as the only clue for obtaining access to that which authentically is [zum eigentlich Seienden], and for defining the Being of such entities. Finally assertion has been accepted from ancient times as the primary and authentic 'locus' of *truth*. The phenomenon of truth is so thoroughly coupled with the problem of Being that our investigation, as it proceeds further, will necessarily come up against the problem of truth; and it already lies within the dimensions of that problem, though not explicitly. The analysis of assertion will at the same time prepare the way for this latter problematic.

In what follows, we give three significations to the term *"assertion."* These are drawn from the phenomenon which is thus designated, they are connected among themselves, and in their unity they encompass the full structure of assertion.

1. The primary signification of "assertion" is *"pointing out"* [*Aufzeigen*]. In this we adhere to the primordial meaning of λόγος as ἀπόφανσις — letting an entity be seen from itself. In the assertion 'The hammer is too heavy,' what is discovered for sight is not a 'meaning,' but an entity in the way that it is ready-to-hand. Even if this entity is not close enough to be grasped and 'seen,' the pointing-out has in view the entity itself and not, let us say, a mere "representation" [Vorstellung] of it— neither something 'merely represented' nor the psychical condition in which the person who makes the assertion "represents" it.

2. "Assertion" means no less than *"predication."* We 'assert' a 'predicate' of a 'subject,' and the 'subject' is *given a definite character* [*bestimmt*] by the 'predicate.' In this signification of "assertion," that which is put forward in the assertion [Das Ausgesagte] is not the predicate, but 'the hammer itself.' On the other hand, that which does the asserting [Das Aussagende] (in other words, that which gives something a definite character) lies in the 'too heavy.' That which is put forward in the assertion in the second signification of "assertion" (that which is given a definite character, as such) has undergone a narrowing of content as compared with what is put forward in the assertion in the first signification of this term. Every predication is what it is, only as a pointing-out. The second signification of "assertion" has its foundation in the first. Within this pointing-out, the elements which are Articulated in predication— the subject and predicate— arise. It is not by giving something a definite character that we first discover that which shows itself— the hammer— as such; but when we give it such a character, our seeing gets *restricted* to it in the first instance, so that by this explicit *restriction*[3] of our view, that which is already manifest may be made *explicitly* manifest in its definite character. In giving something a definite character, we must, in the first instance, take a step back when confronted with that which is already manifest— the hammer that is too heavy. In 'setting down the subject,' we dim entities down to focus in 'that hammer there,' so that by thus dimming them down we may let that which is manifest be seen *in* its own definite character as a character that can be determined.[4] Setting down the subject, setting down the predicate, and setting down the two together, are thoroughly 'apophantical' in the strict sense of the word.

3. "Assertion" means *"communication"* [*Mitteilung*], speaking forth [Heraussage]. As communication, it is directly related to "assertion" in the first and second significations. It is letting someone see with us what we have pointed out by way of giving it a definite character. Letting someone see with us shares with [teilt . . . mit] the Other that entity which has been pointed out in its definite character. That which is 'shared' is our *Being towards* what has been pointed out— a Being in which we see it in common. One must keep in mind that this Being-towards is Being-in-the-world, and that from out of this very world what

has been pointed out gets encountered. Any assertion, as a communication under-stood in this existential manner, must have been expressed.[5] As something communicated, that which has been put forward in the assertion is something that Others can 'share' with the person making the assertion, even though the entity which he has pointed out and to which he has given a definite character is not close enough for them to grasp and see it. That which is put forward in the assertion is something which can be passed along in 'further retelling.' There is a widening of the range of that mutual sharing which sees. But at the same time, what has been pointed out may become veiled again in this further retelling, although even the kind of knowing which arises in such hearsay (whether knowledge that some-thing is the case [Wissen] or merely an acquaintance with something [Kennen]) always has the entity itself in view and does not 'give assent' to some 'valid mean-ing' which has been passed around. Even hearsay is a Being-in-the-world, and a Being towards what is heard.

There is prevalent today a theory of 'judgment' which is oriented to the phe-nomenon of 'validity.'[6] We shall not give an extensive discussion of it here. It will be sufficient to allude to the very questionable character of this phenomenon of 'validity,' though since the time of Lotze people have been fond of passing this off as a 'primal phenomenon' which cannot be traced back any further. The fact that it can play this role is due only to its ontologically unclarified character. The 'problematic' which has established itself round this idolized word is no less opaque. In the first place, validity is viewed as the '*form*' *of actuality* which goes with the content of the judgment, in so far as that content remains unchanged as opposed to the changeable 'psychical' process of judgment. Considering how the status of the question of Being in general has been characterized in the introduc-tion to this treatise, we would scarcely venture to expect that 'validity' as 'ideal Being' is distinguished by special ontological clarity. In the second place, "valid-ity" means at the same time the validity of the meaning of the judgment, which is valid of the 'Object' it has in view; and thus it attains the signification of an '*Objectively valid character*' and of Objectivity in general. In the third place, the meaning which is thus 'valid' *of* an entity, and which is valid 'timelessly' in itself, is said to be 'valid' also in the sense of being valid *for* everyone who judges rationally. "Validity" now means a *bindingness*, or 'universally valid' character.[7] Even if one were to advocate a 'critical' epistemological theory, according to which the subject does not 'really' 'come out' to the Object, then this valid char-acter, as the validity of an Object (Objectivity), is grounded upon that stock of true (!) meaning which is itself valid. The three significations of 'being valid' which we have set forth—the way of Being of the ideal, Objectivity, and binding-ness—not only are opaque in themselves but constantly get confused with one another. Methodological fore-sight demands that we do not choose such unstable concepts as a clue to Interpretation. We make no advance restriction upon the concept of "meaning" which would confine it to signifying the 'content of

judgment,' but we understand it as the existential phenomenon already characterized, in which the formal framework of what can be disclosed in understanding
and Articulated in interpretation becomes visible.

If we bring together the three significations of 'assertion' which we have analysed, and get a unitary view of the full phenomenon, then we may define "*assertion*" as "*a pointing-out which gives something a definite character and which
communicates.*" It remains to ask with what justification we have taken assertion
as a mode of interpretation at all. If it is something of this sort, then the essential
structures of interpretation must recur in it. The pointing-out which assertion
does is performed on the basis of what has already been disclosed in understanding or discovered circumspectively. Assertion is not a free-floating kind of
behaviour which, in its own right, might be capable of disclosing entities in
general in a primary way: on the contrary it always maintains itself on the basis
of Being-in-the-world. What we have shown earlier in relation to knowing the
world, holds just as well as assertion. Any assertion requires a fore-having of
whatever has been disclosed; and this is what it points out by way of giving something a definite character. Furthermore, in any approach when one gives something a definite character, one is already taking a look directionally at what is to
be put forward in the assertion. When an entity which has been presented is given
a definite character, the function of giving it such a character is taken over by that
with regard to which we set our sights towards the entity.[8] Thus any assertion
requires a fore-sight; in this the predicate which we are to assign [zuzuweisende]
and make stand out, gets loosened, so to speak, from its unexpressed inclusion
in the entity itself. To any assertion as a communication which gives something
a definite character there belongs, moreover, an Articulation of what is pointed
out, and this Articulation is in accordance with significations. Such an assertion
will operate with a definite way of conceiving: "The hammer is heavy," "Heaviness
belongs to the hammer," "The hammer has the property of heaviness." When an
assertion is made, some fore-conception is always implied; but it remains for the
most part inconspicuous, because the language already hides in itself a developed
way of conceiving. Like any interpretation whatever, assertion necessarily has
a fore-having, a fore-sight, and a fore-conception as its existential foundations.

But to what extent does it become a *derivative* mode of interpretation? What
has been modified in it? We can point out the modification if we stick to certain
limiting cases of assertion which function in logic as normal cases and as examples of the 'simplest' assertion-phenomena. Prior to all analysis, logic has
already understood 'logically' what it takes as a theme under the heading of the
"categorical statement"— for instance, 'The hammer is heavy.' The unexplained
presupposition is that the 'meaning' of this sentence is to be taken as: "This
Thing—a hammer—has the property of heaviness." In concernful circumspection there are no such assertions 'at first.' But such circumspection has of course
its specific ways of interpreting, and these, as compared with the 'theoretical

judgment' just mentioned, may take some such form as 'The hammer is too heavy,' or rather just 'Too heavy!,' 'Hand me the other hammer!' Interpretation is carried out primordially not in a theoretical statement but in an action of circumspective concern—laying aside the unsuitable tool, or exchanging it, 'without wasting words.' From the fact that words are absent, it may not be concluded that interpretation is absent. On the other hand, the kind of interpretation which is circumspectively *expressed* is not necessarily already an assertion in the sense we have defined. *By what existential-ontological modifications does assertion arise from circumspective interpretation?*

The entity which is held in our fore-having—for instance, the hammer—is proximally ready-to-hand as equipment. If this entity becomes the 'object' of an assertion, then as soon as we begin this assertion, there is already a change-over in the fore-having. Something *ready-to-hand with which* we have to do or perform something, turns into something *'about which'* the assertion that points it out is made. Our fore-sight is aimed at something present-at-hand in what is ready-to-hand. Both *by* and *for* this way of looking at it [Hin-sicht], the ready-to-hand becomes veiled as ready-to-hand. Within this discovering of presence-at-hand, which is at the same time a covering-up of readiness-to-hand, something present-at-hand which we encounter is given a definite character in its Being-present-at-hand-in-such-and-such-a-manner. Only now are we given any access to *properties* or the like. When an assertion has given a definite character to something present-at-hand, it says something about it *as* a "what"; and this "what" is drawn *from that* which is present-at-hand as such. The as-structure of interpretation has undergone a modification. In its function of appropriating what is understood, the 'as' no longer reaches out into a totality of involvements. As regards its possibilities for Articulating reference-relations, it has been cut off from that significance which, as such, constitutes environmentality. The 'as' gets pushed back into the uniform plane of that which is merely present-at-hand. It dwindles to the structure of just letting one see what is present-at-hand, and letting one see it in a definite way. This levelling of the primordial 'as' of circumspective interpretation to the "as" with which presence-at-hand is given a definite character is the specialty of assertion. Only so does it obtain the possibility of exhibiting something in such a way that we just look at it.

Thus assertion cannot disown its ontological origin from an interpretation which understands. The primordial 'as' of an interpretation (ἑρμηνεία) which understands circumspectively we call the "existential-*hermeneutical* 'as'" in distinction from the "*apophantical* 'as'" of the assertion.

## Translator's Notes

1. 'Gegliederte.' The verbs 'artikulieren' and 'gliedern' can both be translated by 'articulate' in English; even in German they are nearly synonymous, but in the former the

emphasis is presumably on the 'joints' at which something gets divided, while in the latter the emphasis is presumably on the 'parts' or 'members.' We have distinguished between them by translating 'artikulieren' by 'Articulate' (with a capital 'A'), and 'gliedern' by 'articulate' (with a lower-case initial).

2. '. . . die Aussage (das "Urteil") . . .'

3. *'Einschränkung.'* The older editions have 'Entschränkung.'

4. '. . . die "Subjektsetzung" blendet das Seiende ab auf "der Hammer da," um durch den Vollzug der Entblendung das Offenbare *in* seiner bestimmbaren Bestimmtheit sehen zu lassen.'

5. 'Zur Aussage als der so existenzial verstandenen Mit-teilung gehört die Ausgesprochenheit."

6. Heidegger uses three words which might conveniently be translated as 'validity': 'Geltung' (our 'validity'), 'Gültigkeit' (our 'valid character'), and 'Gelten' (our 'being valid,' etc.). The reader who has studied logic in English and who accordingly thinks of 'validity' as merely a property of arguments in which the premises imply the conclusion, must remember that in German the verb 'gelten' and its derivatives are used much more broadly, so as to apply to almost anything that is commonly (or even privately) accepted, so that one can speak of the 'validity' of legal tender, the 'validity' of a ticket for so many weeks or months, the 'validity' of that which 'holds' for me or for you, the 'validity' of anything that is the case. While Heidegger's discussion does not cover as many of these meanings as will be listed in any good German dictionary, he goes well beyond the narrower usage of the English-speaking logician. Of course, we shall often translate 'gelten' in other ways.

7. '. . . *Verbindlichkeit,* "Allgemeingültigkeit,"'

8. 'Woraufhin das vorgegebene Seiende anvisiert wird, das übernimmt im Bestimmungsvollzug die Funktion des Bestimmenden.'

# BEING-THERE AND DISCOURSE. LANGUAGE

The fundamental *existentialia* which constitute the Being of the "there," the disclosedness of Being-in-the-world, are states-of-mind and understanding. In understanding, there lurks the possibility of interpretation—that is, of appropriating what is understood. In so far as a state-of-mind is equiprimordial with an act of understanding, it maintains itself in a certain understanding. Thus there corresponds to it a certain capacity for getting interpreted. We have seen that assertion is derived from interpretation, and is an extreme case of it. In clarifying the third signification of assertion as communication (speaking forth), we were led to the concepts of "saying" and "speaking," to which we had purposely given no attention up to that point. The fact that language *now* becomes our theme *for the first time* will indicate that this phenomenon has its roots in the existential constitution of Dasein's disclosedness. *The existential-ontological foundation of language is discourse or talk.*[1] This phenomenon is one of which we have been making constant use already in our foregoing Interpretation of state-of-mind, understanding, interpretation, and assertion; but we have, as it were, kept it suppressed in our thematic analysis.

*Discourse is existentially equiprimordial with state-of-mind and understanding.* The intelligibility of something has always been articulated, even before there is any appropriative interpretation of it. Discourse is the Articulation of intelligibility. Therefore it underlies both interpretation and assertion. That which can be Articulated in interpretation, and thus even more primordially in discourse, is what we have called "meaning." That which gets articulated as such in discursive Articulation, we call the "totality-of-significations" [Bedeutungsganze]. This can be dissolved or broken up into significations. Significations, as what has been Articulated from that which can be Articulated, always carry meaning [. . . sind . . . sinnhaft]. If discourse, as the Articulation of the intelligibility of the "there," is a primordial *existentiale* of disclosedness, and if disclosedness is primarily constituted by Being-in-the-world, then discourse too must have essentially a kind of Being which is specifically *worldly*. The intelligibility of Being-in-the-world—an intelligibility which goes with a state-of-mind—*expresses itself as discourse.* The totality-of-significations of intelligibility is *put into words*. To significations, words accrue. But word-Things do not get supplied with significations.

The way in which discourse gets expressed is language.[2] Language is a totality of words—a totality in which discourse has a 'worldly' Being of its own; and as an entity within-the-world, this totality thus becomes something which we may come across as ready-to-hand. Language can be broken up into word-Things which are present-at-hand. Discourse is existentially language, because that entity whose disclosedness it Articulates according to significations, has, as its kind of Being, Being-in-the-world—a Being which has been thrown and submitted to the 'world.'

As an existential state in which Dasein is disclosed, discourse is constitutive for Dasein's existence. *Hearing* and *keeping silent* [*Schweigen*] are possibilities belonging to discursive speech. In these phenomena the constitutive function of discourse for the existentiality of existence becomes entirely plain for the first time. But in the first instance the issue is one of working out the structure of discourse as such.

Discoursing or talking is the way in which we articulate 'significantly' the intelligibility of Being-in-the-world. Being-with belongs to Being-in-the-world, which in every case maintains itself in some definite way of concernful Being-with-one-another. Such Being-with-one-another is discursive as assenting or refusing, as demanding or warning, as pronouncing, consulting, or interceding, as 'making assertions,' and as talking in the way of 'giving a talk.'[3] Talking is talk about something. That which the discourse is *about* [das *Worüber* der Rede] does not necessarily or even for the most part serve as the theme for an assertion in which one gives something a definite character. Even a command is given about something; a wish is about something. And so is intercession. What the discourse is about is a structural item that it necessarily possesses; for discourse helps to constitute the disclosedness of Being-in-the-world, and in its own structure it is modelled upon this basic state of Dasein. What is talked about [das Beredete] in talk is always 'talked to' ["angeredet"] in a definite regard and within certain limits. In any talk or discourse, there is *something said-in-the-talk* as such [ein *Geredetes* as solches]—something said as such [das . . . Gesagte als solches] whenever one wishes, asks, or expresses oneself about something. In this "something said," discourse communicates.

As we have already indicated in our analysis of assertion,[4] the phenomenon of *communication* must be understood in a sense which is ontologically broad. 'Communication' in which one makes assertions—giving information, for instance—is a special case of that communication which is grasped in principle existentially. In this more general kind of communication, the Articulation of Being-with-one-another understandingly is constituted. Through it a co-state-of-mind [Mitbefindlichkeit] gets 'shared,' and so does the understanding of Being-with. Communication is never anything like a conveying of experiences, such as opinions or wishes, from the interior of one subject into the interior of another. Dasein-with is already essentially manifest in a co-state-of-mind and a co-understanding. In discourse Being-with becomes 'explicitly' *shared*; that is to say, it *is* already, but it is unshared as something that has not been taken hold of and appropriated.[5]

Whenever something is communicated in what is said-in-the-talk, all talk about anything has at the same time the character of *expressing itself* [*Sichaussprechens*]. In talking, Dasein *e*xpresses itself [spricht sich . . . *aus*] not because it has, in the first instance, been encapsulated as something 'internal' over against something outside, but because as Being-in-the-world it is already 'outside' when it understands. What is expressed is precisely this Being-outside—that is to say, the way in which one currently has a state-of-mind (mood), which we have shown to pertain to the full disclosedness of Being-in. Being-in and its state-of-mind are made known in discourse and indicated in language by intonation, modulation, the tempo of talk, 'the way of speaking.' In 'poetical' discourse, the communication of the existential possibilities of one's state-of-mind can become an aim in itself, and this amounts to a disclosing of existence.

In discourse the intelligibility of Being-in-the-world (an intelligibility which goes with a state-of-mind) is articulated according to significations; and discourse is this articulation. The items constitutive for discourse are: what the discourse is about (what is talked about); what is said-in-the-talk, as such; the communication;

and the making-known. These are not properties which can just be raked up empirically from language. They are existential characteristics rooted in the state of Dasein's Being, and it is they that first make anything like language ontologically possible. In the factical linguistic form of any definite case of discourse, some of these items may be lacking, or may remain unnoticed. The fact that they often do *not* receive 'verbal' expression, is merely an index of some definite kind of discourse which, in so far as it is discourse, must in every case lie within the totality of the structures we have mentioned.

Attempts to grasp the 'essence of language' have always taken their orientation from one or another of these items; and the clues to their conceptions of language have been the ideas of 'expression,' of 'symbolic form,' of communication as 'assertion,'[6] of the 'making-known' of experiences, of the 'patterning' of life. Even if one were to put these various fragmentary definitions together in syncretistic fashion, nothing would be achieved in the way of a fully adequate definition of "language." We would still have to do what is decisive here—to work out in advance the ontologico-existential whole of the structure of discourse on the basis of the analytic of Dasein.

We can make clear the connection of discourse with understanding and intelligibility by considering an existential possibility which belongs to talking itself—hearing. If we have not heard 'aright,' it is not by accident that we say we have not 'understood.' Hearing is constitutive for discourse. And just as linguistic utterance is based on discourse, so is acoustic perception on hearing. Listening to . . . is Dasein's existential way of Being-open as Being-with for Others. Indeed, hearing constitutes the primary and authentic way in which Dasein is open for its ownmost potentiality-for-Being—as in hearing the voice of the friend whom every Dasein carries with it. Dasein hears, because it understands. As a Being-in-the-world with Others, a Being which understands, Dasein is 'in thrall' to Dasein-with and to itself; and in this thraldom it "belongs" to these.[7] Being-with develops in listening to one another [Aufeinander-hören], which can be done in several possible ways: following,[8] going along with, and the private modes of not-hearing, resisting, defying, and turning away.

It is on the basis of this potentiality for hearing, which is existentially primary, that anything like *hearkening* [*Horchen*] becomes possible. Hearkening is phenomenally still more primordial than what is defined 'in the first instance' as "hearing" in psychology—the sensing of tones and the perception of sounds. Hearkening too has the kind of Being of the hearing which understands. What we 'first' hear is never noises or complexes of sounds, but the creaking waggon, the motor-cycle. We hear the column on the march, the north-wind, the woodpecker tapping, the fire crackling.

It requires a very artificial and complicated frame of mind to 'hear' a 'pure noise.' The fact that motor-cycles and waggons are what we proximally hear is the phenomenal evidence that in every case Dasein, as Being-in-the-world, already dwells *alongside* what is ready-to-hand within-the-world; it certainly does not dwell proximally alongside 'sensations'; nor would it first have to give shape to the swirl of sensations to provide the springboard from which the subject leaps off and finally arrives at a 'world.' Dasein, as essentially understanding, is proximally alongside what is understood.

Likewise, when we are explicitly hearing the discourse of another, we proximally understand what is said, or—to put it more exactly—we are already with him, in advance, alongside the entity which the discourse is about. On the other hand, what we proximally hear is *not* what is expressed in the utterance. Even in cases where the speech is indistinct or in a foreign language, what we proximally hear is *unintelligible* words, and not a multiplicity of tone-data.[9]

Admittedly, when what the discourse is about is heard 'naturally,' we can at the same time hear the 'diction,' the way in which it is said [die Weise des Gesagtseins], but only if there is some co-understanding beforehand of what is said-in-the-talk; for only so is there a possibility of estimating whether the way in which it is said is appropriate to what the discourse is about thematically.

In the same way, any answering counter-discourse arises proximally and directly from understanding what the discourse is about, which is already 'shared' in Being-with.

Only where talking and hearing are existentially possible, can anyone hearken. The person who 'cannot hear' and 'must feel'[10] may perhaps be one who is able to hearken very well, and precisely because of this. Just hearing something "all around" [Das Nur-herum-hören] is a privation of the hearing which understands. Both talking and hearing are based upon understanding. And understanding arises neither through talking at length [vieles Reden] nor through busily hearing something "all around." Only he who already understands can listen [zuhören].

*Keeping silent* is another essential possibility of discourse, and it has the same existential foundation. In talking with one another, the person who keeps silent can 'make one understand' (that is, he can develop an understanding), and he can do so more authentically than the person who is never short of words. Speaking at length [Viel-sprechen] about something does not offer the slightest guarantee that thereby understanding is advanced. On the contrary, talking extensively about something, covers it up and brings what is understood to a sham clarity— the unintelligibility of the trivial. But to keep silent does not mean to be dumb. On the contrary, if a man is dumb, he still has a tendency to 'speak.' Such a person has not proved that he can keep silence; indeed, he entirely lacks the possibility of proving anything of the sort. And the person who is accustomed by Nature to speak little is no better able to show that he is keeping silent or that he is the sort of person who can do so. He who never says anything cannot keep silent at any given moment. Keeping silent authentically is possible only in genuine discoursing. To be able to keep silent, Dasein must have something to say—that is, it must have at its disposal an authentic and rich disclosedness of itself. In that case one's reticence [Verschwiegenheit] makes something manifest, and does away with 'idle talk' ["Gerede"]. As a mode of discoursing, reticence Articulates the intelligibility of Dasein in so primordial a manner that it gives rise to a potentiality-for-hearing which is genuine, and to a Being-with-one-another which is transparent.

Because discourse is constitutive for the Being of the "there"(that is, for states-of-mind and understanding), while "Dasein" means Being-in-the-world, Dasein as discursive Being-in, has already expressed itself. Dasein has language. Among the Greeks, their everyday existing was largely diverted into talking with one another, but at the same time they 'had eyes' to see. Is it an accident that in both their pre-philosophical and their philosophical ways of interpreting Dasein, they defined the essence of man as ζῷον λόγον ἔχον? The later way of interpreting this definition of man in the sense of the *animal rationale,* 'something living which has reason,' is not indeed 'false,' but it covers up the phenomenal basis for this definition of "Dasein." Man shows himself as the entity which talks. This does not signify that the possibility of vocal utterance is peculiar to him, but rather that he is the entity which is such as to discover the world and Dasein itself. The Greeks had no word for "language"; they understood this phenomenon 'in the first instance' as discourse. But because the λόγος came into their philosophical ken primarily as assertion, *this* was the kind of *logos* which they took as their clue for working out the basic structures of the forms of discourse and its components. Grammar sought its foundations in the 'logic' of this *logos.* But this logic was based upon the ontology of the present-at-hand. The basic stock of 'categories of signification,' which pased over into the subsequent science of language, and which in principle is still accepted as the standard today, is oriented towards discourse as assertion. But if on the contrary we take this phenomenon to have in principle the primordiality and breadth of an *existentiale,* then there emerges the necessity of re-establishing the science of language on foundations which are ontologically more primordial. The task of *liberating* grammar from logic requires *beforehand* a *positive* understanding of the basic a priori structure of discourse in general as an *existentiale.* It is not a task that can be carried through later on by improving and rounding out what has been handed down. Bearing this in mind, we must inquire into the basic forms in which it is possible to articulate anything understandable, and to do so in accordance with significations; and this articulation must not be confined to entities within-the-world which we cognize by considering them theoretically, and which we express in sentences. A doctrine of signification will not emerge automatically even if we make a comprehensive comparison of as many languages as possible, and those which are most exotic. To accept, let us say, the philosophical horizon within which W. von Humboldt made language a problem, would be no less inadequate. The doctrine of signification is rooted in the ontology of Dasein. Whether it prospers or decays depends on the fate of this ontology.

In the last resort, philosophical research must resolve to ask what kind of Being goes with language in general. Is it a kind of equipment ready-to-hand within-the-world, or has it Dasein's kind of Being, or is it neither of these? What kind of Being does language have, if there can be such a thing as a 'dead' language? What do the "rise" and "decline" of a language mean ontologically? We possess a science of language, and the Being of the entities which it has for its theme is obscure. Even the horizon for any investigative question about it is veiled. Is it an accident that proximally and for the most part significations are 'worldly,' sketched out beforehand by the significance of the world, that they are indeed often predominantly 'spatial'? Or does this 'fact' have existential-ontological necessity? and if it is necessary, why should it be so? Philosophical research will have to dispense with the 'philosophy of language' if it is to inquire into the 'things themselves' and attain the status of a problematic which has been cleared up conceptually.

Our Interpretation of language has been designed merely to point out the ontological 'locus' of this phenomenon in Dasein's state of Being, and especially to prepare the way for the following analysis, in which, taking as our clue a fundamental kind of Being belonging to discourse, in connection with other phenomena, we shall try to bring Dasein's everydayness into view in a manner which is ontologically more primordial

## Translator's Notes

1. *'Rede.'* We have translated this word either as 'discourse' or 'talk,' as the context seems to demand, sometimes compromising with the hendiadys 'discourse or talk.' But in some contexts 'discourse' is too formal while 'talk' is too colloquial; the reader must remember that there is no good English equivalent for 'Rede.'

2. 'Die Hinausgesprochenheit der Rede ist die Sprache.'

3. 'Dieses ist redend als zu- und absagen, auffordern, warnen, als Aussprache, Rücksprache, Fürsprache, ferner als "Aussagen machen" und als reden in der Weise des "Redenhaltens."'

4. Reading '. . . bei der Analyse der Aussage . . .' with the older editions. The words 'der Aussage' have been omitted in the newer editions.

5. Das Mitsein wird in der Rede "ausdrücklich" *geteilt, das heisst es ist* schon, nur ungeteilt als nicht ergriffenes und zugeeignetes.'

6. '. . . der Mitteilung als "Aussage" . . .' The quotation marks around 'Aussage' appear only in the newer editions.

7. 'Als verstehendes In-der-Welt-sein mit dem Anderen ist es dem Mitdasein und ihm selbst "hörig" und in dieser Hörigkeit zugehörig.' In this sentence Heidegger uses some cognates of hören ('hearing') whose interrelations disappear in our version.

8. '. . . des Folgens . . .' In the earlier editions there are quotation marks around 'Folgens.'

9. Here we follow the reading of the newer editions: '. . . nicht eine Mannigfaltigkeit von Tondaten.' The older editions have 'reine' instead of 'eine.'

10. The author is here alluding to the German proverb, "Wer nicht hören kann, muss fühlen.' (I.e. he who cannot heed, must suffer.)

# 8

# Hermeneutics and Theology

## Rudolf Bultmann

RUDOLF BULTMANN (1884–1976) was born in Wiefelstede (Oldenburg) in North Germany the son of a Lutheran pastor. At the age of nineteen he enrolled as a student of theology at the University of Tübingen. In 1912—after his *Habilitation*—he became a lecturer (*Privatdozent*) at Marburg. After several years of teaching at various other universities (Breslau, 1916–20; Giessen, 1920–21), he returned to Marburg as professor of New Testament and remained in that city until his retirement in 1951 and his death in 1976. During the period of the Hitler regime Bultmann supported the Confessing Church—a Protestant group opposing Hitler. But he did not actively participate in politics. One of the most important Protestant theologians in this century, Bultmann wrote a number of significant works: among them, *Jesus and the Word* (1926; Eng. trans., 1934), *Theology of the New Testament* (2 vols., 1951–54), *History and Eschatology* (1957), *Jesus Christ and Mythology* (1958), and numerous essays and articles (see Sect. A, Bibl.). Bultmann is best known for his radical program of demythologizing the Scriptures. He contended that the Scriptures contained an existential message cloaked in mythical terms which were a product of the time and place when they were written. It was the task of the interpreter to uncover this existential meaning. The idea and the program of demythologizing originated during the years 1922 to 1928, when Bultmann was in close contact with Martin Heidegger during his Marburg stay. Bultmann derived major inspiration from Heidegger's existential analysis as expounded in *Being and Time*. The hermeneutic dimension of Bultmann's work is evident because it consists of a theory and philosophy of interpretation of Scriptures. The approach developed by him and those who followed his ideas received the name *The New Hermeneutic* (see J. M. Robinson, Sect. B, Bibl.). But Bultmann's importance for hermeneutics is not limited to what is meant or implied by demythologizing. He was familiar not only with the theological history of hermeneutics included in his considerations but the entire tradition of hermeneutic thought and its relevance for the situation of the human sciences as he found them. Thus, he himself made an important contribution to general hermeneutics. Our selections illustrate both aspects of Bultmann's hermeneutics: the one which has to be viewed in connection with his idea of demythologizing; the other, more general one, which arises from his occupation with the problems of interpreting historical texts. It is in the latter that his affinity with the positions of other theoreticians—like Gadamer or Habermas—is best expressed.

# IS EXEGESIS WITHOUT
# PRESUPPOSITIONS POSSIBLE?

The question whether exegesis without presuppositions is possible must be answered affirmatively if "without presuppositions" means "without presupposing the results of the exegesis." In this sense, exegesis without presuppositions is not only possible but demanded. In another sense, however, *no* exegesis is without presuppositions, inasmuch as the exegete is not a *tabula rasa*, but on the contrary, approaches the text with specific questions or with a specific way of raising questions and thus has a certain idea of the subject matter with which the text is concerned!

## I

1. The demand that exegesis must be without presuppositions, in the sense that it must not presuppose its results (we can also say that it must be without prejudice), may be clarified only briefly. This demand means, first of all, the rejection of allegorical interpretation? When Philo finds the Stoic idea of the apathetic wise man in the prescription of the law that the sacrificial animal must be without blemish (*Spec. Leg.* I, 260), then it is clear that he does not hear what the text actually says, but only lets it say what he already knows. And the same thing is true of Paul's exegesis of Deut. 25:4 as a prescription that the preachers of the gospel are to be supported by the congregations (I Cor. 9:9) and of the interpretation in the Letter of Barnabas (9:7 f.) of the 318 servants of Abraham (Gen. 14:14) as a prophecy of the cross of Christ.

2. However, even where allegorical interpretation is renounced, exegesis is frequently guided by prejudices? This is so, for example, when it is presupposed that the evangelists Matthew and John were Jesus' personal disciples and that therefore the narratives and sayings of Jesus that they hand down must be historically true reports. In this case, it must be affirmed, for instance, that the cleansing of the temple, which in Matthew is placed during Jesus' last days just before his passion, but in John stands at the beginning of his ministry, took place twice. The question of an unprejudiced exegesis becomes especially urgent when the problem of Jesus' messianic consciousness is concerned. May exegesis of the gospels be guided by the dogmatic presupposition that Jesus was the Messiah and was conscious of being so? Or must it rather leave this question open? The answer should be clear. Any such messianic consciousness would be a historical fact and could only be exhibited as such by historical research. Were the latter able to make it probable

that Jesus knew himself to be the Messiah, this result would have only relative certainty; for historical research can never endow it with absolute validity. All knowledge of a historical kind is subject to discussion, and therefore, the question as to whether Jesus knew himself as Messiah remains open. Every exegesis that is guided by dogmatic prejudices does not hear what the text says, but only lets the latter say what it wants to hear.

## II

1. The question of exegesis without presuppositions in the sense of unprejudiced exegesis must be distinguished from this same question in the other sense in which it can be raised. And in this second sense, we must say that *there cannot be any such thing as presuppositionless exegesis.* That there is no such exegesis in fact, because every exegete is determined by his own individuality, in the sense of his special biases and habits, his gifts and his weaknesses, has no significance in principle. For in this sense of the word, it is precisely his "individuality" that the exegete ought to eliminate by educating himself to the kind of hearing that is interested in nothing other than the subject matter of which the text speaks. However, the one presupposition that cannot be dismissed is *the historical method* of interrogating the text. Indeed, exegesis as the interpretation of historical texts is a part of the science of history.

It belongs to the historical method, of course, that a text is interpreted in accordance with the rules of grammar and of the meaning of words. And closely connected with this, historical exegesis also has to inquire about the individual style of the text. The sayings of Jesus in the synoptics, for example, have a different style from the Johannine ones. But with this there is also given another problem with which exegesis is required to deal. Paying attention to the meaning of words, to grammar, and to style soon leads to the observation that every text speaks in the language of its time and of its historical setting. This the exegete must know; therefore, he must know the historical conditions of the language of the period out of which the text that he is to interpret has arisen. This means that for an understanding of the language of the New Testament the acute question is, "Where and to what extent is its Greek determined by the Semitic use of language?" Out of this question grows the demand to study apocalypticism, the rabbinic literature, and the Qumran texts, as well as the history of Hellenistic religion.

Examples of this point are hardly necessary, and I cite only one. The New Testament word πνεῦμα is translated in German as *"Geist."* Thus it is understandable that the exegesis of the nineteenth century (e.g., in the Tübingen school) interpreted the New Testament on the basis of the idealism that goes back to ancient Greece, until Hermann Gunkel pointed out in 1888 that the New Testament πνεῦμα meant something entirely different—namely, God's miraculous power and manner of action.[4]

The historical method includes the presupposition that history is a unity in the sense of a closed continuum of effects in which individual events are connected by the succession of cause and effect. This does not mean that the process of history is determined by the causal law and that there are no free decisions of men whose actions determine the course of historical happenings. But even a free decision does not happen without a cause, without a motive; and the task of the historian is to come to know the motives of actions. All decisions and all deeds have their causes and consequences; and the historical method presupposes that it is possible in principle to exhibit these and their connection and thus to understand the whole historical process as a closed unity.

This closedness means that the continuum of historical happenings cannot be rent by the interference of supernatural, transcendent powers and that therefore there is no "miracle" in this sense of the word. Such a miracle would be an event whose cause did not lie within history. While, for example, the Old Testament narrative speaks of an interference by God in history, historical science cannot demonstrate such an act of God, but merely perceives that there are those who believe in it. To be sure, as historical science, it may not assert that such a faith is an illusion and that God has not acted in history. But it itself as science cannot perceive such an act and reckon on the basis of it; it can only leave every man free to determine whether he wants to see an act of God in a historical event that it itself understands in terms of that event's immanent historical causes.

It is in accordance with such a method as this that the science of history goes to work on all historical documents. And there cannot be any exceptions in the case of biblical texts if the latter are at all to be understood historically. Nor can one object that the biblical writings do not intend to be historical documents, but rather affirmations of faith and proclamation. For however certain this may be, if they are even to be understood as such, they must first of all be interpreted historically, inasmuch as they speak in a strange language in concepts of a faraway time, of a world-picture that is alien to us. Put quite simply, they must be *translated,* and translation is the task of historical science.

2. If we speak of translation, however, then the hermeneutical problem at once presents itself.[5] To translate means to make understandable, and this in turn presupposes an understanding. The understanding of history as a continuum of effects presupposes an understanding of the efficient forces that connect the individual historical phenomena. Such forces are economic needs, social exigencies, the political struggles for power, human passions, ideas, and ideals. In the assessment of such factors historians differ; and in every effort to achieve a unified point of view the individual historian is guided by some specific way of raising questions, some specific perspective.

This does not mean a falsification of the historical picture, provided that the perspective that is presupposed is not a prejudice, but a way of raising questions, and that the historian is self-conscious about the fact that his way of asking questions is one-sided and only comes at the phenomenon or the text from the standpoint of a particular perspective. The historical picture is falsified only when a specific way of raising questions is put forward as the only one—when, for example, all history is reduced to economic history. Historical phenomena are many-sided. Events like the Reformation can be observed from the standpoint of church history as well as political history, of economic history as well as the history of philosophy. Mysticism can be viewed from the standpoint of its significance for the history of art, etc. However, some specific way of raising questions is always presupposed if history is at all to be understood.

But even more, the forces that are effective in connecting phenomena are understandable only if the phenomena themselves that are thereby connected are also understood! This means that an understanding of the subject matter itself belongs to historical understanding. For can one understand political history without having a concept of the state and of justice, which by their very nature are not historical products but ideas? Can one understand economic history without having a concept of what economy and society in general mean? Can one understand the history of religion and philosophy without knowing what religion and philosophy are? One cannot understand Luther's posting of the ninety-five theses, for instance, without understanding the actual meaning of protest against the Catholicism of his time. One cannot understand the Communist Manifesto of 1848 without understanding the principles of capitalism and socialism. One cannot understand the decisions of persons who act in history if one does not understand man and his possibilities for action. In short, historical understanding presupposes an understanding of the subject matter of history itself and of the men who act in history.

This is to say, however, that historical understanding always presupposes a relation of the interpreter to the subject matter that is (directly or indirectly) expressed in the texts. This relation is grounded in the actual life-context in which the interpreter stands. Only he who lives in a state and in a society can understand the political and social phenomena of the past and their history, just as only he who has a relation to music can understand a text that deals with music, etc.

Therefore, a specific understanding of the subject matter of the text, on the basis of a "life-relation" to it, is always presupposed by exegesis; and insofar as this is so no exegesis is without presuppositions. I speak of this understanding as a "preunderstanding." It as little involves prejudices as does the choice of a perspective. For the historical picture is falsified only when the exegete takes his preunderstanding as a definitive understanding. The "life-relation" is a genuine one, however, only when it is vital, i.e., when the subject matter with which the text is concerned also concerns us and is a problem for us. If we approach history alive with our own problems, then it really begins to speak to us. Through discussion the past becomes alive, and in learning to know history we learn to know our own present; historical knowledge is at the same time knowledge of ourselves. To understand history is possible only for one who does not stand over against it as a neutral, nonparticipating spectator, but himself stands in history and shares in responsibility for it. We speak of this encounter with history that grows out of one's own historicity as the *existentiell* encounter. The historian participates in it with his whole existence.

This *existentiell* relation to history is the fundamental presupposition for understanding history.[6] This does not mean that the understanding of history is a "subjective" one in the sense that it depends on the individual pleasure of the historian and thereby loses all objective significance. On the contrary, it means that history precisely in its objective content can only be understood by a subject who is *existentiell* moved and alive. It means that, for historical understanding, the schema of subject and object that has validity for natural science is invalid.[7]

Now what has just been said includes an important insight—namely, that historical knowledge is never a closed or definitive knowledge—any more than is the preunderstanding with which the historian approaches historical phenomena. For if the phenomena of history are not facts that can be neutrally observed, but rather open themselves in their meanings only to one who approaches them alive with questions, then they are always only understandable now in that they actually speak in the present situation. Indeed, the questioning itself grows out of the historical situation, out of the claim of the now, out of the problem that is given in the now. For this reason, historical research is never closed, but rather must always be carried further. Naturally, there are certain items of historical knowledge that can be regarded as definitively known—namely, such items as concern only dates that can be fixed chronologically and locally, as, for example, the assassination of Caesar or Luther's posting of the ninety-five theses. But what these events that can thus be dated *mean* as historical events cannot be definitively fixed. Hence one must say that a historical event is always first knowable for what it is—precisely as a historical event—in the future. And therefore one can also say that the future of a historical event belongs to that event.

Naturally, items of historical knowledge can be passed on, not as definitively known, but in such a way as to clarify and expand the following generation's preunderstanding. But even so, they are subject to the criticism of that generation. Can we today surmise the meaning of the two world wars? No; for it holds good that what a historical event means always first becomes clear in the future. It can definitively disclose itself only when history has come to an end.

## III

What are the consequences of this analysis for exegesis of the biblical writings? They may be formulated in the following theses:

(1) The exegesis of the biblical writings, like every other interpretation of a text, must be unprejudiced.

(2) However, the exegesis is not without presuppositions, because as historical interpretation it presupposes the method of historical-critical research.

(3) Furthermore, there is presupposed a "life-relation" of the exegete to the subject matter with which the Bible is concerned and, together with this relation, a preunderstanding.

(4) This preunderstanding is not a closed one, but rather is open, so that there can be an *existentiell* encounter with the text and an *existentiell* decision.

(5) The understanding of the text is never a definitive one; but rather remains open because the meaning of the Scriptures discloses itself anew in every future.

In the light of what has already been said, nothing further is required in the way of comment on the first and second theses.

As regards the third thesis, however, we may note that the preunderstanding has its basis in the question concerning God that is alive in human life. Thus it does not mean that the exegete must know everything possible about God, but rather that he is moved by the *existentiell* question for God—regardless of the form that this question actually takes in his consciousness (say, for example, as the question concerning "salvation," or escape from death, or certainty in the face of a constantly shifting destiny, or truth in the midst of a world that is a riddle to him).

With regard to the fourth thesis, we may note that the *existentiell* encounter with the text can lead to a yes as well as to a no, to confessing faith as well as to express unfaith, because in the text the exegete encounters a claim, i.e., is there offered a self-understanding that he can accept (permit to be given to him) or reject, and therefore is faced with the demand for decision. Even in the case of a no, however, the understanding is a legitimate one, i.e., is a genuine answer to the question of the text, which is not to be refuted by argument because it is an *existentiell* decision.

So far as the fifth thesis is concerned, we note simply that because the text speaks to existence it is never understood in a definitive way. The *existentiell* decision out of which the interpretation emerges cannot be passed on, but must always be realized anew. This does not mean, of course, that there cannot be continuity in the exegesis of Scripture. It goes without saying that the results of methodical historical-critical research can be passed on, even if they can only be taken over by constant critical testing. But even with respect to the exegesis that is based *existentiell* there is also continuity, insofar as it provides guidance for the next generation—as has been done, for example, by Luther's understanding of the Pauline doctrine of justification by faith alone. Just as this understanding must constantly be achieved anew in the discussion with Catholic exegesis, so every genuine exegesis that offers itself as a guide is at the same time a question that must always be answered anew and independently. Since the exegete exists historically and must hear the word of Scripture as spoken in his special historical situation, he will always understand the old word anew. Always anew it will tell him who he, man, is and who God is, and he will always have to express this word in a new conceptuality. Thus it is true also of Scripture that it only is what it is with its history and its future.

## Notes

1. Walter Baumgartner, to whom the following pages are dedicated, has published an essay in the *Schweizerische theologische Umschau*, XI (1941), 17-38, entitled "*Die Auslegung des Alten Testaments im Streit der Gegenwart.*" Inasmuch as I completely agree with what he says there, I hope he will concur if I now attempt to carry the hermeneutical discussion somewhat further.

2. If there is actually an allegory in the text, then, of course, it is to be explained as an allegory. However, such an explanation is not allegorical interpretation; it simply asks for the meaning that is intended by the text.

3. A criticism of such prejudiced exegesis is the chief concern of the essay of W. Baumgartner mentioned above (cf. n. 1).

4. Cf. H. Gunkel, *Die Wirkungen des Heiligen Geist nach der populären Anschauung der apostolischen Zeit und der Lehre des Apostel Paulus* (1888; 3rd ed., 1909).

5. Cf. with the following, my essays, "*Das Problem der Hermeneutik,*" *Glauben und Verstehen,* II (1952), 211-35. [Eng. trans. by J. C. G. Greig in *Essays, Philosophical and Theological* (1955), pp. 234-61], and "*Wissenschaft und Existenz,*" *Ehrfurcht vor dem Leben:* Festschrift for Albert Schweitzer (1954), pp. 30-45; and also *History and Eschatology* (1957), ch. VIII.

6. It goes without saying that the *existentiell* relation to history does not have to be raised to the level of consciousness. By reflection it may only be spoiled.

7. I do not deal here with certain special questions, such as how an *existentiell* relation to history can already be present in the research of grammar, lexicography, statistics, chronology, and geography or how the historian of mathematics or physics participates *existentiell* in the objects of his research. One thinks of Plato!

# THE PROBLEM OF DEMYTHOLOGIZING

I take the term *demythologizing* to mean a *hermeneutic* procedure which inquires after the real content of mythological assertions or texts.

It is presupposed here that myth, to be sure, talks about reality, but in an inadequate way.

Likewise presupposed is a certain understanding of reality.

Now, *reality* can be understood in two senses. Commonly, one understands reality as *the reality of the world perceived through objective representation.* Man finds himself within this world and orients himself by positing himself against it. He counts on his connection to it and calculates how to control it in order to secure his life. This way of perceiving reality is developed in natural science and in technology, which natural science made possible.

This way of perceiving reality is *demythologizing as such* insofar as it rules out the effects of the supernatural powers described in myth, be it the effects of powers which start natural processes and preserve them, or of powers which interrupt natural processes. Thoroughly consistent natural science does not need the "hypothesis of God" (Laplace); the powers which control natural processes are immanent to them. Likewise, natural science eliminates the notion of wonder as a miracle which interrupts the causal nexus of the world-process.

Like all phenomena in the world surrounding him, man can also submit himself to objectifying observation to the extent that he is tangible in the world. He posits himself over against himself and makes himself an object. In this way he reduces his authentic, specific reality to reality in the world. This occurs in "explanatory" psychology (in distinction to *verstehenden* psychology—cf. Dilthey) and in this type of sociology.

This perspective can also come to the fore in the *discipline of history,* and it is likewise the case in positivistic historicism.[1] The historian acts as a subject observing the object, history, and thus takes a stand as spectator outside of the historical time process.

Today there is a growing recognition that there is no such objectivity, because *perceiving the historical process is in itself a historical procedure.* Attaining distance from the object through neutral observation is impossible. The seemingly objective picture of historical processes is always stamped with the personality of the observer, who is himself historical and can never be a spectator standing outside of historical time.

Now, I am not treating something here; namely, that an analogous understanding of the subject-object relationship has also become pervasive in modern science in the recognition that that which is observed is partially formed or modified somehow by its observer. How far the analogy between the modern discipline of history and natural science extends would require special examination. The point here is that the modern understanding of history sees *reality* as the *reality of man existing in history* as opposed to observing it objectifyingly.

Human being is fundamentally different from natural being perceived through objectifying observation. Today we like to designate specifically human being as *existence.*[2] "Existence" does not mean a mere presence, in the sense that plants and animals, too, "exist," but rather, a specifically human mode of being.

Unlike beings of nature, man is not determined by the causal nexus of natural occurrence; rather, he has to take charge of himself, be responsible for himself. This means that human life is history; it leads man through his decisions at every turn into a future in which he chooses himself. The decisions are made according to how a man understands himself and what he sees as the fulfillment of his life. *History* is the realm of human decisions. It becomes understandable if seen as such; i.e., if it is seen that the potentialities for self-understanding have been operative in it. These are the same potentialities as those for contemporary self-understanding and can only be perceived whatsoever as one with these decisions. I call such an interpretation of history *existential interpretation,* since it, stirred by the interpreter's own inquiry into existence, inquires after the understanding of existence which is operative in every instance in history.

Since, in fact, all people emerge from a past in which potentialities for self-understanding already rule, are offered up, or are placed into question, the decision is then always one of *deciding in relation to the past;* indeed, deciding in the final end in relation to man's own past and future.

Now, the decision need not be made consciously and is in most cases unconscious. Indeed, that which is, in fact, the unconscious decision in favor of the past— man in the hands of his past— can appear to be indecisiveness. That means, however, that man can exist authentically or inauthentically. Just this *potentiality for authentic or inauthentic being* belongs to historicity, i.e., to human reality.

If authentic human being is existence, in which man has to take charge of himself and is responsible for himself, then the following belongs to authentic existence: *openness towards the future, the freedom in every instance to become an event* [*die jeweils Ereignis werdende Freiheit*]. Consequently, the reality of historical man is never a settled one like that of animals, which is always entirely what it can be. Man's reality is his history; i.e., it constantly lies before him such that one can say: *future being* is the reality in which man lives.

This becomes clear in the history of mankind in that the historical sense [*Sinn*] of an event first becomes understandable by way of its future outcome. The future is essential to the event. Thus, the sense of historical occurrences will only be decisively understood at the end of history. But since such a retrospective view from the end is impossible for human eyes, a philosophy which endeavors to understand the sense of history is also impossible. It is only possible to speak of the sense of history as the sense of the moment, which is meaningful as a moment of decision.

Now, all decisions are made in concrete situations, and indecisive behavior too— i.e., inauthentic human being— always takes place in concrete situations. If the discipline of history is going to point out the potentialities for self-understanding which come to light in human decisions, it also has to portray concrete situations in past history. But these are only revealed through an objectifying view of the past. As little as this captures the historical sense of a deed or event, it very well can and must try to recognize the simple facts of the deeds and events and to determine "how it was" in *this sense.* And as little as the nexus of human actions is determined by causal necessity, it is very much linked by the consequences of cause and effect. Even free decision results from reasons so as not to be blind arbitrariness. Because of this, it is possible to understand the course of history retrospectively as a closed causal nexus in every instance. An objectifying historical study has to perceive it in this way.

One may now be wondering whether the existential interpretation and the objectifying representation of history are in contradiction to one another; i.e., whether the reality of the one is in contradiction to the reality of the other, so that one would have to speak of two spheres of reality or even of a double truth. That would obviously be a false conclusion; for there is, in fact, only *one reality* and only *one* true assertion about one and the same phenomenon.

The *one* reality can, however, be seen in two aspects corresponding to man's two potentialities: authentic or inauthentic existence. In inauthentic existence, man understands himself in the available world. In authentic existence, he understands himself in the unavailable future. Accordingly, he can study the history of the past objectifyingly and also as an address, insofar as the potentialities for human self-understanding are perceptible and provoke responsible choice.

One has to designate the relationship of the two kinds of self-understanding as *dialectical* insofar as the one does not, in fact, exist without the other. For man, whose authentic life is carried out in decisions, is also a physical being. Responsible decisions are only made in concrete situations in which physical life is also at stake. The decision whereby man chooses himself, his authentic existence, is always simultaneously the decision for a potential physical life. Responsibility for oneself is always simultaneously responsibility for the world and its history. On account of his responsibility, man needs an objectifying view of the world into which he is placed as his available "working world." For that reason, there is repeatedly the temptation or seduction to view the "working world" as authentic reality; to miss the authenticity of existing [*Existieren*] and to secure life by arranging what is available.

Thus, it is completely clear that the existential intepretation of history requires the objectifying study of the historical past. As little as this can capture the historical sense of a deed or event, it can just as little forgo an establishing (as reliable as possible) of the facts. Nietzsche's postulate directed against positivism ("there are no facts, but only interpretation") is erroneous. He is right if one understands "fact" as the complete sense of a historical fact, thus inclusive of its sense and its meaning [*Bedeutung*] in the context of the historical occurrence. A fact in this sense can always only present itself as "interpretation," as the picture drawn by a historian who brings his personality to his work. But an interpretation is obviously not a creation of fantasy. Rather, something is being interpreted by it, namely, the facts, which are (always to some approximate degree) accessible to the historian's objectifying view.

If the above is considered valid, then the *problem of demythologizing with regard to the discipline of history* can be solved. Is the discipline of history, like natural science, demythologizing as such? Yes and no!

The discipline of history demythologizes as such insofar as it understands the historical process, viewed objectifyingly, as a closed nexus of effects. The historian cannot proceed in any other way if he wants to gain certain knowledge of any fact; if, for example, he wants to verify whether a traditional story is really a valid testimony for a fact of the past. He therefore cannot acknowledge that the context of an event is disrupted by the intervention of supernatural powers. He cannot acknowledge as an event any wonder whose cause does not lie within history. History as a factual science cannot, as the biblical scriptures do, speak of the intervening activity of God in the course of history. It can only perceive belief in God's activity, but not God Himself, as a historical phenomenon. It cannot know whether this belief corresponds to a reality, since a reality which lies beyond objectifiably perceivable reality is not within its range. It must view as mythological every discourse which claims to talk about the activities of otherworldly powers as though it were talking about activity which is observable and noticeable in the objectifiably perceivable world before us. Perhaps it can also serve as an argument for the proof of some truths. But, likewise, every discourse about otherworldly spheres which are spatially attached to the perceivable world, like heaven and hell, is held to be mythological.

Now, there is a fundamental difference from natural science with respect to a position on myth: natural science eliminates it, and the discipline of history has to interpret it. It has to inquire into the sense of mythological discourse, which is indeed a historical phenomenon.

The question as to *the sense of mythological discourse* on the whole ought to be easy to answer. Myth strives to speak of a reality which lies beyond objectifiable, observable, and controllable reality. To be sure, it is a reality of decisive importance for man, denoting well-being or calamity, grace or wrath, and demanding respect and obedience.

I can leave out here the etiological myths which endeavor to explain conspicuous formations or appearances in nature. They are only relevant in our context insofar as they allow us to recognize mythological thought as something which grows out of awe, terror, and questioning, and which takes into account the relation between cause and effect. It can be described as primitive scientific thought, be it that some researchers endeavor to reduce mythological thought on the whole down to primitive thought.

This primitive scientific, and in this sense objectifying, thought is indeed inherent to all mythology. But now a fundamental distinction arises. Namely, it is questionable whether, or to what extent, the intention of myth is to give an explanation of the world over against which man observes and calculates, or whether it endeavors to talk about the reality of man himself, i.e., his existence. We are concerned in the present context with myth insofar as it is the expression of a certain understanding of human existence.

*Which understanding of existence?* Well, the following: man finds himself in a world which is full of enigmas and mysteries, and he experiences a fate which is just as enigmatic and mysterious. He is forced to recognize that he is not the master of his life. He realizes that the world and human life have their ground and their limit in a power (or in powers), in a transcendent power, which lies beyond that which he can calculate or control.

Mythological thought, however, naively objectifies the otherworldly as inner-worldly insofar as it, at odds with its authentic intention, imagines the transcendent as spatially distant and its power as quantitatively greater than human capability. In opposition to this, demythologizing endeavors to bring forth the authentic intention of myth; namely, the intention to speak of the authentic reality of man.

Now, is there a *limit to demythologizing*? It is often said that religion, and Christian faith as well, cannot forgo mythological discourse. Why not? It certainly provides religious poetry and cultic and liturgical language with images and symbols. And pious devotion may intuitively and feelingly perceive an inner sense [*Sinngehalt*] in them. The decisive point, however, is that such images and symbols really conceal an inner sense, and philosophical and theological reflection has the task, after all, of clarifying this inner sense. But this, in turn, cannot be expressed in mythological language; otherwise, its sense would in turn, have to be explained—and so ad infinitum.

The claim that myth is indispensable means, however, that there are myths which do not allow for existential interpretation. Thus, it is necessary—at least in certain cases—to talk objectifyingly about the transcendent, the Godhead, since mythological discourse is objectifying language to begin with.

Is this valid? It all gives rise to the question: is *discourse about the activity of God* necessarily mythological discourse, or can and must it also be interpreted existentially?

Since God is not an objectively ascertainable phenomenon in the world, it is only possible to speak of His activity in such a way that one is speaking simultaneously of our existence, which is affected by God's activity. One may wish to call such ways of speaking about God's activity "analogical." This serves to express that the condition of being affected by God has its origin absolutely in God Himself, and because of this, man alone is the suffering and receiving being.

But it must be likewise confirmed that the condition of being affected by God's activity can only be spoken of in the same manner as one can speak of an existentiell event which is not objectively ascertainable or demonstrable.

Now, each and every existential condition of being affected occurs in a concrete situation. Thus, it is obvious or only natural, so to speak, for the affected being to trace this situation back to the activity of God—which is completely legitimate, as long as one does not confuse origin in God's will with causality, which is accessible to objectifying view. This is the proper place to speak of a wonder, and not of a miracle!

Just as it speaks of wonder, faith also speaks of God's activity as His *creation of and sovereignty over nature and history,* and it has to do so. For if man knows himself in his existence to be called and led into life by God's omnipotence, then he also knows that nature and history, within which his life plays itself out, are permeated with God's activity. But this knowledge can only be avowed and never be asserted as a general truth like a natural scientific or a historio-philosophical theory. Otherwise, God's activity would be objectified into a secular process. The testimony to God's creatorship and sovereignty has a legitimate ground only in the existentiell self-understanding of man.

But the testimony therefore contains a *paradox.* For it affirms the paradoxical identity of innerworldly occurrences with the activity of an otherworldly God. Faith indeed affirms that it sees an act of God in an event or in processes which are at the same time ascertainable to objectifying view in the nexus of natural and historical occurrences. For faith, the activity of God is thus a wonder in which the natural nexus of world occurrences is equally preserved [*aufgehoben.*]

But what is special for *Christian faith* is that it sees the activity of God within a certain historical event, which can be objectively ascertained as such, in a very special sense: the revelation of God which calls every man to faith, namely, in the *appearance of Jesus Christ.* The paradox of this affirmation is most aptly expressed in John's testimony: "The word became flesh."

This paradox is obviously of another kind than that which affirms that the activity of God is at all times and everywhere indirectly identical with world-occurrence. For the sense of the Christ-event is the eschatological occurrence through which God has set an end to the world and its history. This paradox is therefore the affirmation that a historical event is simultaneously the eschato-logical event.

Now the question is: can this event be understood as an event which is ever carried out in one's own existence? Or does it remain over against the man called to faith, in the same way that the object is posited over against the subject in secular reality? That would mean that it is an event in the past as the objectifying view of the historian represents, or "recalls," it. If it ought, however, to be understood as an event which ever touches me in my existence, it must be able to be or to become present in another sense.

Just this is contained in its sense as an eschatological event. As such, it cannot be or become an event of the past if indeed historical events can never have the meaning of *ephapax* (once and for all). This belongs to the essence of the Christ-event as an eschatological event.

Therefore, it cannot, like other historical events, be made present through "recollection." It becomes present *in the proclamation* (the Kerygma) which originates in the event itself and which cannot be what it is without it. That means: the proclamation itself is eschatological occurrence. In it, as address, the Jesus

Christ-event becomes present everytime—present as that event which ever touches me in my existence.

*The church* is the carrier of the proclamation, and that same paradox repeats itself here. For in *one* respect, the church is a phenomenon available to objectifying view, but according to its authentic essence, it is an eschatological phenomenon—or better: an eschatological event taking place ever more.

Thus, I agree with Enrico Castelli "que le 'Kerygma' comporte l'être de l'événement (en tant que mystère); et l'éventuelle analyse historique de l'événement n'entame pas la Révélation, parce qu'elle est la Révélation du message et de l'événement (c'est-à-dire de l'histoire) en même temps."[3]

## Translator's Notes

1. The reader should note the following translations of words having to do with "history" throughout the text: *Geschichte* = history; *geschichtlich* and *historisch* = historical; *Geschichlichkeit* = historicity; *Geschichtswissenschaft* = the discipline of history; *Historismus* = historicism; *die historische Wissenschaft* = history as a factual science; *Historiker* = historian.

2. The following terms are translated in accordance with the Macquarrie-Robinson translation of Martin Heidegger's *Sein und Zeit* (*Being and Time* [New York: Harper & Row, 1962]): *Existenz* = existence; *existenzial* = existential; *existenziell* = existentiell. "Existence" in *Being and Time* refers to man's openness toward being in historical time (see section 6 above). "Existential" thus predicates existence, while "existentiell" means "resulting from personal choice," "Existentiell" therefore derives from "existential," which is concerned with the structure of the constitution of *Dasein,* and lays ground for personal choice.

3. ". . . that the 'Kerygma' comprises the essence of the event (in so far as it is mystery); and the possible historical analysis of the event does not do injury to revelation, because it [the analysis] is the revelation of the message and of the event (i.e., of history) at the same time."

# 9

# The Historicity of Understanding

=========== Hans-Georg Gadamer ===========

HANS-GEORG GADAMER (b. 1900) was born in Marburg, where he also studied philosophy and classics. He received his doctorate in 1922 and began teaching at Marburg as an instructor (*Privatdozent*) in 1929, where he became a professor extraordinary in 1937. From 1938 to 1947 he taught at Leipzig, and from 1947 to 1949 at Frankfurt. In 1949 he moved to the University of Heidelberg where he taught until his retirement in 1968. Gadamer, a personal student of Heidegger's, combines in his work a vital interest in Greek thought and culture with a strong inclination toward the German idealist tradition in its different facets. His work in hermeneutics grew out of his historical and philosophical studies and his abiding interest in literature and poetry, both ancient and modern. In *Truth and Method* Gadamer developed an extensive and profound analysis and critique of classical hermeneutic thought in its various manifestations. The concept of the historicity of understanding—which he derived from Heidegger's *Being and Time*—is at the center of his argument. But he is also indebted to Dilthey's methodological studies and interests in the nature and history of the humanities and human sciences. In contrast to Dilthey, however, Gadamer does not wish to secure a methodology for these sciences. Instead, he chose to concentrate his efforts on exposing and criticizing the hermeneutic principles which underlie the humanistic disciplines in their actual history and present-day manifestations. Our first two selections present sections from *Truth and Method*. The first one deals with the important notion of *prejudice* (*Vorurteil*) without which understanding is not possible, according to Gadamer. Because of the attitude of Enlightenment philosophers against prejudice and bias, he believes that we have until now overlooked the positive, or, better, the constitutive character of prejudice in our culture. The concept of effective history (*Wirkungsgeschichte*) is one of equal importance for Gadamer. What he means, in a nutshell, is that no understanding would be possible if the interpreter were not also part of the historical continuum which he and the phenomenon he studies must share.

One of the criticisms leveled against *Truth and Method* by Habermas and the followers of the Frankfurt School concentrated on Gadamer's alleged narrow transcendental interest in hermeneutics and the human sciences. Habermas expressed this criticism in his study *On the Logic of the Social Sciences* (1967). Gadamer replied almost immediately and at length in an essay which constitutes our third selection, *Rhetoric, Hermeneutics, and the Critique of Ideology* (1967). Points of affinity, as well as differences, between the positions of Gadamer and Habermas are brought out in this essay, and the indebtedness of both thinkers to the hermeneutic tradition becomes quite apparent. Habermas's reply to this essay is reprinted below in chapter 10.

# THE DISCREDITING OF PREJUDICE BY THE ENLIGHTENMENT

If we pursue the view that the enlightenment developed in regard to prejudices we find it makes the following fundamental division: a distinction must be made between the prejudice due to human authority and that due to over-hastiness[1]. The basis of this distinction is the origin of prejudices in regard to the persons who have them. It is either the respect in which we hold others and their authority, that leads us into error, or else it is an over-hastiness in ourselves. That authority is a source of prejudices accords with the well-known principle of the enlightenment that Kant formulated: have the courage to make use of your own understanding[2]. Although this distinction is certainly not limited to the role that prejudices play in the understanding of texts, its chief application is still in the sphere of hermeneutics. For the critique of the enlightenment is directed primarily against the religious tradition of christianity, i.e. the bible. By treating the latter as an historical document, biblical criticism endangers its own dogmatic claims. This is the real radicality of the modern enlightenment as against all other movements of enlightenment: it must assert itself against the bible and its dogmatic interpretation[3]. It is, therefore, particularly concerned with the hermeneutical problem. It desires to understand tradition correctly, i.e. reasonably and without prejudice. But there is a special difficulty about this, in that the sheer fact of something being written down confers on it an authority of particular weight. It is not altogether easy to realise that what is written down can be untrue. The written word has the tangible quality of something that can be demonstrated and is like a proof. It needs a special critical effort to free oneself from the prejudice in favour of what is written down and to distinguish here also, as with all oral assertions, between opinion and truth[4].

It is the general tendency of the enlightenment not to accept any authority and to decide everything before the judgment seat of reason. Thus the written tradition of scripture, like any other historical document, cannot claim any absolute validity, but the possible truth of the tradition depends on the credibility that is assigned to it by reason. It is not tradition, but reason that constitutes the ultimate source of all authority. What is written down is not necessarily true. We may have superior knowledge: this is the maxim with which the modern enlightenment approaches tradition and which ultimately leads it to undertake historical research.[5] It makes the tradition as much an object of criticism as do the natural sciences the evidence of the senses. This does not necessarily mean that the "prejudice against preju-dices" was everywhere taken to the extreme consequences of free thinking and atheism, as in England and France. On the contrary, the German enlightenment recognised the "true prejudices" of the christian religion. Since the human in-tellect is too weak to manage without prejudices it is at least fortunate to have been educated with true prejudices.

It would be of value to investigate to what extent this kind of modification and moderation of the enlightenment[6] prepared the way for the rise of the romantic movement in Germany, as undoubtedly did the critique of the enlightenment and the revolution by Edmund Burke. But none of this alters the fundamental facts. True prejudices must still finally be justified by rational knowledge, even though the task may never be able to be fully completed.

Thus the criteria of the modern enlightenment still determine the self-understanding of historicism. This does not happen directly, but in a curious refraction caused by romanticism. This can be seen with particular clarity in the fundamental schema of the philosophy of history that romanticism shares with the enlightenment and that precisely the romantic reaction to the enlightenment made into an unshakeable premise: the schema of the conquest of mythos by logos. It is the presupposition of the progressive retreat of magic in the world that gives this schema its validity. It is supposed to represent the progressive law of the history of the mind, and precisely because romanticism has a negative attitude to this development, it takes over the schema itself as an obvious truth. It shares the presupposition of the enlightenment and only reverses the evaluation of it, seek-ing to establish the validity of what is old, simply because it is old: the "gothic" middle ages, the christian European community of states, the feudal structure of society, but also the simplicity of peasant life and closeness to nature.

In contrast to the enlightenment's belief in perfection, which thinks in terms of the freedom from "superstition" and the prejudices of the past, we now find that olden times, the world of myth, unreflective life, not yet analysed away by con-sciousness, in a "society close to nature," the world of christian chivalry, all these acquire a romantic magic, even a priority of truth.[7] The reversal of the enlighten-ment's presupposition results in the paradoxical tendency to restoration, i.e. the tendency to reconstruct the old because it is old, the conscious return to the un-conscious, culminating in the recognition of the superior wisdom of the primaeval age of myth. But the romantic reversal of this criterion of the enlightenment actually perpetuates the abstract contrast between myth and reason. All criticism of the enlightenment now proceeds via this romantic mirror image of the en-lightenment. Belief in the perfectibility of reason suddenly changes into the perfection of the "mythical" consciousness and finds itself reflected in a paradisic primal state before the "fall" of thought.

In fact the presupposition of a mysterious darkness in which there was a mythical collective consciousness that preceded all thought is just as dogmatic and abstract as that of a state of perfection achieved by a total enlightenment or that of absolute knowledge. Primaeval wisdom is only the counter-image of "primaeval stupidity." All mythical consciousness is still knowledge, and if it knows about divine powers, then it has progressed beyond mere trembling before power (if this is to be regarded as the primaeval state), but also beyond a collective life contained in magic rituals (as we find in the early Orient). It knows about itself, and in this knowledge it is no longer simply "outside itself."[8]

There is the related point that even the contrast between genuine mythical thinking and pseudo-mythical poetic thinking is a romantic illusion which is based on a prejudice of the enlightenment: namely, that the poetic act, because it is a creation of the free imagination, is no longer in any way bound within the religious quality of the myth. It is the old quarrel between the poets and the philosophers in the modern garb appropriate to the age of belief in science. It is now said, not that poets tell lies, but that they are incapable of saying anything true, since they have an aesthetic effect only and merely seek to rouse through their imaginative creations the imagination and the emotions of their hearers or readers.

The concept of the "society close to nature" is probably another case of a romantic mirror-image, whose origin ought to be investigated. In Karl Marx it appears as a kind of relic of natural law that limits the validity of his socio-economic theory of the class struggle.[9] Does the idea go back to Rousseau's description of society before the division of labour and the introduction of property?[10] At any rate, Plato has already demonstrated the illusory nature of this political theory in the ironical account he gives of a "state of nature" in the third book of the *Republic.*[11]

These romantic revaluations give rise to the attitude of the historical science of the nineteenth century. It no longer measures the past by the yardsticks of the present, as if they represented an absolute, but it ascribes their own value to past ages and can even acknowledge their superiority in one or the other respect. The great achievements of romanticism— the revival of the past, the discovery of the voices of the peoples in their songs, the collecting of fairy-tales and legends, the cultivation of ancient customs, the discovery of the world views implicit in languages, the study of the "religion and wisdom of India"— have all motivated the historical research that has slowly, step by step, transformed the intuitive revival into historical knowledge proper. The fact that it was romanticism that gave birth to the historical school confirms that the romantic retrieval of origins is itself based on the enlightenment. The historical science of the nineteenth century is its proudest fruit and sees itself precisely as the fulfilment of the enlightenment, as the last step in the liberation of the mind from the trammels of dogma, the step to the objective knowledge of the historical world, which stands as an equal besides the knowledge of nature achieved by modern science.

The fact that the restorative tendency of romanticism was able to combine with the fundamental concern of the enlightenment to constitute the unity of the historical sciences simply indicates that it is the same break with the continuity of meaning in tradition that lies behind both. If it is an established fact for the enlightenment that all tradition that reason shows to be impossible, i.e. nonsense, can only be understood historically, i.e. by going back to the past's way of looking at things, then the historical consciousness that emerges in romanticism involves a radicalisation of the enlightenment. For the exceptional case of nonsensical tradition has become the general rule for historical consciousness. Meaning that is generally accessible through reason is so little believed that the whole of the past, even, ultimately, all the thinking of one's contemporaries, is seen only "historically." Thus the romantic critique of the enlightenment ends itself in enlightenment, in that it evolves as historical science and draws everything into the orbit of historicism. The basic discrediting of all prejudices, which unites the experiential emphasis of the new natural sciences with the enlightenment, becomes, in the historical enlightenment, universal and radical.

This is the point at which the attempt to arrive at an historical hermeneutics has to start its critique. The overcoming of all prejudices, this global demand of the enlightenment, will prove to be itself a prejudice, the removal of which opens the way to an appropriate understanding of our finitude, which dominates not only our humanity, but also our historical consciousness.

Does the fact that one is set within various traditions mean really and primarily that one is subject to prejudices and limited in one's freedom? Is not, rather, all human existence, even the freest, limited and qualified in various ways? If this is true, then the idea of an absolute reason is impossible for historical humanity. Reason exists for us only in concrete, historical terms, i.e. it is not its own master, but remains constantly dependent on the given circumstances in which it operates. This is true not only in the sense in which Kant limited the claims of rationalism, under the influence of the sceptical critique of Hume, to the a priori element in the knowledge of nature; it is still truer of historical consciousness and the possibility of historical knowledge. For that man is concerned here with himself and his own creations (Vico) is only an apparent solution of the problem set by historical knowledge. Man is alien to himself and his historical fate in a quite different way from that in which nature, that knows nothing of him, is alien to him.

The epistemological question must be asked here in a fundamentally different way. We have shown above that Dilthey probably saw this, but he was not able to overcome the influence over him of traditional epistemology. His starting-point, the awareness of "experience," was not able to build the bridge to the historical realities, because the great historical realities of society and state always have a predeterminant influence on any "experience." Self-reflection and autobiography—Dilthey's starting-points—are not primary and are not an adequate basis for the hermeneutical problem, because through them history is made private once more. In fact history does not belong to us, but we belong to it. Long before we understand ourselves through the process of self-examination, we understand ourselves in a self-evident way in the family, society and state in which we live. The focus of subjectivity is a distorting mirror. The self-awareness of the individual is only a flickering in the closed circuits of historical life. That is why the prejudices of the individual, far more than his judgments, constitute the historical reality of his being.

# THE REHABILITATION OF AUTHORITY AND TRADITION

This is where the hermeneutical problem comes in. This is why we examined the discrediting of the concept of prejudice by the enlightenment. That which presents itself, under the aegis of an absolute self-construction by reason, as a limiting prejudice belongs, in fact, to historical reality itself. What is necessary is a fundamental rehabilitation of the concept of prejudice and a recognition of the fact that there are legitimate prejudices, if we want to do justice to man's finite, historical mode of being. Thus we are able to formulate the central question of a truly historical hermeneutics, epistemologically its fundamental question, namely: where is the ground of the legitimacy of prejudices? What distinguishes legitimate prejudices from all the countless ones which it is the undeniable task of the critical reason to overcome?

We can approach this question by taking the view of prejudices that the enlightenment developed with a critical intention, as set out above, and giving it a positive value. As for the division of prejudices into those of "authority" and those of "over-hastiness," it is obviously based on the fundamental presupposition of the enlightenment, according to which a methodologically disciplined use of reason can safeguard us from all error. This was Descartes' idea of method. Over-hastiness is the actual source of error in the use of one's own reason. Authority, however, is responsible for one's not using one's own reason at all. There lies, then, at the base of the division a mutually exclusive antithesis between authority and reason. The false prejudice for what is old, for authorities, is what has to be fought. Thus the enlightenment regards it as the reforming action of Luther that "the prejudice of human prestige, especially that of the philosophical (he means Aristotle) and the Roman pope was greatly weakened."[12] The reformation, then, gives rise to a flourishing hermeneutics which is to teach the right use of reason in the understanding of transmitted texts. Neither the teaching authority of the pope nor the appeal to tradition can replace the work of hermeneutics, which can safeguard the reasonable meaning of a text against all unreasonable demands made on it.

The consequences of this kind of hermeneutics need not be those of the radical critique of religion that we found, for example, in Spinoza. Rather the possibility of supernatural truth can remain entirely open. Thus the enlightenment, especially in the field of popular philosophy, limited the claims of reason and acknowledged the authority of bible and church. We read in, say, Walch, that he distinguishes between the two classes of prejudice—authority and over-hastiness—but sees in them two extremes, between which it is necessary to find the right middle path, namely a reconciliation between reason and biblical authority. Accordingly, he sees the prejudice from over-hastiness as a prejudice in favour of the new, as a predisposition to the overhasty rejection of truths simply because they are old and attested by authorities.[13] Thus he discusses the British freethinkers (such as Collins and others) and defends the historical faith against the norm of reason. Here the meaning of the prejudice from over-hastiness is clearly reinterpreted in a conservative sense.

There can be no doubt, however, that the real consequence of the enlightenment is different: namely, the subjection of all authority to reason. Accordingly, prejudice from over-hastiness is to be understood as Descartes understood it, i.e. as the source of all error in the use of reason. This fits in with the fact that after the victory of the enlightenment, when hermeneutics was freed from all dogmatic ties, the old division returns in a changed sense. Thus we read in Schleiermacher that he distinguishes between narrowness of view and over-hastiness as the causes of misunderstanding.[14] He places the lasting prejudices due to narrowness of view beside the momentary ones due to overhastiness, but only the former are of interest to someone concerned with scientific method. It no longer even occurs to Schleiermacher that among the prejudices in the mind of one whose vision is narrowed by authorities there might be some that are true—yet this was included in the concept of authority in the first place. His alteration of the traditional division of prejudices is a sign of the fulfilment of the enlightenment. Narrowness now means only an individual limitation of understanding: "The one sided preference for what is close to one's own sphere of ideas."

In fact, however, the decisive question is concealed behind the concept of narrowness. That the prejudices that determine what I think are due to my own narrowness of vision is a judgment that is made from the standpoint of their dissolution and illumination and holds only of unjustified prejudices. If, contrariwise, there are justified prejudices productive of knowledge, then we are back with the problem of authority. Hence the radical consequences of the enlightenment, which are still contained in Schleiermacher's faith in method, are not tenable.

The distinction the enlightenment draws between faith in authority and the use of one's own reason is, in itself, legitimate. If the prestige of authority takes the place of one's own judgment, then authority is in fact a source of prejudices. But this does not exclude the possibility that it can also be a source of truth, and this is what the enlightenment failed to see when it denigrated all authority. To be convinced of this, we only have to consider one of the great forerunners of the European enlightenment, namely Descartes. Despite the radicalness of his methodological thinking, we know that Descartes excluded morality from the total reconstruction of all truths by reason. This was what he meant by his provisional morality. It seems to me symptomatic that he did not in fact elaborate his definitive morality and that its principles, as far as we can judge from his letters to Elizabeth, contain hardly anything new. It is obviously unthinkable to prefer to wait until the progress of modern science provides us with the basis of a new morality. In fact the denigration of authority is not the only prejudice of the enlightenment. For, within the enlightenment, the very concept of authority becomes deformed. On the basis of its concept of reason and freedom, the concept of authority could be seen as diametrically opposed to reason and freedom: to be, in fact, blind obedience. This is the meaning that we know, from the usage of their critics, within modern dictatorships.

But this is not the essence of authority. It is true that it is primarily persons that have authority; but the authority of persons is based ultimately, not on the subjection and abdication of reason, but on recognition and knowledge—knowledge, namely, that the other is superior to oneself in judgment and insight and that for this reason his judgment takes precedence, i.e. it has priority over one's own. This is connected with the fact that authority cannot actually be bestowed, but is acquired and must be acquired, if someone is to lay claim to it. It rests on recognition and hence on an act of reason itself which, aware of its own limitations, accepts that others have better understanding. Authority in this sense, properly understood, has nothing to do with blind obedience to a command. Indeed, authority has nothing to do with obedience, but rather with knowledge. (It seems to me that the tendency towards the acknowledgement of authority, as it emerges in, for example, Karl Jaspers' *Von der Wahrheit*, pp. 766ff. and Gerhard Krüger, *Freiheit und Weltverwaltung*, pp. 231ff., is not convincing unless the truth of this statement is recognised.) It is true that authority is necessary in order to be able to command and find obedience. But this proceeds only from the authority that a person has. Even the anonymous and impersonal authority of a superior which derives from the command is not ultimately based on this order, but is what makes it possible. Here also its true basis is an act of freedom and reason, which fundamentally acknowledges the authority of a superior because he has a wider view of things or is better informed, i.e. once again, because he has superior knowledge.[15]

Thus the recognition of authority is always connected with the idea that what authority states is not irrational and arbitrary, but can be seen, in principle, to be true. This is the essence of the authority claimed by the teacher, the superior, the expert. The prejudices that they implant are legitimised by the person himself. Their validity demands that one should be biased in favour of the person who presents them. But this makes them then, in a sense, objective prejudices, for they bring about the same bias in favour of something that can come about through other means, e.g. through solid grounds offered by reason. Thus the essence of authority belongs in the context of a theory of prejudices free from the extremism of the enlightenment.

Here we can find support in the romantic criticism of the enlightenment; for there is one form of authority particularly defended by romanticism, namely tradition. That which has been sanctioned by tradition and custom has an authority that is nameless, and our finite historical being is marked by the fact that always the authority of what has been transmitted—and not only what is clearly grounded—has power over our attitudes and behaviour. All education depends on this, and even though, in the case of education, the educator loses his function when his charge comes of age and sets his own insight and decisions in the place of the authority of the educator, this movement into maturity in his own life does not mean that a person becomes his own master in the sense that he becomes free of all tradition. The validity of morals, for example, is based on tradition. They are freely taken over, but by no means created by a free insight or justified by themselves. This is precisely what we call tradition: the ground of their validity. And in fact we owe to romanticism this correction of the enlightenment, that tradition has a justification that is outside the arguments of reason and in large measure determines our institutions and our attitudes. It is even a mark of the superiority of classical ethics over the moral philosophy of the modern period that it justifies the transition of ethics into "politics," the art of right government, by the indispensability of tradition.[16] In comparison with it the modern enlightenment is abstract and revolutionary.

The concept of tradition, however, has become no less ambiguous than that of authority, and for the same reason, namely that it is the abstract counterpart to the principle of the enlightenment that determines the romantic understanding of tradition. Romanticism conceives tradition as the antithesis to the freedom of reason and regards it as something historically given, like nature. And whether the desire is to be revolutionary and oppose it or would like to preserve it, it is still seen as the abstract counterpart of free self-determination, since its validity does not require any reasons, but conditions us without our questioning it. Of course, the case of the romantic critique of the enlightenment is not an instance of the automatic dominance of tradition, in which what has been handed down is preserved unaffected by doubt and criticism. It is, rather, a particular critical attitude that again addresses itself to the truth of tradition and seeks to renew it, and which we may call "traditionalism."

It seems to me, however, that there is no such unconditional antithesis between tradition and reason. However problematical the conscious restoration of traditions or the conscious creation of new traditions may be, the romantic faith in the "growth of tradition," before which all reason must remain silent, is just as prejudiced as and is fundamentally like the enlightenment. The fact is that tradition is constantly an element of freedom and of history itself. Even the most genuine and solid tradition does not persist by nature because of the inertia of what once existed. It needs to be affirmed, embraced, cultivated. It is, essentially, preservation, such as is active in all historical change. But preservation is an act of reason, though an inconspicuous one. For this reason, only what is new, or what is planned, appears as the result of reason. But this is an illusion. Even where life changes violently, as in ages of revolution, far more of the old is preserved in the supposed transformation of everything than anyone knows, and combines with the new to create a new value. At any rate, preservation is as much a freely-chosen action as revolution and renewal. That is why both the enlightenment's critique of tradition and its romantic rehabilitation are less than their true historical being.

These thoughts lead to the question of whether in the hermeneutic of the human sciences the element of tradition should not be given its full value. Research in the human sciences cannot regard itself as in an absolute antithesis to the attitude we take as historical beings to the past. In our continually manifested attitude to the past, the main feature is not, at any rate, a distancing and freeing of ourselves from what has been transmitted. Rather, we stand always within tradition, and this is no objectifying process, i.e. we do not conceive of what tradition says as something other, something alien. It is always part of us, a model or exemplar, a recognition of ourselves which our later historical judgment would hardly see as a kind of knowledge, but as the simplest preservation of tradition.

Hence in regard to the dominant epistemological methodologism we must ask if the rise of historical consciousness has really detached our scientific attitude entirely from this nature attitude to the past. Does understanding in the human sciences understand itself correctly when it relegates the whole of its own historicality to the position of prejudices from which we must free ourselves? Or does "unprejudiced science" have more in common than it realises with that naive openness and reflection in which traditions live and the past is present?

At any rate understanding in the human sciences shares one fundamental condition with the continuity of traditions, namely, that it lets itself be addressed by tradition. Is it not true of the objects of its investigation—just as of the contents of tradition—that only then can its meaning be experienced? However much this meaning may always be a mediated one and proceed from a historical interest, that does not seem to have any relation to the present; even in the extreme case of "objective" historical research, the proper realisation of the historical task is to determine anew the meaning of what is examined. But the meaning exists at the beginning of any such research as well as at the end: as the choice of the theme to be investigated, the awakening of the desire to investigate, as the gaining of the new problematic.

At the beginning of all historical hermeneutics, then, the abstract antithesis between tradition and historical research, between history and knowledge, must be discarded. The effect of a living tradition and the effect of historical study must constitute a unity, the analysis of which would reveal only a texture of reciprocal relationships.[17] Hence we would do well not to regard historical consciousness as something radically new—as it seems at first—but as a new element within that which has always made up the human relation to the past. In other words, we have to recognise the element of tradition in the historical relation and enquire into its hermeneutical productivity.

That there is an element of tradition active in the human sciences, despite the methodological nature of its procedures, an element that constitutes its real nature and is its distinguishing mark, is immediately clear if we examine the history of research and note the difference between the human and natural sciences with regard to their history. Of course no finite historical effort of man can completely erase the traces of this finiteness. The history of mathematics or of the natural sciences is also a part of the history of the human spirit and reflects its destinies. Nevertheless, it is not just historical naiveté when the natural scientist writes the history of his subject in terms of the present stage of knowledge. For him errors and wrong turnings are of historical interest only, because the progress of research is the self-evident criterion of his study. Thus it is of secondary interest only to see how advances in the natural sciences or in mathematics belong to the moment in history at which they took place. This interest does not affect the epistemic value of discoveries in the natural sciences or in mathematics.

There is, then, no need to deny that in the natural sciences elements of tradition can also be active, e.g. in that particular lines of research are preferred at particular places. But scientific research as such derives the law of its development not from these circumstances, but from the law of the object that it is investigating.

It is clear that the human sciences cannot be described adequately in terms of this idea of research and progress. Of course it is possible to write a history of the solution of a problem, e.g. the deciphering of barely legible inscriptions, in which the only interest was the ultimate reaching of the final result. Were this not so, it would not have been possible for the human sciences to have borrowed the methodology of the natural ones, as happened in the last century. But the analogy between research in the natural and in the human sciences is only a subordinate element of the work done in the human sciences.

This is seen in the fact that the great achievements in the human sciences hardly ever grow old. A modern reader can easily make allowances for the fact that, a hundred years ago, there was less knowledge available to a historian, who therefore made judgments that were incorrect in some details. On the whole, he would still rather read Droysen or Mommsen than the latest account of the particular subject from the pen of a historian living today. What is the criterion here? Obviously one cannot simply base the subject on a criterion by which we measure the value and importance of research. Rather, the object appears truly significant only in the light of him who is able to describe it to us properly. Thus it is certainly the subject that we are interested in, but the subject acquires its life only from the light in which it is presented to us. We accept the fact that the subject presents itself historically under different aspects at different times or from a different standpoint. We accept that these aspects do not simply cancel one another out as research proceeds, but are like mutually exclusive conditions that exist each by themselves and combine only in us. Our historical consciousness is always filled with a variety of voices in which the echo of the past is heard. It is present only in the multifariousness of such voices: this constitutes the nature of the tradition in which we want to share and have a part. Modern historical research itself is not only research, but the transmission of tradition. We do not see it only in terms of the law of progress and verified results; in it too we have, as it were, a new experience of history, whenever a new voice is heard in which the past echoes.

What is the basis of this? Obviously we cannot speak of an object of research in the human sciences in the sense appropriate to the natural sciences, where research penetrates more and more deeply into nature. Rather, in the human sciences the interest in tradition is motivated in a special way by the present and its interests. The theme and area of research are actually constituted by the motivation of the enquiry. Hence historical research is based on the historical movement in which life itself stands and cannot be understood teleologically in terms of the object into which it is enquiring. Such an object clearly does not exist at all in itself. Precisely this is what distinguishes the human sciences from the natural sciences. Whereas the object of the natural sciences can be described idealiter as what would be known in the perfect knowledge of nature, it is senseless to speak of a perfect knowledge of history, and for this reason it is not possible to speak of an object in itself towards which its research is directed.

# THE PRINCIPLE OF EFFECTIVE-HISTORY

The fact that the interest of the historian is directed not only towards the historical phenomenon and the work that has been handed down but also, secondarily, towards their effect in history (which also includes the history of research) is regarded in general as a mere supplement to the historical problematic that, from Hermann Grimm's *Raffael* to Gundolf and beyond, has given rise to many valuable insights. To this extent, effective-history is not new. But that this kind of effective-historical approach be required every time that a work of art or an element of the tradition is led from the twilight region between tradition and history to be seen clearly and openly in terms of its own meaning—this is a new demand (addressed not to research, but to methodological consciousness itself) that proceeds inevitably from the analysis of historical consciousness.

It is not, of course, a hermeneutical requirement in the sense of the traditional concept of hermeneutics. I am not saying that historical enquiry should develop this effective-historical problematic that would be something separate from that which is concerned directly with the understanding of the work. The requirement is of a more theoretical kind. Historical consciousness must become aware that in the apparent immediacy with which it approaches a work of art or a tradition, there is also contained, albeit unrecognised and hence not allowed for, this other element. If we are trying to understand a historical phenomenon from the historical distance that is characteristic of our hermeneutical situation, we are always subject to the effects of effective-history. It determines in advance both what seems to us worth enquiring about and what will appear as an object of investigation, and we more or less forget half of what is really there—in fact, we miss the whole truth of the phenomenon when we take its immediate appearance as the whole truth.

In our understanding, which we imagine is so straightforward, we find that, by following the criterion of intelligibility, the other presents himself so much in terms of our own selves that there is no longer a question of self and other. Historical objectivism, in appealing to its critical method, conceals the involvement of the historical consciousness itself in effective-history. By the method of its foundational criticism it does away with the arbitrariness of cosy re-creations of the past, but it preserves its good conscience by failing to recognise those presuppositions—certainly not arbitrary, but still fundamental—that govern its own approach to understanding, and hence falls short of reaching that truth which, despite the finite nature of our understanding, could be reached. In this historical objectivism resembles statistics, which are such an excellent means of propaganda because they let facts speak and hence simulate an objectivity that in reality depends on the legitimacy of the questions asked.

We are not saying, then, that effective-history must be developed as a new independent discipline ancillary to the human sciences, but that we should learn to understand ourselves better and recognise that in all understanding, whether we are expressly aware of it or not, the power of this effective-history is at work. When a naive faith in scientific method ignores its existence, there can be an actual deformation of knowledge. We know it from the history of science as the irrefutable proof of something that is obviously false. But looking at the whole situation, we see that the power of effective-history does not depend on its being recognised. This, precisely, is the power of history over finite human consciousness, namely that it prevails even where faith in method leads one to deny one's own historicality. The demand that we should become conscious of this effective-history is pressing because it is necessary for scientific consciousness. But this does not mean that it can be fulfilled in an absolute way. That we should become completely aware of effective-history is just as hybrid a statement as when Hegel speaks of absolute knowledge, in which history would become completely transparent to itself and hence be raised to the level of a concept. Rather, effective historical consciousness is an element in the act of understanding itself and, as we shall see, is already operative in the choice of the right question to ask.

Effective-historical consciousness is primarily consciousness of the hermeneutical situation. To acquire an awareness of a situation, however, is always a task of particular difficulty. The very idea of a situation means that we are not standing outside it and hence are unable to have any objective knowledge of it.[18] We are always within the situation, and to throw light on it is a task that is never entirely completed. This is true also of the hermeneutic situation, i.e. the situation in which we find ourselves with regard to the tradition that we are trying to understand. The illumination of this situation—effective-historical reflection—can never be completely achieved, but this is not due to a lack in the reflection, but lies in the essence of the historical being which is ours. To exist historically means that knowledge of oneself can never be complete. All self-knowledge proceeds from what is historically pre-given, what we call, with Hegel, "substance," because it is the basis of all subjective meaning and attitude and hence both prescribes and limits every possibility of understanding any tradition whatsoever in terms of its unique historical quality. This almost defines the aim of philosophical hermeneutics: its task is to move back along the path of Hegel's phenomenology of mind until we discover in all that is subjective the substantiality that determines it.

Every finite present has its limitations. We define the concept of "situation" by saying that it represents a standpoint that limits the possibility of vision. Hence an essential part of the concept of situation is the concept of "horizon." The horizon is the range of vision that includes everything that can be seen from a particular vantage point. Applying this to the thinking mind, we speak of narrowness of horizon, of the possible expansion of horizon, of the opening up of new horizons etc. The word has been used in philosophy since Nietzsche and Husserl[19] to characterise the way in which thought is tied to its finite determination, and the nature of the law of the expansion of the range of vision. A person who has no horizon is a man who does not see far enough and hence overvalues what is nearest to him. Contrariwise, to have an horizon means not to be limited to what is nearest, but to be able to see beyond it. A person who has an horizon knows the relative significance of everything within this horizon, as near or far, great or small. Similarly, the working out of the hermeneutical situation means the achievement of the right horizon of enquiry for the questions evoked by the encounter with tradition.

In the sphere of historical understanding we also like to speak of horizons, especially when referring to the claim of historical consciousness to see the past in terms of its own being, not in terms of our contemporary criteria and prejudices, but within its own historical horizon. The task of historical understanding also involves acquiring the particular historical horizon, so that what we are seeking to understand can be seen in its true dimensions. If we fail to place ourselves in this way within the historical horizon out of which tradition speaks, we shall misunderstand the significance of what it has to say to us. To this extent it seems a legitimate hermeneutical requirement to place ourselves in the other situation in order to understand it. We may ask, however, whether this does not mean that we are failing in the understanding that is asked of us. The same is true of a conversation that we have with someone simply in order to get to know him, i.e. to discover his standpoint and his horizon. This is not a true conversation, in the sense that we are not seeking agreement concerning an object, but the specific contents of the conversation are only a means to get to know the horizon of the other person. Examples are oral examinations, or some kinds of conversation between doctor and patient. The historical consciousness is clearly doing something similar when it places itself within the situation of the past and hence is able to acquire the right historical horizon. Just as in a conversation, when we have discovered the standpoint and horizon of the other person, his ideas become intelligible, without our necessarily having to agree with him, the person who thinks historically comes to understand the meaning of what has been handed down, without necessarily agreeing with it, or seeing himself in it.

In both cases, in our understanding we have as it were, withdrawn from the situation of trying to reach agreement. He himself cannot be reached. By including from the beginning the other person's standpoint in what he is saying to us, we are making our own standpoint safely unattainable. We have seen, in considering the origin of historical thinking, that in fact it makes this ambiguous transition from means to ends, i.e. it makes an end of what is only a means. The text that is understood historically is forced to abandon its claim that it is uttering something true. We think we understand when we see the past from a historical standpoint, i.e. place ourselves in the historical situation and seek to reconstruct the historical horizon. In fact, however, we have given up the claim to find, in the past, any truth valid and intelligible for ourselves. Thus this acknowledgement of the otherness of the other, which makes him the object of objective knowledge, involves the fundamental suspension of his claim to truth.

The question is, however, whether this description really corresponds to the hermeneutical phenomenon. Are there, then, two different horizons here, the horizon in which the person seeking to understand lives, and the particular horizon within which he places himself? Is it a correct description of the art of historical understanding to say that we are learning to place ourselves within alien horizons? Are there such things as closed horizons, in this sense? We recall Nietzsche's complaint against historicism that it destroyed the horizon bounded by myth in which alone a culture is able to live.[20] Is the horizon of one's own present time ever closed in this way, and can a historical situation be imagined that has this kind of closed horizon?

Or is this a romantic reflection, a kind of Robinson Crusoe dream of the historical enlightenment, the fiction of an unattainable island, as artificial as Crusoe himself for the alleged primary phenomenon of the solus ipse? Just as the individual is never simply an individual, because he is always involved with others, so too the closed horizon that is supposed to enclose a culture is an abstraction. The historical movement of human life consists in the fact that it is never utterly bound to any one standpoint, and hence can never have a truly closed horizon. The horizon is, rather, something into which we move and that moves with us. Horizons change for a person who is moving. Thus the horizon of the past, out of which all human life lives and which exists in the form of tradition, is always in motion. It is not historical consciousness that first sets the surrounding horizon in motion. But in it this motion becomes aware of itself.

When our historical consciousness places itself within historical horizons, this does not entail passing into alien worlds unconnected in any way with our own, but together they constitute the one great horizon that moves from within and, beyond the frontiers of the present, embraces the historical depths of our self-consciousness. It is, in fact, a single horizon that embraces everything contained in historical consciousness. Our own past, and that other past towards which our historical consciousness is directed, help to shape this moving horizon out of which human life always lives, and which determines it as tradition.

Understanding the past, then, undoubtedly requires an historical horizon. But it is not the case that we acquire this horizon by placing ourselves within a historical situation. Rather, we must always already have a horizon in order to be able to place ourselves within a situation. For what do we mean by "placing ourselves" in a situation? Certainly not just disregarding ourselves. This is necessary, of course, in that we must imagine the other situation. But into this other situation we must also bring ourselves. Only this fulfills the meaning of "placing ourselves." If we place ourselves in the situation of someone else, for example, then we shall understand him, i.e. become aware of the otherness, the indissoluble individuality of the other person, by placing ourselves in his position.

This placing of ourselves is not the empathy of one individual for another, nor is it the application to another person of our own criteria, but it always involves the attainment of a higher universality that overcomes, not only our own particularity, but also that of the other. The concept of the "horizon" suggests itself because it expresses the wide, superior vision that the person who is seeking to understand must have. To acquire a horizon means that one learns to look beyond what is close at hand— not in order to look away from it, but to see it better within a larger whole and in truer proportion. It is not a correct description of historical consciousness to speak, with Nietzsche, of the many changing horizons into which it teaches us to place ourselves. If we disregard ourselves in this way, we have no historical horizon. Nietzsche's view that historical study is deleterious to life is not directed, in fact, against historical consciousness as such, but against the self-alienation that it undergoes when it regards the method of modern historical science as its own true nature. We have already pointed out that a truly historical consciousness always sees its own present in such a way that it sees itself, as it sees the historically other, within the right circumstances. It requires a special effort to acquire an historical horizon. We are always affected, in hope and fear, by what is nearest to us, and hence approach, under its influence, the testimony of the past. Hence it is constantly necessary to inhibit the overhasty assimilation of the past to our own expectations of meaning. Only then will we be able to listen to the past in a way that enables it to make its own meaning heard.

We have shown above that this is a process of distinguishing. Let us consider what this idea of distinguishing involves. It is always reciprocal. Whatever is being distinguished must be distinguished from something which, in turn, must be distinguished from it. Thus all distinguishing also makes visible that from which something is distinguished. We have described this above as the operation of prejudices. We started by saying that a hermeneutical situation is determined by the prejudices that we bring with us. They constitute, then, the horizon of a particular present, for they represent that beyond which it is impossible to see. But now it is important to avoid the error of thinking that it is a fixed set of opinions and evaluations that determine and limit the horizon of the present, and that the otherness of the past can be distinguished from it as from a fixed ground.

In fact the horizon of the present is being continually formed, in that we have continually to test all our prejudices. An important part of this testing is the encounter with the past and the understanding of the tradition from which we come. Hence the horizon of the present cannot be formed without the past. There is no more an isolated horizon of the present than there are historical horizons. Understanding, rather, is always the fusion of these horizons which we imagine to exist by themselves. We know the power of this kind of fusion chiefly from earlier times and their naive attitude to themselves and their origin. In a tradition this process of fusion is continually going on, for there old and new continually grow together to make something of living value, without either being explicitly distinguished from the other.

If, however, there is no such thing as these horizons that are distinguished from one another, why do we speak of the fusion of horizons and not simply of the formation of the one horizon, whose bounds are set in the depths of tradition? To ask the question means that we are recognising the special nature of the situation in which understanding becomes a scientific task, and that it is necessary to work out this situation as a hermeneutical situation. Every encounter with tradition that takes place within historical consciousness involves the experience of the tension between the text and the present. The hermeneutic task consists in not covering up this tension by attempting a naive assimilation but consciously bringing it out. This is why it is part of the hermeneutic approach to project an historical horizon that is different from the horizon of the present. Historical consciousness is aware of its own otherness and hence distinguishes the horizon of tradition from its own. On the other hand, it is itself, as we are trying to show, only something laid over a continuing tradition, and hence it immediately recombines what it has distinguished in order, in the unity of the historical horizon that it thus acquires, to become again one with itself.

The projecting of the historical horizon, then, is only a phase in the process of understanding, and does not become solidified into the self-alienation of a past consciousness, but is overtaken by our own present horizon of understanding. In the process of understanding there takes place a real fusing of horizons, which means that as the historical horizon is projected, it is simultaneously removed. We described the conscious act of this fusion as the task of effective-historical consciousness. Although this task had been obscured by aesthetic historical positivism in the train of romantic hermeneutics, it is, in fact, the central problem of hermeneutics. It is the problem of application that exists in all understanding.

## Notes

1. *Praeiudicium auctoritatis et precipitantiae,* which we find as early as Christian Thomasius's *Lectiones de praeiudiciis* (1689/90) and his *Einleitung der Vernunftlehre,* chap. 13, ## 39/40. Cf. the article in Walch's *Philosophisches Lexikon* (1726), p. 2794ff.

2. At the beginning of his essay, "Beantwortung der Frage: Was ist Aufklärung?" (1784).

3. The enlightenment of the classical world, the fruit of which was Greek philosophy and its culmination in sophism, was quite different in nature and hence permitted a thinker like Plato to use philosophical myths to convey the religious tradition and the dialectical method of philosophising. Cf. Erich Frank, *Philosophische Erkenntnis und religiöse Wahrheit,* p. 31ff., and my review of it in the *Theologische Rundschau* 1950 (pp. 260–266). Cf. also Gerhard Krüger, *Einsicht und Leidenschaft,* 2nd ed. 1951.

4. A good example of this is the length of time it has taken for the authority of the historical writing of antiquity to be destroyed in historical studies and how slowly the study of archives and the research into sources have established themselves (cf. R. G. Collingwood, *Autobiography* [Oxford, 1939], chap. 11, where he more or less draws a parallel between the turning to the study of sources and the Baconian revolution in the study of nature).

5. Cf. what we said about Spinoza's theological-political treatise above.

6. As we find, for example, in C. F. Meier's *Beiträge zu der Lehre von den Vorurteilen des menschlichen Geschlechts,* 1766.

7. I have analysed an example of this process in a little study on Immermann's "Chiliastische Sonette" (*Die Neue Rundschau,* 1949).

8. Horkheimer and Adorno seem to me right in their analysis of the "dialectic of the enlightenment" (although I must regard the application of sociological concepts such as "bourgeois" to Odysseus as a failure of historical reflection, if not, indeed, a confusion of Homer with Johann Heinrich Voss [author of the standard German translation of Homer], who had already been criticised by Goethe).

9. Cf. the reflections on this important question by G. von Lukács in his *History and Class Consciousness* (London, 1969; orig. 1923).

10. Rousseau, *Discours sur l'origine et les fondements de l'inégalité parmi les hommes.*

11. Cf. the present author's *Plato und die Dichter*, p. 12f.

12. Walch, *Philosophisches Lexicon* (1726), p. 1013.

13. Walch, *op. cit.*, p. 1006ff. under the entry *Freiheit zu gedenken*. See p. 257 above.

14. Schleiermacher, *Werke I*, 7, p. 31.

15. The notorious statement, "The party (or the Leader) is always right" is not wrong because it claims that a certain leadership is superior, but because it serves to shield the leadership, by a dictatorial decree, from any criticism that might be true. True authority does not have to be authoritarian.

16. Cf. Aristotle's *Eth. Nic.*, book 10, chap. 9.

17. I don't agree with Scheler that the pre-conscious pressure of tradition decreases as historical study proceeds (*Stellung des Menschen im Kosmos*, p. 37). The independence of historical study implied in this view seems to me a liberal fiction of a sort that Scheler is generally able to see through. (Cf. similarly in his *Nachlass I*, p. 228ff., where he affirms his faith in the historical enlightenment, or that of the sociology of knowledge).

18. The structure of the concept of situation has been illuminated chiefly by K. Jaspers (*Die geistige Situation der Zeit*) and Erich Rothacker.

19. Nietzsche, *Unzeitgemässe Betrachtungen II*, at the beginning.

# RHETORIC, HERMENEUTICS, AND THE CRITIQUE OF IDEOLOGY: METACRITICAL COMMENTS ON *TRUTH AND METHOD*

It is the task of a philosophical hermeneutics to reveal the full scope of the hermeneutical dimension of human experience and to bring to light its fundamental significance for the entirety of our understanding of the world, in all the forms which that understanding takes: from interpersonal communication to social manipulation, from the experience of the individual as a member of society to his experience of that society itself, from the tradition comprised of religion and law, art and philosophy, to the liberating, reflective energy of the revolutionary consciousness. Even so, the individual scholar necessarily begins from limited experiences and limited fields of experience. Insofar as it dealt with the theory of the human sciences,[1] for example, my own endeavor was closely linked to Dilthey's philosophical development of the heritage of German Romanticism; at the same time, however, it was based on a new, much broader foundation— namely, the experience of art, which replies to the historical alienation of the human sciences with its own persistent and triumphant claim to contemporaneity. In approaching the subject as I did, I had in view a kind of truth which goes questioningly behind and in anticipation before all knowledge—a kind of truth which I hoped to bring to light in terms of the essentially linguistic character of all human experience, the consummation and the burden of which is its constantly self-renewing contemporaneity. Still, it was inevitable that the phenomenon which had served as my point of departure should exert a special force even in my analysis of the universal linguistic character of man's relationship to the world, and that it should do so, moreover, in a way which reflected the intellectual and historical origin of the hermeneutical problem itself. The problem had been touched off by the written tradition, a tradition which had become foreign through fixity, longevity, and the distance of time. Thus, it was natural to take the many-layered problem of translation as a model of the linguisticality of man's relationship to the world and to develop the general problem of how that which is foreign becomes ours in terms of the structures of translation.

Nevertheless, what O. Marquard has called the *Sein zum Texte*[2] does not exhaust the hermeneutic dimension—unless the word "text" is taken to mean, above and beyond its narrower sense, the text which "God has written with His own hand," the *liber naturae,* and thus to embrace all scientific knowledge as well, from physics to sociology and anthropology. And even then the model of translation is by no means broad enough to encompass the manifold significance of language in human affairs. To be sure, one can demonstrate in the reading of this greatest of all "books" the pattern of tension and resolution which structures understanding and understandability—perhaps even the understanding mind itself; and in this respect it is impossible to have any doubt about the universality of the hermeneutic problem. It is no secondary topic; hermeneutics is no mere handmaiden to the human sciences of the Romantic period.[3]

At the same time, however, the universal phenomenon of human linguisticality unfolds itself in other dimensions as well. As a result, the concerns of hermeneutics make themselves felt in other fields which also have to do with the linguisticality of the human experience. Some of these were touched upon in *Truth and Method* itself. Thus, effective historical consciousness (*wirkungsgeschichtliches Bewusstsein*)[4] was presented there, in several phases of its history, as the conscious illumination of the human idea of language; it extends, however, as Johannes Lohmann has since shown in his book *Philosophy and Linguistics*[5] and in a discussion of my own work in *Gnomon,*[6] into still further and entirely different dimensions. Taking up the history of "the coinage of the concept 'language' in Occidental thought" which I had sketched, Lohmann extends it both forwards and backwards along the vast time-line of linguistic history: backwards, in that he examines the "emergence of the 'concept' as the intellectual medium by means of which the immediate 'subsumption' of given objects under thought forms becomes possible" (714), seeing in the "stem-inflected" character of Old Indo-European the grammatical form of the concept—a form which finds its most visible expression in the copula—and in this manner identifying the possibility of theory as the most distinctive invention of the Western world; forwards, in that he once again interprets the intellectual history of the Western world in terms of the development of linguistic form, in particular in terms of the transition from stem-inflected to word-inflected languages—a development which makes science possible in the modern sense, as a kind of knowledge which puts the world at our disposal.

Rhetoric further attests to truly universal linguisticality—and that of a kind which is by its very nature antecedent to hermeneutics in the limited sense and which represents something like the positive pole to the negative of textual explication. The connections between rhetoric and hermeneutics which I had noted in my book are susceptible to expansion in numerous ways, as can be seen from the wealth of additions and corrections which Klaus Dockhorn has offered in the *Göttingischen Gelehrten-Anzeigen*.[7] Linguisticality, however, is finally so deeply woven into the sociality of human existence that the validity and limits of the hermeneutical inquiry must also occupy the theoretician of the social sciences. Thus Jürgen Habermas[8] has recently brought philosophical hermeneutics to bear as well on the logic of the social sciences, evaluating it in terms of the epistemological interests of the social sciences.

It seems imperative, then, to take up the topic of the mutually pervasive and interdependent claims to universality embodied in rhetoric, hermeneutics, and sociology and to throw some light on the various kinds of legitimacy to which each can lay claim. It is all the more important to do so, since in all three—most visibly in the first two—the claim to scientific endeavor is itself attended by a certain equivocality, in which the reference to praxis plays a determining role.

For it is manifestly true that rhetoric is not simply a theory of forms of speech and means of persuasion, but can be developed to the level of practical mastery without any theoretical reflection on the means of which it avails itself. By the same token, the art of understanding [hermeneutics]—whatever its ways and means may be—obviously does not depend directly on the deliberateness with which it follows its rules. Here, too, a natural capability which everyone has transforms itself into an ability in the exercise of which one surpasses all others, and theory at best can only say why. In both cases, theory is an afterthought to that from which it is abstracted and which we call praxis. And yet for all that, the one art belongs to the period of the earliest Greek philosophy, while the other is a consequence of the modern breakdown of firm bonds with tradition and the effort to hold fast to that which was in the process of vanishing and deliberately to preserve it.

The first history of rhetoric was written by Aristotle. We have only fragments. It is clear, however, that Aristotle's theory of rhetoric was developed as the realization of a program originally drawn up by Plato. Behind all the specious claims put forward by contemporary teachers of oratory, Plato had discovered a genuine task which only the philosopher, the dialectician, was in a position to carry out: namely, to obtain mastery of truly illuminatory speech in such a manner that the appropriate arguments were brought forward in regard to the specific receptivity of the souls of those to whom they were directed. That is an enlightening theoretical statement of the task of rhetoric, which nevertheless involves two Platonic assumptions: (1) that only he who is at home with the truth (i.e., the Ideas) knows how to find unerringly the "plausible" *pseudos* represented by the rhetorical argument; and (2) that the rhetorician must be equally knowledgeable and at home with the souls on which he hopes to work. Aristotelian rhetoric is preeminently a working out of the latter concern. There, the theory of the correspondence between speech and soul which Plato had called for in the *Phaedrus* culminates in an anthropological approach to the art of speaking.

The theory of rhetoric was the long-term result of a controversy which had been touched off by the intoxicating and alarming invasion of a new art of speaking and a new concept of education which we now refer to as sophism. At that time, rhetoric, in the form of an uncanny new knowledge which showed the way to turn everything topsy-turvy, had streamed from Sicily into an Athens socially and politically stratified but animated by a younger generation easily led astray. Thus, it became imperative to teach this great dictator (as Georgias calls rhetoric) obedience to a new master. From Protagoras to Isocrates it was the claim of the masters of rhetoric not only to teach public speaking but to form as well the sound civic consciousness which promised political responsibility. However, it was Plato who first laid down the principles on the basis of which the new, universally disruptive art of speaking—Aristophanes has portrayed that for us vividly enough—found its limit and its legitimate place. To that the philosophical dialectic of the Platonic Academy attests with the same force as the Aristotelian foundation of logic and rhetoric.

The history of understanding is no less ancient and venerable. If one acknowledges hermeneutics to exist wherever a true art of understanding is in evidence, one would have to begin, if not with Nestor in the *Iliad,* then certainly with Odysseus. Then, too, one could usefully make reference to the new sophistic movement in education, which actually practiced the explication of famous passages of poetry and skillfully elaborated them as pedagogical examples; and one could distinguish between the practice of the Sophists and a Socratic hermeneutics, as Gundert has done.[9] Even so, that is far from being a *theory* of understanding; and indeed it seems to be generally characteristic for the emergence of the hermeneutical problem as such that a situation must exist where something remote has to be brought nearer, a strangeness overcome, a bridge built between "once" and "now." Accordingly, the hour appointed to a theory of understanding arrived with the modern period, which had become conscious of its distance from antiquity. Something of that consciousness was already present in the theological claims brought forward by Protestant biblical exegesis and its principle of *sola scriptura*, but its true development took place as historical consciousness matured during the Enlightenment and the Romantic period and so established a broken relationship with all tradition. In keeping with the circumstances surrounding its historical development, hermeneutical theory quite naturally oriented itself to the task of explicating "expressions of life fixed in writing" [Dilthey], even though Schleiermacher's theoretical formulation of hermeneutics included understanding as it occurs in the spoken dialogue of personal conversation. Just the opposite is true of rhetoric, which focused its attention on the immediate impact of the spoken word; and if it ventured into the paths of skillful written expression as well and so developed the doctrine of style and stylistics, the true vocation of rhetoric lay not in reading but in speaking. The equivocal position occupied by the prepared address, of course, already shows the tendency to ground the art of speaking in the permanency of written forms of expression and so to detach it from its original situation. At this point, then, rhetoric begins to merge with poetics, whose linguistic objects are so thoroughly art that they can be transferred without loss from spoken to written form and vice versa.

Rhetoric as such, however, is tied to the immediacy of its effect. In this connection, Klaus Dockhorn has shown with impressive and thoroughgoing scholarship the extent to which the excitation of the emotions has been seen as the most important tool of persuasion from Cicero and Quintilian to the English political rhetoricians of the eighteenth century. Now the excitation of the emotions, which is the essential task of the orator, has only the most shadowy kind of role to play in the written expressions which become the object of hermeneutical endeavor; and this is precisely the distinction upon which everything rests. The listener is carried away by the orator. The cogency of the speaker's arguments overwhelms him, critical reflection is and should be held in abeyance by the persuasive power of the speech. In the reading and explication of something written, however, the audience is so remote and so detached from the writer, from his mood, his immediate aims, and his unstated assumptions, that the act of grasping the sense of the text takes on the character of autonomous production, one which for its part is more like the art of the speaker than the attitude of his audience. With this in mind, it is not hard to see why the theoretical tools of the art of explication are extensively borrowed from rhetoric—a point which I made in several instances and which Dockhorn has explored on a broader basis.

And where else, indeed, should theoretical reflection on the art of understanding turn than to rhetoric, which from the earliest days of the tradition has been the sole champion of a claim to truth which vindicates the plausible, the *eikos* (verisimilar), and that which is illuminating to common sense against science's claim to proof and certainty? To convince and to illuminate without being able to prove, that clearly is just as much the goal and measure of understanding and explication as it is of rhetoric and the art of persuasion—nor is this vast realm of illuminating convictions and prevailing opinions in the least diminished, gradually or otherwise, by the progress of science, however great that may be; on the contrary, it expands to take in every new advance in scientific knowledge, in order to claim it for itself and bring it into conformity with its own nature. The ubiquitousness of rhetoric is truly unlimited; for only through rhetoric does science become a social factor in our lives. What would we know of modern physics, which so visibly transforms our lives, from physics alone? All presentations of physics which are directed beyond professional circles (and perhaps one ought to say: which do not confine themselves to a very small circle of initiated specialists) owe their effect to the rhetorical element. As Henri Gouhier, especially, has shown,[10] even Descartes, that great and passionate advocate of method and certainty, is in all of his works a writer who handles the tools of rhetoric with consummate skill. There can be no doubt about the fundamental function of rhetoric within the social life. Every science which would be of practical significance is dependent on its resources. Nor is the function of hermeneutics less universal; for the incomprehensibility or susceptibility to misinterpretation of received texts which originally called it into existence is only a special case of that which is to be met with in every human orientation to the world as the *atopon,* the "strange," as that which cannot be accommodated by the customary ordered expectations of experience. And just as, with the advance of knowledge, the *mirabilia* are no sooner understood than they lose their strangeness, so, too, every successful appropriation of tradition resolves itself into a new, distinct familiarity in which tradition belongs to us and we are a part of it. The two flow together into one world which unites in itself both history and the present, the particular experience and the shared, and which achieves its linguistic articulation in the discourse between one man and another. Not in rhetoric alone, then, but in the phenomenon of understanding as well, the universality of human linguisticality proves itself to be an intrinsically limitless element which carries everything within it—not merely the cultural heritage transmitted through language, but *everything* pure and simple; for nothing that is can remain outside the realm of interpretation and intelligibility in which we have our common being. Hence the validity of Plato's fundamental assertion that he who beholds things in the mirror of speech becomes aware of them in their full and undiminished truth. And there is an equally profound and accurate insight to be had from Plato's doctrine that all cognition is first what it is only as re-cognition; for a "first" cognition is as little possible as a first word. Even the freshest and most original perception, whose ramifications still seem entirely unforeseeable, is what it truly was only when its consequences have been worked out, its connections with existing knowledge established, and when it has been absorbed into the medium of intersubjective understanding.

Thus the rhetorical and the hermeneutical aspects of human linguisticality interpenetrate each other at every point. There would be no speaker and no such thing as rhetoric if understanding and agreement were not the lifeblood of human relationships. There would be no hermeneutical task if there were no loss of agreement between the parties to a "conversation" and no need to seek understanding. The connection between hermeneutics and rhetoric ought to serve, then, to dispel the notion that hermeneutics is somehow restricted to the aesthetic-humanistic tradition alone and that hermeneutical philosophy has to do with a "life of the mind" which is somehow opposed to the world of "real" life and propagates itself only in and through the "cultural tradition."

It is in keeping with the universality of the hermeneutical approach that its implications must be considered for the logic of the social sciences as well. Accordingly, Habermas has taken up the analysis of "effective historical consciousness" and of the model of "translation" in *Truth and Method* and given them a positive role to play in overcoming the positivistic paralysis of social scientific logic and the historical naiveté of its fundamental assumptions about the nature of language. Such reference to hermeneutics, therefore, is made on the avowed premise that it should serve the methodology of the social sciences. That is a presupposition of the greatest moment, and one of course which severs Habermas's approach from the traditional grounds of the hermeneutic problematic, in the aesthetically oriented human sciences of the Romantic period. To be sure, the methical alienation which is of the essence in modern science is employed as well throughout the "humanities."[11] The opposition which the title of *Truth and Method* implies was never meant to be absolute (see the Preface to the second edition, p. xv). Nevertheless, the human sciences were chosen as the starting point of the analysis because they have to do with experiences in which it is a matter not of method or science but, on the contrary, of experiences which lie outside of science—among them the experience of the culture which bears the imprint of science's own historical tradition. The hermeneutical experience is fully operative only in such instances, nor can it be itself the object of methodical alienation; on the contrary, it necessarily precedes methodical alienation, in that it assigns to science the questions with which it occupies itself and thereby makes possible for the first time the application of its methods. The modern social sciences, on the other hand, to the extent that they recognize hermeneutical reflection as unavoidable, nevertheless claim to raise understanding, as Habermas puts it, "from a pre-scientific pursuit to the rank of a conscious procedure" through "controlled alienation"—as it were, through the "methodical cultivation of cleverness" (172/174).

Now it has long since been the way of science to accomplish through teachable and controllable modes of procedure what also accrues to individual cleverness on occasion, though in uncertain and uncontrollable ways. If awareness of the hermeneutical considerations involved in the interpretive human sciences leads to methodical contrivances which are beneficial to the work of the social sciences (which would not "understand" but would rather try to get hold of the real structure of society scientifically by drawing upon the truisms which have deposited themselves in linguisticality), then that would certainly be a scientific gain. At the same time, hermeneutical reflection will not allow the social sciences to limit it to this function within science, nor, especially, will it be restrained from applying hermeneutical reflection anew to the methodological alienation practiced by the social sciences—even if, in the process, it once again invites positivist devaluation of hermeneutics. Yet let us see first how the hermeneutical problematic makes its influence felt within the bounds of social scientific theory and how it looks in that role.

First, there is the "linguistic approach" (124ff.). If linguisticality is the distinctive province and embodiment of hermeneutical consciousness, then it is natural to see in linguisticality, as the basic constitutive element of human sociality, the reigning a priori of the social sciences—an a priori from which are derived ad absurdum the behaviorist and positivistic theories which view society as an observable and controllable functional whole. That seems clear enough inasmuch as human society lives in institutions which, understood as such, are traditionalized, reformed—in short, are determined by the self-conception of the individuals who comprise the society. Habermas thus sees the value of hermeneutics for social scientific statements in the fact that, unlike Wittgenstein's theory of language games and Winch's[12] interpretation of them as a linguistic a priori, the insights to be had from the concept of historical involvement enable one to establish a legitimate relationship between the communicative approach and the investigative field of the social sciences.

If, however, Habermas undertakes the analysis of the preconceptions and the inherent prejudice which accompany all human thought and action, the demand which he makes on hermeneutical reflection is fundamentally different. To be sure, he says, effective historical consciousness, which attempts to reflect upon its own prejudices and controls its own preconceptions, puts an end to the naive objectivism which falsifies both the positivistic theory of science and the phenomenological and language analytical approaches to the social sciences as well. But what, he asks, is such reflection able to accomplish in its own right? Among other things, he notes, there is the problem of universal history—that is, the conception of a goal in history which arises inevitably out of the conceptions of goal implicit in social action. If hermeneutical reflection rests content with the general observation that it is impossible to transcend the limitations of one's own point of view, then it is without consequence. To be sure, he says, such considerations call into question the validity of a full-blown philosophy of history, but historical consciousness will nevertheless constantly project a preconceived universal history out of its own orientation to the future. What good is it to know that such projections are provisional and repeatedly subject to revision?

In situations where hermeneutical reflection actually comes into play, however, what does it do? In what relationship does "effective historical consciousness" stand to the tradition of which it becomes conscious? Now my thesis is—and I believe—that the thing hermeneutics teaches us, as a necessary consequence of recognizing the contingency and finitude which are inseparable from historical involvement, is to see through the dogmatic antithesis between ongoing "autochthonous" tradition, on the one hand, and its reflective appropriation on the other. Behind such an antithesis lurks a dogmatic objectivism which deforms the very concept of reflection itself. Even in the interpretive sciences, the one who does the understanding can never reflect himself out of the historical involvement of his hermeneutical situation so that his own interpretation does not itself become a part of the subject at hand. The historian, even the historian of the so-called critical school, so little dissolves ongoing traditions—for example, nationalistic ones—that, on the contrary, he is really engaged, as a national historian, in their formation and development. And most important of all, the more consciously he reflects upon his hermeneutical conditionality, the more engaged he becomes. Droysen, who saw through the "eunuchlike objectivity" and the methodological naiveté of the historians, was himself highly influential when it came to the nationalism of nineteenth-century middle-class culture—in any event, more influential than Ranke's epical consciousness, which sought to inculcate instead the apoliticality appropriate to a state based on higher authority alone. The act of understanding is itself an event. Only a naive, unreflective historicism will see in the historical-hermeneutical sciences something absolutely new which puts an end to the power of tradition.

In *Truth and Method* I sought to furnish unequivocal proof for the constant process of mediation by means of which societal tradition perpetuates itself in terms of linguisticality, which is at once the medium and the register of all understanding. To this Habermas replies that the process of mediation profoundly alters the medium of knowledge through reflection—an insight, as Habermas would have it, which is itself the perpetual legacy bequeathed us by German idealism out of the spirit of the eighteenth century. Although Hegelian reflection, as it appears in my work, no longer culminates in an absolute consciousness, the "idealism of linguisticality," which exhausts itself in mere "cultural tradition"—in its hermeneutical appropriation and continuation—nevertheless remains tragically impotent vis-à-vis the concrete whole of the living social network, which is woven not of language alone but of work and domination as well. Hermeneutical reflection, Habermas concludes, must pass over into a critique of ideologies.

With this, Habermas touches upon the main motive behind sociology's interest in epistemology. Rhetoric (as theory) took its stand against the enchantment of consciousness through the power of speech, in that it insisted on the distinction between the matter of fact, or the true, and the plausible or apparently true which its adherents are taught to produce; hermeneutics endeavors to reestablish a disrupted intersubjective agreement through the dialectical exchange of ideas and, in particular, to free an alienated epistemology from false objectivism and return it to its hermeneutical foundations. Similarly, there is an emancipatory interest at work in sociological reflection as well which undertakes to disperse external and internal social compulsions by bringing them to the level of consciousness. Insofar as these compulsions seek to legitimize themselves in and through language, the critique of ideologies (itself, of course, an act of reflection which makes use of the powers of language) becomes an exposure of "deception with language" (178).

In the realm of psychoanalytical therapy, Habermas argues, one finds further evidence of the emancipatory power of reflection for social life. When we see through repression, we rob false compulsions of their power; and just as in psychotherapy, as the end result of a reflective educational process, the meaning of all motives for action would coincide with that which they have for the patient himself—an end result which is, of course, limited in the psychoanalytical situation by the therapeutic task and therefore represents here only a theoretical concept—so, by analogy, social reality, too, would be hermeneutically comprehensible only in such a fictive final state. In reality, the life of society is a web of understandable motives and concrete compulsions. It is the task of social research to disentangle that web through a continuing educational process and set it free for action.

One cannot deny that this socio-theoretical conception has its logic. It seems questionable, however, whether the role of hermeneutics is not unjustly restricted when its limits are defined in terms of a conjunction between all motives for action and their understood meaning. Indeed, the hermeneutical problem is so universal and so fundamental for all interpersonal experience, both of history and of the present, precisely because meaning can be experienced even where it was not the conscious intention of its author. It abridges the universality of the hermeneutical dimension when a realm of understandable meaning ("cultural tradition") is set off against other determinants of social reality, identifiable solely as concrete factors. As if every ideology, as a false linguistic consciousness, presented itself only in the garb of understandable meaning and could not also be *understood* in its "true" sense—for example, as an expression of the interests of dominance. The same thing is true of the unconscious motives which the psychoanalyst brings to consciousness.

Here the choice of the experience of art and of the human sciences as the starting point for the development of the hermeneutical dimension in *Truth and Method* appears to have made an appreciation of its true compass more difficult. Certainly, even the so-called "universal" exposition in the third part of the book is too sketchy and one-sided. In light of the subject matter, however, and in particular of the way the hermeneutical problem was posited, it seems altogether absurd that the concrete factors of work and dominance should be seen as lying outside the scope of hermeneutics. What else are the prejudices with which hermeneutical reflection concerns itself? Where else shall they originate if not in work and dominance? In the cultural tradition? To be sure, there, too. But of what is that tradition compounded? The idealism of linguisticality were a grotesque absurdity indeed—if it would extend beyond its mere methodological function. Habermas says at one point: "Hermeneutics bangs from within, so to speak, against the walls of tradition" (177). There is some truth to that, if by "from within" he means to indicate the opposite of a position taken up "from without"— one which does not enter into our interpretational world, intelligible or unintelligible, but persists instead in the detached observation of external alterations (as opposed to individual actions). That my position amounts to the same thing as an absolutization of cultural tradition, however, seems to me an erroneous supposition. It means only: to want to understand everything which will allow itself to be understood. That is the proper meaning of the statement: "Being which can be understood is language."

It does not mean nor does it entail confinement to a world of meaning which, as a "knowing of the known" (A. Boeckh),[13] were a kind of secondary object of knowledge, with the appropriation of that which is already known, the wealth of the "cultural tradition," serving as a supplement to the economic and political realities which preeminently determine the life of society. On the contrary, everything that is reflects itself in the mirror of language. In language and only in language are we confronted by that which we encounter nowhere else, because it is we ourselves (not merely that which we believe to be true and which we know about ourselves). When all is said and done, language is no mirror at all, nor is that which we catch sight of in it a mere reflection of our own and of all existence. Rather, it is the continual definition and redefinition of our lives, in the concrete dependencies of work and dominance as well as in all the other dependencies which make up our world. Language is not the ultimate anonymous subject, discovered at last, in which all social-historical processes and actions are grounded, and which presents itself and the totality of its activities, its objectifications, to the gaze of the detached observer; rather, it is the game in which we are all participants. None less so than any other. Each of us is "it," and it is always our turn. That is true whenever we understand something, and especially so when we see through prejudices or unmask pretenses which disguise the truth. Yes, there most of all we "understand." When at last we have got to the bottom of something which seemed to us strange and unintelligible, when we have managed to accommodate it within our linguistically ordered world, then everything falls into place, just as it does with a difficult chess problem, where only the solution renders the necessity of the absurd setup intelligible, down to the very last piece on the board.

But does that mean that we understand only when we see through some subterfuge and expose false presumption? Habermas appears to assume so. At the very least, reflection seems to demonstrate its power for him only in such instances—and its powerlessness when we get stuck in the web of language and spin it out further. Indeed, he assumes that reflection, as practiced in the hermeneutical sciences, "upsets the dogmatics of the practical life." Conversely, it seems to him insupportable and a betrayal of the heritage of the Enlightenment to say that elucidation of the biases inherent in understanding can lead to an acknowledgement of authority—of a dogmatic force! It may well be that conservatism (not the conservatism of Burke's generation, but that of a generation which has seen three great upheavals in German history, not one of them involving a revolutionary upset of the established social order) lends itself to the recognition of a truth easily overlooked. In any case, it is a desire to throw some light on the problem at hand and not a mere "deep-seated conviction" (174) which leads me to sever authority and reason from the abstract antithetical relationship they have for the Enlightenment, with its emancipatory frame of mind, and to insist instead on their essentially ambivalent relationship.

The Enlightenment's abstract antithesis between authority and reason seems to me to mistake the truth, and to do so with fatal consequences—namely, because one thereupon ascribes a power to reflection which it does not have and so mistakes the true dependencies involved through false *idealism*. Granted, authority exercises dogmatic force in countless forms, from the system of education, through the chain of command in army and government, to the power structures of political and evangelistic movements. But this view of the obedience rendered to authority can never explain why it should express itself in power *structures* and not in the disorder which characterizes the exercise of force alone. As I see it, then, there are compelling reasons for viewing acknowledgment as the determining factor in true authority relationships. The question is simply: on what does this acknowledgement rest? In many cases, to be sure, such acknowledgement is really nothing much more than a yielding of the powerless to force, but that is not true obedience and does not rest on authority. One need only study representative instances of the loss or decline of authority to see what authority is and whence it derives its life. Not from dogmatic force, but from dogmatic acknowledgment. What, however, is dogmatic acknowledgment, if not this: that one concedes to authority a superiority in knowledge and judgment and on that ground believes that it is just. On that alone, authority "rests." It prevails, therefore, not because it is blindly obeyed, but because it is "freely" acknowledged.

It is an undue imputation, though, to suppose that I thought there were no such thing as loss of authority and emancipatory critique. Whether one can really say that loss of authority comes about *through* emancipatory critique and reflection, or ought to say, instead, that loss of authority manifests itself *in* critique and emancipation is a question which may be let drop and which perhaps involves a distinction without a difference after all. The point at issue is simply whether reflection always dissolves substantial relationships or can equally well result in their conscious acceptance and adoption. In this regard, my treatment of the process of learning and education (in reference to Aristotelian ethics) is seen by Habermas in a remarkably one-sided way. The notion that, in the educational process, tradition as such should be and remain the sole ground for the assessment of prejudices—a view which Habermas attributes to me—flies directly in the face of my thesis that authority rests on knowledge and understanding. The individual who has come of age can—but need not!—adopt on the basis of insight that which he adhered to out of obedience alone. Tradition itself is no proof of validity, at any rate not in instances where reflection demands proof. But that is the point: where does reflection demand proof? Everywhere? The finiteness of human existence and the intrinsic particularity of reflection seem to me to make that impossible. Ultimately, it is a question of whether the function of reflection is defined in terms of a conscious awareness which confronts current practice and prevailing opinion with other possibilities—so that one can discard something established in favor of other possibilities but can also consciously adopt that which tradition presents him with de facto—or whether reflection and conscious awareness always dissolve the status quo. When Habermas says that "what was mere domination can be stripped from authority [by which I understand: what was not authority in the first place] and dissolved into powerless coercion by insight and rational decision" (176), then I no longer know what we are arguing about. At most, whether the "rational decision" involved can be made (on the strength of what progress!) with the help of one of the social sciences or not. Of that, however, I shall have more to say later on.

From the point of view of a hermeneutical reflection, Habermas's concept of reflection and bringing to consciousness seems heavily burdened by its own dogmatism, and here I could wish that the hermeneutical reflection I have argued for had come into play. From Husserl (in his doctrine of anonymous intentionalities) and from Heidegger (in his demonstration of the ontological abridgement inherent in the idealist concepts of subject and object) we have learned to see through the false objectification with which the concept of reflection is loaded. There is surely an inward reversion of intentionality which in no way raises that which is thus "reflected" upon to the level of a thematic object. Of that, Brentano (drawing on Aristotelian insights) was already aware. I fail to see how one were to grasp the enigmatic mode of existence of language at all, if not on the basis of that assumption. One must (to use J. Lohmann's terms) distinguish between "effective" reflection, which takes place in the unfolding of language itself, and the explicit and thematic reflection which has evolved within the linguistic history of the Western world and which, in that it makes everything into an object, has created, in modern science, the presuppositions of the planetary civilization of tomorrow.

With what extraordinary emotion Habermas defends the empirical sciences against the charge of being an arbitrary language game! Who has challenged their claim to necessity— seen from the point of view of the ability to exercise technical control over nature? At most, the researcher himself will disclaim the technical motivation of his work in the interest of his relationship to the science itself— and with full subjective right. But no one will deny that the practical application of modern science profoundly alters our world, and with it our language. Indeed, "also our language." That in no way means— Habermas's imputations notwithstanding— that the material existence of practical life is determined by the linguistic articulation of consciousness; it means simply that there is no social reality, with all its concrete compulsions, which does not also exhibit itself in a linguistically articulated consciousness. Reality does not happen "behind the back of language" (179); it happens behind the backs of those who live in the subjective opinion that they understand the world (or no longer understand it), and it happens in language as well.

Seen from this point of view, of course, the concept of an "autochthonous" or "natural" order of things— which Marx set in uncritical opposition to the working world of modern class society and which Habermas, too, is fond of using ("the autochthonous substance of tradition," but also "the causality of autochthonous relationships" [173/4]— takes on a highly questionable aspect. Indeed, that is sheer romanticism— and such romanticism creates an artificial gulf between tradition and reflection grounded in historical consciousness. The "idealism of linguisticality" at least has the distinction of not lapsing into that kind of thinking.

Habermas's critique culminates in an attack on the immanentism of transcendental philosophy, calling it into question by reference to the same historical conditions on which its arguments are based. In fact, a central problem. Anyone who takes the finiteness of human existence seriously and who constructs neither a "consciousness in general" nor an *intellectus archetypus* or transcendental ego to serve as the repository and reference point for all authority will not be able to avoid the question of how his own thinking, as transcendental, is empirically possible. So far as the hermeneutical dimension I have developed is concerned, however, I see no real difficulty in that respect.

Pannenberg's highly useful discussion of my work[14] has led me to see what a fundamental difference there is between Hegel's claim to find reason in history and those constantly self-renewing, constantly antiquated conceptions of universal history, in the framing of which one always behaves as if he were "the last historian" (166). To be sure, the nature and validity of Hegel's claim to a philosophy of world history is open to debate. He, too, knew that "the footsteps of our pall-bearers can already be heard at the door," and one can find that, in spite of all one's reservations about world-historical speculation, there is a compelling kind of certainty about the root idea of universal human freedom itself which one can no more dismiss than he can dismiss consciousness itself. All the same, the claim which every historian must make by virtue of his need to tie the meaning of all events to a "today" of his own (and to the future of that "today") is a fundamentally different and much more modest one than Hegel's. No one can deny that history presupposes futurity, and to that extent a conception of universal history is unavoidably one of the dimensions of contemporary historical consciousness, "from a practical point of view." But does it do justice to Hegel to restrict the meaning of his work to an expression of this interpretational need which makes itself felt in every present? "From a practical point of view"—that no one today goes beyond such a claim is understandable in view of the ingrained consciousness of our own finitude and a mistrust of the dictatorship of the concept. But does one seriously want to reduce Hegel to practical terms?

So far as I can see, my discussion with Pannenberg comes to a dead end on this point; for Pannenberg has no desire to renew Hegel's claim either—only it does make a difference, of course, that for the Christian theologian the "practical point of view" involved in every conception of universal history has its fixed point of reference, its "today" so to speak, in the absolute historicity of the Incarnation.

Still the question remains. If the hermeneutical problematic expects to hold its own ground against the universality of rhetoric on the one hand, and the topicality of the critique of ideologies on the other, it must make a case for its own universality, and that precisely over against modern science's claim to absorb hermeneutical reflection into itself and make it subservient to science (through the "methodological cultivation of cleverness"). It will be able to do that only if, instead of taking refuge in the immanence of transcendental reflection, it is able to show in its own right what such reflection accomplishes over against—and not merely within the purview of—modern scientific knowledge.

Because the task of hermeneutical reflection is ultimately the same as that of all other efforts to provide self-conscious awareness of ourselves and our world, its worth will have to make itself felt first of all in terms of its contributions to scholarly and scientific knowledge themselves. Clearly, reflection on a prevailing preconception brings something before me which otherwise happens behind my back. Something—not everything. For effective historical consciousness is inescapably more existence than it is consciousness. That does not mean, however, that it can escape ideological ossification without constantly striving toward self-conscious awareness. Only by virtue of such reflection can I escape being a slave to myself, am I able to judge freely of the validity or invalidity of my preconceptions—even if "freely" means only that from my encounter with a prejudiced view of things I am able to come away with nothing more than yet another conception of them. This implies, however, that the prejudices which govern my preconception are always at stake along with it—to the extent, indeed, of their abandonment, which of course can always mean mere rehabilitation as well. For that is the inexhaustible power of experience, that in every process of learning we constantly form a new preconception.

In the fields which served as the starting point for my hermeneutical studies, the arts and the philological-historical sciences, it is easy to show the kind of effect hermeneutical reflection has. Consider, for example, the way the autonomy of style study in art history has been shaken by hermeneutical reflection on the concept of art—or on the concepts of individual periods and styles; how iconography pressed to the fore from its peripheral position; and the influence hermeneutical reflection on the concepts of experience (*Erlebnis*) and expression (*Ausdruck*) has had on literary criticism—if only in the form of a more conscious pursuit of scholarly trends long since emergent. (Interaction is also a form of influence.) It goes without saying that the shaking of fixed prejudices gives promise of an advancement in knowledge, for it makes new questions possible; indeed, we experience on an every day basis what historical scholarship is able to gain from an awareness of the history of ideas. In these fields I hope to have demonstrated how the alienation brought about by historicism is mediated through a "fusing of horizons." Then, too, thanks to Habermas's astute observations, the contribution of hermeneutics has made itself felt within the social sciences as well, in particular through a confrontation between the hermeneutical dimension and the preconceptions involved not only in the positivistic philosophy of science but in an aprioristic phenomenology and a universal linguistics as well.

But the function of hermeneutical reflection is not exhausted by the role it plays within the sciences themselves. Inherent in all modern sciences is a deep-rooted alienation, which they impose on natural consciousness and which, in the form of the concept of method, has been a part of reflective consciousness since the formative stage of modern science. Hermeneutical reflection cannot claim to do anything about that; it can, however, by elucidating for the sciences the ruling preconceptions of the moment, uncover new avenues of inquiry and thus indirectly be of service to the work of methodology. And, beyond that, it can bring to consciousness what the methodology of the sciences exacts in payment for the progress it makes possible: how much screening and abstraction it demands, and how, in the process, it leaves natural consciousness perplexed behind it—which nevertheless, in its role as consumer of the inventions and information acquired through science, perpetually follows in its wake. Or, to use Wittgenstein's terms: the "language games" of science remain related to the metalanguage represented by the mother tongue. The findings of science, travelling through modern channels of information and then, after due (many times after unduly great) delay, via the schools and education, become at last a part of the social consciousness. In this way, they give articulation to "socio-linguistic" realities.

For the natural sciences as such, of course, all that is largely irrelevant. The true natural scientist already knows full well how particular is the realm of knowledge encompassed by his field, compared with the whole of human reality. He does not take part in the deification of it which the public forces upon him. And yet that is all the more reasons why the public—and the scientist who goes before the public—stands in need of hermeneutical reflection on the presuppositions and the limits of science. The so-called *Humaniora*, by contrast, are still able to convey their knowledge to the general consciousness with ease—insofar as they still reach it at all—since the objects of that knowledge belong immediately to the cultural tradition and to the subject matter of conventional education. But the modern social sciences stand in an inherently and peculiarly strained relationship to the object of their knowledge, the social reality—a relationship which has a special need for hermeneutical reflection. For the methodical alienation to which the social sciences are indebted for their progress is brought to bear in their work on the whole of the human and social world, a world which thus finds itself exposed to scientific disposition in planning, management, organization, development—in short, in a multitude of offices which determine from the outside, so to speak, the life of every individual and every group within the society. The social engineer, who looks after the operation of the social machine, thus seems sundered from the society, of which he is nevertheless a member.

Clearly, that is a role which is unacceptable to a hermeneutically reflected sociology. In a lucid analysis of the logic of the social sciences, Habermas has resolutely worked out the distinctive epistemological interest which sets the sociologist apart from the social technician. It is, he says, an emancipatory interest, which aims only at reflection, and he makes reference in this connection to the example of psychoanalysis.

In fact, the role which hermeneutics has to play in the setting of a psychoanalysis is a fundamental one; and since, as I have already emphasized, unconscious motives lie well within the scope of hermeneutical theory—more, since psychotherapy can be described as the work of "unfolding interrupted processes of education into a complete history (which can be recounted)" (189)—hermeneutics and the circle of language, which is closed in conversation, have their place there, as I believe I have learned above all from the work of J. Lacan.

Nevertheless, it is clear that that is not the end of the matter. The categories of interpretation worked out by Freud make a distant but nevertheless real claim to the character of genuine natural-scientific hypotheses—that is, to constitute a knowledge of operative laws. One would expect that to be reflected in the role methodical alienation plays within psychoanalysis, and so it is. Although a successful analysis receives its own validation from the results it produces, the claim to knowledge of psychoanalysis as a discipline is by no means a matter that can be decided on pragmatic grounds alone. That means, however, that it is manifestly open to further hermeneutical reflection. What, it must be asked, is the relationship between the knowledge of the psychoanalyst and his professional position within the social reality, of which he is, after all, a member? That he inquires behind superficial explanations, breaks through obstacles to self-understanding, sees through the repressive effect of social taboos—all these things are part and parcel of the emancipatory reflection in which he engages with his patients. But if he exercises the same kind of reflection in situations and in fields where his role as doctor is not legitimately involved, where he is himself a participant in the social game, then he steps out of his social role. The person who "sees through" his playing partners to something beyond the understandings involved in their relationship—that is, does not take the game they are playing seriously—is a spoilsport whom one avoids. The emancipatory power of reflection to which the psychoanalyst lays claim thus has its limit—a limit which is defined by the larger social consciousness in terms of which analyst and patient alike understand themselves, along with everyone else. For hermeneutical reflection teaches us that social community, with all its tensions and disruptions, leads us back time and again to a social understanding, by virtue of which it continues to exist.

In light of such considerations, however, Habermas's analogy between psychoanalytical and sociological theory becomes problematic. For where is the latter to find its limit? Where in Habermas's scheme of things does the patient stop and the social partnership step in in its unprofessional right? Behind and beyond which self-interpretation of the social consciousness—and every custom is such a self-interpretation—appropriate for one to inquire and go (perhaps out of desire for revolutionary change), and which not? Such questions are apparently unanswerable. The inevitable consequence seems to be that the emancipatory consciousness cannot stop short of the dissolution of every obligation to restraint—and thus that its guiding light must be the vision of an anarchistic utopia. This, of course, seems to me a hermeneutically false consciousness.

## Notes

1. [Editor's note] *Geisteswissenschaften.* For a definition of the meaning of this term in the German hermeneutic tradition see "Introduction," pp. 23f.

2. Cf. O. Marquand at the Heidelberger Philosophiekongress 1966.

3. [Editor's note] That is of the human sciences as conceived by the historians of the Romantic era in Germany, for example, Savigny, Schleiermacher, Ranke.

4. [Editor's note] Literally, "consciousness of the history of effects"—consciousness not only of the effect a given work, event, or idea has on subsequent history and thus on the preconceptions of the interpreter, but consciousness as well of the effect produced by the confrontation between the point of view (or "horizon") of the interpreter and that of the material which he attempts to understand. For a more complete explanation of the concept, see the previous selection, pp. 267–73, and the "Introduction" to this volume, p. 38f.

5. [Editor's note] *Philosophie und Sprachwissenschaft,* Erfahrung und Denken: Schriften zur Förderung der Beziehung zwischen Philosophie und Einzelwissenschaften, 15 (Berlin, 1965).

6. *Gnomon* XXXVII (1965), pp. 709-18.

7. *Göttingische Gelehrten-Anzeigen* CCXVII, Heft 3/4 (1966), pp. 169-206.

8. Jürgen Habermas, "Zur Logik der Sozialwissenschaften," *Philosophische Rundschau*, Beiheft 5 (1967), pp. 149-80.

9. Hermann Gundert in *Hermeneia*, Festschrift für Otto Regenbogen—1952.

10. Henri Gouhier, "La résistance au vrai. . . ," in *Retorica e Barocco*, (ed. E. Castelli; Roma, 1955).

11. [Editor's note] Gadamer uses the English term "the humanities" here.

12. [Editor's note] Peter Winch, *The Idea of a Social Science* (London, 1958).

13. [Editor's note] See "Introduction" to this volume, p. 21.

14. Wolfhart Pannenberg, "Hermeneutik und Universalgeschichte," in *Zeitschrift für Theologie und Kirche* 60 (1963), pp. 90-121. Eng. trans. in *History and Hermeneutic*, (ed. Rob. W. Funk and G. Ebeling; New York: Harper & Row, 1967), pp. 122-52.

15. Jacques Lacan, *Écrits* (Paris: Éditions du Seuil, 1966.

# 10

# Hermeneutics and the
# Social Sciences

===================== Jürgen Habermas =====================

JÜRGEN HABERMAS (b. 1929) studied first at the University of Bonn where he earned a doctorate in 1954. For the next five years he worked as an assistant in the Institute for Social Research (*Institut für Sozialforschung*) in Frankfurt under Adorno and Horkheimer. In 1961 he received his second doctorate (*Habilitation*) at Mainz and began teaching at the University of Heidelberg during that same year. He became a professor of philosophy at Frankfurt in 1964, and joined the Max Planck Institute in Starnberg near Munich in 1971, to concentrate more fully on his research and writing. Habermas's work, with its numerous philosophical, historical-critical, and sociological concerns, has many implications for hermeneutics in both its theoretical and practical aspects. His first important book, *Communication and the Evolution of Society* (1962; Eng. trans. 1979), demonstrated new ways by which the production and reception of literary works, and the change in aesthetic and ideological attitudes, can be studied in precise historical and sociological terms. In *Knowledge and Human Interests* (1968; Eng. trans. 1976) Habermas rethought from a new point of view some of the central problems which had occupied philosophers and human scientists during the past 150 years. His efforts display an astute interpretive mastery of the hermeneutic tradition in which the book itself also participates. Habermas's "reply" to Gadamer, therefore, cannot be read simply as a polemical statement by a neo-Marxian thinker against the views of an allegedly idealist metaphysical philosopher. It is a statement which reveals, above all, the hermeneutic dimensions of Habermas's own thought and the extent to which hermeneutics plays an essential part in his conception of the social sciences. The essay was first published by Habermas in 1970 in the *Festschrift* dedicated to Gadamer on his seventieth birthday.

# ON HERMENEUTICS' CLAIM
# TO UNIVERSALITY

## I

Hermeneutics refers to a "capability" which we acquire to the extent that we come to "master" a natural language— with the art of understanding the meaning of linguistic communication and, in the case of disrupted communication, of making it understandable. Understanding of meaning focuses on the semantic content of speech, but also on the meaning contained in written forms of expression or in nonlinguistic symbol systems, so far as such meanings can, in principle, be "recovered" in speech. Not by accident do we speak of the "art" of understanding and of making something understandable, for the interpretive capability which every speaker has at his command can be stylized, even developed to the level of an artistic ability. The art of interpretation is the counterpart of the art of convincing and persuading in situations where practical questions are brought to decision. Indeed, the same thing that is true of hermeneutics is true of rhetoric as well; for rhetoric, too, rests on a capability which belongs to the communicative competence of every speaker but can be artificially developed into a special skill. Rhetoric and hermeneutics have their origin in arts which take in hand the methodical training and development of a natural capability.[1]

Philosophical hermeneutics is a different matter: it is not an art but a critique— that is, it brings to consciousness in a reflective attitude experiences which we have of language in the exercise of our communicative competence and thus in the course of social interaction with others through language. Because rhetoric and hermeneutics have to do with the teaching and disciplined development of communicative competence, hermeneutical reflection has been able to draw upon their realm of experience. But [hermeneutical] reflection on (1) skillful understanding and explication, on the one hand, and (2) convincing and persuading, on the other, serves in the interest not of an art but of a philosophical inquiry into the structures of colloquial communication.

(1) From the characteristic experience of the art of understanding and explication, philosophical hermeneutics has learned that the resources of a natural language are in principle sufficient to clarify the meaning of any configuration of symbols, however foreign and inaccessible it may at first be. We can translate from any language into any other language. We can place the objectifications of the most remote period and the most alien culture in understandable relationship to the familiar (that is, previously understood) context of our own surroundings.

At the same time, of course, the factual distance from foreign traditions forms part of the horizon of every natural language. And then, too, the long since understood context of familiar surroundings can at any time be revealed as something questionable; it is the potentially unintelligible. Only the two moments taken together encompass the whole of the hermeneutical experience. The inter-subjectivity of colloquial understanding is in principle as limitless as it is fragmentary: limitless, because it can be enlarged at will; fragmentary, because it can never be exhaustively constructed. That is as much true of contemporary communication within a socio-culturally homogeneous language community as it is of communication which takes place over the distance between different classes, cultures, and time periods.

The hermeneutical experience raises to the level of consciousness the relationship between the speaking subject and language. The speaking subject can make use of the reflexive property of natural language metacommunicatively in order to paraphrase modifications of any kind. Indeed, it is possible to construct hierarchies of formal languages on the foundation of the colloquial language, which in each case serves as the "ultimate" metalanguage. These are related to each other as object-language to meta-language to meta-meta-language, and so forth. The formal construction of such languages precludes ad hoc stipulation, commentary on, or alteration of the rules of application for individual statements. And the logic of classes forbids metacommunication about statements within a formal language on the level of that object-language itself. Both, however, are possible in colloquial language. The system of a natural language is not closed but permits ad hoc stipulation, commentary on, or alteration of the rules of application for any given expression. And metacommunication in natural languages can make use only of the same language which is being spoken about as object: for every natural language is its own meta-language. On that rests the reflexivity of natural languages, which makes it possible, in contrast to class-logic languages, for the semantic content of linguistic expressions to carry, along with the manifest message, an indirect message as to its application. That is true, for instance, of the metaphorical use of language. Owing to the reflexive structure of natural languages, then, the native speaker has at his command a unique realm of meta-communicative free play.

The obverse of this freedom of movement is a palpable bondage to linguistic tradition. Natural languages are informal, and for that reason speaking subjects cannot come face to face with their language as they could with a closed system. Language competence remains, as it were, behind the backs of those who make use of it: they can be certain about the meaning of something only to the extent that they also remain dependent, explicitly, on a context which has been, on the whole, dogmatically transmitted and, implicitly, long since preestablished. Hermeneutical understanding cannot enter into a question without prejudice; on the contrary, it is unavoidably biased by the context in which the understanding subject has first acquired his schemata of interpretation. Such a preconception can be thematized; it must be assayed as part of the question at hand in every hermeneutically conscious analysis. But even the modification of the unavoidable anticipations involved in understanding does not break through the objectivity of the language vis-à-vis the speaking subject: in the process of learning, he merely forms a new preconception, which in turn becomes the reigning preconception at the next hermeneutical step. That is the meaning of Gadamer's statement: "Effective historical consciousness is inescapably more existence than it is consciousness."[2]

(2) From the characteristic experience of the art of convincing and persuading, on the other hand, philosophical hermeneutics has learned that the medium of colloquial communication serves not only to exchange messages but as well to shape and alter the attitudes which inform behavior. Rhetoric has traditionally been seen as the art of producing a consensus on questions which cannot be decided on the basis of compelling proof. Classical antiquity thus reserved to rhetoric the realm of the merely "plausible," as opposed to that in which the truth of statements is discussed on theoretical grounds. It is a matter, then, of practical questions—questions which can be reduced to decisions about the acceptance or rejection of standards, of criteria of evaluation and norms of behavior. When such decisions are made rationally, they are arrived at by means which are neither theoretically compelling nor merely arbitrary; instead, they are motivated by convincing speech. In the notable ambivalence between conviction and persuasion which attaches to the consensus produced by rhetoric, one sees not merely the element of force, which to the present day remains an ineradicable part of any consensus—as, indeed, it has always been of processes aimed at the shaping of volition through discussion; that same equivocality is also circumstantial evidence that practical questions can be decided only through dialogue and therefore remain bound to the context of the colloquial language. Rationally motivated decisions are reached only on the basis of a consensus which is produced through convincing speech, and that means: in dependence on the cognitively *and* expressively appropriate resources of representation in colloquial language.

The rhetorical experience, too, teaches us something about the relationship between the speaking subject and his language. The speaker can make use of the creativity of natural language to respond spontaneously to changing states of affairs and to define new situations through fundamentally unpredictable expressions. In formal terms, that presupposes a language structure which, with the help of a finite number of elements and in conformity with general rules, makes it possible to produce and to understand an infinite number of statements. This productivity, however, is by no means limited to the short-term production of individual statements, but extends as well to the long-term process of shaping colloquially formulated schemata of interpretation—schemata which not only make experience possible but prejudice it at the same time. The skillful use of language which brings about a consensus in the decision of practical questions marks only the point at which we consciously attempt to take a hand in this natural process and see what we can do to change ingrained schemata of interpretation, to learn (and teach others) to see things understood on the basis of tradition differently and to judge them anew. This type of insight draws its innovational power from its ability to choose the right word. Owing to the creativity of natural languages, then, the native speaker has at his command a unique power over the practical consciousness of corporate bodies of men—a power which, as the long history of sophism shows, can be used for the purpose of obfuscation and agitation as well as for enlightenment.

The obverse of this power is, of course, a specific powerlessness of the speaking subject vis-à-vis familiar language games. Anyone who wishes to modify a language game must participate in it first. That, in turn, is possible only through internalization of the rules which define the language game. Acclimating oneself to linguistic traditions thus demands, at least potentially, the kind of effort that is involved in a process of socialization: the "grammar" of language games must become a constituent part of the personality structure. Indeed, skillful speech owes its power over the practical consciousness to the fact that a natural language cannot be adequately grasped as a system of rules for the production of systematically ordered and semantically meaningful configurations of symbols; for it is also immanently and compellingly dependent on the context established by actions and gestural forms of expression. The rhetorical experience thus teaches us to see the connection between language and praxis. Colloquial communication would not just be incomplete, but impossible outside of a context that is grammatically regulated and includes certain shared standards of interaction, as well as the accompanying or intermittent presence of experiential expressions. Language and behavior interpret each other reciprocally: indeed, that idea is already present in Wittgenstein's conception of the language game, in which the game is also a way of life. The grammar of language games, understood as a complete life-praxis, governs not only the combination of symbols but the interpretation of linguistic symbols through actions and expressions.[3]

Philosophical hermeneutics, then—and my remarks are intended only to call this to mind—develops the insights into the structure of natural languages which are to be derived from a reflective use of communicative competence: *Reflexivity and objectivity are as fundamental to language as creativity and the integral relationship between language and life-praxis.* A reflective knowledge of this sort, which comprises the "hermeneutical consciousness," is obviously different from the artistic expertise which goes into disciplined understanding and speaking themselves. But hermeneutics is equally distinct from linguistics.

Linguistics does not concern itself with communicative competence and hence with the ability of the native speaker to take part in colloquial communication by understanding and speaking; it limits itself to "linguistic competence" in the narrower sense—a term introduced by Chomsky[4] to characterize the ability of an ideal speaker who has full command of the abstract rule system of a natural language. The concept of a language system, in which language is understood as *langue,* leaves out of account the pragmatic dimension in which *langue* is transformed into *parole.* Hermeneutics, by contrast, concerns itself with the experiences of the speaker in this dimension. Further, the goal of linguistics is a reconstruction of the rule system which underlies the production of all the various grammatically correct and semantically meaningful elements of a natural language, whereas hermeneutics reflects on the principal experiences of a communicatively competent speaker (whose linguistic competence is tacitly presupposed). I should like to establish the distinction between rational reconstruction and self-reflection on an intuitive basis alone.

In the process of *self-reflection,* the subject becomes aware of unconscious presuppositions which underlie accomplishments he has taken for granted. Thus, hermeneutical consciousness is the result of a self-reflection in which the speaking subject becomes aware of his inherent freedoms and dependencies in regard to language. In the process, the naive consciousness is rid of a subjectivist as well as an objectivist illusion, under which it labors. Self-reflection throws light on experiences the speaking subject meets with in the use of his communicative competence, but it cannot define that competence. Rational *reconstruction* of a linguistic rule system, on the other hand, serves to define linguistic competence. It makes rules explicit of which the native speaker has an implicit command; but it does not, properly speaking, make the speaker aware of unconscious presuppositions. The subjectivity of the speaker, within the horizon of which the experience of reflection is alone possible, remains fundamentally untouched. One can say that a successful linguistic reconstruction raises the speech apparatus, which functions unconsciously, into consciousness; to do so, however, would be an inexact use of language. The consciousness of the person engaged in the act of speaking, in other words, is unchanged by such linguistic knowledge.

If philosophical hermeneutics, then, has as little to do with the art of understanding and speaking as it does with linguistics, if it yields as little for the prescientific use of communicative competence as it does for the scientific study of language, wherein lies the significance of the hermeneutical consciousness?

There are four respects in which hermeneutics is significant for the various branches of knowledge and the interpretation of their findings. (1) Hermeneutical consciousness demolishes the objectivistic self-conception of the traditional human sciences. Given the bond between the interpreting scholar and the hermeneutical situation from which he starts, it follows that impartiality of understanding cannot be secured by abstraction from preconceived ideas, but alone through reflection on the effective historical relationship in which the knowing subject always stands to its object.[5] Further, (2) hermeneutical consciousness calls to the attention of the social sciences problems which arise from the symbolic "fore-structuring" of their investigative field. When data is gathered through colloquial communication instead of controlled observation, theoretical concepts can no longer be operationalized within the framework for empirical measurement provided by the prescientifically established language game. The problems which arise at the level of measurement recur at the level of theory formation: the choice of a categorical framework and of theoretical predications necessarily corresponds to a tentative prejudgment of the investigative field itself.[6] (3) Hermeneutical consciousness has a bearing as well on the scientistic self-conception of the natural sciences, though not, of course, on their method. The insight that the natural language always plays the role of an "ultimate" metalanguage for all theories expressed in formal language explains the epistemological rank of colloquial language in the research process. The legitimation of decisions which determine the choice of research strategies, the construction of theories and the methods of their verification, and consequently the course of "scientific progress," is dependent upon discussions within the research community. Such discussions conducted at the metatheoretical level, however, are bound inexorably to the context of natural languages and to the explicational mode of colloquial communication. Hermeneutics can show why, on this metatheoretical level, a consensus can be reached which is indeed rationally motivated but never compelling. Finally, (4) a realm of interpretation which demands hermeneutical consciousness as no other has today become a social reality: namely, the translation of momentous scientific information into the language of the social world at large: "What would we know of modern physics, which so visibly transforms our lives, from physics alone? All presentations of physics which are directed beyond professional circles owe their effect to the rhetorical element. . . . Every science which would be of practical significance is dependent on rhetoric" (p. 279).

The functions which have accrued to scientific and technical progress and which it performs in the maintenance and operation of developed industrial societies illustrate the objective need to set useful technical knowledge in rational relationship to the practical consciousness of the everyday world. This need, I believe, hermeneutics attempts to meet with its claim to universality; for then and only then is hermeneutical consciousness able to prepare the way for the reintegration "even of the experience of science into our own, our common and human experience of life,"[7] if one may point with justice to "the universality of human linguisticality as an inherently limitless element which carries everything within it—not merely the cultural heritage transmitted through language" (p. 279). Gadamer refers to Plato's remark that he who beholds things in the mirror of speech becomes aware of them in their full and undiminished truth— "everything that is reflects itself in the mirror of language" (p. 279).

Precisely that historical force, however, which first elicited the efforts of a philosophical hermeneutics is at variance with Plato's assertion. For obviously modern science can legitimately claim that it arrives at true statements about "things," not by paying attention to the mirror of human speech, but by proceeding on the basis of a monologue: by advancing theories, in other words, which are formulated in its own language and supported by controlled observation. Because the hypothetical-deductive systems of statements one finds in science are not part of the elements of speech, the information which can be derived from them stands apart from the world of everyday life which is articulated in natural language. Doubtless the transposition of useful technical knowledge into the context of the world at large requires us to render monologically produced meaning understandable in the dimension of speech, and thus in the dialogue of everyday language; and to be sure such a translation poses a hermeneutical problem. But it is a problem which is new to hermeneutics itself. Hermeneutical consciousness originates in reflection on our activity *within* natural language, while the interpretation of the sciences for the world at large must mediate *between* natural language *and* monological language systems. This process of translation oversteps the boundaries of the art of rhetoric and hermeneutics, which had to do merely with the culture constituted in and handed down through colloquial language. If hermeneutics is to go beyond the hermeneutical consciousness which has been developed in the reflective exercise of that art, it must elucidate the conditions which make it possible to withdraw, as it were, from the dialogical structure of colloquial language and to use language monologically instead, for rigorous formation of theories and for the organization of rational goal-oriented behavior.

I would like to insert a thought parenthetically at this point. The genetic epistemology of Jean Piaget[8] lays bare the language-independent roots of operational thinking. To be sure, such thinking can reach full development only on the strength of an integration into the linguistic rule system of the cognitive schemata which originate prelinguistically in the sphere of instrumental action. However, there are ample indications that language is merely "superimposed" on categories such as space, time, causality, and substance, and on rules which govern the combination of symbols according to the laws of formal logic—both of which have a *pre*linguistical foundation. On this hypothesis, it would be possible to explain the monological use of language for the organization of rational goal-oriented behavior and the construction of scientific theories: in such cases natural language could be seen as freed, so to speak, from the structure of intersubjectivity—as functioning, in other words, without its dialogical element and severed from [colloquial] communication, subject only to the conditions of operative intelligence.[9] This complex of questions still awaits its resolution; whatever the outcome, however, it will be relevant for the answer to our question. If it proves true that operative intelligence originates in prelinguistic cognitive schemata and therefore can employ language instrumentally, then hermeneutics' claim to universality finds a limit in the language systems of science and in theories of rational choice. On this presupposition, in other words, it is possible to offer a plausible explanation why monologically erected language systems, while they cannot be interpreted without reference to a natural language, can nevertheless be "understood" without involvement in the hermeneutical problematic: for on that presupposition the conditions of understanding were not the same thing as the conditions of colloquial communication. That would only be the case when the content of rigorous theories were translated into the context of speech in the everyday world.

That, however, is a problem I cannot deal with; I would like to put the question of the validity of hermeneutics' claim to universality a different way. Is it possible to have an understanding of colloquial configurations of symbols themselves that is not bound by the hermeneutical presuppositions of context-dependent processes of understanding, that in this sense cheats the natural language of its role as ultimate metalanguage? Since hermeneutical understanding must always proceed ad hoc and cannot be developed into a scientific method (can at most reach the level of an art through discipline and training), this question is equivalent to asking whether there can be a theory appropriate to the structure of natural languages which provides the basis for a methodologically ensured understanding of meaning.

I see two avenues of inquiry which we might pursue with promise of finding an answer.

On the one hand, we meet with nontrivial limits to the application of hermeneutical understanding in cases of the sort that psychoanalysis and, insofar as they involve collective behavior, the critique of ideologies undertake to explain. Both fields of endeavor have to do with colloquial objectifications in which the subject who so expresses himself is unaware of his own intentions. Such expressions can be grasped as parts of a systematically distorted communication. They can be understood only to the extent that the general conditions which govern the pathology of colloquial communication are known. A theory of colloquial communication, consequently, must first open the way to pathologically buried meaning. If the claim to produce such a theory were to prove valid, an explanatory understanding were then possible which would be able to pass beyond the limits of hermeneutical understanding of meaning.

On the other hand, the advocates of a generative linguistics have been engaged for more than a decade in a renewed search for a universal theory of natural language. The goal of such a theory is the rational reconstruction of a rule system which would adequately define universal linguistic competence. If this program were to be carried out in such a way that one could assign a structural description from the theoretical language unequivocally to every element of a natural language, then the structural descriptions expressed in the theoretical language would be able to take the place of hermeneutical understanding of meaning.

This problem, too, I am unable to deal with in the present context. In the pages that follow I shall limit myself to the question of whether a critical science like psychoanalysis, through a theoretically grounded semantic analysis, can elude the bondage of trained interpretation to the natural competence of colloquial communication and thus render hermeneutics' claim to universality invalid. This investigation will help us to specify in what sense it is nevertheless possible to defend the fundamental hermeneutical thesis: that we cannot transcend, to use Gadamer's romantic phraseology, "the conversation that we are."

# II

Hermeneutical consciousness is incomplete so long as it has not incorporated into itself reflection on the limit of hermeneutical understanding. The limit experience of hermeneutics is defined by specifically unintelligible expressions. Such specific unintelligibility cannot be overcome by the exercise, however artful, of naturally acquired communicative competence; its refractoriness may be taken as an indication that it is not to be explained alone in terms of the structure of colloquial communication which hermeneutics brings to consciousness. In such a case, it is not the objectivity of the linguistic tradition, the limitations imposed on linguistic understanding of the world by its own horizons, or the potential unintelligibility of the apparently obvious that presents the primary obstacle to interpretive effort.

When confronted with difficulties in comprehension which arise from a large distance between cultures, time periods, or social classes, we can say in principle what additional information we would have to have at our disposal in order to understand: we know that we must make out an alphabet, familiarize ourselves with the lexicon, or derive context-specific rules of application. In the attempt to throw light hermeneutically on unintelligible configurations of meaning, we can know, within the limits of everyday colloquial communication, what we do not (yet) know. Such hermeneutical consciousness proves inadequate in the case of systematically distorted communication: here the unintelligibility results from a faulty organization of speech itself. Openly pathological disturbances of speech— of the sort, for example, which appear in psychotics— hermeneutics can neglect without damage to its conception of itself; for so long as pathological cases alone elude the grasp of hermeneutics, its sphere of application remains coincidental with the limits of normal colloquial communication. The self-conception of hermeneutics can be shaken only if it becomes apparent that systematically distorted patterns of communication also occur in "normal"— that is to say, in pathologically inconspicuous— speech. That, however, is true in the case of pseudocommunication, in which a disruption of communication is not recognizable by the parties involved. Only a newcomer to the conversation notices that they misunderstand each other. Pseudocommunication produces a system of misunderstandings which remain opaque because they are seen in the light of a false consensus. Now we have learned from hermeneutics that so long as we have to do with a natural language we are always interested participants and cannot escape from the role of the reflective playing partner. We thus have no universal criterion at our disposal which would tell us when we are caught up in the false consciousness of a pseudonormal understanding and are viewing something merely as the kind of difficulty which hermeneutics can clarify, when in fact it requires systematic explanation. The limit experience of hermeneutics thus consists in the discovery of systematically produced misunderstandings—without at first being able to "comprehend" them.

Freud has thoroughly explored systematically displaced communication in order to delimit a sphere of specifically unintelligible expressions. He consistently views the dream as the "normative model" of such phenomena. The phenomena themselves extend from harmless pseudocommunication and routine blunders to the pathological symptoms of neuroses, mental illnesses, and psychosomatic disturbances. In his cultural-theoretical works Freud expands his conception of systematically distorted communication, using the insights gained from clinical phenomena as a key to pseudonormality—that is, to the hidden pathology of entire social systems. We will concentrate at the outset on the most thoroughly elucidated kinds of neurotic symptoms.

There are three criteria which serve to define neurotically distorted, or specifically unintelligible, expressions. On the level of linguistic symbols, distorted communication makes itself felt through the application of rules which deviate from the rule system of public language. This can affect the semantic content of individual expressions and entire fields of meaning; in extreme cases, syntax, too, is involved. Freud notes, in particular, condensation, displacement, agrammaticality, and the role of "representation through the opposite" in dream-texts. On the behavioral level, a distorted language game makes itself felt through rigidity and compulsive repetition. Stereotyped patterns of behavior occur in situations with like emotive stimuli. Such inflexibility is an indication that the semantic content of the symbol has lost its linguistic independence of situation. Finally, when we look at the system of distorted communication as a whole, the inherent discrepancy between the different levels of communication becomes conspicuous: the usual congruence between linguistic symbolism, actions, and attendant [gestural] expressions has collapsed. Neurotic symptoms provide only the most refractory and tangible evidence of such dissonance. Regardless of the level of communication on which the symptoms appear, whether in linguistic expression, on the level of gestural symbolism, or on the level of compulsive behavior, a content excommunicated from the public use of language asserts itself against the will of the speaker. This content brings to expression a meaning which is unintelligible according to the rules of public communication, one which, in this sense, has become private, and which remains inaccessible even to the speaker himself, who is nevertheless its "author." In the self, a communication block subsists between the language competent ego which participates in intersubjectively established language games and that "foreign land within" (Freud) which manifests itself in the symbolism of private or primitive language.

Alfred Lorenzer, who has investigated the analytical conversation between doctor and patient from a point of view which sees psychoanalysis as an analysis of language,[10] thinks of the depth-hermeneutical deciphering of specifically unintelligible objectifications as an understanding of analogically related "scenes." Regarded hermeneutically, the goal of analytical interpretation is thus the elucidation of the unintelligible meaning of symptomatic expressions. In cases where neuroses are involved, such expressions are part of a deformed language game in which the patient becomes an "actor"—that is, he plays out an unintelligible scene, contravening accepted behavioral expectations in a conspicuously stereotypical way. The analyst attempts to make the meaning of the symptomatic scene intelligible by establishing its relationship to analogous scenes in the transference situation. Such scenes hold the key to the enciphered relationship between the symptomatic scene the adult patient plays outside the analysis and an original scene from early childhood; for in the transference situation the patient forces the doctor into the role of the conflict-invested primary reference person. The doctor, in the role of reflective supporting actor, can interpret the transference situation as a repetition of early childhood scenes and so compile a lexicon of the private meanings attached to the patient's symptomatic expressions. Scenic understanding, then, is based on the discovery that the patient conducts himself in his symptomatic scenes as he does in certain well-defined transference ones; its goal is the reconstruction of the original scene, authenticated by an act of self-reflective insight on the part of the patient.

Typically, as Lorenzer has shown in reference to the phobia of Freud's "Little Hans," the original scene is a situation in which the child is exposed to and attempts to ward off an intolerable conflict. The attempt to ward off the conflict is accompanied by a process of *desymbolization* and the formation of a symptom. The child excludes the experience of the conflict-laden object relation from public communication (thereby rendering it inaccessible to his own ego as well); he sunders the conflict-laden portion of the object representation and desymbolizes to some extent the meaning of the relevant reference person. The gap which is left in the semantic field is filled by the symptom, in that an apparently normal symbol takes the place of the sundered symbolic content. The symbol in question, however, has the conspicuousness of a symptom, for it has taken on a private meaning and can no longer be used in accordance with the rules of public language. Scenic understanding—which establishes the equivalencies of meaning among the elements of three different patterns (the everyday scene, the transference scene, and the original scene) and thus does away with the specific unintelligibility of the symptom—therefore aids in the process of *resymbolization*—that is, in the reintroduction into public communication of the sundered symbolic content. The latent meaning of the present-day situation becomes understandable through reference to the unscrambled significance of the infantile original scene. Scenic understanding, therefore, makes it possible to "translate" the meaning of the pathologically rigid pattern of communication—a meaning which was previously inaccessible in public communication but nevertheless had a determining effect on behavior.

Scenic understanding is distinct from simple hermeneutical understanding by virtue of its explanatory power; it unlocks the meaning of specifically unintelligible expressions only insofar as it can also successfully reconstruct the original scene and thus bring to light the conditions responsible for the genesis of the difficulty itself. The What—the meaningful content of the systematically distorted expression—cannot be "understood" if the Why—the origin of the symptomatic scene in the conditions responsible for the systematic distortion itself—cannot be "explained" at the same time.

Understanding, of course, can assume an explanatory function in the strict sense only if its analysis of meaning does not rely solely upon the trained application of communicative competence but procedes on the basis of theoretical hypotheses as well. I can point to two indications that scenic understanding is based on theoretical presuppositions which are in no way the spontaneous outgrowth of the natural competence of a native speaker.

First, scenic understanding is linked to an experimental design which is inherently hermeneutical. Freud's basic principle of analysis ensures a communication between doctor and patient which, in its own way, fulfills experimental conditions: virtualization in psychoanalysis of the real life situation and free association on the part of the patient, together with goal-inhibited reaction and reflective participation on the part of the analyst make it possible to realize a transference situation which can serve as a basis for comparison in the process of translation. Second, the preconception which the analyst brings to the analysis is directed to a small selection of possible constructions—namely, to conflict-disturbed early childhood object relations. The linguistic material which emerges from conversations with the patient is classified according to a narrowly circumscribed context of possible meanings. This context consists of an overall interpretation of early childhood models of interaction, which is keyed to a phase-specific developmental history of the personality. Both factors suggest that scenic understanding cannot be thought of, like hermeneutics, as a theory-free application of communicative competence, itself the necessary precondition for all possible theories.

The theoretical hypotheses which are tacitly presupposed by depth-hermeneutical analysis of language may be seen as falling into three different groups: (1) the psychoanalyst has a preconceived notion of the structure of undistorted colloquial communication; (2) he traces the systematic distortion of communication back to the confusion of two distinct developmental-historical stages, prelinguistic and linguistic, in the organization of symbols; (3) he explains the origin of the deformation with the help of a theory of deviational processes of socialization which draws upon the connection between models of early childhood interaction and the formation of personality structures. There is no need here to develop systematically the theoretical hypotheses themselves. I would, however, like to comment briefly on the groups I have mentioned.

1. The first set of theoretical hypotheses has to do with the structural conditions which must be met for colloquial communication to be considered "normal."

(a) In a nondeformed language game, expressions on all three levels of communication are congruent: linguistically symbolized expressions, expressions represented in actions, and those embodied in physical expressions do not contradict each other but supplement each other metacommunicatively. Intentional contradictions, which carry a message of their own, are normal in this regard. Further, in the normal form of colloquial communication a portion of the extra verbal meanings must be intentional—that is, capable of being verbalized. The portion itself is socio-culturally variable, but constant within a given language community.

(b) Normal colloquial communication conforms to intersubjectively valid rules: it is public. Communicated meanings are identical, in principle, for all members of the language community. Verbal expressions are constructed in conformity with the operative grammatical rule system and are context-specific in application; for extraverbal expressions, which are not grammatically regulated, there is also a lexicon which, within defined limits, is socio-culturally variable.

(c) In normal discourse, the speakers are conscious of the categorical distinction between subject and object. They differentiate between external and internal discourse and separate the private from the public world. In addition, differentiation between reality (*Sein*) and appearance (*Schein*) is further dependent on the speaker's ability to discriminate between the linguistic symbol, the meaning it carries (significatum), and the object to which the symbol refers (referent, denotatum). Only on such a basis is a situation-independent application (decontextualization) of linguistic symbols possible. The speaking subject comes to master the distinction between reality and appearance to the extent that language itself takes on for him a distinct reality, separate from the objects it denotes, the circumstances it represents, and from private experiences as well.

(d) In normal colloquial communication an intersubjectivity, which serves to guarantee identity is formed and preserved in the relationship between mutually recognizant individuals. While the analytical use of language allows one to identify matters of fact (and thus to categorize objects by means of the identification of distinctive qualities, the subsumption of individual members under classes, and the inclusion of large quantities), the reflexive use of language guarantees a relationship between the speaking subject and the language community which cannot be adequately described by means of the analytical operations just named. The intersubjectivity of the world in which the subjects live together by virtue of colloquial communication alone is not a universal, to which individuals can be subordinated the same way members are to their classes. Rather, the relationship between I, Thou (another I), and We (I and other I's) is established only through an analytically paradoxical feat. The parties to a conversation identify themselves simultaneously with two irreconcilable roles; in so doing, they guarantee the identity not only of the I but that of the group as well. The One (I) asserts vis-à-vis the Other (Thou) his absolute nonidentity; at the same time, however, both also recognize their common identity, in that they mutually acknowledge each other as unique individuals. As a result, they are once again bound by a commonality (We), a group—which in turn asserts its individuality vis-à-vis other groups, so that the same relationship which exists between individuals establishes itself as well on the level of intersubjectively bound collectives.[11]

The specific element in linguistic intersubjectivity resides in its ability to serve as a basis for communication between individual members of the language community. In the reflexive use of language, our use of unavoidably universal categories to represent something inalienably individual is such that, to a certain extent, we metacommunicatively revoke (and at the same time confirm, with reservations) the direct messages involved. And we do so in order to bring to expression, indirectly, that which is nonidentical in the I—a nonidentity which is not absorbed by the universal definitions used to express it, yet can come to representation only through them.[12] The analytical use of language is embedded in its reflexive use; for the intersubjectivity of colloquial understanding cannot be sustained without a mutual self-representation on the part of the speaking subjects. To the extent that the speaker has command of those indirect messages on the metacommunicative level, he differentiates between essence and appearance. We can come to an understanding about facts directly; but the subjectivity which we encounter when we speak to one another merely "appears" in direct messages. The speaker's categorical sense of the indirect form of the message in which something inexpressibly individual is nevertheless brought to expression is merely ontologized in the concept of an essence which exists in its appearances.

(e) Finally, normal discourse is distinctive in that the categories of substance and causality, space and time have different meanings, according to whether they are applied to objects in the world or to the linguistically constituted world of the speaking subjects themselves. The interpretive schematism "substance" has a different meaning for the identity of objects which can be analytically and thus unequivocally categorized than it has for speaking and acting subjects, whose I-identity, as shown, altogether escapes analytically unequivocal operations. The causal interpretive schematism leads to the concept of "cause" when applied to empirical chains of events, and to the concept of "motive" when applied to a configuration of intentional actions. Similarly, space and time are also schematized differently when applied to physically measurable properties of objects and events than they are when applied to the intersubjective experience of configurations of symbolically mediated interactions. In the first instance, the categories serve as a system of coordinates for controlled observation of the outcome of instrumental behavior, in the latter as the referential framework for the subjective experience of social space and historical time. The compass of intersubjective experience alters complementarily with that of the experience of objectivized objects and events.

2. The second set of hypotheses has to do with the interrelationship between two genetically successive stages in the organization of symbols.

(a) The earlier symbol organization, the content of which resists transposition into grammatically regulated communication, can be brought to light only by means of data gathered from the study of pathological speech and through the analysis of dream material. In such cases, one has to do with symbols which control behavior and not merely with signs, for the symbols have genuine significative function: they represent interactional experiences. In other respects, however, this paleosymbolic layer is without any of the properties of normal discourse.[13] Paleosymbols are not installed in a grammatical rule system. They are not ordered elements and do not appear in configurations which can be grammatically transformed. For that reason, the mode of operation of prelinguistic symbols has been compared with that of analog, as opposed to digital, computers. Freud himself notes the absence of logical relationships in his dream analyses. He points in particular to "representations through the opposite," which have preserved on the linguistic level the genetically earlier characteristic of a unification of logically incompatible—that is, antithetical—meanings.[14] Prelinguistic symbols are heavily laden with emotion and center in each case on definite scenes. There is no division between linguistic symbol and gestural expression. The bond to a particular context is so strong that the symbol cannot vary freely with actions.[15] Although paleosymbols constitute a prelinguistic groundwork for the intersubjectivity of corporate life and concerted action, they do not, strictly speaking, permit public communication. For the meanings they carry are low in stability and high in private content: they are not yet able to support an intersubjectively binding identity of meanings. The privatism of prelinguistic symbol organization, which plays a conspicuous role in all forms of pathological speech, is traceable to the fact that the distance between sender and addressee and the distinction between symbolic sign, semantic content, and referent, which are characteristic of colloquial communication, have not yet developed. The levels of reality represented by reality and appearance, by public and private worlds, cannot yet be clearly differentiated by means of paleosymbols (Adualism).

Finally, prelinguistic symbol organization does not permit an analytically satisfactory categorization of the experienced objective world. Among the communicative and cognitive disorders of psychotics,[16] one finds two extreme kinds of symptomatic deficiencies; in both cases, analytical operations having to do with class formation are disturbed. In the one instance, a fragmentational pattern is present which makes it impossible to collect scattered individual elements into classes on the basis of general criteria; in the other, an amorphous pattern which makes it impossible to analyze aggregates of superficially similar and vaguely related things. The ability to use symbols is not wholly lost. In both cases, however, the inability to construct hierarchies of classes and to identify the members of classes testifies to a breakdown in the analytical use of language. The second variant, to be sure, suggests that an archaic kind of class formation is possible with the help of prelinguistic symbols. In any event, we find in early stages of ontogenetic and phylogenetic development, as well as in instances of pathological speech, so-called primary classes, which are not formed abstractly on the basis of the identity of properties. Instead, the aggregates are made up of concrete objects—concrete in view of the fact that, irrespective of their identifiable properties, they are incorporated into a holistic, subjectively compelling motivational context. Animistic world-views are articulated in accordance with such primitive classes. Since holistic intentional contexts cannot be constructed in the absence of interactional experiences, there is some ground for the hypothesis that atavistic forms of intersubjectivity are in fact developed at the stage of prelinguistic symbol organization. Paleosymbols, on the other hand, are clearly developed in interactional contexts, prior to the time they are assimilated into a grammatical rule system and linked to operative intelligence.

(b) The symbol organization here described, which genetically precedes language, is a theoretical construction. We cannot observe it. Psychoanalytical deciphering of systematically distorted communication, however, presupposes such a construction, in that depth-hermeneutics grasps deviations from normal discourse either as compulsive regression to earlier stages of communication or else as a penetration of the earlier form of communication into language. Taking the analyst's experiences with neurotic patients as his starting point, Alfred Lorenzer, as we have noted, sees the significance of psychoanalysis in terms of its ability to reintegrate sundered symbolic content, as a private language which produces a constriction in public communication, into the common use of language. The work of analysis, which reverses the process of repression, aids in "resymbolization"; repression itself can thus be understood as "desymbolization." Repression, which operates as a defense mechanism and which comes to light in the patient's flightlike resistance to apt interpretations on the part of the analyst, is carried out in and through language; otherwise it would be impossible to reverse the defensive process hermeneutically, even via the analysis of language. The fugitive ego, which, when faced with a conflict, must submit to the demands of the outside world, conceals itself from itself, in that it purges representation of the undesirable impulse from the text of its everyday self-understanding. Through such censorship, the representation of the prohibited love-object is excommunicated from public use of language and banished, as it were, to the genetically earlier stage of paleosymbols.

The hypothesis that neurotic behavior is paleosymbolically controlled and only rationalized subsequently through a linguistic construction offers an explanation as well for the characteristic symptoms of this type of behavior—for pseudo-communicative value, stereotyping, and compulsiveness, for emotional cathexis, expressive content, and rigid bonding to concrete situations.

If repression, then, can be understood as desymbolization, a language analytical explanation is also to hand for the complementary defense mechanisms—namely, for projection and denial, which are directed not against the self but against the outside world. While in the former case the public use of language is garbled by symptoms which have formed to take the place of excommunicated language elements, in the latter case the distortion results directly from the uncontrolled penetration into language of paleosymbolic offshoots. Here the goal of language analysis is not a transformation of desymbolized content into linguistically artic-ulated meaning, but a consciously effected excommunication of prelinguistic xenocysts. In both cases, the systematic distortion of colloquial communication can be traced to the encapsulation, like foreign bodies, of paleosymbolically linked semantic content in the linguistically regulated application of symbols. The task of language analysis is to break up the syndrome—that is, to isolate the two layers of language.

In processes which lead to the coining of new words and phrases, on the other hand, a genuine integration of the two layers takes place: in the creative use of language the potential meaning bound up in the paleosymbolic is publicly re-covered and placed at the disposal of a grammatically regulated application of symbols.[17] Such a transference of semantic content from the prelinguistic to the linguistic state of aggregation widens the sphere of communicative behavior at the expense of behavior which is unconsciously motivated. Success in the creative use of language is marked by emancipation.

Wit is a different matter. The laughter with which we react, almost compul-sively, to the humor of wit records the liberating experience of the passage from paleosymbolic to linguistic thinking; the unmasked equivocality of wit is comic in that, by this means, the raconteur lures us into regression to the stage of prelinguistic symbolism—for example, into confounding identity and similarity —and at the same time carries us past the faulty thinking of that regression. Our laughter is laughter of relief. In the reaction to wit, which allows us to repeat, in principle and tentatively, the precarious passage over the archaic boundary which separates prelinguistic from linguistic communication, we assure ourselves of the control we have acquired over the perils inherent in a surmounted stage of consciousness.

3. Unlike simple hermeneutical understanding, depth-hermeneutics, which clarifies the specific unintelligibility of systematically distorted communication, can no longer be grasped, strictly speaking, in terms of the model of translation. For the controlled "translation" of prelinguistic symbolism into language

eliminates obscurities which originate not within language but with language itself: the structure of colloquial communication, which forms the basis for every translation, is thus itself involved. Consequently, depth-hermeneutical understanding requires a systematic preconception which has to do with language as a whole, whereas hermeneutical understanding begins, in each case, from a preconception defined by the tradition which is formed and altered within linguistic communication. The theoretical hypotheses which have to do with (1) the two stages of symbol organization and (2) the processes of de- and resymbolization, penetration of paleosymbolic elements into language, and conscious excommunication of these xenocysts, as well as the linguistic integration of prelinguistic symbolic content—these theoretical hypotheses can be classified according to a structural model which Freud derived from fundamental experiences with the analysis of defense processes. The constructs "ego" and "id" interpret the analyst's experiences with *resistance* on the part of the patient.

Ego is the agency which carries out the tasks of reality testing and impulse censorship. Id is the name for that part of the self which is isolated from the ego and to which we gain access, through its manifestations, in connection with defense processes. The id manifests itself *indirectly* through the symptoms which fill the gaps left in the normal use of language by desymbolization, and *directly* through the delusory paleosymbolic elements imported into language by projection and denial. Now the clinical encounter with "resistance" which makes the constructs of ego and id necessary also shows that the activity of the defending agency proceeds for the most part unconsciously. Freud therefore institutes the category "superego": a defense system alien to the ego which is comprised of abandoned identification with the expectations of primary reference persons. All three categories, ego, id, and superego, are therefore linked to the specific meaning of a systematically distorted communication which the doctor and patient enter into with the object of setting in motion a dialogical process of enlightenment and of leading the patient to self-reflection. Metapsychology can be grounded only as metahermeneutics.[18]

The model of agencies relies implicitly on a model of deformations in colloquial intersubjectivity: the dimensions which the id and superego define for the structure of personality clearly correspond to those of structural deformations in the intersubjectivity of unconstrained communication. The structural model which Freud introduced as the categorical framework of metapsychology is therefore reducible to a theory of deviations in communicative competence.

Now metapsychology consists principally of hypotheses about the origination of personality structures. And that, too, is accounted for by the metahermeneutical role the psychoanalyst must play. The analyst's *understanding,* as we have seen, owes its explanatory power to the fact that a systematically inaccessible meaning can be elucidated only to the extent that the origin of the loss of meaning can be *explained.* The construction of the original scene makes both things possible at once: it opens the way to an understanding of the meaning of the deformed language game and explains at the same time the origin of the deformation itself. Scenic understanding, therefore, presupposes metapsychology as a theory which explains the *origin* of the structures ego, id, and superego. On the sociological level, the counterpart of metapsychology is a theory which explains the acquisition of the basic traits of role behavior. Both theories, however, are part of a metahermeneutics which traces the psychological rise of personality structures and the acquisition of the basic traits of role behavior back to the development of communicative competence, and that means: to the socializing assimilation of forms which govern the intersubjectivity of colloquial intelligibility. We have thus arrived at an answer to the question which served as our point of departure: explanatory understanding, as a depth-hermeneutical deciphering of specifically inaccessible expressions, presupposes not only, as simple hermeneutical understanding does, the trained application of naturally acquired communicative competence, but a theory of communicative competence as well. Such a theory concerns itself with the forms of the intersubjectivity of language and the causes of their deformation. I do not maintain that, at present, a theory of communicative competence has been satisfactorily undertaken, much less explicitly developed. Freud's metapsychology would have to be freed of its scientistic misconception of itself before it could serve fruitfully as part of a metahermeneutics. I do maintain, however, that any depth-hermeneutical interpretation of systematically distorted communication, whether it takes place in the analytical exchange between doctor and patient or informally, must implicitly presuppose exacting theoretical hypotheses of the sort which can be developed and grounded only within the framework of a *theory of communicative competence.*

## III

What follows from the foregoing so far as hermeneutics' claim to universality is concerned? Would it not be true of the theoretical language of a metahermeneutics —a question which must be asked in reference to every theory—that a given, nonreconstructed colloquial language remains its ultimate metalanguage? And would not the application of the universal interpretations derived from such a theory to a given material in colloquial language have as much need as before of ordinary hermeneutical understanding, which no generalized technique of scientific analysis can replace? It would no longer be necessary to answer either question without circumstance in terms of hermeneutics' claim to universality if the knowing subject, who to be sure must always draw upon his previously acquired linguistic competence, were able to assure himself of that competence expressly through a theoretical reconstruction. We have left this problem of a universal theory of natural languages out of consideration. Even without such a theory to hand, however, we can call to witness the competence which the analyst (and the critic of ideology) must actually have at his command in deciphering specifically unintelligible expressions. Indeed, *the implicit knowledge of the determinants of systematically distorted communication,* which is presupposed by the depth-hermeneutical use of communicative competence, *is enough to call into question the ontological self-conception of hermeneutics* which Gadamer explicates, following Heidegger.

The context-dependency of understanding which hermeneutics brings to consciousness and which compels us in each case to begin from a preconception supported by tradition and to develop constantly, in every process of learning, a new preconception, Gadamer attributes ontologically to an insuperable primacy of the linguistic tradition.[19] Gadamer poses the question: "Is the phenomenon of understanding adequately defined if I say: understanding means avoiding misunderstanding? Does not, in truth, every misunderstanding presuppose the existence of something like a "standing agreement"?[20] On the affirmative answer to this question we agree; not, however, on the way in which that prior consensus is to be defined.

Gadamer, if I am correct, is of the opinion that the hermeneutical elucidation of unintelligible or misunderstood expression must always refer back to a prior consensus which has been reliably worked out in the dialogue of a convergent tradition. This tradition, however, is objective for us, in the sense that it cannot be confronted with a claim to the truth on principle. The inherently prejudiced nature of understanding renders it impossible—indeed, makes it seem pointless—to place in jeopardy the factually worked out consensus which underlies, as the case may be, our misconception or lack of comprehension. Hermeneutically, we are obliged to have reference to concrete preunderstandings which, ultimately, can be traced back to the process of socialization, to the mastery of and absorption into common contexts of tradition. None of the contexts involved is off-limits to criticism as a matter of principle, but none of them can be called into question abstractly. That would be possible only if we could look at a consensus produced through mutual understanding from the sidelines, as it were, and could subject it, behind the backs of the participants, to renewed demands for legitimation. But we can make demands of this sort to the face of the participants only by entering into a conversation with them. In so doing, we resubmit ourselves to the hermeneutical obligation of accepting for the time being—as a standing agreement—whatever consensus the resumed conversation may lead to as its resolution. The attempt to cast doubt, abstractly, on this agreement—which is, of course, contingent—as a false consciousness is pointless, since we cannot transcend the conversation which we are. From this, Gadamer infers the ontological precedence of linguistic tradition over criticism of all sorts: we can, it follows, bring criticism to bear only on given individual traditions, since we ourselves are part of the encompassing traditional context of a language.

Such considerations seem plausible at first. They are upset, however, by the depth-hermeneutical insight that a consensus, apparently worked out on a "rational" basis, may equally well be the product of pseudocommunication. As Albrecht Wellmer has pointed out, this same antitraditional insight comes to general expression in the heritage of the Enlightenment. In all matters touching agreement, the Enlightenment demands that reason be established as the principle of unconstrained communication, as opposed to the experienced reality of a communication distorted by force: "The Enlightenment knew what hermeneutics forgets: that the 'conversation' which, according to Gadamer, we 'are' is also a nexus of force and for precisely that reason is not a conversation. . . . The claim to universality of the hermeneutical approach can be upheld only if one starts from the recognition that the context of tradition, as the locus of possible truth and real accord, is at the same time the locus of real falsehood and the persistent use of force."[21]

The standing agreement which Gadamer envisions as the consequence of every failure to agree could legitimately be equated with a real accord on the matter in question only if we were able to say for certain that every consensus worked out in the medium of linguistic tradition is arrived at unconstrainedly and without distortion. We know from depth-hermeneutics, however, that the dogmatism of the traditional context is the vehicle not only for the objectivity of language in general, but for the repressiveness of a power relationship which deforms the intersubjectivity of understanding as such and systematically distorts colloquial communication. For that reason, every consensus in which interpretation terminates stands under the suspicion of having been pseudocommunicatively compelled: the ancients called it delusion when misunderstanding and misunderstanding of one's self blithely perpetuated themselves in the guise of real accord. Clearly, insight into the prejudicial structure of understanding yields nothing when it comes to the pitfall of identifying the factually produced consensus with the true one. Instead, it leads to the ontologization of language and to the hypostatization of the traditional context. A critically self-aware hermeneutics, on the other hand, one which differentiates between insight and delusion, assimilates the metahermeneutical knowledge concerning the conditions which make systematically distorted communication possible. It links understanding to the principle of rational discourse, so that truth can be guaranteed only by *that* consensus which might be reached under the idealized conditions to be found in unrestrained and dominance-free communication, and which could, in the course of time, be affirmed to exist.

As K.-O. Apel has rightly emphasized, hermeneutical understanding is conducive to a critical confirmation of the truth only to the extent that it subordinates itself to a regulative principle which requires universal communicative agreement within an unlimited community of interpretation.[22] Only this principle, in other words, is able to ensure that the hermeneutical effort will not stop short before it has seen through deception (in the case of a forced consensus) and systematic displacement (in the case of apparently accidental misunderstanding). If under-standing of meaning is not to remain indifferent to the idea of truth a fortiori, we must envisage, along with the concept of a truth which measures itself against the idealized concurrence to be reached in unlimited and dominance-free communi-cation, the structure of a corporate life in unconstrained communication. Truth is the inherent and proper constraint upon unconstrained universal acknowledg-ment; such acknowledgment, however, is inseparable from the notion of an ideal forum—and that means way of life—in which unconstrained universal agreement is possible. In this respect, critical understanding of meaning necessarily demands the formal anticipation of right living. As G. H. Mead has said: "Universal discourse is the formal ideal of communication. If communication can be carried through and made perfect, then there would exist the kind of democracy . . . in which each individual would carry just the response in himself that he knows he calls out in the community. That is what makes communication in the significant sense the organizing process in the community."[23] An idea of the truth which measures itself against true consensus implies an idea of the true life. We can also say: it includes the idea of a coming of age. Only the formal anticipation of the idealized conversation as a future way of life guarantees the ultimate, contra-factual standing agreement which unites us provisionally, and on the basis of which any factual agreement, if it be a false one, can be criticized as a false consciousness.

It is true that we are not in a position to call for that regulative principle of understanding, much less to ground it, until such time as we can demonstrate that the anticipation of eventual truth and right living is constitutive for every non-monological linguistic agreement. To be sure, the fundamental experience of metahermeneutics makes us aware that critique—namely, a penetrating under-standing which is not deflected by delusion—takes its bearings from the concept of ideal concurrence and in this respect is guided by the regulative principle of rational discourse. However, since we not only entertain that formal anticipation in every incisive understanding, but must do so in principle, we cannot appeal to the evidence of experience alone. In order to provide legitimate grounds for the validity of critical understanding, we must develop the implicit knowledge by which a depth-hermeneutical analysis of language is always guided into a theory which makes it possible to derive from the logic of colloquial language the prin-ciple of rational discourse as the necessary regulator of every actual discourse, be it ever so displaced.

Meanwhile, even apart from anticipation of a general theory of natural lan-guages, the present considerations are sufficient to call into question two views, both of which follow, not indeed from hermeneutics itself, but from what seems to me a false ontological conception of hermeneutics.

1. Gadamer has used hermeneutical insight into the prejudicial structure of understanding to rehabilitate prejudice. He sees no antithesis between authority

and reason. The authority of tradition, he says, does not prevail blindly but through the reflective acknowledgment of those who, standing within the tradition, interpret it and continue its development through application. In his reply to my critique,[24] Gadamer once again makes his position clear:

> Granted, authority exercises force in countless forms. . . . But this view of the obedience rendered to authority can never explain why it should express itself in power *structures* and not in the disorder which characterizes the exercise of force alone. As I see it, then, there are compelling reasons for viewing acknowledgement as the determining factor in true authority relationships. . . . One need only study representative instances of the loss or decline of authority to see what authority is and whence it derives its life. Not from dogmatic force, but from dogmatic acknowledgement. What, however, is dogmatic acknowledgement, if not this: that one concedes to authority a superiority in knowledge and judgment [p. 285].

Dogmatic acknowledgment of any tradition—and that means the acceptance of its claim to the truth—can, of course, be equated with knowledge itself only if the tradition in question somehow guarantees freedom from constraint and from restriction in agreement about tradition itself. Gadamer's argument presupposes that legitimating acknowledgment and the agreement in which authority is grounded are brought about without force. Experience with systematically distorted communication militates against that presupposition. Moreover, force achieves permanence through precisely the objective illusion of freedom from force which characterizes a pseudocommunicative agreement. I call a force which is legitimated in that way, as Max Weber does, authority. Without the proviso, on principle, of universal and dominance-free agreement, therefore, it is impossible to differentiate in a fundamental way between dogmatic acknowledgment and true consensus. Reason, as the principle of rational discourse, is the rock on which existing authorities split, not the one on which they were founded.

2. If, however, the antithesis between authority and reason proclaimed by the Enlightenment is valid and cannot be rescinded hermeneutically, then the attempt to impose fundamental restrictions on the interpreter's claim to enlightenment becomes problematic as well. Gadamer has further used hermeneutical insight into the prejudicial structure of understanding to restrict the quest for enlightenment to the horizon of prevailing convictions. According to Gadamer, the superior knowledge of the interpreter finds its limit in the recognized and traditionally ingrained convictions of the socio-cultural life-world to which he himself belongs:

> What, it must be asked, is the relationship between the knowledge of the psychoanalyst and his professional position within the social reality, of which he is, after all, a member? That he inquires behind superficial explanations,

breaks through obstacles to self-understanding, sees through the repressive effect of social taboos—all these things are part and parcel of the emancipatory reflection into which he leads his patients. But if he exercises the same kind of reflection in situations and in areas where his role as a doctor is not legitimately involved, where he is himself a participant in the social game, then he abandons his social role. The person who "sees through" his playing partners to something beyond the understandings involved in their relationship—that is, does not take the game they are playing seriously—is a spoilsport whom one avoids. The emancipatory power of reflection to which the psychoanalyst lays claim thus has its limit—a limit which is defined by the larger social consciousness in terms of which analyst and patient alike understand themselves, along with everyone else. For hermeneutical reflection teaches us that social community, with all its tensions and disruptions, leads us back time and again to a social understanding by virtue of which it continues to exist [p. 290f.].

Nevertheless, we have good reason to suspect that the background consensus of established traditions and language games can be a consciousness forged of compulsion, a result of pseudocommunication, not only in the pathologically isolated case of disturbed familial systems, but in entire social systems as well. The freedom of movement of a hermeneutical understanding widened into critique, therefore, ought not be linked to the free play available within the tradition and prevailing convictions. Because a depth-hermeneutics pledged to the regulative principle of rational discourse must seek and can find the natural historical traces of disturbed communication even in fundamental concurrences and acknowledged legitimations, it would be incompatible with its methodological approach to privatize its claim to enlightenment and to restrict the critique of ideologies to the role of a procedure institutionalized in the doctor-patient relationship. Enlightenment, which effects a radical understanding, is always political. To be sure, critique, too, remains bound to the traditional context which it reflects. When it comes to monological self-certainty, which critique merely arrogates to itself, Gadamer's hermeneutical objection is valid. There is no corroboration for depth-hermeneutical interpretation outside of the self-reflection of all parties involved—a self-reflection which is found in and carried out through dialogue. In fact, the hypothetical status of all general interpretations gives rise in each case to compelling a priori restrictions when it comes to the choice of mode, according to which critical understanding's claim to enlightenment is to be redeemed.[25]

Perhaps under the present circumstances there is a more pressing need to call attention to the limits of critique's false claim to universality than to those of the claim to universality of hermeneutics. So far as it is a matter of clarifying a dispute about validity, however, the latter, too, stands in need of critical appraisal.

## Notes

1. The word "natural" is used here in the same sense that it is used to distinguish "natural" from "artificial" languages.

2. H.-G. Gadamer, "Rhetorik, Hermeneutik, [und] Ideologiekritik," in *Kleine Schriften I* (Tübingen, 1967), pp. 113-30. [In this volume, pp. 174–92. Subsequent references to Gadamer's essay are to the translation in the present collection and are cited parenthetically in the text.]

3. See the author's *Erkenntnis und Interesse* (Frankfurt am Main, 1968), pp. 206ff. *[Knowledge and Human Interest,* trans. Jeremy J. Shapiro (Boston, 1971).]

4. Noam Chomsky, *Aspects of the Theory of Syntax* (Cambridge, MA, 1965).

5. Gadamer demonstrates this point in the Second Part of *Truth and Method.*

6. See the author's *Zur Logik der Sozialwissenschaften, Philosophische Rundschau,* Beiheft 5 (1967): Chapter III.

7. H.-G. Gadamer, "Die Universalität des hermeneutischen Problems," in *Kleine Schriften I,* p. 109. ["The Universality of the Hermeneutical Problem," trans. David E. Linge, in *Philosophical Hermeneutics,* ed. Linge (Berkeley, 1976).]

8. See H. G. Furth's excellent study, *Piaget and Knowledge* (Englewood Cliffs, 1969).

9. This view is further supported by Lorenzen's proposed operative construction of logic. His scheme would explain why the elements of the calculus of statements can be introduced language-independently, in the sense that the natural language used to introduce them is called upon in an auxillary capacity only, for didactic purposes, but need not be presented systematically. See P[aul] Lorenzen, *Normative Logic and Ethics* (Mannheim, 1969). Also, K. Lorenz and J. Mittelstrass, "Die Hintergehbarkeit der Sprache," *Kantstudien* 58 (1967): 187-208.

10. A. Lorenzer, *Sprachzerstörung und Rekonstruktion: Vorarbeiten zu einer Metatheorie der Psychoanalyse* (Frankfurt, 1970).

11. This is reflected as well in our relationship to foreign languages. In principle, we can acquire a mastery of any foreign language because all natural languages are reducible to a universal generative rule system. And yet we learn a foreign language only to the extent that we recapitulate, virtually at least, the same process of socialization the native speaker goes through, and thereby, again virtually, become part of an individual language community: a natural language is something universal only as something concrete.

12. On the concept of the nonidentical, see T. W. Adorno, *Negative Dialektik* (Frankfurt, 1966). *[Negative Dialectics,* trans. E. B. Ashton; (New York, 1973).]

13. See S[ilvano] Arieti, *The Intrapsychic Self* (New York, 1967), especially Chapters 7 and 16. Also H. Werner and B. Kaplan, *Symbol Formation* (New York, 1967), and Paul Watzlawick, J. H. Beavin, and D. D. Jackson, *Pragmatics of Human Communication* (New York, 1967), especially Chapters 6 and 7.

14. Representations through the opposite, or words with antithetical meanings, of course, are not merely examples of agrammaticality; they are probably the record as well of primal situations involving behavioral and attitudinal ambivalence, an ambivalence which has become chronic with the dedifferentiation of the impulse system and the breakdown of class-specific responses, and which has been caught up and stabilized through

prelinguistic symbolism. See A[rnold] Gehlen, *Urmensch und Spätkultur* (Bonn, 1956) and A. S. Diamond, *The History and Origin of Language* (London, 1959).

15. Lorenzer (in *Kritik des psychoanalytischen Symbolbegriffs* [Frankfurt, 1970], p. 87ff.) finds the same characteristics in the unconscious representations which govern neurotic kinds of behavior: confusion of experiential expression and symbol, close coordination with a particular kind of behavior, scenic content, context dependency. The unconscious schemata are part of concretely established interactions; they are "correlational stereotypes."

16. See Arieti, p. 286ff.; Werner and Kaplan, p. 253ff.; and L. C. Wynne, "Denkstörung und Familienbeziehung bei Schizophrenen," *Psyche*, May 1965, p. 82ff.

17. Arieti, p. 327ff.

18. See *Erkenntnis und Interesse*, p. 260ff.

19. On Gadamer's metacritique of my arguments against the ontological construction of hermeneutical consciousness in the Third Part of *Truth and Method* (*Zur Logik der Sozialwissenschaften,*, pp. 172–80), see, more recently, C[laus] v. Bormann, "Die Zweideutigkeit der hermeneutischen Erfahrung," *Philosophische Rundschau* 16 (1969): 92ff.

20. Gadamer, "Die Universalität des hermeneutischen Problems," *Kleine Schriften*, I, p. 104.

21. A[lbrecht] Wellmer, *Kritische Gesellschaftstheorie und Positivismus* (Frankfurt am Main, 1969), p. 48f. [*Critical Theory of Society,* trans. John Cumming (New York, 1971).]

22. K.-O. Apel, "Szientismus oder transzendentale Hermeneutik?" in *Hermeneutik und Dialektik*, ed. Rüdiger Bubner et al (Tübingen, 1970), p. 105.

23. G. H. Mead, *Mind, Self, Society* (Chicago, 1934), p. 327.

24. *Zur Logik der Sozialwissenschaften*, p. 174ff.

25. See the Introduction to the author's *Protestbewegung und Hochschulreform* (Frankfurt, 1969), p. 43n.6.

# 11

# Perspectives for a
# General Hermeneutic Theory

## ══════════════ Karl-Otto Apel ══════════════

KARL-OTTO APEL (b. 1922) was born in Düsseldorf and studied at the University of Bonn
where he received a doctorate in 1950. He obtained his second degree (*Habilitation*) in
Mainz in 1961 and subsequently became professor of philosophy at Kiel (1962-69). From
1969 to 1972 he taught at Saarbrücken. He has been holding a chair for philosophy at the
University of Frankfurt since 1972. In his work Apel first combined the historical-
philosophical traditions of Dilthey and his teacher Rothacker with a phenomenological
orientation derived from Husserl and Heidegger. His field of interest include the philosophy and history of science and the humanities, the history of thought, hermeneutics,
social theory, linguistics, and the philosophy of language. Over the years he became
increasingly interested in bridging the gulf between the Continental and the Anglo-Saxon
approaches to philosophy. Many of his works can be seen as an effort to mediate between
the hermeneutic-humanistic and the analytical-empiricist outlooks. He was one of the first
writers to point out and to investigate in detail the affinities between ordinary language
philosophy—notably of the late Wittgenstein—and the hermeneutic tradition on the Continent. The following essay was first published in 1968 and summarizes Apel's long standing
occupation with hermeneutic philosophy and the methodology of the human and social
sciences. He argues for the development of what he terms an anthropological-
epistemological basis for all theory formation. In contradistinction to Gadamer, Apel is
keenly interested in going beyond transcendental analysis and critique and in exploring and
clarifying practical methodological issues. Hermeneutics is always a part of existing
systems of knowledge and cannot be divorced from them, except for theoretical considerations. Apel does not subscribe to the notion of the mutually exclusive character of the
scientific and the hermeneutic attitudes, but instead believes in their complimentary nature.
Both the sciences of nature and the sciences of man and society arise from the common
ground of a shared a priori which Apel identifies as the linguistic (or speech) community
of communication.

# Scientistics, Hermeneutics, Critique of Ideology: An Outline of a Theory of Science from an Epistemological-Anthropological Point of View

*Introduction: The epistemological-anthropological inquiry*
The following study is conceived of as a programmatic sketch. If one compares its title with its subtitle, it becomes apparent that the notion "science" [*Wissenschaft*] in "theory of science" [*Wissenschaftslehre*] is obviously intended to be broader than the notion "science" [*scientia*] (= "science" in English or French) which is contained in "scientistics" [*Szientistik*], since the proposed "theory of science" is intended to comprise not only "scientistics" but also "hermeneutics" and the "critique of ideology." Indeed, in the following sketch the attempt is made to demonstrate the possibility of a conception with respect to the theory of science which is at least methodologically relevant and which nonetheless is not restricted to the "logic of science."

The basis for the postulated extension of the notion of science is to be provided by an extension of traditional "epistemology" in favor of an "epistemological anthropology." By an "epistemological anthropology" I mean an approach which extends the Kantian inquiry into the "conditions of the possibility" of knowledge: so that not only are conditions indicated for an objectively valid, unified idea of the world for a "consciousness as such," but also all conditions which make a scientific inquiry possible as a meaningful one.

The meaning of the inquiry of physics, for example, cannot, in my opinion, be made comprehensible by recourse to "unifying" (synthetic) functions of consciousness ("categories") alone. Both a linguistic "agreement" among scientists on the understanding of the meaning of nature and the possibility of a realization of the inquiry through an instrumental intervention into nature are also presupposed. In this instrumental intervention into nature, which is an a priori presupposition of every experiment, the bodily world-engagement through the sense organs, itself already presupposed in prescientific experience, is made precise: man's "measuring of himself" "with" nature becomes the "measurement" of experimental science. Thus, for example, the prescientific notion of "heat" corresponds to the organism's "measuring of itself" with its surroundings; the notion "temperature," on the other hand, corresponds to the instrumentally precise "measurement intervention" of the thermometer and the scientific language game which has its "paradigm" in the thermometer.[1] Modern scientists have not only approached nature with an a priori schema of regular processes in thought (i.e., in the temporally and spatially schematizing imagination), as Kant had already noted, but have also placed this schema into a real relation with nature in the form of an instrumental apparatus, i.e., as an artificial nature. Only by means of this technological intervention, which translated the human inquiry into the language of nature, so to speak, were scientists able, to use Kant's words, "to compel nature to answer their questions."[2] The fact that this is a condition of the possibility of physical knowledge which is a necessary complement to the categorical synthesis as a function of the understanding and which constitutes an integral moment of the physicalist language game was made particularly clear, in my opinion, by Einstein's semantic revolution in the definition of the fundamental concepts of physics. As a consequence, the meaning of "simultaneity," for example, had to be so defined as to take into account the technological-material conditions of the measurement of simultaneity. Natural constants such as the speed of light therefore belong to the "paradigms" of the language game of the theory of relativity; one speaks of "material" or "physical conditions of the possibility of experience."[3]

On the one hand, the conditions of the possibility and validity of knowledge indicated above cannot be deduced from the logical functions of consciousness alone; on the other hand, they can also not be attributed to the object of knowledge under investigation, since they are already presupposed by all knowledge of objects. The Cartesian subject-object relation is not sufficient for the foundation of an epistemological anthropology: a pure consciousness of objects, taken in itself, is not able to extract meaning from the world. In order to achieve a meaning-constitution, consciousness, which is in its essence "eccentric,"[4] must engage itself centrically, i.e., bodily, in the here and now. Every meaning-constitution refers back to an individual perspective, which corresponds to a standpoint, and, that is to say, to a bodily engagement of the cognitive consciousness.

But, surprisingly enough, not only is each particular individual constitution of possible meaning mediated by an actual engagement of the cognitive consciousness, but also the intersubjective validity of each meaning-constitution.

That is to say, it is only through linguistic signs that my meaning intentions are mediated with the possible meaning intentions of others in such a way that I can really "mean" something. In other words, I have valid meaning intentions only because a language exists in which not only my own meaning intentions are secured. This agreement with others on possible meaning intentions, which to a certain degree has always been achieved in the "meanings" of language, is a condition of the possibility of the unification of empirical data in the Kantian "synthesis of apperception"; in addition, however, it opens up an empirical dimension of its own.

Namely, from an epistemological-anthropological point of view, linguistic signs no more belong to the objects of knowledge than do the sense organs or the technological instruments by means of which the sense organs are able to intervene into external nature, since signs too, as a condition of the possibility of all meaning intentions, are themselves presupposed in order that objects of knowledge may be constituted. Nor, on the other hand, can language, as a sign medium, be reduced to the logical conditions of consciousness for knowledge. Rather, language too, like the material-technological intervention that belongs to the presuppositions of experimental natural science, refers back to a particular subjective a priori which had not been taken into consideration in traditional Cartesian epistemology. I would like to call it the "bodily a priori" of knowledge.[5]

The bodily a priori of knowledge, as it appears to me, stands in a complementary relationship with the a priori of consciousness, i.e., both conditions of the possibility of knowledge necessarily supplement one another in the totality of knowledge, but in the actual process of cognition either the *bodily a priori* or the a priori of consciousness takes precedence: "knowledge through reflection: and "knowledge through engagement" are diametrically opposed. For example, I cannot extract a significant aspect from the world and at the same time reflect upon the standpoint that I must take in doing so. All experience—including even the theoretically guided, experimental experience of natural science—is primarily knowledge through bodily engagement; all theory formation is primarily knowledge through reflection.[6]

Now, insofar as an epistemological anthropology regards man's bodily engagement as a necessary condition of all knowledge, it can and must, in my opinion, elevate still another condition of knowledge to the status of an a priori: namely, a particular *cognitive interest* corresponds to the manner of the bodily engagement of our knowledge.[7] Thus, for example, a technological cognitive interest corresponds a priori to the experimental engagement of modern physics.

This is not to say that psychologically ascertainable motives of technological utility belong to the conditions of the possibility and the validity of scientific theory formation. Such motives are doubtless by no means characteristic of the subjective mentality of the major theoretical scientists. The inquiry into such motives, however, in my opinion, completely misses the problem of the a priori valid interconnection of technology and science and thus the question of the necessary interest which makes this particular type of knowledge possible in the first place. This interest appears to me to lie solely in the prior linkage of the inquiry of modern physics to the possibility of operational verification which it presupposes in principle. This linkage corresponds to the bodily a priori of modern physics that lies in the presupposition of an instrumental intervention through which the inquiry of man can be brought to bear upon nature. The modern scientist *must* be guided by a technological interest in the sense of this a priori linkage of his inquiry to instrumental verification. It is this supra-individual, quasi-objective linkage which differentiates his cognitive interest from that of the philosophy of nature of the Greeks and the Renaissance, and, in turn, from that of Goethe and the Romantics. And it is above all this methodically relevant interest which distinguishes the whole of the exact sciences from the essentially different practical interest and world engagement which lies at the basis of the so-called "cultural sciences."[8]

With this I come to the main topic of my lecture. Presupposing the epistemological-anthropological categories outlined above, I would like to take up once again the old controversy of the relationship between the natural sciences and the cultural sciences—a problem which has recently become even more complicated by the development of the "behavioral" sciences—and, if possible, bring it nearer to a resolution. The solution which I have in mind is expressed in the trichotomy of the title: "scientistics," "hermeneutics," "critique of ideology." It is to be shown that the various methodical approaches of the currently practiced empirical sciences can be defined and related to one another within the framework of this methodological trichotomy. My argumentation takes two parts: the first and more comprehensive part is concerned with the assertion of a complementarity between "scientistics" and "hermeneutics" (in other words, between the natural sciences based on explanation and the cultural sciences based on understanding). This complementarity-thesis is critically directed against the idea of a "unified science." The second part is concerned with a dialectical mediation of "explanation" and "understanding" in the approach of the critique of ideology.

I. *The complementary relationship of scientism and hermeneutics (Critique of the idea of a unified science)*

Whoever currently advocates a theory of science which presupposes a priori differentiated cognitive interests must take issue with the opposing presuppositions of the positivist or neopositivist thesis of "unified science."[9] It is essential first to analyze these presuppositions from an epistemological-anthropological point of view.

If one compares the neopositivist theory of science which is dominant today with Kant's epistemology, it becomes apparent that the inquiry into the conditions of the possibility of knowledge is not expanded, as in the epistemological anthropology which I proposed, but rather, on the contrary, reduced as much as possible. While Kant regarded a "transcendental logic," whose particular problem was the constitution of experience through a "categorical synthesis," as necessary for the philosophical clarification of the conditions of the possibility of experience, neopositivism believes that it can make do with formal logic in its expanded and mathematically precise form and, with its help, deduce all knowledge from "the" empirical data. The problem of a synthetic constitution of the empirical data itself is not supposed to be of any consequence, at least not in the consistent form of a neopositivistically conceived "logic of knowledge."[10]

The resulting reduction of the inquiry into the presuppositions of knowledge becomes fully clear only when we bear in mind the fact that our epistemological anthropology, in following Kant, had made the constitution of the empirical data itself dependent not only on the synthetic function of the human understanding as such, but also on an engaged world-understanding, i.e., on a *meaning-constitutive cognitive interest.*

Neopositivism, on the other hand, would like to eliminate the question of cognitive interest, like the question of evaluation, at least from the problems of the foundations of the logic of science. It would like to see in these questions secondary problems of cognitive psychology or the sociology of knowledge, i.e., questions which can be thematized as purely factual problems by interest-free, purely theoretical thematizations of facts, cognitive operations which obey fundamentally the same methodology, the unified "logic of science."

Proceeding from these assumptions, neopositivism is inclined to see in the so-called "transcendental" conditions of knowledge, insofar as these are made responsible for a dissimilar constitution of empirical data in different sciences, an ideological mixture of theoretical insights and unacknowledged practical objectives. As far as the theoretical insights are concerned, these are considered to belong to empirical psychology or sociology, as already indicated. As for the practical objectives, they are to be subject to a critique of ideology, which itself, as a component of a unified science, is supposed to be free from practical interests.

The presuppositions of the idea of a "unified science" just indicated can be illustrated by the way in which neopositivism judges the distinction attempted by Dilthey and others between the natural sciences based on "causal explanation" and the cultural sciences based on the "understanding of meaning."[11]

To the extent that this distinction lays claim to an epistemological status, it is declared by the neopositivists to be ideologically suspect metaphysics, according, say, to the following pattern. The title "cultural sciences" from within and a merely external "explaining" reveal that here certain objective domains (of human life) are to be withdrawn from the impartial grasp of explanatory science ("science" itself) and made into the preserves of a secularized theology of the spirit (as derived from Hegel or Schleiermacher).

In spite of this, however, according to neopositivism there is a correct psychological finding in the distinction between "explaining" and "understanding." We are able to "internalize" certain causal relations between events of the outer world—to experience them from within as it were—namely, those which are known as stimulus and response in the behavior of organisms: for example, a fearful man's flight in the face of a hostile attack or a threatening natural event, or an angry man's attack in the same situation, a freezing man's search for warmth, a hungry man's search for food, and the like. We are familiar with such behavioral responses from within to some extent and, on their basis, with more complex ones too, and we are therefore accustomed to interpolating them automatically into our mental construction of events of the outer world.

The following example is from T. Abel,[12] who, in his essay "The Operation called 'Verstehen,'" has analyzed understanding in the light of the theory of science of neopositivism.

If I see, for example, that upon a sudden drop in temperature my neighbor rises from his desk, chops wood, and lights a fire in his fireplace, then I automatically interpolate that he has been feeling chilly and seeks to bring about a condition through which he will get warm. Such "interpolation," Abel maintains, is called "understanding." However, according to him this by no means provides us with a particular scientific method which could logically be distinguished from that of causal explanation according to laws, since the logical point of empathic understanding consists in the fact that through the "internalization" of the observed behavior we arrive at the representation of a "behavior maxim," which exactly corresponds to a "hypothesis" for a possible causal explanation of the behavior. If the hypothesis set up in this way can be objectively verified, then we do in fact have an "explanation." The difference between "understanding" and "explaining" thus consists in the fact that "understanding" is equivalent to only one aspect of the *logical* operation of explaining: the setting up of a hypothesis. However, according to the view of the neopositivist "logic of science," this heuristic aspect does not constitute the scientific character of the operation of explanation, since, taken in itself, it cannot be justified logically, but rather at best only psychologically. The psychological feeling of certainty which may accompany the finding of behavior maxims in the process of understanding corresponds logically only to the *possible* correctness of a hypothesis. Only the deduction of verifiable test implications from the hypothesis, thus to a certain extent a prognostic testing, constitutes the scientific character of an "explanation." Thus, Abel concludes in agreement with the theory of explanation of Hempel and Oppenheim,[13] the "understanding" of the so-called "cultural sciences" remains on the perimeters of science; it is irrelevant for the "logic of science."

What then is to be said from an epistemological-anthropological point of view to this reduction of understanding and, with it, of the so-called "cultural sciences" to a prescientific heuristics in the service of explanatory sciences, of "science" itself?

First of all, we could point skeptically to the difficulties of the neopositivist conception which have been demonstrated in recent decades by the advocates of a unified "logic of science" themselves. Among these, for example, is the observation that a historian's obtaining an explanatory hypothesis with the help of understanding cannot by its very nature be conceived of as a subsumption of events or states of affairs under general laws, nor confirmed like one.

This is the result reached in 1957 by William Dray,[14] when he examined the thesis of Karl Popper that the "individualizing," historical sciences differ from the "generalizing," natural sciences not in their logic of explanation, but rather simply psychologically—namely, in that they are primarily interested not in the setting up of general hypotheses, but in the specific initial- or boundary-conditions, which, in conjunction with the assumption of certain trivial laws, can be introduced as causes for particular events.[15] Dray asserts, in opposition to this view, that historical explanations do not fulfill the condition of subsumption under general laws for certain fundamental reasons and offers the following example. A historian could perhaps explain the unpopularity of Louis XIV at the time before his death by stating that the king pursued policies detrimental to the French national interests. If this were a causal explanation in the sense of the "logic of science," then a logician would have to be able to explicitly formulate the general law which the historian implicitly assumed, such as: "Rulers who pursue policies detrimental to their subjects' interest become unpopular."

The historian in the meantime might object that this supposition was incorrect, and he might also object to any attempt at the specification of a hypothesis as unsatisfactory, with the exception perhaps of the following formulation: "Any ruler pursing policies and in circumstances exactly like those of Louis XIV would become unpopular."

This statement—which does not deduce the particular explanandum from a general explanans, but rather has recourse to a particular in the explanans itself— is not, however, from a logical point of view, a general hypothesis at all, but rather only the formal assertion of the necessity of a particular event, lacking any explanatory value.

It thus becomes apparent that the historian's explanation cannot in any case be regarded as a *deductive-nomological* explanation. Nor, however, can it be regarded as an *inductive-nomological* explanation, which derives from laws only the statistical probability of an event-type, since such an explanation of the "empirical social sciences" in principle falls short of the historian's claim of explaining the "necessity" of a particular event. On what then is the specifically *historical explanation* of its plausibility based? Dray offers the following points for consideration. A historical explanation does establish a relationship between an event and necessary conditions for the occurrence of that event. But these conditions (1) are not sufficient conditions for the prognosis of the event; (2) hold as necessary conditions only within the context of a given total situation.

What lies behind these qualifications?

Ad 1:

That the conditions introduced by the historian are not sufficient for a prognosis stems in the end from the fact that all events which the historian "explains" are mediated in their *constitution* by the intentions of the acting individuals. To this extent, conditions for these events are not "causes," but rather "rationales" of actions. As such, however, they must be "understood" by the historian from the situation of the acting individuals; they cannot be treated in the logic of the explanation of events in the same way as causal conditions in the context of a prognosis on the basis of laws. Hypotheses can be falsified by negative instantiations, but behavior maxims, which refer to conditions in terms of rationales, cannot be falsified by facts.

With this we would admittedly again be in a position where T. Abel could object that insofar as understandable behavior maxims cannot be falsified by facts they have no explanatory value either, rather, they express merely a behavioral possibility.

Ad 2:

Here, however, Dray's other point helps us along. Historical explanations do disclose necessary conditions of events (actions), but only within the context of a given total situation.

This thesis does in fact provide an indication of the positive function of "understanding" as a decisive condition of the possibility of a so-called "historical explanation." This can best be made clear by contrasting it with Abel's theory of understanding.

In his analysis of understanding, Abel completely overlooked the problem of the hermeneutical connection between the human behavior which is to be understood and the preunderstanding of the world-data to which that behavior intentionally relates. The data appear to him to be given in more or less the same way as are events in the cognitive situation of the natural sciences; understanding then consists only in the interpolation of an internally experienced connection into the objectively explainable regular connection of facts. This analysis thus corresponds to a prelanguage-analytical theory of understanding,[16] a theory which fails to take into account the insight of the later Wittgenstein, according to which the empirical data themselves are constituted only within the context of a language game. Understanding is regarded here only as a psychologically relevant auxiliary function in the connection of data, not, however, as a condition of the possibility of the data itself. In contrast, a language-hermeneutical analysis would proceed from the fact that understandable human behavioral reactions, as language-related intentional formations, themselves possess the characteristic property of understanding, and it would have to conclude from this that the world-data within whose context the behavior which is to be understood occurs must itself be understood from the intentional understanding of precisely that behavior. The world is no longer the "being of things, insofar as they form a regular connection [in the sense of natural science]" (Kant), but rather the "total situation" of a certain "being-in-the-world" (Heidegger) in which we can participate through linguistic understanding.

This brings us back to Dray's answer to the question of the conditions of the possibility of a historical factual explanation which is not deducible from general laws. According to Dray, this derives its necessity from the consideration of a given total situation from which the antecedent conditions of the factual explanation must first be understood as possible reasons for intentional actions. How does such understanding occur de facto in the historical sciences? How do the historical sciences attain that pragmatically sufficient certainty which Dray allows to enter into the factual explanation as a situationally conditioned necessity?

Early hermeneutics (Schleiermacher, Droysen, Dilthey) spoke of the historian's having to project himself back into the total situation of the actions to be understood. This statement is true in a metaphorical sense. But how, to come back to Dray's example, does the historian project himself back into the total situation from which the French populace judged Louis XIV's policies shortly before his death? How are the facts of a past situation of human activity constituted for the historian in the first place?

In accordance with the presuppositions of the world-understanding of objective unified science, we would come to the following remarkable conclusion. From all of the events which actually occurred in the time preceding Louis XIV's death, the historian must select those which are relevant as conditions for the actions of Louis XIV's contemporaries. In actuality, however, the historian will not proceed in this way, since he neither knows "all the events which actually occurred" before the death of Louis XIV, nor can he find them out from anyone. They exist only in the metaphysics of positivism. That is to say, the natural sciences can infer only certain classes of events of the time of Louis XIV from their semantic world-understanding: for example, earthquakes, solar eclipses, and the like. In many cases, these can be related to specific constellations of human action which have been historically handed down. The natural sciences and the historical sciences are able to work together in the dating of so-called prehistoric finds, for example.

The historian, however, obtains his primary orientation regarding events of the past from a different "language game" than does the scientist, to use Wittgenstein's term. It is a language game which has already been played before the actually scientific language game of the historian: that of the transmission of culture, or, better still, that of a particular, itself historically thematizable transmission of culture. The historian's scientific language game then consists in a critical examination and supplementation of this primary transmission. Because of this, however, he is fundamentally dependent on the credibility of linguistic transmission—for example, narratives of events which have been handed down in oral or written form. In order to examine these narratives in detail (through so-called source criticism) he must however presuppose them in principle as a medium of communication with a former human "being-in-the-world." It is from the situational horizon of these transmitted "histories," which he understands from the situational horizon of "the" history within which he himself belongs,[17] that the historian actually obtains the "data" which are relevant in terms of antecedent conditions for a "historical explanation" of events. The plausible connection of these data with the event to be explained at a given time consists then in a new narration of a history in which as many events as possible, mediated by the situational relationships of the persons involved, are related to one another.[18]

Thus the process of the hermeneutically mediated recollection of events and their relations can in principle no more be brought to a conclusion than the process of the verification of scientific hypotheses; but, like the latter, it attains a pragmatically sufficient validity within a given research situation.

It appears to me that it is from this perspective that the result reached by W. Dray in his analysis of an example of a historical explanation best becomes comprehensible. Dray writes: "The force of the explanation of Louis XIV's unpopularity in terms of his policies being detrimental to French interests is very likely to be found in the detailed description of the aspirations, beliefs, and the problems of Louis's subjects. Given these men and their situation, Louis and his policies, their dislike of the king was an appropriate response."[19]

The distinction reached by Dray between a logic of "historical explanation," based on the explication of situations of action, and a logic of scientific explanation, which deduces from hypotheses, however, is still not able to properly illuminate the difference and the complementary relationship between the natural sciences and the cultural sciences, between scientific and hermeneutical method. Political history is really not the proper place to make fully clear the epistemological-anthropological meaning of hermeneutical presuppositions which we indicated, is still primarily a science which explains facts and objectifies events in a temporal framework. The "understanding" of meaning still functions here as an aid in the explanation of the fact that certain events have occurred as a consequence of other events, whether or not this objective connection, in contrast to the causal nexus of natural science, is mediated by the understanding of rationales, emotional dispositions, socially binding behavioral expectations, institutionalized values or individual objectives. (This makes it comprehensible why positivists have again and again equated the notion of the motive of an action with that of the cause of a process.[20] A motive, however, before it can be objectified as a cause, must first be understood in a completely different manner, in accordance with its meaning contents. The inquiry of political history does however display a certain undeniable analogy to the causal analysis of natural science in its a priori tie to the objectification of temporal events.)

In contrast, the genuinely hermeneutical inquiry, in my opinion, stands in a *complementary* relationship to the scientific objectification and explanation of events. Both inquiries are mutually exclusive and thereby supplement one another. This structural relationship can best be made clear if we take up the question of the linguistic conditions of the possibility and validity of natural science and think it through to its conclusion from the standpoint of an epistemological anthropology. A scientist cannot *by* himself explain something *for* himself alone.[21] In order even to know "what" he is to explain, he must already have come to an understanding with others on the matter. As C. S. Peirce recognized, a semiotic community of interpretation always corresponds to the community of experimentation of natural scientists.[22] Now, such an agreement on the intersubjective level can never be replaced by a procedure of objective science, precisely because it is a condition of the possibility of objective science; thus we encounter here an absolute limit to any program of objective-explanatory science. Linguistic agreement as to what one means and what one intends to do is *complementary* to objective science in the sense defined above.

We have now only to demonstrate that this intersubjective agreement, which cannot be replaced by any method of objective science, can nonetheless become a topic of scientific inquiry. In other words, it is to be demonstrated that not only the "descriptive" and "explanatory" sciences, operating under the assumption of the subject-object-relation, but also the "sciences of intersubjective understanding," operating under the assumption of the intersubjectivity-relation, are possible, indeed necessary. Their inquiry should then have a relation to the pre-scientific communication of man which is similar to that of causally explaining science to a so-called "working knowledge" (Scheler) as a preliminary stage. This is in fact the case. It appears to me that man has fundamentally two equally important, not identical, but rather *complementary* cognitive interests: (1) one which is determined by the necessity of a technological praxis on the basis of insight into natural laws; (2) one which is determined by the necessity of a morally relevant social praxis.

The latter is directed toward an agreement as to the possibility and the norms of a meaningful human being-in-the-world, which is also presupposed by technological praxis. This interest in coming to an understanding on meaning relates not only to communication among contemporaries but also to communication of the living with past generations in the form of the mediation of tradition.[23] Indeed, it is only by means of this communicative mediation of tradition that man attains the accumulation of technological knowledge and the deepening and enrichment of his knowledge of possible *meaning-motivations* which gives him his superiority over animals.

The process of the communication of tradition, above all when it encounters a crisis, is in fact the epistemological-anthropological locus in which the so-called hermeneutical sciences can arise and have actually arisen in advanced European and Asian civilizations. Their core is formed by the "philologies," in the broadest sense of the word, i.e., including literary studies. These sciences must not be regarded as mere auxiliary sciences of history—as often happens in objectivistic theories of science—as if the interpretation of texts of the transmission of culture were meant only to provide information on events of the past. The "classical" or canonical texts of the transmission of culture (religious, philosophical, poetic, legal literary documents) are not primarily "sources" for the historian which the philologist is merely to edit. The "philologies" are rather the true hermeneutical cultural sciences in that they are primarily concerned not with processes in time and space, but with the "interpretation" of "meaning," which only has its vehicle, its conditio sine qua non, in such spatio-temporal events.[24]

The "bodily a priori" of knowledge (p. 323 above) reveals itself in the problems of the foundations of the hermeneutical cultural sciences not as the presupposition of an instrumental intervention into nature, but as the dependence of the intersubjective manifestation of meaning on an "expression" which is perceptible to the sense: in linguistic, for example, as the phonologically thematizable articulation of possible meaning in the speech sound. This physical expression of intersubjectively communicable meaning can, of course, in the limiting case, say in a formal language, become an inflexible "semiotic instrument." Once language does become a pure "semiotic instrument," the understanding of meaning is no longer dependent on the individual interpretation of the physical expression, but rather only on the participation in the conventional establishment of the (syntactic and semantic) rules of a semiotic system. But even here the semiotic instrument still serves as a vehicle for the "understanding of meaning"; it is the result which is fixed in its form through a prior agreement within the "community of interpretation," a community to which the architects of formal languages must also belong.

This much for the first main thesis toward a theory of science which does not proceed as is usual from the subject-object-relation as the sole presupposition and dimension of thematization of human knowledge. In the final analysis, the above assertion of a *complementarity* of the scientific and the hermeneutical sciences proceeds from the fact that the existence of a community of communication is a presupposition for all knowledge in the subject-object dimension and that the function of this community of communication— as an intersubjective metadimension for the objective description and explanation of world-data— can and must become the topic of scientific knowledge.

The American Hegelian J. Royce formulated this insight as follows, in reference to the founder of pragmatism, C. S. Peirce. Man must not only "perceive" sense data and "conceive" ideas in his interchange with nature; he must also "intercept" ideas in a constant interchange with the other members of a historical "community." In the case of the verification of opinions, for example, a determination of the "cash value" of ideas by means of experimental operations leading to perceptions of sense data is not sufficient; rather, the "nominal value" of the ideas which are to be verified must first be determined by means of "interpretation." In this process A makes clear to B what C means, in a fundamentally triadic relation. The same holds true for so-called solitary thought, in which I (A) must make clear to myself (B) what my present idea, opinion, intention (C) means. This triadic mediation-process of interpretation guarantees the historical continuity of knowledge insofar as A represents the present which communicates to the future (B) the meaning or opinion of the past (C).[25]

The essential problem of the philosophical foundation of hermeneutics, i.e., the theory of the scientific interpretation of meaning (which is intended or at least expressed) can, in my opinion, be formulated with the following question: is there a *methodical abstraction* by means of which a scientific thematization of intended or expressed meaning becomes possible on the level of intersubjective understanding?

The philosophical founders of hermeneutics in the nineteenth century (Schleiermacher and Dilthey) answered this question in the affirmative and replied to the following effect. A progressive, universally valid objectivation of meaning is possible by an abstraction from the question of the truth or the normative claim of the meaning utterances which are to be understood, e.g., the transmitted texts. It is here that the similarities between the cultural sciences based upon understanding and the likewise objective and progressive natural sciences are said to lie. Thus, according to their theoretical intentions, the normatively nonbinding, but scientifically universally valid understanding of the hermeneutical "sciences of the human spirit" takes the place of the normatively binding understanding of the prescientific process of the communication of tradition.

If the practical (existential) consequences of this conception are taken seriously, it leads to the problem of nihilistic "historicism," which Dilthey himself had clearly recognized and which the writer Robert Musil, in reference to the thought of Nietzsche, later brought under the heading "The Man without Qualities."[26] Indeed, a man who had scientifically objectified all binding truths and norms and had gathered them all together into the simultaneity of an "imaginary museum" of merely passively understood meaning would be like a being who was incapable of gaining any qualities, a pure "man of possibility," as Musil also says, a man who would be unable to actualize his life. He would have lost all ties to tradition and it would have been the historical-hermeneutical sciences themselves which would have reduced him to just this ahistorical state. They themselves—i.e., their neutralizing objectivation of binding norms and truths—would have taken the place of effective tradition and, thus, of history itself.[27]

In recent times, it has been H.-G. Gadamer in particular, who, proceeding from Heidegger's hermeneutics of existence and, like Heidegger himself, from Dilthey's life-philosophical approach (i.e., not from his objectivist-historicist approach), has questioned the presuppositions of the historicist foundations of the cultural sciences.[28] Gadamer disputes the meaningfulness and the possibility of a methodical-progressive objectivation of meaning in the hermeneutical sciences which leads to the weakening of the force of historical tradition. He sees in this idea a seduction by the scientific methodical ideal which even Dilthey had failed to recognize. And he goes so far as to make the revocation of all methodical abstractions a precondition of the philosophical analysis of meaning in the hermeneutical sciences. According to Gadamer, hermeneutical understanding cannot disregard the decision of the normative question or the question of truth, as Schleiermacher had demanded; whether it wants to or not, it must include an "application" to the practical life-situation, hence a historical-existential engagement, as a condition of its possibility and validity. As a model for a philosophical analysis of the integral function of understanding, Gadamer recommends the applied understanding of written law by a judge or of a drama by its director. Here understanding does not dissolve the binding force of tradition, but rather mediates it with the present. According to Gadamer this is *also* the task of the historical-hermeneutical sciences: he equates the model of the competent interpreter, with whom the cultural scientist might identify, in its essential hermeneutical structural features with the model of the director or the judge.

In my opinion, however, one cannot regard the issue of a historicist or an existential-hermeneutical foundation of meaning in the cultural sciences simply as a choice between alternatives.

It appears to me that the strong point of Gadamer's "philosophical hermeneutics" lies in its critique of the objectivistic methodical ideals of historicism, but that he goes too far when he disputes the meaningfulness of a methodical-hermeneutical abstraction from the question of truth and equates the model of the judge or the director with that of the interpreter. In my opinion, Gadamer is correct in pointing out that the historicity of the interpreter belongs to the conditions of the possibility of understanding in the cultural sciences, that it is not a Cartesian or Kantian subject or consciousness as such which makes the world progressively accessible as an objective construction, but rather that the present being-in-the-world must understand itself in its possibilities from the tradition which is to be assimilated. To this extent the conception of a weakening of the force of historical tradition through the "imaginary museum" of meaning objectified in the cultural sciences is an illusion. Its dubiousness lies in the fact that the cultural scientist conceals or suppresses the inevitable dependence of his understanding on his own historical engagement and thus, instead of helping to bring about the desired dedogmatization of the understanding of meaning, only contributes to its ideologization.

Nevertheless, it appears to me that a scientific understanding of meaning in the sense of philological hermeneutics—like any procedure of a single science—presupposes a *methodical abstraction*. This methodical abstraction is already present in the prescientific domain in the situation of the interpreter. The function of the interpreter, as it results from the division of labor within the process of the communication of meaning in real life situations, is itself completely different from that of the director or even the judge. The methodical interpretative work of the historian of law is also completely different from that of the judge, even if they both clearly do not serve the objective neutralization of the meaning of law in an "imaginary museum" but are both indeed rightly integrated by Gadamer into the process of the practically applied communication of tradition. One would certainly have to admit that membership in a historical situation of life-praxis is also presupposed by the scientific interpreter of texts as a condition of the possibility of his understanding. To this extent, not only reflective detachment but also prereflective engagement belong to hermeneutical understanding. Even the prereflective engagement of the scientific interpreter, however, is essentially different from that of the director or the judge.

The concern of the director, and even more so that of the judge, lies primarily in the application of understanding to the situation in which he is involved. In his creative interpretation he will therefore have to assume responsibility for the truth or normative binding force of the meaning which is to be understood to a much higher degree than, say, a historian of law who interprets the canonical texts of Roman law. The primary concern of the historian of law is the meaning of a text which is difficult to understand in its original intention; and in this already lies an abstraction from the question of normative binding force. This question is delegated to the practitioner of law, who, in the division of labor within the process of the communication of tradition, has assumed the function of the "application" of understanding. The historian of law would certainly not presume that by linguistic and historical studies he could make himself contemporaneous with the public of the texts of the *corpus juris,* as Schleiermacher had demanded as a condition of the final identification with the author; but he would be even less likely to renounce Schleiermacher's hermeneutic ideal in favor of a conscious actualization of understanding.[29] Gadamer correctly demands of the interpreter of texts that he follow the effective history of the text, which essentially co-constitutes his own historical situation and thus also the conditions of the possibility of his understanding. But in the case of the scientific interpreter, this following of the effective history through an interval of time would not take place in the interest of the application of understanding, but rather in the interest of Schleiermacher's methodical ideal of making oneself contemporaneous with that which is to be understood.

This sheds new light on the question (which has been disputed since Nietzsche's "untimely" meditation, "On the Use and Abuse of History") of whether historical understanding can lead to the weakening of the force of history as an effective process of the communication of tradition. We have already denied this possibility above (with Gadamer) in the sense that the cultural scientist cannot presume to be able to take a neutral standpoint outside of history. To this extent, the force of history as a means for the communication of tradition exists in the age of historicism as it did before. On the other hand, the element of truth which lies in the talk of the weakening of the force of tradition through historical understanding must not be overlooked. This is admittedly not a matter of the weakening of the force of history as a process of the weakening of the communication of tradition per se, but rather of the historical process of the weakening of the force of certain particular "traditions" (in terms of contents) of the preindustrial or prescientific age.[30] It is in this revolutionary crisis, a crisis which is much more sharply noticeable for the non-European cultures of the twentieth century than for nineteenth-century Europe, that the crux of the problem of nihilistic historicism lies. And this problem is nevertheless of such a concrete nature that it cannot be dismissed as a pseudoproblem by the formally correct demonstration on the part of existential analysis that hermeneutical understanding cannot divorce itself from the context of the historical process of the communication of tradition.

The process of the communication of tradition, without which man would indeed never be able to exist, must in fact assume a different form in our posthistorical age than in the time prior to the rise of the historical-hermeneutical cultural sciences. The immediacy of the dogmatic-normative (institutionally established and socially binding) "application" of the understanding of tradition— as it functioned up into the time of the Enlightenment in Europe and up into the present in most non-European cultures—cannot be restored. The process of the communication of tradition must become a complicated, scientifically mediated process once the objectification and distancing of the meaning which is to be understood are made possible through a hermeneutical abstraction from normative validity, even if these are only provisional. And in my opinion it is also an illusion to believe that the hermeneutical cultural sciences on their own could perform the function of the communication of tradition, a function which they themselves have necessarily made even more complicated, or that to do so they would only need to give up all positivistic self-understanding and consciously integrate themselves into the functional context of intercultural understanding, and, more particularly, into the process of the communication of tradition. The hermeneutical cultural sciences are in my opinion just as ideologically corrupted by the (existentialist or Marxist) demand for a binding application of their understanding as by the positivistic suppression of historical engagement as a condition of the possibility of their understanding of meaning. If there is to be a rational integration of the results of the hermeneutical sciences at all, if this is not to be left to art or existential self-understanding, then this task can be taken over only by philosophy, specifically, by the philosophy of history. The philosophy of history, however, cannot base itself solely on the historical-hermeneutical cultural sciences in the resolution of this problem. It must also draw upon a further large group of sciences and a methodical way of thought which is reducible neither to scientific nor to hermeneutical inquiry.

With this I come to the second thesis of my outline of a theory of science. Unfortunately, I can indicate the requisite considerations here only in the form of rough outlines and very speculative assertions.

II. *The philosophical resolution of the problem of historicism*
*through a dialectical mediation of objective-scientistic*
*and hermeneutical methods in the critique of ideology*

For an adequate philosophical assessment of the so-called problem of historicism it appears useful to me to choose as a reference point the situation of the non-European cultures rather than ours in the West. Those cultures which have had to adopt the technological-industrial form of life and its scientific bases from

Europe, and which still have to do so, are forced into a much more radical detachment and alienation from their traditions than we are. It would hardly occur to them to compensate for the break with the past by means of hermeneutical reflection alone. In addition to a hermeneutical reflection on their own traditions and on foreign traditions, they are faced from the start with the necessity of having to work out a quasiobjective system of reference based on a philosophy of history which will enable them to integrate their own position into the world-historical and human-planetary connection which was created without their doing by European-American civilization. Because of their inevitable alienation from their own traditions, they have also been made aware of the fact that intellectual meaning-interpretations of the world (such as religious-moral value systems, for example) must be understood in close connection with social forms of life (institutions). What they therefore are seeking above all is a philosophical-scientific orientation to mediate the hermeneutical understanding of their own tradition and foreign meaning-traditions through sociological analyses of past and current economic and social orders. It is primarily this situation which makes comprehensible the power of fascination which Marxism holds on the intellectuals of developing countries.

What lesson then can the theory of science learn from an illustration of the problem of historicism on the basis of the situation of the non-European cultures?

Let us first sketch the answer to this question in a speculative language, to which I would like to attribute at least a heuristic value. The spirit does not descend into time as such, as Hegel suggests in his system of historical idealism, but rather enters on the basis of a mediation with the natural history of man which continues in his social behavior. In other words, when Gadamer makes the "productivity of time" responsible for the fact that the guiding idea of classical hermeneutics must remain an illusion[31] — the idea of making oneself contemporaneous and finally identifying oneself with the author of the text which is to be understood— it appears to me that in all human life-utterances the obscure impact of what is not intended and what cannot yet be intended is to blame for this "productivity" which disturbs our understanding— i.e., the fact that for the time being nonunderstandable natural history still continues in understandable intellectual history.

If men were transparent to themselves in their motives of action or at least in the meaning-conceptions of their literary works, then the act of making oneself contemporaneous in understanding, the reciprocal identification of individual monads (Schleiermacher, in reference to Leibniz), the "elevated talk of the spirits" of all illustrious authors which succeeds in overcoming time (Petrarch, Bembo) would in principle be possible. In other words: if men were transparent to themselves in their intentions, then only two complementary cognitive interests would be justified: the scientific interest in the technologically relevant knowledge of nature, and the hermeneutical interest in the intersubjective agreement on the possible meaning-motivations of life. But up to now, neither have men "made" their socio-political history, nor are their so-called intellectual convictions, as they are set down in linguistic documents, a pure expression of their intellectual "intentions." All results of their intentions are, at the same time, the results of de facto life-forms which they have not as yet been able to incorporate into their self-understanding. It appears to me that efforts at hermeneutical identification, especially with authors of spatially and temporally distant cultures, are frustrated by this obscure intrusion of the natural history of man into human cultural history. For just this reason, all understanding, to the extent that it does succeed, has to understand an author better than he understands himself, in that it reflectively surpasses the author in his world- and self-understanding (in Hegel's sense) and does not merely reconstruct his spiritual experiences by reexperiencing them in his imagination (Schleiermacher, Dilthey). Such an understanding, however, not only has a limit in the finitude and the deficient self-transparency of the interpreter: it also encounters contradictions in the life-utterances which are to be understood, whether within the transmitted texts themselves or between these texts and the corresponding actions of their authors. These are contradictions which cannot be resolved by hermeneutical methods that make implicit meaning explicit, but which are dependent on the intermixture of sense and nonsense and intended actions and naturally determined reactions, and which therefore impose a limit upon "understanding." A philosophy of history which was conceived of merely as an integration of the hermeneutical "cultural sciences" would necessarily encounter here that which was actual but meaningless, or that which was contingent as the simply irrational. But precisely those actual and contingent factors of human history (including the history of ideas) which cannot as yet be eliminated in intersubjective understanding, because, as motives, they are not subjectively transparent but only effective in actuality, *can* be analyzed with the means of a quasiobjective explanatory science.

In every human dialogue there comes some point where one of the participants no longer attempts to take the other hermeneutically seriously in his intentions, but rather attempts to distance him objectively as a quasinatural event, a point where he no longer attempts to sustain the unity of language in communication, but rather attempts to evaluate what the other says as a symptom of an objective factual situation which he can explain from without in a language in which the partner does not participate. This partial suspension of hermeneutical communication in favor of objective cognitive methods is characteristic of the relationship of a physician to his patient, particularly that of a psychotherapist to a neurotic. In my opinion, this model of partially suspended communication can be made just as productive for the foundation of a theory of science as the positive model for conversation. That is to say, the philosopher of history who wishes to solve the problem of historicism must not only combine the hermeneutical function of the interpreter with an application to praxis in order to mediate tradition with the present, as Gadamer demands; he must also assume the objectively distancing cognitive attitude of the physician (or, better yet, that of the psychotherapist) toward the behavior and the meaning-claims of tradition and of his contemporaries. This is what he does in fact do when he draws upon not only the results of the hermeneutical methods of the so-called "cultural sciences," but also the objective structural analyses of the empirical social sciences for an explanation of, for example, interest-constellations in political history or the history of ideas which cannot be proved by literary means.

Here we are once again directed back to the problem of "historical explanation" in its curious intermediate position between hermeneutics and scientistics. We have already stressed above that political history, despite its dependence on the hermeneutical understanding of meaning intentions, explains events which have actually taken place in an objectifiable temporal order and is thus in a way analogous to natural science. In our earlier example of an "historical explanation," however, we presumed that the objective connection of events which the historian reaches is mediated by the understanding of the intentions of the people involved. This will always be the case whenever the historian takes people fully seriously as subjects of their actions and opinions: for example, when he seeks to answer the question of the causes of a war solely on the basis of remarks from the responsible politicians on their motives of action. The opposite case, however, is also conceivable: that the understanding of reasons for actions is methodically mediated by an analysis of objectively effective factors of which the responsible men of action were not at all conscious as meaning-motives. An analysis of this sort was accomplished for the clarification of the causes of World War I by Hallgarten's book on the world-economic situation of imperialism.[32] Here the official motivations of the politicians were ignored to a certain extent and the demonstrable needs of largescale industry interested in markets were set in their place as causal factors.

A more exact methodological analysis would of course show that the empirical investigations which aid the sociologically oriented historian in the quasiobjective determination of states of interest are far removed from resembling the methods of obtaining data in the natural sciences. Business reports, balance sheets, price lists, computations and the like are in the final analysis also understandable "texts" in which human intentions find their expression. Correspondingly, one could very easily demonstrate in the case of so-called social-psychological behavioral science that its statistical investigations can always be traced back to hermeneutical operations for the gathering of data, such as interviews, for example.[33] But the crucial point of the quasiscientific cognitive achievements of sociological and psychological behavioral science is completely missed by a demonstration of its constantly present hermeneutical presuppositions. In my opinion, this lies in the alienation of the traditional self-understanding of individuals and human communities through theory-formations which interpret human life-utterances in a language in which the original authors of these life-utterances cannot directly participate (and which they are also unable to translate into their own language by means of philological operations). Compared to hermeneutical understanding, which is fundamentally directed at the preservation, and indeed the deepening of communication, psychological and social-psychological behavioral analyses can function just like causal explanations according to laws which have been applied to the object from without. This is shown above all by the fact that they make possible a technological domination over their object, just like the prognostically relevant knowledge of natural science: for example, the manipulation of the employee by the manager versed in industrial psychology, of the consumer by the advertising expert, and of the voter by the politician schooled in public opinion polls.

At this point the theoretical self-understanding of the behavioral sciences does in fact become a morally relevant factor in history. If one were actually to assess the quasiobjective cognitive achievements of the behavioral sciences as the beginning of a universal science of man, as neopositivism has done, one would logically have to see their goal in the preservation and the expansion of the domination of man over man. This of course presupposes that human behavior will never become fully predictable, otherwise social engineers would no longer be able to put to use their knowledge of social domination. In any event, even the naive legitimation of the fragmentarily attainable knowledge of social control through the philosophical self-understanding of scientists can itself have dire practical consequences.

Fortunately, the "reaction" of human subjects to the results of behavioral explanation—a "reaction" which in the natural sciences is in principle impossible— shows that there must be a fundamental mistake in the scientistic self-understanding of the social-psychological sciences. Such "reactions," which counter behavioral "explanation" with a new type of behavior, also provide us with an indication of how the quasiobjective cognitive achievements of the behavioral sciences are to be meaningfully integrated into an (epistemological-anthropological) theory of science.

That is to say, the sole explanation of the fact that men are able to react to the causal-analytical explanation of their behavior with a new type of behavior lies in the insight that men can convert the language of the psychological-sociological "explanation" into the language of a deepened self-understanding which in turn alters their motivation structure and thus pulls the rug out from under the "explanation." This brings us back to the model of psychotherapy described above. In this remarkable cognitive model the two moments

(1) the objectively distanced behavioral "explanation," which presupposes a partial break in communication, and

(2) the subsequent "integration" [*Aufhebung*] of the "explanation" into a deepened self-understanding

are in fact dialectically mediated. With the help of psychoanalytical theory-formation:

(1) The physician recognizes the quasinatural, explainable, and even predictable mode of action of repressed meaning-motives. To this extent he makes the patient into an object.

(2) At the same time, however, he seeks to "neutralize" [*aufheben*] the explainable causal force insofar as he understands the meaning of the repressed motives and communicatively provokes the patient into using this interpretation of meaning to revise his autobiographical self-understanding.

As we have already indicated, the model of psychotherapy can be transferred to the relationship between the philosophy of history and the self-understanding of human society. (Indeed, a real connection could actually exist between the quasinatural causal processes of a particular social praxis and the neurotic symptoms of the individuals of that society. The inability (1) to deduce certain social behavioral patterns from causally effective needs and (2) to reconcile such needs with the meaning-traditions of society could further contribute to individuals' repression of the motives immanent in these needs.)

It appears to me that these considerations lead us to the methodological demand for a dialectical mediation of social-scientific "explanation" and historical-hermeneutical "understanding" of meaning-traditions according to the regulative principle of an *Aufhebung* of the irrational moments of our historical being. Social-scientific "explanations" should be founded here (and published) in such a way that they not give the knowing power over the unknowing, but rather so that they provide us all with a challenge to transform causally explainable behavioral patterns into understandable action by means of self-reflection. The technical term for this dialectical mediation of "understanding" and "explaining" is "critique of ideology." As a "psychoanalysis" of human social history and as a "psychotherapy" for the current crisis of human action, it appears to me to represent the only meaningful logical foundation and moral justification for the objectively explanatory sciences of man.[34]

Its guiding cognitive interest corresponds to the bodily a priori of a psychosomatic self-diagnosis and self-therapy of man. The regulative principle of this cognitive engagement would not be the liberation of the mind from the body or the cognitive abolition and transcendence (*Aufhebung*) of the material in the absolute idea, but rather the pure expression of the spiritual in the physical, the "humanization of nature" and the "naturalization of man."

## Notes

1. It is a central thought in the later Wittgenstein that fixed natural phenomena, as well as artificial measures, instruments, or even work procedures together with their material

conditions co-constitute the "depth-grammar" of a language game as "models" or "paradigms" and to such an extent also codetermine the so-called a priori valid "essential structure" of our world-understanding. Recently this idea has been made productive for an understanding of the history of science by T. S. Kuhn (*The Structure of Scientific Revolutions,* Chicago, 1962). Here, however, Kuhn terms precisely that which Wittgenstein designates by "language game" a "paradigm"—namely, the quasi-institutional unity of language usage, behavior (work procedures, instrumental technology) and world-understanding (theory formation) which has been interwoven in life-praxis. I would like to see an illustration of the epistemological-anthropological concretization of epistemology which I postulated in such a conception, a conception which, in the case of Kuhn, as similarly with Wittgenstein, represents a practical cognitive a priori established through a systematic practice. I have one reservation, however: it appears to me that Kuhn, like Wittgenstein, has underestimated the logical connection among the various "paradigms" or "language games," which, during the progress of natural science, has accentuated the cognitive a priori of eccentric, nonengaged reflection in the form of increasingly more comprehensive theory formations. On the complementarity of reflection and engagement see below.

2. Cf. Kant, *Critique of Pure Reason,* B. XII f. Kant himself implicitly suggests here the instrumental a priori which we postulated, and in his "Opus postumum" he again takes up the problem of a bodily a priori as a transcendental condition of physical experience, a problem which was skipped over in the "Critique of Reason." Cf. K. Hübner, "Leib und Erfahrung in Kants Opus Postumum" (*Zeitschrift für philosophische Forschung, 7,* 1953, p. 204ff.) Further, K. G. Hoppe, *Die Objektivität der besonderen Naturerkenntnis. Eine Untersuchung über das Opus postumum von Kant.* Diss. Kiel, 1966. [Editor's note: Actually, Kant (op. cit., p. xii) is referring to reason and not to scientists and says that "reason (*die Vernunft*) must compel nature to answer her questions" (Max Mueller's translation).]

3. Cf. P. Mittelstaedt, *Philosophische Probleme der modernen Physik,* Mannheim, 1963, p. 15 passim.

4. Cf. H. Plessner on the "eccentric positionality" of man in *Die Stufen des Organischen und der Mensch,* Berlin and Leipzig, 1928.

5. Cf. K.-O. Apel, "Das Leibapriori der Erkenntnis (eine Betrachtung im Anschluß an Leibnizens Monadenlehre)"; in *Archiv für Philosophie, 12,* 1963, pp. 152–72.

6. The characteristic nature and the absolute necessity of engaged knowledge have been worked out by E. Rothacker in his treatise *Die dogmatische Denkform in den Geisteswissenschaften und das Problem des Historismus* (Mainz/Wiesbaden, 1954). O. Becker in his book *Größe und Grenze der mathematischen Denkweise* (Freiburg/Munich, 1959) has elucidated the significance of eccentric reflection for the establishment of increasingly more comprehensive relativity or transformation theories by means of the law of "pythagorean necessity" (renunciation of intuitively significant knowledge in favor of mathematically abstract generality), p. 30ff.

7. Cf. J. Habermas, "Erkenntnis und Interesse," in *Merkur,* 1965, pp. 1139–43. Further, K.-O. Apel. "Die Entfaltung der sprachanalytischen Philosophie und das Problem der 'Geisteswissenschaften,'" in *Philosophische Jahrbücher, 72.* Jg., 1965, p. 255.

8. The thesis of *technological cognitive interest* by no means asserts that the *truth* -claim of scientific knowledge can be *instrumentally reduced*. In opposition to such a pragmatism in the manner of Nietzsche, James, and Dewey, and later taken up by M. Scheler, we must emphasize along with C.S. Peirce, that merely the possible *meaning* of experimental knowledge is opened up and delimited a priori through the verification-context of a technological praxis. In accordance with its *meaning, human* knowledge cannot be the knowledge of objects on the part of a "consciousness as such," but rather only the knowledge of a bodily engaged and practically interested being. It is in this, in my opinion, that the epistemological-anthropological radicalization and transformation of Kantian epistemology lies; we cannot meaningfully conceive of any knowledge other than one which is *meaningful for us* and thus to such an extent possibly *true*. Cf. my "Introduction" to C. S. Peirce, *Schriften* I and II, Frankfurt, 1967 and 1970, on the "meaning-critical" transformation of epistemology.

9. Cf. the work published in the journal *Erkenntnis* (1930–38) and continued in the United States in the *Journal of Unified Science* (1939) and in the *International Encyclopedia of Unified Science* (1938ff.).

10. Which of course has seldom been advocated since Popper's *Logic of Scientific Discovery*. Instead, the "language-analytical" approach of modern neopositivism, effective since the early Wittgenstein, has again focussed attention on the problem of a transcendental constitution of the meaning of the so-called "data" in terms of the problem of necessary linguistic conventions. Cf. K.-O. Apel, "Die Entfaltung der 'sprachanalytischen' Philosophie und das Problem der 'Geisteswissenschaften,'" in *Philosophische Jahrbücher*, 72, Jg., 1965, pp. 239–89.

11. My characterization of the positivist critique of ideology in such matters makes use of E. Topitsch, *Sozialphilosophie zwischen Ideologie und Wissenschaft* (Neuwied, 1961) as a point of departure.

12. In H. Feigel and M. Brodbeck, eds., *Readings in the Philosophy of Science,* New York, 1953, pp. 677–88.

13. In H. Feigl and M. Brodbeck, eds., op. cit., p. 319ff.

14. W. Dray, *Laws and Explanation in History,* Oxford, 1957.

15. Cf. K. R. Popper, *The Open Society and its Enemies*, Vol. II, 5th ed., London, 1966.

16. The theoretical reflection of the nineteenth century on the difference between the "natural sciences" and the "cultural sciences" was initially psychologically oriented, like the positivism of J. S. Mill to which it was reacting: i.e., one spoke of the "cultural sciences" as "understanding" life as an expression of the inner man, whereas the natural sciences were seen as "describing" the nonunderstandable "backdrop of life" (Dilthey) from without and "explaining" it according to laws which had been discovered inductively. Today, where the positivistic program of "unified science" occurs in a language-analytical formulation (so as not to appear as a metaphysical reductive theory), philosophical "hermeneutics" has every reason to likewise accept this new basis of argumentation. It can then refute the positivistic thesis of objective-analytical unified science from its own language-analytical presuppositions, without having recourse to the terminology of a metaphysics of the spirit (or of life). (Cf. K.-O. Apel in *Philosophische Jahrbücher*, op. cit.). The distinction between "objectivations of the spirit" (Hegel, Dilthey) which are understandable

from within, on the one hand, and "natural processes" which are explainable from without, on the other, can be replaced—or, concretized, if you will—by the distinction between those "objects" with which the investigator can enter into linguistic communication and those with which no such communication is possible. He must thematize the latter, as data, from the linguistic preconception of theories which have been applied from without; the former confront him together with the data of their situational world from a linguistic world-understanding to which they themselves, as communication partners, contribute. The behavioral explanations applied to "mute" objects can only be verified through observations; hermeneutical "hypotheses" of understanding, on the other hand, are verified primarily through the answers of the communication partner. Even "texts" can "answer." It is interesting to note in this connection that N. Chomsky, the founder of so-called "generative" or "transformational" grammar, has shown that even a language usage which appears to be easily objectifiable as an anonymous-subconscious group behavior cannot be described without an understanding communication with a "competent speaker." It is not possible to decide whether someone is "speaking" at all or according to which rules he proceeds solely on the basis of external observations, as, for example, on the basis of statistical distributional criteria, as the behavioristically oriented Bloomfield school assumed. See Chomsky's articles in J. A. Fodor and J. J. Katz, eds., *The Structure of Language,* Englewood Cliffs, New Jersey, 1964. An answer to the question posed by Wittgenstein as to how one can decide if someone is following a rule leads to a similar result. Cf. P. Winch, *The Idea of a Social Science and its Relation to Philosophy,* London, 4th ed., 1965. On Chomsky and Winch, cf. also J. Habermas, *Zur Logik der Sozialwissenschaften,* Tübingen, 1967 (5th enlarged ed. Frankfurt am Main, 1982).

17."History as such" would be a senseless ontological hypostatization according to Heidegger and Wittgenstein. There is only "our particular" history!

18. In his *Analytical Philosophy of History* (Cambridge, 1965), A. C. Danto differentiates in this sense between historical explanations as "narrative explanations" and the deductive explanations of natural science. The phenomenologist W. Schapp *(In Geschichten verstrickt. Zum Sein von Mensch und Ding,* Hamburg, 1953) had earlier developed a similar approach. H. Lübbe in his essay "Sprachspiele und Geschichten" *(Kantstudien,* Vol. 52, 1960/61) previously compared this phenomenological-hermeneutical approach with the "analytical philosophy" proceeding from Wittgenstein.

19. Dray, op. cit., p. 134.

20. Cf., for example, Stegmüller, *Hauptströmungen der Gegenwartsphilosophie,* 3rd ed., Stuttgart, 1965, p. 457f. In addition cf. Apel in *Philosophische Jahrbücher,* 72 Jg., 1965, p. 254f.

21. Cf. Wittgenstein's thought experiments on the problem of a "private language," in *Philosophical Investigations,* I, §§ 197ff., 199, 243, 256.

22. Cf. my "Introduction" to C. S. Peirce, *Schriften* I and II.

23. Cf. H.-G. Gadamer's interpretation of the hermeneutical cultural sciences from the functional context of the process of the communication of tradition in *Wahrheit und Methode,* Tübingen, 2nd ed., 1965. In addition, cf. K.-O. Apel in *Hegelstudien,* Vol. 2, Bonn, 1963, pp. 314–22.

24. Cf. E. Rothacker, "Sinn und Geschehnis," in *Sinn und Sein,* Tübingen, 1960, pp. 1–9.

25. Cf. J. Royce, *The Problem of Christianity*, New York, 1913, II, p. 146ff. In addition, cf. K.-Th. Humbach, *Das Verhältnis von Einzelperson und Gemeinschaft nach Josiah Royce*, Heidelberg, 1962, p. 110ff.

26. Cf. E. Heintel, "Der Mann ohne Eigenschaften und die Tradition," in *Wissenschaft und Weltbild*, 1960, pp. 179–94.

27. Cf. J. Ritter, "Die Aufgabe der Geisteswissenschaften in der modernen Gesellschaft," in *Jahresschrift 1961 der Gesellschaft zur Förderung der Westfälischen Wilhelms-Universität zu Münster*, pp. 11–39. In addition, cf. H. Schelsky, *Einsamkeit und Freiheit*, Hamburg, 1963, pp. 278ff.

28. Cf. H.-G. Gadamer, op. cit.

29. In my opinion, E. Betti (*Die Hermeneutik als allgemeine Methodik der Geisteswissenschaften*, Tübingen 1962) is correct in opposing the implied demand for actualization as it appears to be directed to the cultural "scientist" in existential hermeneutics.

30. The opposition between the position of Gadamer on the one hand and that of J. Ritter and Schelsky on the other appears to me in fact to rest partially on the ambiguity of the notion of "tradition."

31. Cf. Gadamer, op. cit., p. 279ff.

32. G. W. F. Hallgarten, *Imperialismus vor 1914*, 2 vols., 1951.

33. This has been pointed out in particular by H. Skjervheim in his treatise *Objectivism and the Study of Man* (Oslo: Universitätsforlaget, 1959). For a discussion of the difficulties which result from the conversion of communicative experience into quantitative data in the social sciences, cf. J. Habermas, "Zur Logik der Sozialwissenschaften," *Sonderheft 5 der Philosophischen Rundschau*, Tübingen, 1967, p. 95ff.

34. For a developement and critical discussion of the theoretical model sketched here, cf. P. Winch, *The Idea of a Social Science*, London, 1958; J. Habermas, *Erkenntnis und Interesse*, Frankfurt, 1971; G. Radnitzky, *Contemporary Schools of Metascience*, 2nd ed., Göteborg, 1970; K.-O. Apel, "Communication and the Foundation of the Humanities," in *Acta Sociologica*, Vol. 15, Nr. 1, 7–26; K.-O. Apel et al., *Hermeneutik und Ideologiekritik*, Frankfurt, 1971.

# Bibliography

## Section A: Works by and about the Authors Represented

### KARL-OTTO APEL

Apel, Karl-Otto. *Analytic Philosophy of Language and the Geisteswissenschaften.* Dordrecht (Holland): D. Reidel, 1967.
———. "The Apriori of Communication and the Foundation of the Humanities." In *Man and World. An International Philosophical Review* 5 (1972) 3–37.
———. *Die Idee der Sprache in der Tradition des Humanismus von Dante bis Vico.* 2d ed. Bonn: Bouvier, 1975.
———. *Towards a Transformation of Philosophy.* London/Boston: Routledge & Kegan Paul, 1980. Eng. trans. of *Transformation der Philosophie.* Vol. 1: *Sprachanalytik, Semiotik, Hermeneutik.* Vol. 2: *Das Apriori der Kommunikationsgemeinschaft.* Frankfurt: Suhrkamp, 1973.
———. *Das Verstehen. Eine Problemgeschichte als Begriffsgeschichte.* Archiv für Begriffsgeschichte. Vol. 1. Bonn, 1955.

Bleicher, Joseph. *Contemporary Hermeneutics.* Chapter 7. (Section B)
Dallmayr, Fred R. "Hermeneutics and Historicism: Reflections on Winch, Apel, and Vico." In *The Review of Politics* 39 (1977) 60–81.
Radnitzky, Gerard. *Contemporary Schools of Metascience.* Vol. 2. (Section B)

### PHILIP AUGUST BOECKH

Boeckh, Philip August. *On Interpretation and Criticism.* Trans. and ed. John Paul Pritchard. Norman, OK: University of Oklahoma Press, 1968. Partial Eng. trans. of *Enzyklopädie und Methodologie der philologischen Wissenschaften.* Ed. by E. Bratuscheck. 2d ed. Leipzig: Teubner, 1886.

Klassen Grover, Julie Anne. "August Boeckh's *Hermeneutik* and its relation to contemporary scholarship." Ph.D. diss., Stanford University, 1972.
Rodi, Frithjof. "'Erkenntnis des Erkannten'—August Boeckhs Grundformel der hermeneutischen Wissenschaften." In *Philologie und Hermeneutik.* Ed. Flashar, Grinder, Horstmann, 68–83. (Section C)

347

Steinthal, Heyman. "Darstellung und Kritik der Boeckschen Enzyklopädie und Methodologie der Philologie." *Zeitschrift für Völkerpsychologie und Sprachwissenschaft* 11 (1880) 303-26.
Strohschneider-Kohrs, Ingrid. "Textauslegung und hermeneutischer Zirkel. Zur Innovation des Interpretationsbegriffes von August Boeckh." In *Philologie und Hermeneutik*. Ed. Flashar, Grinder, Horstmann. Pp. 84-102. (Section C)
Wach, Joachim. *Das Verstehen.* (Section C)

RUDOLF BULTMANN

Bultmann, Rudolf. *Essays. Philosophical and Theological.* Trans. J. C. G. Greig. London: SCM Press; New York: Macmillan, 1955. Specifically: "The Problem of Hermeneutics," 234-61.
———. *Existence and Faith: Shorter Writings of Rudolf Bultmann.* Selected, trans. and intro. Schubert M. Ogden. New York: Meridian Books, 1960.
———. *Faith and Understanding.* Ed. and intro. Robert W. Funk. Trans. Louise Pettibone Smith. New York: Harper & Row, 1969. Eng. trans. of vol. 1 of *Glauben und Verstehen.* 4 vols. Tübingen: J. C. B. Mohr (Paul Siebeck), 1961-1965.
———. *Jesus and the Word.* Trans. Louise Pettibone Smith and E. Huntress. New York: Charles Scribner's Sons, 1934, 1958.
———. *Theology of the New Testament.* 2 vols. Trans. K. Grobel. New York: Charles Scribner's Sons, 1951-1955.

Bleicher, Joseph. *Contemporary Hermeneutics.* Chapter 4 (Section B)
Bornkamm, Günther. "Die Theologie Rudolf Bultmanns in der neueren Diskussion. Zum Problem der Entmythologisierung und Hermeneutik." In *Theologische Rundschau* New Series (N.F.) (1963) 33-141. (This report on Bultmann criticism also offers an extensive bibliography prepared by E. Brandenburger, pp. 33-46.)
Fuchs, Ernst. *Hermeneutik.* Bad Cannstatt: R. Müllerschön, 1963.
Macquarrie, John. *An Existentialist Theology. A Comparison of Heidegger and Bultmann.* London: SCM Press, 1955.
Malet, André. *The Thought of Rudolf Bultmann.* Trans. from the French by R. Strachan. Pref. Rudolf Bultmann. Doubleday, 1971, c. 1969.
Ogden, Schubert M. *Christ without Myth. A Study Based on the Theology of Rudolf Bultmann.* New York: Harper and Brothers, 1961.
Roberts, Robert Campbell. *Rudolf Bultmann's Theology: A Critical Interpretation.* Grand Rapids, MI: Eerdmans, 1976.

JOHANNES MARTIN CHLADENIUS

Chladenius, Johann Martin. *Einleitung zur richtigen Auslegung vernünftiger Reden und Schriften.* Facsimile reprint of the Leipzig edition of 1742. With an introduction by Lutz Geldsetzer. Vol. 5 of the Series Hermeneutica, Instrumenta Philosophica. Düsseldorf: Stern Verlag, 1969.

Friedrich, Christoph. *Sprache und Geschichte. Untersuchungen zur Hermeneutik von Johann Martin Chladenius.* Meisenheim am Glan, 1978.

Geldsetzer, Lutz. "Preface" to Chladenius's *Einleitung* (1742). 1969, IX–XXIX.

Gadamer, Hans-Georg. *Truth and Method.* (Section A)

Henn, Claudia. "'Sinnreiche Gedanken.' Zur Hermeneutik des Chladenius." *Archiv für Geschichte der Philosophie* 58 (1976) 240–63.

Müller, Hans. *Johann Martin Chladenius (1710–1759).* Berlin, 1917. Vaduz (Liechtenstein): Kraus repr., 1965.

Szondi, Peter. *Einführung in die literarische Hermeneutik.* Ed. J. Bollack and H. Stierlin. Frankfurt a/M., 1975. Pp. 27–97.

Wach, Joachim. *Das Verstehen.* Vol. 3. (Section B)

## WILHELM DILTHEY

Dilthey, Wilhelm. *Gesammelte Schriften.* Göttingen-Stuttgart: Vandenhoeck & Ruprecht, 1914–1977. 18 volumes.

———. "Der Aufbau der geschichtlichen Welt in den Geisteswissenschaften" ("The Construction of the Historical World in the Human Sciences"). *Gesammelte Schriften.* Vol. 7.

———. "The Development of Hermeneutics." In *Selected Writings.* Ed., trans., and intro. H. P. Rickman. Cambridge: Cambridge University Press, 1976.


Bollnow, Otto Friedrich. *Dilthey, eine Einführung in seine Philosophie.* 2d ed. rev. Stuttgart: Kohlhammer, 1955.

Ermarth, Michael. *Wilhelm Dilthey: The Critique of Historical Reason.* Chicago: University of Chicago Press, 1978.

Hodges, H. A. *The Philosophy of Wilhelm Dilthey.* London: C. Routledge & Kegan Paul, 1952.

Ineichen, Hans. *Erkenntnistheorie und geschichtlich-gesellschaftliche Welt: Diltheys Logik der Geisteswissenschaften.* Frankfurt a/M.: Klostermann, 1975.

Makreel, Rudolf. *Dilthey, Philosopher of the Human Studies.* Princeton: Princeton University Press, 1975.

Misch, Georg. *Lebensphilosophie und Phänomenologie: Eine Auseinandersetzung der Diltheyschen Richtung mit Heidegger und Husserl.* Leipzig, Berlin: Teubner, 1931.

Mueller-Vollmer, Kurt. *Towards a Phenomenological Theory of Literature. A Study of Wilhelm Dilthey's Poetik.* The Hague: Mouton, 1963.

Plantinga, Theodore. *Historical Understanding in the Thought of Wilhelm Dilthey.* Toronto, Buffalo, London: University of Toronto Press, 1980.

Rickman, H. P. *Wilhelm Dilthey. Pioneer of the Human Studies.* Berkeley, Los Angeles, London: University of California Press, 1979.

Tuttle, Howard Nelson. *Wilhelm Dilthey's Philosophy of Historical Understanding: A Critical Analysis.* Leiden: E. J. Brill, 1969.

Wellek, René. "Wilhelm Dilthey." In *A History of Modern Criticism. 1750–1950.* Vol. 5. New Haven and London: Yale University Press, 1965. Pp. 320–335.

## JOHANN GUSTAV DROYSEN

Droysen, Johann Gustav. *Outline of the Principles of History.* Trans. and intro. E. Benjamin Andrews. Boston: Ginn & Co., 1897. Partial translation of *Historik: Vorlesungen über Enzyklopädie und Methodologie der Geschichte.* Ed. R. Hübner. 8th ed. Munich: R. Oldenbourg, 1977.

———. *Historik. Band I: Rekonstruktion der ersten vollständigen Fassung der Vorlesungen (1857) Grundriss der Historik.* . . . Historical and critical edition by Peter Leyh. Stuttgart-Bad Cannstatt: Fromann-Holzboog, 1977. (First volume of the planned complete edition of Droysen's theoretical writings.)

Gooch, G. P. *History and Historians in the Nineteenth Century. With a new introduction by the author.* Boston: Beacon Press, 1959. Pp. 125-31.

Hübner, R. "Preface" to J. G. Droysen's *Historik.* (See above.) Pp. ix-xxi.

Iggers, Georg G. *The German Conception of History: The National Tradition of Historical Thought from Herder to the Present.* Middletown, CT: Wesleyan University Press, 1968. Pp. 104-19.

Rüsen, Jörn. *Begriffene Geschichte: Genesis und Begründung der Geschichtstheorie J. G. Droysens.* Paderborn: Schöningh, 1969. (Diss., University of Chicago).

Spieler, Karl-Heinz. *Untersuchungen zu Johann Gustav Droysens "Historik."* Berlin: Duncker und Humblot, 1970.

Wach, Joachim. *Das Verstehen.* Vol. 3. (Section B)

White, Hayden V. Review essay on Droysen's *Historik* in *History and Theory.* Vol. XIX, 1 (1980) 73-93.

## HANS-GEORG GADAMER

Gadamer, Hans-Georg. *Dialogue and Dialectic: Eight Hermeneutical Studies on Plato.* Trans. and intro. P. Christopher Smith. New Haven: Yale University Press, 1980.

———. *Hegel's Dialectic. Five Hermeneutical Studies.* Trans. and intro. P. Christopher Smith. New Haven: Yale University Press, 1976.

———. "Hermeneutik." In *Historisches Wörterbuch der Philosophie.* Vol. 3. Ed. J. Ritter et al. Darmstadt: Wissenschaftl. Buchgesellschaft. 1974, 1061-1073.

———. *Kleine Schriften.* 3 vols. Vol. 1: *Philosophie und Hermeneutik.* Vol. 2: *Interpretationen.* Vol. 3: *Idee und Sprache.* Tübingen: J. C. B. Mohr (Paul Siebeck), 1967-72.

———. *Philosophical Hermeneutics.* Trans. and ed. David E. Linge. Berkeley: University of California Press, 1976.

———. *Poetica: Ausgewählte Essays.* Frankfurt a/M.: Insel, 1977.

———. *Theorie Diskussion.* (Section C) [Contains the exchange with Habermas].

———. *Truth and Method.* Trans. Garret Barden and William G. Doerpel. New York: Seabury Press, 1975. Eng. trans. of *Wahrheit und Methode: Grundzüge einer philosophischen Hermeneutik.* 3d enlg. ed. Tübingen: J. C. B. Mohr (Paul Siebeck), 1972.

Bleicher, Joseph. *Contemporary Hermeneutics.* Chapters 5 and 6 (Section B)

Bormann, C. von. In *Theorie Diskussion*. Pp. 83–119. (Section B)
Hirsch, E. D. 1967. (Section B)
Hoy, D. C. 1978. (Section B)
Madison, G. B. In *Seminar* (1978). Pp. 393–424. (Section C)
Mendelson, Jack. "The Habermas Gadamer Debate." *New German Critique* 18 (1979) 44–73.
Palmer, R. E. 1969. Pp. 162–217. (Section B)
Pöggeler, O. In *Hermeneutische Philosophie* (1972) 41ff. (Section C).
Sandkühler, H. J. 1973. Pp. 62–83. (Section B)
Zimmerli, Walter Ch. "Ist die kommunikationstheoretische Wende ein Ausweg aus dem Hermeneutikstreit?" Ed. Simon-Schaefer and Zimmerli, 1975. Pp. 95–122. (Section B)

JÜRGEN HABERMAS

Habermas, Jürgen. *Communication and the Evolution of Society*. Trans. and intro. Thomas McCarthy. Boston: Beacon Press, 1979.
——. *Knowledge and Human Interest*. Trans. J. J. Shapiro. Boston: Beacon Press, 1971. Eng. trans. of *Erkenntnis und Interesse*. Frankfurt a/M.: Suhrkamp, 1968.
——. *Legitimation Crisis*. Trans. Thomas McCarthy. Boston: Beacon Press, 1975.
——. *Zur Logik der Sozialwissenschaften*. 5th enlg. ed. Frankfurt a/M.: Suhrkamp, 1982. The edition now includes the essay "Der Universalitätsanspruch der Hermeneutik" ("On Hermeneutic's Claim to Universality").
——. *Theory and Practice*. Trans. John Viertel. Boston: Beacon Press, 1973.

Apel, K.-O. In *Towards a Transformation of Philosophy*. (Section A)
Adorno, Th. W., Popper, K., et al. *The Positivist Dispute in German Sociology*. Adey and David Frisby. London: Heinemann, 1976.
Bubner, R. In *Theorie Diskussion* (1971) 160–209. (Section C)
Kortian, Garbis. *Metacritique: the Philosophical Argument of Jürgen Habermas*. Trans. John Raffan. Intro. Charles Taylor and Alan Montefiori. Cambridge, England: Cambridge University Press, 1980.
McCarthy, Thomas A. *The Critical Theory of Jürgen Habermas*. Cambridge, MA: MIT Press, 1978.
Mendelson, Jack. See under Gadamer.

MARTIN HEIDEGGER

A complete edition of Heidegger's works is being published by the Vittorio Klostermann publishing house of Frankfurt, West Germany. The plan calls for publication in four sections: (1) Published writings 1914–1970. (2) Lecture courses 1923–1944. (3) Unpublished studies 1919–1967. (4) Papers and notes. Sections 1 and 2 to comprise 55 volumes.

Martin Heidegger. *Being and Time.* Trans. John Macquarrie and Edward Robinson. New York: Harper & Row, 1962. Eng. trans. of *Sein und Zeit,* now vol. 2 of section 1 of the *Complete Edition.* Ed. F.-W. von Herrmann. Frankfurt a/M.: Klostermann, 1977.
———. *The Basic Problems of Phenomenology.* Trans., intro., and lexicon Albert Hofstadter. Bloomington, IN: Indiana University Press, 1982.
———. *Basic Writings. Nine Key Essays.* Ed. with an intro. David Farrell Krell. New York: Harper & Row, 1977.
———. *On the Way to Language.* Trans. Peter D. Hertz. New York: Harper & Row, 1971.
———. *Poetry, Language and Thought.* Trans. and intro. Albert Hofstadter. New York: Harper & Row, 1971.


Apel, K.-O. *Towards a Transformation of Philosophy.* (Section A)
Bove, Paul. *Destructive Poetics: Heidegger and Modern American Poetry.* New York: Columbia University Press, 1980.
Gadamer, Hans-Georg. In *Seminar* (1976) 37–40. (Section C).
Gelven, Michael. *A Commentary on Heidegger's "Being and Time."* New York: Harper & Row, 1970.
Gethmann, C. F. *Verstehen und Auslegung: das Methodenproblem in der Philosophie Martin Heideggers.* Bonn: Bouvier, 1974.
*Heidegger and Modern Philosophy. Critical Essays.* Ed. Michael Murray. New Haven and London: Yale University Press, 1978. Contains a special section: "Hermeneutics and Language" as well as a complete bibliography of Heidegger in English up to 1978.
Herrmann, F. W. von. *Subjekt und Dasein. Interpretationen zu "Sein und Zeit."* Frankfurt a/M.: Klostermann, 1974.
Marx, Werner. *Heidegger and the Tradition.* Trans. Theodore Kisiel and Murray Greene. Intro. Th. Kisiel. Evanston, IL: Northwestern University Press, 1972.
*On Heidegger and Language.* Ed. J. Kockelmans. Evanston, IL: Northwestern University Press, 1972.
Palmer, R. O. 1969. (Section B)
Pöggeler, Otto. *Heidegger. Perspektiven zur Deutung seines Werks.* Cologne: Kiepenheuer & Witsch, 1969.
Prauss, Gerold. *Erkennen und Handeln in Heidegger's "Sein und Zeit."* Freiburg, Munich: Alber, 1977.
Robinson, James McConkey. *The Later Heidegger and Theology.* Ed. J. M. Robinson and John B. Cobb, Jr. New York: Harper & Row, 1963.
Schmitt, Richard. *Martin Heidegger on Being Human: An Introduction to "Sein und Zeit."* New York: Random House, 1969.
Steiner, George. *Martin Heidegger.* Middlesex, England; New York: Penguin Books, 1980.


WILHELM VON HUMBOLDT


Humboldt, Wilhelm von. *Gesammelte Schriften.* Ed. A. Leitzmann et al. Prussian Academy of Sciences. 17 vols. Berlin: B. Behr, 1903–1916. Rpt. Berlin: de Gruyter, 1968.

———. *Humanist without Portfolio: An Anthology of the Writings of Wilhelm von Humboldt.* Ed. and trans. Marianne Cowan. Detroit: Wayne State University Press, 1963.

———. *The Limits of State Action.* Ed. J. W. Burrow. London: Cambridge University Press, 1969.

———. *Linguistic Variability and Intellectual Development. Introduction to the Kawi Work.* Trans. G. C. Buck and F. A. Raven. Coral Gables, FL: University of Miami Press, 1971.

Borsche, Tilman. *Sprachansichten. Der Begriff der menschlichen Rede in der Sprachphilosophie Wilhelm von Humboldts.* Stuttgart: Klett-Cotta, 1981.

Cassirer, Ernst. *The Philosophy of Symbolic Forms.* 3 vols. New Haven: Yale University Press, 1961. [Vol. 1 devoted to Humboldt's theory of language.]

Chomsky, Noam. *Cartesian Linguistics. A Chapter in the History of Rationalist Thought.* New York and London: Harper & Row, 1966.

Gadamer, H.-G. *Truth and Method.* (Section A)

Heeschen, Volker. *Die Sprachphilosophie Wilhelm von Humboldts.* Bochum, 1972. (Ph.D. diss.)

Mueller-Vollmer, Kurt. "From Poetics to Linguistics: Wilhelm von Humboldt and the Romantic Idea of Language." In *Le Groupe de Coppet. Actes et documents du deuxieme Colloque de Coppet, 1974.* Paris and Geneva: Champion and Slatkine, 1977. Pp. 195–215.

Sweet, Paul R. *Wilhelm von Humboldt. A Biography.* 2 vols. Columbus, OH: Ohio State University Press, 1978 (vol 1.); 1980 (vol. 2). [Contains an extensive bibliography.]

Wach, Joachim. *Das Verstehen.* (Section B)


EDMUND HUSSERL


Edmund Husserl. *Husserliana—Gesammelte Werke [Collected Works].* The Hague: M. Nijhof, 1950– [23 volumes to date].

———. *The Crisis of European Sciences and Transcendental Phenomenology: An Introduction to Phenomenological Philosophy.* Trans. and intro. David Carr. Evanston, IL: Northwestern University Press, 1970.

———. *Logical Investigations.* 2 vols. Trans. J. N. Findlay (from the second German edition). London: Routledge & Kegan Paul; New York: The Humanities Press, 1976.

———. *The Phenomenology of Internal Time Consciousness.* Ed. Martin Heidegger. Trans. James S. Churchill. Intro. Calvin O. Schrag. Bloomington, IN: Indiana University Press, 1964.


Buck, Günther. "The Structure of Hermeneutic Experience and the Problems of Tradition." *New Literary History* 10/1 (1978) 31–47.

Castilla Lázaro, Ramón. *Zu Husserls Sprachphilosophie und ihren Kritikern.* Berlin, 1967. (Ph.D. diss.)

Derrida, Jacques. *Speech and Phenomena, and Other Essays on Husserl's Theory of Signs.* Trans. and intro. David B. Allison. Evanston, IL: Northwestern University Press, 1973.

Findlay, J. N. "Preface" of E. Husserl, *Logical Investigations.* Vol. 1. London: Routledge & Kegan Paul, 1970. Pp. 1–40.

Kockelmans, Joseph J., ed. *Phenomenology. The Philosophy of Edmund Husserl and Its Interpretation.* Garden City, NY: Anchor Books (Doubleday), 1967.

Luckmann, Thomas. "The Constitution of Language in the World of Everyday Life." In *Life-World and Consciousness. Essays for Aron Gurwitsch.* Ed. Lester E. Embree. Evanston, IL: Northwestern University Press, 1972. Pp. 469–88.

Mohanty, J. N. *Edmund Husserl's Theory of Meaning.* The Hague: Martinus Nijhoff, 1964.

Natanson, Maurice. *Edmund Husserl. Philosopher of Infinite Tasks.* Evanston, IL: Northwestern Univeristy Press, 1973. [Contains extensive bibliography (pp. 209–21) of works in English by and about Husserl.]

Orth, Ernst W. *Bedeutung, Sinn, Gegenstand. Studien zur Sprachphilosophie Edmund Husserls und Richard Hönigswalds.* Bonn: Bouvier, 1967.

Ricoeur, Paul. *Husserl. An Analysis of His Phenomenology.* Evanston, IL: Northwestern University Press, 1967.

Sokolowski, R. *Husserlian Meditations. How Words Present Things.* Evanston, IL: Northwestern University Press, 1974.

## ROMAN INGARDEN

Ingarden, Roman. *The Cognition of the Literary Work of Art.* Trans. from the German by Ruth Ann Crowley and Kenneth R. Olson. Evanston, IL: Northwestern University Press, 1973. Trans. of *Vom Erkennen des literarischen Kunstwerks.* Tübingen: M. Niemeyer, 1976.

―――. *The Literary Work of Art. An Investigation on the Borderline of Ontology, Logic, and Theory of Literature. With an Appendix on the Functions of Language in the Theater.* Trans. and intro. George G. Grabowicz. Evanston, IL: Northwestern University Press, 1973. Eng. trans. of *Das literarische Kunstwerk.* 2d enlg. ed. Tübingen: M. Niemeyer, 1960.

Colomb, G. G. "Roman Ingarden and the Language of Art and Science." *Journal of Aesthetics and Art Criticism* 35/1 (1976/77) 7–13.

*For Roman Ingarden: Nine Essays in Phenomenology.* S'Gravenhage: M. Nijhoff, 1959.

Falk, Eugene H. *The Poetics of Roman Ingarden.* Chapel Hill, NC: North Carolina University Press, 1981.

Fizer, John. "'Actualization' and 'Concretization' as Heuristic Devices in the Study of Literary Art." *Yearbook of Comparative Criticism* Vol. 10, *Literary Criticism and Philosophy.* Ed. Joseph P. Strelka. University Park and New York: The Pennsylvania State University Press, 1983. Pp. 65–77.

Rudnik, Hans. H. "Roman Ingarden: Aesthetics of Literature." *Colloquia Germanica* 8 (1974) 1–14.

Warning, Rainer. "Rezeptionsästhetik als literaturwissenschaftliche Pragmatik." In *Rezeptionsästhetik*. Ed. R. Warning, 1975. Pp. 9–41. (Section C)


FRIEDRICH DANIEL ERNST SCHLEIERMACHER

Schleiermacher, F. D. E. *Hermeneutics: The Handwritten Manuscripts by F. D. E. Schleiermacher*. Ed. Heinz Kimmerle. Trans. James Duke and Jack Forstman. Missoula, MT: Scholars Press, 1977. Eng. trans. of the second German edition; Heidelberg: Carl Winter, 1974.
——. "Hermeneutics: Outline of the 1819 Lectures." [partial translation] Trans. Jan Wojcik and Roland Haaas. *New Literary History* [issue on literary hermeneutics] 10/1 (1978) 1–16.
——. *Hermeneutik und Kritik*. Mit einem Anhang sprachphilosophischer Texte Schleiermachers. Ed. and intro. Manfred Frank. Frankfurt a/M.: Suhrkamp, 1977. The most complete and authoritative edition of Schleiermacher's hermeneutics.

Benson, John Edward. "Schleiermacher's Hermeneutics" (Ph.D. diss., Columbia University, 1967).
Brandt, Richard B. *The Philosophy of Schleiermacher. The Development of his Theory of Scientific and Religious Knowledge*. New York and London: Harper & Brothers, 1941.
Forstman, Jack. *A Romantic Triangle: Schleiermacher and Early German Romanticism*. Missoula, MT: Scholars Press, 1977.
Frank, Manfred. *Das individuelle Allgemeine. Textstrukturierung und -interpretation nach Schleiermacher*. Frankfurt a/M.: Suhrkamp, 1977.
Gadamer, H.-G. "The Problem of Language in Schleiermacher's Hermeneutics." Trans. David Linge. In *Schleiermacher as Contemporary*. Ed. R. Palmer and J. Edie. New York: Herder & Herder, 1970. *Journal for Theology and Church*. Vol. 6.
Szondi, Peter. "L'herméneutique de Schleiermacher." *Poétique* 2 (1970) 141–55.
Van Franken, Dora. "Friedrich Schleiermacher as a Critic." (Ph.D. diss., Stanford University, 1972).
Wach, Joachim. *Das Verstehen*. (Section B)


### Section B: General

Abel, Th. "The Operation Called 'Verstehen.'" *American Journal of Sociology* 54. Reprinted in *Readings in the Philosophy of Science*. Ed. H. Feigl and M. Brodbeck. New York: Appleton-Century-Crofts, 1952.
Ackrill, J. L., trans. *Aristotle's Categories and De Interpretatione*. Translation with notes by the translator. London: Clarendon Press, 1966.
Albert, H. *Transzendentale Träumereien: Karl-Otto Apels Sprachspiele und Sein Hermeneutischer Gott*. Hamburg: Hoffmann und Campe, 1975.
Altenhofer, Norbert. "Geselliges Betragen-Kunst-Auslegung. Anmerkungen zu Peter Szondis Schleiermacher Interpretation und zur Frage einer Materialen Hermeneutik."

*Studien zur Entwicklung einer Materialen Hermeneutik.* Munich: W. Fink Verlag, 1974. Pp. 165-211.

Altieri, Charles. "The Hermeneutics of Literary Indeterminacy: A Dissenting From the Orthodoxy." *New Literary History* 10 (1978-79) 71-99.

Bauman, Zygmunt. *Hermeneutic and Social Science.* New York: Columbia University Press, 1978.

Baumer, Franklin L. *Modern European Thought: Continuity and Change in Ideas, 1600-1950.* New York: Macmillan Publishing Co., 1977.

Betti, Emilio. *Allgemeine Auslegungslehre als Methodik der Geisteswissenschaften.* Tübingen: Mohr (Siebeck), 1967.

———. *Die Hermeneutik als allgemeine Methodik der Geisteswissenschaften.* Tübingen: Mohr (Siebeck), 1962.

———. "Problematik einer allgemeinen Auslegungslehre als Methode der Geisteswissenschaften." *Hermeneutik als Weg heutiger Wissenschaften.* Pp. 15-30. (See Section C)

———. *Teoria generale della interpretazione.* Milan: A. Guiffrè, 1955.

Binswanger, Ludwig. *Grundformen und Erkenntnis menschlichen Daseins.* Munich and Basel: Ernst Reinhardt Verlag, 1962.

Bleicher, Josef. *Contemporary Hermeneutics: Hermeneutics as Method, Philosophy, and Critique.* London: Routledge & Kegan Paul, 1980 (paperback, 1982, 1983). [Contains an English translation of Habermas's essay "Der Universalitätsanspruch der Hermeneutik" under the title "The Hermeneutic Claim to Universality," pp. 181-211.]

Bollnow, O. F. *Das Verstehen: Drei Aufsätze zur Theorie der Geisteswissenschaften.* Mainz: Kircheim, 1949.

Brandt, Reinhard. *Die aristotelische Urteilslehre: Untersuchungen zur "Hermeneutik."* Marburg: Görich und Weiershäuser, 1965.

Brinkmann, Hennig. *Mittelalterliche Hermeneutik.* Tübingen: Niemeyer, 1980.

Bubner, Rüdiger. "Transzendentale Hermeneutik?" In *Wissenschaftstheorie in den Geisteswissenschaften. Konzeptionen, Vorschläge, Entwürfe.* Ed. R. Simon Schaefer and W. Ch. Zimmerli. Hamburg: Hoffmann und Campe, 1975.

Buck, Günter. "Hermeneutics of Texts and Hermeneutics of Action." *New Literary History* 4/1 (1980) 87-96.

Chomsky, Noam. *Aspects of the Theory of Syntax.* Cambridge, MA: MIT Press, 1965.

Cicourel, Aaron. *Cognitive Sociology: Language and Meaning in Social Interaction.* New York: The Free Press (Macmillan), 1974.

Dannhauer, Johann Donrad. *Idea boni interpretis (1670).* Strassbourg: n.p., 1670.

Diderot/d'Alembert. "Interpretation." *Encyclopédie.* Vol. 8. 1765.

Dray, W. H. "Explaining What Is History." In *Theories of History.* Ed. P. Gardiner. Glencoe, IL: The Free Press, 1959.

———. *Laws and Explanations in History.* Cambridge: Oxford University Press, 1957.

Ebeling, G. "Hermeneutik." *Religion in Geschichte und Gegenwart.* 3d ed. 1959. Pp. 242-62.

Ernesti, Jul. Heinrich. *Compendium Hermeneuticae Profanae.* Leipzig: n.p., 1699.

Fischer-Lichte, Erika. *Bedeutung. Probleme einer semiotischen Hermeneutik und Aesthetik.* Munich: C. H. Beck, 1979.

Fish, Stanley. "Literature in the Reader: Affective Stylistics." *New Literary History* 1 (1970) 123-62.

Frank, Mannfred. "Was heisst 'einen Text verstehen'?" In *Texthermeneutik. Aktualität, Geschichte, Kritik*. 1979. Pp. 58-77. (See Section C)

Freundlieb, Dieter. *Zur Wissenschaftstheorie der Literaturwissenschaft: eine Kritik der transzendentalen Hermeneutik*. Munich: Fink Verlag, 1978.

Funke, G. "Problem und Theorie der Hermeneutik: Auslegen, Verstehen in E. Bettis 'Teoria generale della interpretazione.'" In *Studi in Onore di Emilio Betti*. Milan: A. Giuffrè, 1962.

Glowinski, Michael. "Reading, Interpretation, Reception." *New Literary History* (Anniversary Issue II) 9 (1980) 76-81.

Hass Jaeger, H.-E. "Studien zur Frühgeschichte der Hermeneutik." *Archiv für Begriffsgeschichte* 18 (1974) 35-84.

Hirsch, E. D. *The Aims of Interpretation*. Chicago: University of Chicago Press, 1978.

———. *Validity in Interpretation*. New Haven and London: Yale University Press, 1967.

Howard, Roy. J. *Three Faces of Hermeneutics: An Introduction to Current Theories of Understanding*. Berkeley, Los Angeles, London: University of California Press, 1982.

Hoy, David Couzens. *The Critical Circle. Literature, History, and Philosophical Hermeneutics*. Berkeley: University of California Press, 1978.

Hufnagel, E. *Einführung in die Hermeneutik*. Stuttgart, Berlin, Cologne, Mainz: Kohlhammer, 1976.

Humphrey, Laurentius. *De ratione interpretandi libris III*. Basel: n.p., 1559.

Japp, Uwe. *Hermeneutik. Der theoretische Diskurs, die Literatur und die Konstruktion ihres Zusammenhanges in den philologischen Wissenschaften*. Munich: W. Fink Verlag, 1977.

Kamper, Dietmar. "Hermeneutik-Theorie einer Praxis?" *Zeitschrift für allgemeine Wissenschaftstheorie* 5 (1974) 39-53.

Kimmerle, Heinz. "Die Funktion der Hermeneutik in den positiven Wissenschaften." *Zeitschrift für allgemeine Wissenschaftstheorie* 5 (1974) 54-73.

———. *Philosophie der Geisteswissenschaften als Kritik ihrer Methoden*. Den Haag: Martinus Nijhoff, 1978.

Kunne-Ibsch, Elrud. "Rezeptionsforschung: Konstanten und Varianten eines literaturwissenschaftlichen Konzepts in Theorie und Praxis." *Amsterdamer Beiträge* (1974) 1-36.

Labroisse, Gerd. "Überlegungen zu einem Interpretations-Modell." *Amsterdamer Beiträge* (1974) 149-61.

Landgrebe, Ludwig. "Vom geisteswissenschaftlichen Verstehen." *Zeitschrift für philosophische Forschung* 6 (1951/1952) 3.

Leibfried, E. *Kritische Wissenschaft vom Text*. Stuttgart: Metzler, 1970.

Levi, Albert William. "De interpretatione: Cognition and Context in the History of Ideas." *Critical Inquiry* 3/1 (1976) 153-78.

Licher, Edmund. "Kommunikationstheoretische Aspekte der Analyse einiger Gedichte Bertolt Brechts." *Amsterdamer Beiträge* (1974) 163-211.

Linge, David E. "Dilthey and Gadamer: Two Theories of Historical Understanding." *Journal of the American Academy of Religion* 41 (1973) 536-53.

Lipps, Hans. "Untersuchungen zur hermeneutischen Logik." *Werke*. Bd. 2, 1975. 2 Auflage. Frankfurt a/M.: Klostermann, 1959.

Marx, Karl and Friedrich Engels. *The German Ideology. Part One.* Ed. and with introduction by C. J. Arthur. New York: International Publishers, 1970.

———. *Studienausgabe in 4 Bänden.* Vol. I: Philosophie. Ed. W. I. Fetscher. Frankfurt: Fischer Taschenbuch Verlag, 1976.

Meier, Georg Friedrich. *Versuch einer allgemeinen Auslegungskunst.* Halle, 1757; rpt. Düsseldorf: Stern Verlag, 1965.

Meinecke, Friedrich. *Historicism: The Rise of a New Historical Outlook.* Trans. J. E. Anderson. Foreword by Sir Isaiah Berlin. London: Routledge & Kegan Paul, 1972.

Mueller-Vollmer, Kurt. "Fichte und die romantische Sprachtheorie." In *Die gegenwärtige Darstellung der Philosophie Fichte.* Ed. K. Hammermacher. Hamburg: F. Meiner, 1981. Pp. 442–61.

———. "Interpretation: Discourse or Discipline? A Phenomenological View." *Monatshefte* 71/4, 379–86.

———. "Understanding and Interpretation: Toward a Definition of Literary Hermeneutics." In *Literary Criticism and Philosophy, Yearbook of Comparative Criticism* 10 (1983) 41–77.

Nassen, Ulrich. *Studien zur Entwicklung einer materialen Hermeneutik.* Munich: Wilhelm Fink Verlag, 1979.

Outhwaite, William. *Understanding Social Life. The Method Called Verstehen.* New York: Holmes and Meier, 1976.

Palmer, Richard O. *Hermeneutics. Interpretation Theory in Schleiermacher, Dilthey, Heidegger, and Gadamer.* Evanston, IL: Northwestern University Press, 1969.

Radnitzky, Gerard. *Contemporary Schools of Metascience.* 2 vols. 2d. ed.; Göteborg: Akademiförlaget/Gumpert, 1968. 3d. enlg. ed.; Chicago: Regherl, 1973.

Pöggeler, O. "Hermeneutik und semantische Phänomenologie." *Philosophische Rundschau* 13 (1965) 1–39.

Reisinger, P. "Über die Zirkelstruktur des Verstehens in der traditionellen Hermeneutik." *Philosophisches Jahrbuch* 81 (1974) 88–104.

Ricoeur, Paul. *Freud and Philosophy. An Essay in Interpretation.* Trans. Denis Savage. New Haven and London: Yale University Press, 1970.

———. *Interpretation Theory: Discourse and the Surplus of Meaning.* Fort Worth, TX: The Texas Austin University Press, 1976.

———. "The Model of the Text: Meaningful Action Considered as a Text." *Social Research* 38/3 (1971) 529–62.

Riedel, Manfred. *Verstehen oder Erklären? Zur Theorie und Geschichte der hermeneutischen Wissenschaften.* Stuttgart: Klett-Cotta, 1978.

Robinson, James M. *The New Hermeneutic.* Ed. J. M. Robinson and John B. Cobb. New York: Harper and Row, 1964.

Rothacker, Erich. *Einleitung in die Geisteswissenschaften.* 2d. ed. Tübingen: J. C. B. Mohr, 1930.

———. *Logik und Systematik der Geisteswissenschaften.* Bonn: Bouvier, 1948.

Rüsen, Jörn. *Für eine erneuerte Historik. Studien zu Theorie der Wissenschaft.* Stuttgart-Bad Constatt: Fromann-Holzboog, 1976.

Sandkühler, Hans Jörg. *Praxis und Geschichtsbewusstsein. Studien zur materialistischen Dialektik, Erkenntnistheorie und Hermeneutik.* Frankfurt: Suhrkamp Verlag, 1973.

Simon-Schaefer, Roland and Walter Zimmerli. *Theorie zwischen Kritik und Praxis. Jürgen Habermas und die Frankfurter Schule.* Stuttgart-Bad Canstatt: Friedrich Fromann Verlag, 1975.

Schutz, Alfred. *The Phenomenology of the Social World.* Evanston, IL: Northwestern University Press, 1967.

Seebohm, Th. M. "Der Zirkel in der Hermeneutik." In *Zur Kritik des hermeneutischen Verstehens.* Bonn: Bouvier, 1972.

Siemek. M. G. "Marxism and the Hermeneutic Tradition." *Dialectics and Humanism* 2 (1975) 87-103.

Simmel, Georg. *Vom Wesen der historischen Verstehens.* Berlin: E. S. Mittler, 1918.

Stegmüller, Wolfgang. *Main Currents in Contemporary German, British, and American Philosophy.* Trans. E. Blumberg. Bloomington, IN: Indiana University Press, 1970.

Steinmetz, Horst. "Rezeption und Interpretation. Versuch einer Abgrenzung." *Amsterdamer Beiträge* (1974) 37-81.

Szondi, Peter. "Introduction to Literary Hermeneutics." *New Literary History* 10/1 (1978) 17-29, partial translation of *Einführung in die literarische Hermeneutik.* Frankfurt a/M.: Suhrkamp T. B., 1975.

———. "L'Herméneutique de Schleiermacher." *Poétique* 2 (1970) 141-55.

———. "Über philologische Erkenntnis." In *Schriften.* Vol. 1. Frankfurt a/M.: Suhrkamp, 1978.

Taylor, Charles. *The Explanation of Behavior.* New York: Humanities Press, 1964.

———. "Interpretation and the Science of Man." *Review of Metaphysics* 25 (1971) 3-51.

Thibaut, Anton Friedrich Justus. *An Introduction to the Study of Jurisprudence, Being a Translation of the General Part of Thibaut's 'System des Pandektenrechts.'* With notes and illustrations by N. Lindsey. Philadelphia: T. and J. W. Johnson, 1855.

———. *Theorie der logischen Auslegung des römischen Rechts* (1806). Introduction by Lutz Geldsetzer. Rpt. Düsseldorf: Stern Verlag Janssen und Co., 1966.

Todorov, Tzvetan. *Symbolisme et interprétation.* Paris: Éditions du Seuil, 1978.

Tyler, Stephen A. *The Said and the Unsaid. Mind, Meaning, and Culture.* New York-San Francisco-London: Academic Press, 1978.

*Vico. Selected Writings.* Ed. and trans. Leon Pompa. Cambridge, London, New York, etc.: Cambridge University Press, 1982.

Von Wright, Georg Henrik. *Explanation and Understanding.* Ithaca, NY: Cornell University Press, 1971.

Wach, Joachim. *Das Verstehen. Grundzüge einer Geschichte der hermeneutischen Theorie im 19. Jahrhundert.* 3 vols. Tübingen: J. C. B. Mohr, 1926-1933.

Weber, Max. *Economy and Society: An Outline of Interpretive Sociology.* Ed. by G. Roth and C. Wittich. Berkeley, Los Angeles, London: University of California Press, 1978.

Weimar, Klaus. *Historische Einleitung zur literaturwissenschaftlichen Hermeneutik.* Tübingen: J. C. B. Mohr, 1975.

Whitehead, Alfred North. *Modes of Thought.* 1938. Rpt. New York: The Free Press, 1968.

Winch, Peter. *The Idea of a Social Science and Its Relation to Philosophy.* London: Routledge & Kegan Paul, 1958.

Wittgenstein, Ludwig. *Philosophical Investigations*. Trans. G. E. M. Anscombe. Oxford: B. Blackwell, 1958.

Wolff, Christian. *Vernünftige Gedanken. Von den Kräften des menschlichen Verstandes und ihrem richtigen Gebrauche. Gesammelte Werke*. Sect. 1, vol. 1. Ed. H. W. Arndt. Hildesheim: Olms, 1965.

———. *Philosophia rationalis sive logica. Methodo scientifica, pertractata*. 2d. ed. Frankfurt and Leipzig: n.p., 1732.

Zedler, J. H. "Hermeneutik." *Grosses vollständiges Universallexicon aller Künste und Wissenschaften*. Vol. 12. Halle and Leipzig: J. H. Zedler, 1735. Pp. 1729–33.

Zimmermann, Jörg. *Wittgensteins sprachphilosophische Hermeneutik*. Frankfurt a/M.: Vittorio Klostermann, 1975. *Philosophische Abhandlungen*. Vol. 46.

## Section C: Anthologies and Essay Collections

*Essays of Explanation and Understanding: Studies in the Foundations of the Humanities and Social Sciences*. Ed. J. Manninen and R. Tuomela. Dordrecht, Holland: Boston: D. Reidel Publishing Co., 1976.

*Giambattista Vico's Science of Humanity*. Ed. Giorgio Tagliacozzo and Donald Phillip Verene. Baltimore and London: The Johns Hopkins University Press, 1976.

*Hermeneutik als Weg heutiger Wissenschaft*. Ed. V. Warnach. Salzburg-Munich: Anton Pustet, 1971.

*Hermeneutik und Dialektik*. Festschrift für H.-G. Gadamer. Ed. Bubner, Cramer, and Wiehl. 2 vols. Tübingen: J. C. B. Mohr, 1970.

*Hermeneutische Philosophie: Zehn Aufsätze*. Ed. O. Pöggeler. Munich: Nymphenburger Verlagshandlung, 1972.

"Literary Hermeneutics." Special Issue of *New Literary History* 10/1 (1978).

*The New Hermeneutic*. Ed. James M. Robinson and John B. Cobb, Jr. New York: Harper and Row, 1964.

*Philologie und Hermeneutik im 19. Jahrhundert. Zur Geschichte und Methodologie des Geisteswissenschaften*. Ed. H. Flashar, K. Gründer, A. Horstmann. Göttingen: Vandenhoeck & Ruprecht, 1979.

*Qu'est-ce qu'un texte? Eléments pour une herméneutique*. Ed. E. Barbotin. Paris: Librairie José Corti, 1975.

*Rezeptionsästhetik. Theorie und Praxis*. Ed. R. Warning. Munich: Fink Verlag, 1975.

"Rezeption-Interpretation. Beiträge zur Methodendiskussion." *Amsterdamer Beiträge zur neueren Germanistik*. Ed. Gerd Labroisse. Vol. 3. 1974.

*Seminar: Die Hermeneutik und die Wissenschafte*. Ed. H.-G. Gadamer and G. Boehm. Frankfurt a/M.: Suhrkamp, 1978.

*Seminar: Philosophische Hermeneutik*. Ed. H.-G. Gadamer and G. Boehm. Frankfurt a/M.: Suhrkamp, 1976.

*Sprachanalyse und Soziologie. Die sozialwissenschaftliche Relevanz von Wittgensteins Sprachphilosophie*. Ed. R. Wiggershaus. Frankfurt a/M.: Suhrkamp, 1975.

*Studien zur Entwicklung einer Materialen Hermeneutik*. Ed. U. Nassen. Munich: Fink Verlag, 1979.

*Subjective Understanding in the Social Sciences.* Ed. Marzello Truzzi. Reading, MA: Addison-Wesley, 1974.
*Texthermeneutik. Aktualität, Geschichte, Kritik.* Ed. U. Nassen. Paderborn: Schöningh, 1979.
*Theorie Diskussion: Hermeneutik und Ideologiekritik.* With contributions by Apel, Borman, Bubner, Gadamer, Giegel, Habermas. Frankfurt a/M.: Suhrkamp, 1971.
*Understanding and Social Inquiry.* Ed. F. Dallmayr and T. McCarthy. Notre Dame, IN: Notre Dame University Press, 1977.
*Verstehende Soziologie. Grundzüge und Entwicklungstendenzen.* Ed. W. L. Bühl. Munich: Nymphenburger Verlagshandlung, 1972.
*Vico and Contemporary Thought.* Ed. Giorgio Tagliacozzo, Michael Mooney, Donald Phillip Verene. Atlantic Highlands, NJ: Humanities Press, 1979, c. 1976.
*Wissenschaftstheorie der Geisteswissenschaften.* Ed. R. Simon-Schäfer and W. Ch. Zimmerli. Hamburg: Hoffmann und Campe, 1975.

## Section D: Bibliographies

Most entries under Section C contain (often extensive) bibliographical information. In addition, the following titles are of particular relevance.

*Bibliographic Guide to Hermeneutics and Critical Theory.* Ed. W. C. Gay and P. Eckstein. *Cultural Hermeneutics* 2 (1975).
*Bibliographie der Hermeneutik und ihrer Anwendungsbereiche seit Schleiermacher.* Ed. N. Henrichs. Düsseldorf: Philosophia Verlag, 1972.
*See also:*
Betti, Emilio. *Allgemeine Auslegungslehre.* 1967. (Section B)
Gadamer, H.-G. *Wahrheit und Methode.* 3d ed. 1972. (Section A)
Bleicher, J. *Contemporary Hermeneutics.* 1980. (Section B)

# Acknowledgments

We gratefully acknowledge permission to reprint or publish in English for the first time the following materials:

Karl-Otto Apel, "Szientistic, Hermeneutik, Ideologiekritik: Entwurf einer Wissenschaftslehre in erkenntnisanthropologischer Sicht." In *Transformation der Philosophie*. Vol. 2: *Das Apriori der Kommunikationsgemeinschaft*, pp. 96–127. Frankfurt a/M: Suhrkamp Verlag, 1973. Translated by Linda Gail DeMichiel and published by permission of Routledge & Kegan Paul PLC.
August Boeck. *On Interpretation and Criticism*, pp. 43–46, 47–61, and 121–31. Translated, and with an introduction by John Paul Pritchard. Copyright 1968 by University of Oklahoma Press. Reprinted by permission of University of Oklahoma Press.
Rudolf Bultmann. *Existence and Faith: Shorter Writings of Rudolf Bultmann*, pp. 289–96 and 314–15. Selected, translated, and introduced by Schubert M. Ogden. Copyright © 1960 by Meridian Books, Inc. Reprinted by arrangement with The New American Library Inc., New York, N.Y.
———. "Zum Problem der Entmythologiesierung." In *Glauben und Verstehen: Gesammelte Aufsätze*, Vol. 4, pp. 128–37. 3rd ed. Tübingen: J. C. B. Mohr (Paul Siebeck), 1975. Translated by Barbara F. Hyams and published by permission of J. C. B. Mohr (Paul Siebeck).
Johann Martin Chladenius. *Einleitung zur richtigen Auslegung vernünftiger Reden und Schriften*, pp. 82–111, 181–97, and 201–5. Facsimile reprint of the Leipzig edition of 1742. With an introduction by Lutz Geldsetzer. Düsseldorf: Stern-Verlag Janssen & Co., 1969. Translated by Carrie Asman-Schneider and published by permission of Stern-Verlag Janssen & Co.
Wilhelm Dilthey. *Selected Writings*, pp. 208–12, 219–31. Edited, translated, and introduced by H. P. Rickman. Cambridge: Cambridge University Press, 1976. Reprinted by permission of Cambridge University Press.
Johann Gustav Droysen. *Historik: Vorlesungen über Enzyklopädie und Methodologie der Geschichte*, pp. 149–56 and 340–43. Edited by Rudolf

364     *Acknowledgments*

Hübner. 4th ed. Munich: R. Oldenbourg, 1960. Translated by Carrie Asman-Schneider and published by permission of R. Oldenbourg Verlag.
——. *Outline of the Principles of History* (*Grundriss der Historik*), pp. 9–16. Translated by E. Benjamin Andrews. Boston: Ginn & Co., 1897.
Hans-Georg Gadamer. *Truth and Method*, pp. 241–53 and 267–74. Translation edited by Garrett Barden and John Cumming. English translation copyright © 1975 by Sheed and Ward Ltd. New York: Continuum Publishing Co., 1980.
——. "Rhetorik, Hermeneutik und Ideologiekritik—Metakritische Erörterungen zu Wahrheit und Methode." In *Kleine Schriften*, Vol. 1, pp. 113–30. 2nd ed. Tübingen: J. C. B. Mohr (Paul Siebeck), 1976. Translated by Jerry Dibble and published by permission of J. C. B. Mohr (Paul Siebeck).
Jürgen Habermas. "Der Universalitätsanspruch der Hermeneutik." In *Hermeneutik und Ideologiekritik: Theorie-Diskussion*, pp. 120–59. Frankfurt a/M: Suhrkamp Verlag, 1971. Translated by Jerry Dibble and published by permission of Suhrkamp Verlag.
Martin Heidegger. *Being and Time*, pp. 182–201, 203–10. Translated by John Macquarrie and Edward Robinson. Copyright © 1962 by SCM Press Ltd. Reprinted by permission of Harper and Row Publishers, Inc., and Basil Blackwell Publisher Ltd.
Wilhelm von Humboldt. "Über die Aufgabe des Geschichtsschreibers." In *Gesammelte Schriften*, Vol. 4, pp. 35–56. Edited by A. Leitzmann. Berlin: B. Behr Verlag, 1905. Translated by Linda Gail DeMichiel.
——. "Nature and Properties of Language." In *Linguistic Variability and Intellectual Development: Introduction to the Kawi Work*, pp. 33–40. Translated by George C. Buck and Frithjof A. Raven. Coral Gables, FL: University of Miami Press, 1971.
Edmund Husserl. *Logical Investigations*, Vols. 1 and 2, pp. 269–82 and 299–311. Translated by J. N. Findlay from the 2nd German ed. London: Routledge & Kegan Paul; New York: Humanities Press, 1976. Reprinted by permission of Routledge & Kegan Paul Ltd. and Humanities Press, Inc., Atlantic Highlands, N.J.
Roman Ingarden. *The Cognition of the Literary Work of Art*, pp. 5–14 and 19–41. Translated by Ruth Ann Crowley and Kenneth B. Olson. Evanston, IL: Northwestern University Press, 1973. Reprinted by permission of Northwestern University Press.
Friedrich D. E. Schleiermacher. *Hermeneutics: The Handwritten Manuscripts by F. D. Schleiermacher*, pp. 95–122, 127–33, and 147–51. Edited by Heinz Kimmerle. Translated by James Duke and Jack Forstman. Missoula, MT: Scholars Press, 1977. Reprinted by permission of the American Academy of Religion.

# Indexes

## Index of Subjects

Account, 4, 7f., 20, 55, 59, 64–71, 80, 114, 252, 259, 267, 322, 328. *See also* Description; History; Narrative; Story
Act (of), 9–11, 16, 22, 25, 28–31, 34, 38, 40, 42, 74, 79, 96, 105, 112, 127, 130, 152, 154, 162, 167f., 172–77, 180f., 184–86, 190–92, 195, 198f., 202, 204–8, 212, 244, 254, 259, 263, 265, 269, 273, 282, 298, 304. *See also* Interpretation; Speaking; Speech; Understanding
Action(s), 26, 29, 42, 59, 67, 79, 113, 115, 128, 135, 141, 153f., 157, 163, 167, 232, 243f., 261, 265, 281, 283f., 297, 306, 308, 328–30, 337–39, 341
Aesthetics, aesthetic, aesthetical, aesthetically, 5, 9, 23, 30, 32, 37, 46, 98, 129, 134, 187, 189, 193, 196, 205, 208, 259, 273, 279f., 293
Allegory, allegorical, 78f., 139–42, 162, 242
Ambiguity, ambiguous, ix, 5, 12, 27, 39, 42, 60f., 166, 170, 174, 183, 228, 264, 270
Analysis, to analyze, 23f., 28, 31, 33, 35f., 40, 43, 57, 99, 134, 136, 142, 146, 148, 152, 158, 166, 182–84, 191–93, 204, 212, 221, 228, 231, 235f., 239, 241, 246, 255f., 258, 266, 268, 273–75, 279f., 290, 296, 301, 304f., 309–12, 315, 320, 324, 326, 328, 330, 332f., 336–40. *See also* Existential; Life
Analytic(al), 24, 42, 44, 50, 122, 224, 281, 304, 306–10, 312, 320, 328, 340, 343f.

Ancient, 9, 18, 54, 132, 139–42, 228, 243, 256, 259
Ancients, 5, 140, 314
Anthropology, anthropological, 23, 26, 98, 275, 277, 320
Antiquity, 1f., 20f., 58, 62, 85, 146, 278, 296
Apprehension, to apprehend, 31, 149, 151, 155–57, 165, 173, 189–96, 200, 202, 205–9. *See also* Comprehension; Understanding
Art, 5f., 9, 12, 21f., 27, 30f., 52, 60–62, 72–77, 81–83, 87, 93, 95, 97, 107, 109–13, 115, 126, 133–36, 140, 154f., 161, 164, 167, 178, 187–97, 205–9, 211–13, 264, 267, 270, 274–79, 283, 289, 294, 296, 298, 300f., 336. *See also* Interpretation; Understanding
Artist, 15, 99, 109–11, 117, 130, 159
Artistic, 5, 73, 94, 109f., 134f., 140f., 144, 154, 157, 161, 189, 193, 208f., 294, 297
*Ars Critica*, 2, 19
Assertion, 145, 149, 154, 162, 168, 172, 178, 192, 197, 205, 207, 211, 222, 228–32, 234–36, 238, 248, 251, 257, 279, 299, 324, 332. *See also* Clause; Proposition; Sentence; Statement
Audience, 10, 78, 278. *See also* Listener; Public; Reader; Spectator
Authenticity, authentic, 2, 19, 218, 228, 236f., 249–51, 253
Author, authorial, xi, 4–9, 11, 21, 33, 37, 44, 56f., 59, 64f., 68–71, 73, 78–81, 83–88, 90, 92, 94–97, 127, 129, 134, 136,

365

143, 156, 161, 164, 194–96, 198–200, 202f., 206, 210–12, 231, 233f., 236, 238f., 243f., 253, 259, 275, 279f., 282–87, 294f., 300f., 303–5, 309–12, 314f., 318f., 322f., 328, 332, 337f., 340, 343; games, 281, 284, 286, 289, 297, 299, 304, 306, 312, 317, 321f., 328f., 342–44; meta-, 289, 295, 299, 301, 312. *See also* Linguistic; Foreign tongue; Mother tongue; Speech

Latin, 84, 89, 203

Law, 3, 48, 56, 59, 63, 93, 98, 155f., 164, 242, 274, 334f.; roman, 3, 47, 135, 335. *See also* Jurisprudence; Legal

Law(s), 24, 99, 103, 106, 113–17, 123, 133–35, 139, 153, 162f., 170, 244, 258f., 266f., 269, 290, 300, 326–28, 331, 340, 342f. *See also* Rules

Legal/Judicial, 3, 18, 23, 27, 47, 61, 87, 155f., 331

Letter/Epistle, 55, 78f., 94, 126f., 138, 160, 242, 263

Lexicon, 57, 137, 302, 304, 306

Liberal arts, 6

Life, 10, 20, 23–26, 28, 34f., 37, 51, 57, 67, 75, 101–3, 108, 110, 114, 116, 120, 124, 126, 131, 143, 148–51, 153f., 158–61, 165, 186, 214, 236, 245, 247, 249–51, 253f., 259, 267, 271, 279f., 283–85, 287, 290, 299f., 305, 308, 315f., 325, 333, 342; utterance, -expressions, 25–27, 152–157, 161, 163, 278, 337–40, 343; mental, 11, 27, 151, 157, 159, 160, 162f., 166. *See also* Lived experience

Linguist, 13f., 30, 38

Linguistic, 2f., 9–14, 16, 19–22, 25, 31, 35, 39–41, 44f., 75–77, 81, 86f., 89f., 98f., 102f., 138, 163, 169, 189, 196f., 199f., 207f., 236, 275f., 278f., 281, 283f., 286f., 289, 294f., 297f., 300–3, 305–8, 310–15, 320, 322, 328–32, 335, 338. *See also* Competence; Understanding

Linguisticality, 9–11, 13, 35, 39f., 43, 75, 275f., 279–82, 284, 287, 299

Linguistics, 13, 46, 275, 289, 297f., 301, 320

Listener, 14, 16, 55f., 59f., 69, 102f., 237, 272, 278. *See also* Audience; Reader; Public

Literary, 20, 22–24, 28, 30f., 40f., 95, 136–38, 143, 188, 331, 339; criticism (critics), ix, 30, 32, 35f., 289; studies, 31, 40, 45, 331; scholars, ix, 28, 38, 187; theory, 30, 187

Literature, 14, 23, 30f., 55, 60, 72, 79, 84f., 95, 97f., 113, 134, 136, 139, 256

Lived experience/*Erlebnis*, 25f., 149–51, 153, 158f., 162, 289. *See also* Inner experience

Logic, 1, 3f., 6, 29, 41f., 44, 46, 74, 97, 123, 132f., 146, 153f., 163, 165f., 169, 187, 197, 231, 233, 238, 256, 276f., 280, 283, 290, 295, 300, 315, 321, 324–27, 330

Logical, logically, 22, 25, 28f., 111, 122, 126, 132f., 144–46, 152f., 156, 159, 162, 165f., 168, 171f., 175, 182, 189, 197f., 216, 231, 308, 322f., 326f., 340f.

Logician, 186, 327

Lyric, lyrical, 78, 137f., 140, 159, 188

Manuscript, 10, 72, 134, 214

Mathematical, 110f., 145, 147, 163, 168, 182, 190, 201, 324

Meaning, to mean, ix, 3–9, 14, 18–22, 25, 27–33, 36, 39–43, 45, 55–57, 59–61, 63, 78f., 81–83, 86–93, 102, 105, 111, 127, 134f., 137, 140–43, 146, 149f., 153, 155f., 165–67, 171–80, 182–86, 188, 191f., 195, 197–207, 210–12, 214, 219, 224–26, 228–30, 234, 241, 243, 245–47, 252, 260, 262–65, 268–72, 283f., 287f., 294f., 301–8, 311f., 317f., 321f., 330, 332–34, 336–40, 341, 343; allegorical, 140, 142; constitutive, conferring, 28, 175, 177, 184, 194, 325; figurative, 78f., 88; fulfillment, 30, 175, 271; intention, intended, 4f., 78, 175–78, 181, 183f., 186, 202, 204, 248, 322f., 334; literal, 3, 78f., 88, 135–37, 141, 221. *See also* Intention; Sense; Significance

Meaningfulness, meaningful, 29f., 56, 170, 178, 181, 204, 224, 321, 333f., 340, 343

Meaningless, 15, 30, 63, 150, 182, 224f., 338

Mental 10, 12, 14, 24, 31, 51, 102, 108, 114, 120, 152–57, 160–62, 169f., 172, 175–77, 179, 185, 197; act, 202–4, 207,

Unity, 9, 28, 82, 87–89, 94, 96, 100, 102, 114, 128, 149, 151f., 155f., 167, 169f., 176, 192, 196, 212, 217, 244, 260, 266, 338, 342. *See also* Circle; Whole and its parts

Utterance, to utter, 5–7, 10f., 13–14, 26, 29, 121f., 138, 171, 211, 236–38, 270, 333, 335. *See also* Expression; Life–expression; Language; Speech; Writing

Valid, 4, 46, 135, 169, 189f., 230, 252, 257, 270, 301, 306, 317, 321, 333

Validity, to validate, validation, x, 22, 24, 29, 131, 146, 149, 153, 162, 190, 230, 233, 246, 257–59, 264, 276, 279, 281, 286–88, 290, 301, 315, 317, 322f., 330, 333, 336

Value, to value, 22, 82, 124, 130, 133, 143f., 149, 151, 155, 158, 164, 189f., 193, 209, 225, 259, 261, 267, 272, 281, 310, 327f., 330, 332

Verification, to verify, 50, 61, 85, 125, 127, 129, 210f., 252, 267, 299, 323, 326, 330, 332, 344

Verse, 146, 181, 184, 196

*Verstehen. See* Understanding

Viewpoint, 9, 11, 45, 66, 70, 77, 105, 128, 165, 210. *See also* Perspective; Point of view; Standpoint

Whole (cohesion, totality, unity of a work) and its parts, 2, 8, 15f., 19, 35, 84f., 87, 92, 94, 103–9, 112–14, 118, 122, 126, 141f., 144, 147, 151, 157f., 163f., 166, 194, 202–5, 212. *See also* Circle; Part; Unity

Work(s), 4, 6, 8, 10ff., 14, 18, 21f., 24, 28, 31, 33, 41f., 55–58, 60–63, 68, 77, 82, 84, 90, 92f., 95–97, 106f., 131, 134–39, 141–43, 155, 158f., 187–89, 191–98, 205, 209, 214, 266, 268, 279, 287f., 290f., 293, 303; of art, 7, 9, 31, 134, 136, 154, 187–93, 195, 197, 205, 267f.; literary, 4, 14, 23, 28, 30f., 41, 52, 143, 159, 187–96, 202–13, 337; scientific, 188f., 193, 205f., 209

World, 19, 23f., 29f., 33f., 63–65, 79, 87, 105, 107, 112, 116f., 119f., 123–26, 152f., 155, 161, 164, 202, 206f., 211, 215–19, 221, 223–25, 229, 237–39, 249, 251, 253f., 260, 271, 273–76, 279, 284, 286–88, 290, 299, 301, 306–10, 321–25, 328f., 334, 337–39, 342, 344; history, 17f., 49, 112–15, 287; mind-constructed, of the mind, 149, 151, 155–58, 160; view, picture, 12, 14, 36, 104f., 244, 259, 309

Writer, ix, xi, 3, 6–8, 10, 32, 39, 54, 56, 70, 81, 92f., 135f., 138, 140, 142, 154, 278f.

Writing, to write, written, xi, 4–6, 10, 13–15, 21, 27, 36f., 46, 54–57, 62f., 69, 73, 79–81, 84f., 87, 90, 93–95, 98, 102, 109, 118, 126f., 127, 135, 137, 148, 160f., 171, 183, 187f., 194f., 202, 210, 244, 246, 257, 273, 275, 278, 294, 329, 334. *See also* Speaking; Speech

## Index of Persons

Abel, T., 325, 326, 328
Adorno, T. W., 38, 293
Aeschylus, 118, 141
Ajdukiewicz, Kasimir, 211
Albert, Hans, 38
Alexander the Great, 118
Apel, Karl-Otto, 25, 43–46, 314, 320–45
Aristotle, 1, 3, 62, 277, 286
Aristophanes, 118, 141, 277 ·
Ast, F., 20, 132

Bacon, Francis, 12, 16

Baldus, 63
Bartholus, 63
Baur, F. C., 124
Bembo, Pietro, 337
Bentley, Richard, 144
Benveniste, Émile, 210
Bergson, Henri, 187
Bernhardi, 13
Binswanger, Ludwig, 36
Boeckh, Philip August, 9, 11, 20–23, 25, 31, 32, 38, 40, 45, 46, 132–47, 161, 162, 284